Advanced Businesses in Industry 6.0

Mohammad Mehdi Oskounejad
Azad University of the Emirates, UAE

Hamed Nozari
Azad University of the Emirates, UAE

A volume in the Advances in
Business Information Systems and
Analytics (ABISA) Book Series

Published in the United States of America by
IGI Global
Business Science Reference (an imprint of IGI Global)
701 E. Chocolate Avenue
Hershey PA, USA 17033
Tel: 717-533-8845
Fax: 717-533-8661
E-mail: cust@igi-global.com
Web site: http://www.igi-global.com

Library of Congress Cataloging-in-Publication Data

Names: Oskounejad, Mohammad, 1952- editor. | Nozari, Hamed, 1984- editor.
Title: Advanced businesses in industry 6.0 / edited by Mohammad Oskounejad,
    Hamed Nozari.
Description: Hershey, PA : Business Science Reference, [2024] | Includes
    bibliographical references and index. | Summary: "The main purpose of
    this book is to develop the concept of ultra-advanced industry 6.0,
    express the opportunities ahead, and evaluate the challenges in the
    ultra-smart environment of life"-- Provided by publisher.
Identifiers: LCCN 2024010198 (print) | LCCN 2024010199 (ebook) | ISBN
    9798369331088 (hardcover) | ISBN 9798369344514 (paperback) | ISBN
    9798369331095 (ebook)
Subjects: LCSH: Technological innovations--Economic aspects. |
    Industries--Technological innovations. | Artificial
    intelligence--Industrial applications.
Classification: LCC HC79.T4 A287 2024 (print) | LCC HC79.T4 (ebook) | DDC
    338/.064--dc23/eng/20240313
LC record available at https://lccn.loc.gov/2024010198
LC ebook record available at https://lccn.loc.gov/2024010199

This book is published in the IGI Global book series Advances in Business Information Systems and Analytics (ABISA) (ISSN: 2327-3275; eISSN: 2327-3283)

British Cataloguing in Publication Data
A Cataloguing in Publication record for this book is available from the British Library.
All work contributed to this book is new, previously-unpublished material.

The views expressed in this book are those of the authors, but not necessarily of the publisher.
For electronic access to this publication, please contact: eresources@igi-global.com.

Advances in Business Information Systems and Analytics (ABISA) Book Series

ISSN:2327-3275
EISSN:2327-3283

Editor-in-Chief: Madjid Tavana, La Salle University, USA

MISSION

The successful development and management of information systems and business analytics is crucial to the success of an organization. New technological developments and methods for data analysis have allowed organizations to not only improve their processes and allow for greater productivity, but have also provided businesses with a venue through which to cut costs, plan for the future, and maintain competitive advantage in the information age.

The **Advances in Business Information Systems and Analytics (ABISA) Book Series** aims to present diverse and timely research in the development, deployment, and management of business information systems and business analytics for continued organizational development and improved business value.

COVERAGE

- Business Process Management
- Management Information Systems
- Geo-BIS
- Data Strategy
- Big Data
- Business Intelligence
- Business Systems Engineering
- Statistics
- Decision Support Systems
- Business Decision Making

IGI Global is currently accepting manuscripts for publication within this series. To submit a proposal for a volume in this series, please contact our Acquisition Editors at Acquisitions@igi-global.com or visit: http://www.igi-global.com/publish/.

Titles in this Series

For a list of additional titles in this series, please visit:
http://www.igi-global.com/book-series/advances-business-information-systems-analytics/37155

Intelligent Optimization Techniques for Business Analytics
Sanjeev Bansal (Amity Business School, Amity University, Noida, India) Nitendra Kumar (Amity Business School, Amity University, Noida, India) and Priyanka Agarwal (Amity Business School, Amity University, Noida, India)
Business Science Reference • © 2024 • 357pp • H/C (ISBN: 9798369315989) • US $270.00

Data-Driven Business Intelligence Systems for Socio-Technical Organizations
Pantea Keikhosrokiani (University of Oulu, Finland)
Business Science Reference • © 2024 • 490pp • H/C (ISBN: 9798369312100) • US $265.00

Utilizing AI and Smart Technology to Improve Sustainability in Entrepreneurship
Syed Far Abid Hossain (BRAC University, Bangladesh)
Business Science Reference • © 2024 • 370pp • H/C (ISBN: 9798369318423) • US $290.00

Strengthening Industrial Cybersecurity to Protect Business Intelligence
Saqib Saeed (Department of Computer Information Systems, College of Computer Science and Information Technology, Imam Abdulrahman Bin Faisal University, Saudi Arabia) Neda Azizi (Torrens University, Australia) Shahzaib Tahir (Department of Information Security, College of Signals, Pakistan & National University of Sciences and Technology, Islamabad, Pakistan) Munir Ahmad (School of Computer Science, National College of Business Administration and Economics, Lahore, Pakistan) and Abdullah M. Almuhaideb (Department of Networks and Communications, College of Computer Science and Information Technology, Imam Abdulrahman Bin Faisal University, Saudi Arabia)
Business Science Reference • © 2024 • 373pp • H/C (ISBN: 9798369308394) • US $275.00

AI and Data Analytics Applications in Organizational Management
Tereza Raquel Merlo (University of North Texas, USA & Merlo Management Consulting, USA)
Business Science Reference • © 2024 • 317pp • H/C (ISBN: 9798369310588) • US $300.00

For an entire list of titles in this series, please visit:
http://www.igi-global.com/book-series/advances-business-information-systems-analytics/37155

701 East Chocolate Avenue, Hershey, PA 17033, USA
Tel: 717-533-8845 x100 • Fax: 717-533-8661
E-Mail: cust@igi-global.com • www.igi-global.com

Table of Contents

Detailed Table of Contents

Chapter 1

    Reza Tavakkoli-Moghaddam, University of Tehran, Iran
    Hamed Nozari, Azad University of the Emirates, UAE
    Aminmasoud Bakhshi-Movahed, Iran University of Science and
        Technology, Iran
    Ali Bakhshi-Movahed, Iran University of Science and Technology, Iran

In today's modern world, new things are determined for the generations of industry, especially Industry 6.0. The industrial revolutions are the key factors in changing and transforming the conditions for society. Industrial revolution, society, marketing, and factories have their generations. Time determines the new and old generations. Also, in this chapter, the conceptual framework explores the evolution of smart factories into the next phase, which is called Smart Factory 6.0. Integrating cutting-edge Industry 4.0 technologies can be one of the most important facets of this title. The new technologies can be artificial intelligence, the internet of things, and machine learning. All the new technologies in the chapter can help provide structure of papers. The proposed framework aims to enhance manufacturing efficiency, agility, and adaptability. By elucidating key components (e.g., intelligent automation, and digital twins), this framework provides a roadmap for organizations seeking to leverage the transformative potential of Smart Factory 6.0 in the contemporary industrial landscape.

Chapter 2

Technologies are increasingly changing everything. The modern world needs modern concepts for sure. The concept of industry and business has rapidly changed in recent years. Industry 6.0 (I 6.0) includes many subjects like business and marketing. Marketing 6.0 (M 6.0) has its position in modern concepts in the modern world. Of course, the implementation of M 6.0 can be a sophisticated topic, but applying the sixth generation of marketing can widely make a more comfortable life for many people like participants in the supply chain, marketers, and customers. M 6.0 can rightfully be an effective version of marketing. This generation of marketing leads to some magnificent advantages which is demonstrated in this research. The advantages of M 6.0 lead to the evolution in sales and more convenience for people. The current people of the world live much easier than the previous ones, and it is definite that for people who will live in the future world, equipment, facilities, and modern science will position them in a more beautiful life according to the smart technologies.

Chapter 3

The agriculture industry has experienced new developments due to the world's population increasing and the lack of food. For this reason, farmland management is done by artificial intelligence and the internet of things with the aim of agriculture industry smartization. Quantity and quality product improvement, energy consumption optimization, reducing emissions, and reducing the number of workers in the production process are the results of advanced industrialization in agriculture. In this regard, the production of healthy and sustainable food seems vital, because nutritional health is one of the lofty goals of the modern industrial revolution. Supply chain cycle improvement of the agriculture industry to increase sustainability and environmental security is one of the concepts that will be important in Industry 6.0.

Chapter 4

*Mohammad Hadi Aliahmadi, Iran University of Science and
Technology, Iran
Aminmasoud Bakhshi Movahed, Iran University of Science and
Technology, Iran
Ali Bakhshi Movahed, Iran University of Science and Technology, Iran
Hamed Nozari, Azad University of the Emirates, UAE
Mahmonir Bayanati, Islamic Azad University, Tehran, Iran*

The processes and dimensions of the development of the health system are some of the most important parts of a healthy society. The positive vision formation for people toward a society's health system requires trust, honesty, specialization, and two-way interactions between people and the healthcare system. Hospitals as a physical environment symbolize society's health system. As much as this physical environment reflects a more efficient and developing image of society in appearance, process, logistics, and infrastructure, the physical and mental peace of people will be improved. For this purpose, health systems and hospitals must adapt to current industrial and technological conditions. The smart hospital is one of the concepts that is developed in this field. In this chapter, due to the importance of hospital smartization, Industry 6.0 has been integrated with the smart hospital, and Hospital 6.0 has been propounded.

Chapter 5

*Ali Bakhshi Movahed, Iran University of Science and Technology, Iran
Aminmasoud Bakhshi Movahed, Iran University of Science and
Technology, Iran
Hamed Nozari, Azad University of the Emirates, UAE
Maryam Rahmaty, Islamic Azad University, Chalous, Iran*

The importance of the financial system in the industry is not only related to the organization itself but also depends on the industry's network. Technological developments, growth in industry, and increasing use of new technology in human life have changed the organization's financial system. One of the most important factors in the necessity of financial development is the issue of network security, monetary systems, banking systems, and privacy of customers and users. For this purpose, it will be considered to improve the quality level and speed of this process to pursue financial claims. Along with the industrial developments of different generations and the continuous and universal use of Industry 4.0 technologies, the financial and banking system also needs to be updated and mastered to reduce cybercrime and prevent financial fraud and bank stolen. This chapter examines the financial system by analyzing the financial security criteria and achieving Financial Security 6.0.

Chapter 6

Hamed Nozari, Azad University of the Emirates, UAE
Adel Pourghader Chobar, Department of Industrial Engineer, Islamic
Azad University, Qazvin, Iran

In today's era, businesses are mixed with technologies. Industry 4.0 added the presence of roaming technologies with the power of extracting, analyzing, and fast data calculations to businesses. Therefore, the data with high transparency and accuracy increased the performance power of the marketing department and adopted powerful strategies. In the fifth generation of the emerging industry, in addition to analytical power, stability, resilience, and human-centeredness, the capabilities of transformative technologies have also been added. For this reason, marketing by refining the data that comes from the actions of humans, multiplied intelligence. Examining this ability in smart Marketing 5.0 will have tremendous effects on the entire supply chain and the value chain of organizations. Therefore, this research has tried to examine the dimensions and components of fifth-generation marketing. In this regard, an analytical framework is also provided for the smart marketing system. This framework has been approved by some active experts in the field of marketing.

Chapter 7

Manjit Kour, Chandigarh University, India
Rajinder Kour, CGC Technical College, India

Numerous sectors have been transformed by artificial intelligence (AI), and marketing is no exception. The rise of artificial intelligence (AI) influencers, or virtual people powered by cutting-edge AI algorithms, is one of the newest trends in marketing. These AI influencers are upending conventional marketing approaches and changing how firms interact with their target markets. AI influencers have developed into valuable marketing tools for companies looking to engage customers in a social environment thanks to their increased personalisation, expanded reach, and affordability. The world of social media marketing has been significantly altered by AI and influencer marketing, and this trend is expected to continue. This study examines how AI influencers are revolutionising brand promotion, reshaping the marketing environment, and creating a new industry in this chapter.

Digital marketing strategies play a crucial role in today's business world and have become an indispensable component of many sectors. The main objective of this study is to assess digital marketing strategies in the retail sector with multiple criteria decision making (MCDM) methods. Bayesian BWM (B-BWM) is utilized in the study to identify the weights of the criteria and fuzzy TOPSIS method is utilized to assess digital marketing strategies implemented in the retail sector. Based on the methodology used, customer satisfaction, customer loyalty, and competitive position in the market are the most important criteria that are taken into account in the selection of digital marketing strategies. Moreover, search engine optimisation and influencer marketing are the most suitable digital marketing strategies in the retail sector. The findings from this study could serve as a guide for evaluating digital marketing strategies in the retail sector.

With regard to the increasing number of international industries and integrated industries and the vertical and horizontal globalization of industries and the challenges that exist in this direction on the way of world trade, a lot of motivation has been created to share the different dimensions of the two fields of information technology and chain management. In this direction, steps should be taken to meet industrial needs and industrial technologies. Blockchain technology has been able to gain a high position in this regard in the opinion of industry managers and researchers in the world. Therefore, suitable opportunities for research and identification of operational applications have been provided. In this research, the development of blockchain-based global supply chains has been investigated and evaluated. Investing in blockchain is one of the most important tools for growing competitive advantage in process-oriented businesses with large financial flows in today's era.

This chapter investigates the commercial applications of blockchain technology and how it affects the banking industry and other industries through the use of cryptocurrencies. It first examines the functioning of blockchain technology and identifies its benefits for business and economic transactions. It then explores the impact of this technology on financial operations and beyond. Through synthesizing knowledge from various fields such as technology, economics, finance, and politics, the chapter establishes four scenarios for the future of blockchain technology. The results of the study show that blockchain technology is still in the early stages of altering many businesses, but it has already had a significant impact on the financial industry. The chapter finds that blockchain technology's benefits in terms of security, efficiency, transparency, and accountability are undeniable, and it has the capacity to completely transform the way we conduct transactions and interact with organizations.

Modern services like e-commerce, which emerged from the technological revolution, are some of the many domains that greatly contributed to business thriving by reducing costs, saving time, and increasing productivity by enabling companies and individuals to execute their financial transactions electronically. However, the remarkable rise of financial transactions due to the massive adoption of internet bank services, FinTech innovation, and e-commerce has increased the risk of malicious attacks aiming to perform fraudulent activities. Data mining and artificial intelligence are approaches that have widely been used as fraud detection techniques. Researchers have taken advantage of such methods to discover abnormal activities through which fraudsters intend to violate the law. In this research, the authors first introduce different types of financial fraud in e-commerce systems, then review various data mining methods to deal with them. Finally, the most efficient techniques regarding different types of fraud that can be applied to detect anomalies have been identified.

Chapter 12

D. Renuka Devi, Stella Maris College (Autonomous), India
T. A. Swetha Margaret, Stella Maris College (Autonomous), India
K. Avanthika, Stella Maris College (Autonomous), India

AI and robotics are tremendously growing in the industry. It is going to affect the human labor in the coming decades. Artificial intelligence and robotics are rapidly being adapted by the industry. So, there is a need for humans to be competitive to survive in the growing industry. Due to the enormous demand for intelligent robots across all industries globally, employment in the field of artificial intelligence is growing along with this technology. The ample opportunity to understand the impact of these technology and preempt their negative effect is closing rapidly. In order to cope with these technological changes, humans are expected to be proactive rather than being reactive. So, this chapter discusses the technological aspects as well as the societal norms it's affecting. The aim is to increase awareness in understanding and rapidly adapting the significance of these technologies to help in formation of policies and regulation that maximize the uses and benefits of this technological evolution and minimize the possible danger it could do to the society.

Chapter 13

S. C. Vetrivel, Kongu Engineering College, India
T. Gomathi, Gnanamani College of Technology, India
K. C. Sowmiya, Sri Vasavi College, India
V. Sabareeshwari, Amrita School of Agricultural Sciences, India

This chapter examines the evolving landscape of marketing in the contemporary business environment, with a particular focus on the sixth wave of marketing (Marketing 6.0). This wave represents a paradigm shift towards unprecedented customer-centricity, where businesses are compelled to align their strategies with the ever-changing expectations and preferences of the modern consumer. The chapter begins by providing a comprehensive overview of the historical progression of marketing, from its inception to the current era, highlighting the pivotal shifts that have shaped each phase. It then meticulously explores the core principles and characteristics that define the Marketing 6.0 era, emphasizing the pivotal role of technology, data analytics, and artificial intelligence in reshaping the marketing landscape. Furthermore, the chapter addresses the key challenges and opportunities faced by businesses as they strive to adopt customer-centric excellence in Marketing 6.0.

Preface

The world is evolving every day. Technologies are developing every day. Complex processes are managed. Industrial generations are also becoming more advanced every day. The fourth industrial generation or fourth industry emerged with the introduction of transformative technologies. Technologies such as the Internet of Things, artificial intelligence and blockchain technology along with various social platforms have revolutionized the industry. Processes changed with the presence of these technologies. Businesses found capabilities that they did not have before. The ability to extract data was created that was not possible before. Analytical capabilities were created that no one had imagined before. But the sudden emergence of technologies and bombardment of information also brought refinements. These polishes always caused worries for mankind. Therefore, the fifth industrial generation was developed as an academic definition. A stable, forward-looking and resilient look was added to the technologies. In the fifth generation, special attention has been paid to security challenges. But what will the sixth generation be like? A generation that hasn't happened yet. It seems that in the 6th industrial generation, the power and ability to analyze the work will be equal. The speed of calculations will be quantum. But this ultimate digitization and the growth of computing speed will happen in an environment with maximum security, that is, maximizing the power and ability to store and calculate data in the safest possible state. so that human life is not endangered. In this book, an attempt has been made to take a brief look at some concepts and definitions related to the advancements of technological leaps. We hope this book is for those interested in technology.

ORGANIZATION OF THE BOOK

Chapter 1: In this chapter, the focus is on the evolution of smart factories into Smart Factory 6.0, a phase marked by the integration of cutting-edge Industry 4.0 technologies. The conceptual framework delves into how technologies like artificial intelligence, the Internet of Things, and machine learning are reshaping manufacturing efficiency, agility, and adaptability. Through elucidating key components such as intelligent automation and digital twins, the chapter provides a roadmap for organizations aiming to leverage the transformative potential of Smart Factory 6.0.

Chapter 2: Chapter 2 delves into the rapidly changing landscape of marketing, particularly with the emergence of Marketing 6.0 (M 6.0). It explores how the sixth generation of marketing, characterized by modern concepts and strategies, offers significant advantages such as evolution in sales and enhanced convenience for stakeholders across the supply chain. By examining the implementation and benefits of M 6.0, the chapter highlights its potential to revolutionize marketing practices and improve lives through smart technologies.

Chapter 3: This chapter investigates the role of artificial intelligence and the Internet of Things in smartening the agriculture industry to meet the challenges posed by increasing population and food scarcity. It explores how advanced industrialization in agriculture leads to improvements in product quantity and quality, energy consumption optimization, and sustainability efforts. Additionally, the chapter emphasizes the importance of supply chain cycle improvement for achieving sustainability and environmental security in Industry 6.0.

Chapter 4: Chapter 4 focuses on the development of smart hospitals within the broader context of Industry 6.0. It examines how integrating Industry 6.0 principles into healthcare systems can improve both physical and mental well-being by enhancing processes, logistics, and infrastructure. The chapter underscores the importance of adapting health systems to current industrial and technological conditions, presenting the concept of Hospital 6.0 as a pivotal aspect of smartizing the health sector.

Chapter 5: This chapter scrutinizes the evolving landscape of the financial system within Industry 6.0, emphasizing the necessity of updating financial and banking systems to mitigate cybercrime and ensure financial security. By analyzing financial security criteria and proposing strategies to achieve Financial Security 6.0, the chapter addresses the challenges posed by technological developments and the continuous evolution of Industry 4.0 technologies.

Chapter 6: Chapter 6 delves into the transformative capabilities of Smart Marketing 5.0, which integrates transformative technologies with powerful data analytics to drive marketing strategies. By examining the dimensions and components of fifth-generation marketing and providing an analytical framework for Smart Marketing 5.0, the chapter demonstrates its profound impact on supply chains and organizational value chains.

Chapter 7: This chapter explores the emerging trend of AI influencers and their impact on reshaping the marketing environment. By examining how AI influencers leverage cutting-edge AI algorithms to engage customers and personalize marketing efforts, the chapter highlights their potential as valuable marketing tools. It underscores how AI influencers are revolutionizing brand promotion and reshaping the marketing landscape, particularly in the realm of social media marketing.

Chapter 8: Chapter 8 evaluates digital marketing strategies in the retail sector using Multiple Criteria Decision-Making methods. Through methodologies like Bayesian BWM and fuzzy TOPSIS, the chapter identifies key criteria such as customer satisfaction and competitive positioning in selecting digital marketing strategies. It provides insights into the most suitable strategies, including search engine optimization and influencer marketing, to guide decision-making in the retail sector.

Chapter 9: This chapter investigates the development of blockchain-based global supply chains and their role in enhancing competitive advantage in process-oriented businesses. By analyzing the operational applications of blockchain technology, the chapter underscores its potential to address challenges in international industries and improve industrial technologies within the framework of Industry 6.0.

Chapter 10: Chapter 10 examines the commercial applications of blockchain technology and its impact on the banking industry and beyond. Through synthesizing knowledge from various fields, the chapter establishes scenarios for the future of blockchain technology and highlights its benefits in terms of security, efficiency, transparency, and accountability. It underscores blockchain's potential to transform transactions and interactions with organizations across industries.

Chapter 11: This chapter addresses the increasing risk of financial fraud in e-commerce systems and explores data mining methods for fraud detection. By introducing different types of financial fraud and reviewing techniques to detect anomalies, the chapter provides insights into combating fraudulent activities in the digital realm. It underscores the importance of leveraging data mining and artificial intelligence to ensure the security of financial transactions in e-commerce.

Chapter 12: Chapter 12 examines the growing impact of artificial intelligence and robotics on industries and human labor. It discusses the need for proactive adaptation to technological changes and emphasizes the importance of understanding both the technological aspects and societal implications. The chapter aims to increase awareness and facilitate the formulation of policies and regulations to maximize the benefits of technological evolution while minimizing potential risks to society.

Chapter 13: This chapter delves into the paradigm shift towards customer-centricity in Marketing 6.0 and its implications for businesses in the contemporary business environment. By providing an overview of the historical progression of marketing and exploring core principles of Marketing 6.0, the chapter highlights the role of technology, data analytics, and artificial intelligence in reshaping marketing strategies. It addresses the challenges and opportunities businesses face as they strive for customer-centric excellence in Marketing 6.0.

Preface

Mohammad Mehdi Oskounejad
Azad University of the Emirates, UAE

Hamed Nozari
Azad University of the Emirates, UAE

Chapter 1
A Conceptual Framework for the Smart Factory 6.0

Reza Tavakkoli-Moghaddam
https://orcid.org/0000-0002-6757-926X
University of Tehran, Iran

Hamed Nozari
https://orcid.org/0000-0002-6500-6708
Azad University of the Emirates, UAE

Aminmasoud Bakhshi-Movahed
https://orcid.org/0000-0003-3259-5419
Iran University of Science and Technology, Iran

Ali Bakhshi-Movahed
Iran University of Science and Technology, Iran

ABSTRACT

In today's modern world, new things are determined for the generations of industry, especially Industry 6.0. The industrial revolutions are the key factors in changing and transforming the conditions for society. Industrial revolution, society, marketing, and factories have their generations. Time determines the new and old generations. Also, in this chapter, the conceptual framework explores the evolution of smart factories into the next phase, which is called Smart Factory 6.0. Integrating cutting-edge Industry 4.0 technologies can be one of the most important facets of this title. The new technologies can be artificial intelligence, the internet of things, and machine learning. All the new technologies in the chapter can help provide structure of papers. The proposed framework aims to enhance manufacturing efficiency, agility, and adaptability. By elucidating key components (e.g., intelligent automation, and digital twins), this framework provides a roadmap for organizations seeking to leverage the transformative potential of Smart Factory 6.0 in the contemporary industrial landscape.

DOI: 10.4018/979-8-3693-3108-8.ch001

1. INTRODUCTION

As a traditional insight, the process of production is managed by the factories in their way. Additionally, not only the process is changed but precisely also, the whole policy of factories can change. The previous generation of factories provides the previous generation of production. It is obvious that the more implementation of factories, the more use of production will happen. Smart factories emphasize data privacy and security, workforce training, intellectual property rights, and collaboration and partnership.

Passing time builds new or old generations and the new generations will build new concepts for the world in the future. New generations of every concept can automatically generate other new concepts. There is a trend of emerging new concepts in Industry Revolution and marketing. Also, technology can help the process of updating and can be a strong initiator in this field. Smart technology can make a different and new process in the factories. The process will also be easier in the whole world of industry by applying new technologies. Furthermore, technology should be transformed into a new path. As an attractive insight, smart people make smart cities (Kannan et al., 2024). Also, smart factories will appear after all this progress with the help of intelligence.

There is a collaboration between Industry 4.0 technologies and smart supply. As a practical insight, examining patterns in Supply Chain 4.0 and its implementation within the wood construction sector can be an example (Gharaibeh et al., 2024). On one hand, Industry 4.0 technologies can help the process of production. There are tools (e.g., AI, IoT, blockchain, and big data) in the structure of cutting-edge technologies that can be effective in updating production systems. By updating the production systems of factories, the whole production lines of smart factories will be transformed into a modern flow. On the other hand, there is smart supply in the factories. When advanced technologies are applied in the supply chain process, the whole chain of production will transform in a way that the top management will be fully satisfied with.

In addition, security and privacy will be performed better. The reason is about the accuracy of new technologies. Meanwhile, Industry 5.0 has some effects on the sixth generation of the industry. Moreover, Industry 5.0 is characterized by three significant attributes, namely, a focus on human-centricity, sustainability, and resiliency (Huang et al., 2022). In the results of the stated paragraphs, Industry 6.0 will emerge all around the world. it signifies the subsequent stage of industrial development. It entails the amalgamation of cutting-edge technologies like artificial intelligence, robotics, the Internet of Things (IoT), big data analytics (BDA), and automation into the realm of manufacturing and production processes

Smart Factory 6.0 will be at the final layer of this story. It helps to level up the obstacles of setup in all the factories to increase efficiency, productivity, and adaptability. The primary goal of Smart Factory 6.0 is to establish connected and smart manufacturing conditions where machines, systems, and humans can collaborate truly. Also, Cobots can strongly help workers in factories too. Cobots, also referred to as collaborative robots, are a distinct category of robotic systems that have advanced to function alongside both humans and workers. Smart manufacturing is where cobots work alongside humans (Wang et al., 2024) and They can engage more and more in the whole process of the production system and they can have a role in the implementation and setup of the systems that create and increase the production line. In summary, the integration of digital technologies and automation helps to facilitate operation management.

In Fig. 1, the smart transformation is presented for readers. By observing this, it can easily understand what story is in the background of the smart factory 6.0.

Figure 1. Smart transformation

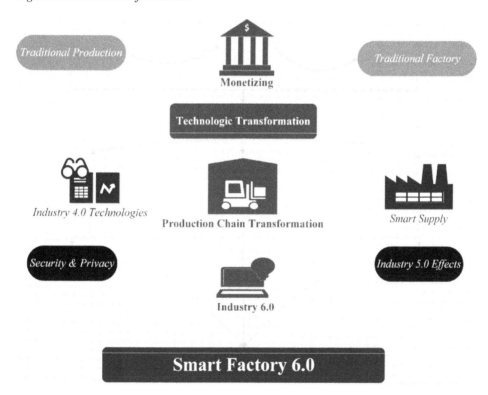

2. LITERATURE REVIEW

This study presents the sixth generation of the Industrial Revolution and the sixth generation of smart factories.

2.1. Industry 6.0

Researchers are now starting to contemplate Industry 6.0, an innovative notion, as a progression beyond Industry 5.0 (Singh et al., 2024). The main aim of Industry 6.0 is to establish smart manufacturing amenities, facilities, and interconnected networks of suppliers that signify exceptional productivity, adaptability, and connectivity. This emerging phase of industrialization is expected to bring about key success in sustainability. However, the capacity to customize and personalize products and services according to individual requirements is not limited. The thing that matters is to apply customization and personalization because the new generation of people likes this topic. The research can examine the impacts of factories on customization capacity (Bego & Mattos, 2024).

Historically, the stated Proposition can be a crucial topic for the ancestors. The people who lived in the past tended to be customized but the old generation of equipment was not enough to provide suitable conditions for them. As an answer to these types of issues, the Industrial Revolution generation appears. So as a long-term insight, the Industrial Revolution generation will transform everything that is around us. Also, one of the bold signs of the difference between industrial revolutions is the concept of customization in Industry 5.0 is a prospective insight (ElFar et al., 2021).

Thus, the sixth industrial generation put itself on the way to industrialization. It means that all processes, people, and things will be transformed in a new way in the background of technology (Nozari, 2024). The whole process of decision-making will be transformed in the factories and the people will be able to feel the differences.

2.2. Smart Factory 6.0

According to the definition, Smart Factory 6.0 encompasses the idea of a sophisticated automated manufacturing facility that integrates emerging technologies and digital systems. Smart Factory 6.0 consists of IoT, AI, ML, robotics, blockchain, big data analytics, quantum computing, and cloud computing. These technologies make some processes easier. The real-time collection, analysis, and decision-making of data will be performed as easily as possible. Also, smart manufacturing can generate fresh employment prospects in programming, data analysis, and robotics (Tyagi et al., 2024). So, there is an explanation of how Smart Factory 6.0 can apply advanced technologies.

There is a story in the processes of the smart factory that advanced technology is narrating. The concepts are gathered by IoT analyzed by AI checked by blockchain and accelerated by quantum computing. IoT can centralize the scattered data. it is important to be done in the field of production that data should be collected through the new technologies. Nowadays AI can analyze the gathered data and create a meaningful connection between them. The role of blockchain in this process is to ensure that the collected data will be transparent and healthy. Also, the role of quantum computing is to increase the speed of analysis, by using that the safety of the whole process will be guaranteed for factories.

The whole scheduling process for production will be done with the information of IoT. The maintenance process will be done and controlled automatically and when the alarms will be activated in the crash times. Then, the product will be sent for distribution and marketing. In this step, the product is in the way of retailer places for sales and marketing. In the end, the customers will receive the products, and automatically the process of inventory control will happen. Factories according to this spotless cycle can manage their warehouses in an optimum way. All these cycles are performed by upgrading the process, people, and things. Also, the concept of artificial intelligence of everything (AIOE) is the background of all these concepts.

2.2.1 Supply and Procurement

First, we must be aware of the significance of supply and procurement. These two concepts are integral aspects of the business process. The challenging factor in supply is choosing the best ones. The process of examining the best suppliers and using them in the supply chains as a true position always matters for factories. Also, Efficient supply management entails some different activities that are formed as the processes of factories. They include sourcing, inventory management, and logistics.

Procurement and providing materials are the two important signs for factories that want to be the best ones in their field. By using new technologies this dream comes to true. Indeed, factory members can do what they would done before in a much better way. procurement specifically means providing goods or services from some external sources. procurement involves some activities such as identifying requirements, sourcing suppliers, and negotiating contracts.

So, supply and procurement both play vital roles in ensuring that an organization possesses the essential resources to operate effectively and meet customer demands. Thus, the topic of Supply and procurement encompasses raw materials, administrative requirements, and the equipment of the factory. All these concepts will be explained in the following for readers who are eager to understand the next generation of industry.

- **Raw materials supply:** Raw materials are found in their original state and undergo a series of production processes to be transformed into the finished products. By background of smart factory 6.0, the transition of material from the suppliers to the Production warehouse will be easier and faster than in the past. the utilization of intelligent technologies like AI, IoT, and automation enables a more optimized handling of raw materials. In summary, supplying raw materials to new generations is under the meticulous insight of the authors of this paper.

- **Administrative requirements:** With the advent of technologies and new generations, the administrative bureaucracy will be transformed. There will be some new instructions and policies in the factories and workers and people will perform according to these structures. People will be assessed according to the stated policies too. Also. It will be difficult for employees to perform their careers wrong.

- **Factory equipment:** Indeed, the facilities and equipment of all factories can demonstrate whether they work in an old way or not. According to the instructions of factories and their processes, the whole mechanism of the factories will be transformed in the new generation. For sure, for the implementation of the equipment of Smart Factory 6.0, sufficient context is needed. Sufficient context can provide a positive atmosphere for factories. In summary, new technologies need new equipment to develop the whole systems of factories from machines to procedures.

2.2.2. Warehousing

In the new decades, the warehousing issue has been an important and determining factor. It is vital to manage the materials for warehouses. In addition, smart warehouses within the realm of Smart Factories 6.0 are furnished with sensors and IoT devices, which offer instantaneous data regarding variables (e.g., temperature, humidity, and storage conditions). These kinds of variables are more meaningful for fast-moving consumer goods (FMCG) products. If variables like temperature are not managed properly, the warehouse's principles will face more challenges. Also, many tools ensure the preservation of the stored materials. In a smart factory 6.0, the warehousing process is modified by leveraging data analytics and intelligent systems.

- **Based on orders at the moment:** The demands are predicted based on algorithm models and new technologies. ML can help in this field. To this trend and story, the warehouses will be managed in smart factories properly. Furthermore, the products are ordered and then at the same time in smart factories and warehouses of them. The sensors and smart devices are used in the warehouses. Technology is applied in the whole process and plays a key role here.

- **More storage capacity:** Also, in the smart factory and the sixth generation the capacity will be greater. In this generation, the storage will be more equipped because of the use of technologies. After the customer registers the order, the products will be prepared to send and the inventory control will be performed as well as possible.

2.2.3. Production

Production 6.0 examines the subsequent iteration of manufacturing procedures distinguished by sophisticated technologies and automation. It is based on the principles of Industry 4.0 by smart technologies. Moreover, production 6.0 places significant emphasis on the utilization of data analytics and predictive algorithms to enhance production scheduling. The sixth generation of factories has some effects on the production process in smart factories. Additionally, IoT as a modern technology can help the factories in collecting valid data and information from the production lines. Analyzing these data and extracting knowledge from them can be the important point of using these technologies. In summary, the quality can be controlled for products and the maintenance can be performed in a very nice and safe way. This process will be protected by blockchain and some other new technologies.

- **Quality approval of products:** Control and approving the quality of finished products have always been a challenging issue all around the world in factories. So, this subject matters in smart factories. Customer satisfaction is connected to the quality maintenance of factories. Smart factories need to have always the best quality of products because according to the research, their clients of them are tended to have high-quality products. IoT always plays a key role in collecting data from production lines in smart factories. By excavating these data, the quality can be easily controlled.
- **Maintenance:** In the smart factories, the whole process of maintenance is done in an automatically way. The alarms are activated at the right time and the problem will be solved automatically. Systems enable to management of the whole process of operation in factories. Furthermore, the smart factory can act in a way that the previous generations could not act like that.

2.2.4. Financial Control

Financial problems will be less than in the past in the factories. In the context of a smart factory 6.0, financial control encompasses some activities including budgeting and financial forecasting of the overall financial performance. Managing the accounting part of companies by using new technologies like big data can create a new way of predicting future events. Smart Factories 6.0 utilize AI, ML, and BDA to gather and examine extensive quantities of data on financial transactions, production expenses, and resource utilization. So, in this part, the importance of AI can be stated.

- Management Accounting: In smart Factories 6.0, management accounts harnesses advanced technologies and data analytics to furnish instantaneous financial insights, facilitate decision-making procedures, and propel ongoing enhancements in both operational and financial efficacy.
- Analysis of financial conditions with AI: The situation of every factory is important for the top management and its employees. In particular, the financial condition is more important than the many other aspects of the company. Smart technologies can create an atmosphere for people who are trying to build a situation that can easily live in. Without money it is impossible. So, without suitable management in financial conditions, factories cannot be on their true path. AI can help factories and build smart factories in the world.

2.2.5. Distribution

In a smart factory 6.0, distribution involves delivering goods to customers or sales outlets using advanced technologies and data-centric systems. This improves efficiency and effectiveness. In a smart factory 6.0, intelligent systems enhance distribution by monitoring and tracking products in real time using IoT devices, sensors, and RFID tags. This improves inventory management, demand forecasting, and delivery routing, resulting in more efficient distribution operations.

Smart Factories 6.0 uses automation and robotics to optimize distribution. This includes automated sorting, packaging, and labeling systems, as well as autonomous vehicles or drones for transportation. These technologies minimize errors, improve speed and precision, and enhance overall efficiency. Data analytics and AI in Smart Factories 6.0 optimize distribution networks by analyzing past data, customer preferences, and market trends. AI algorithms make informed decisions about inventory allocation, order fulfillment, and route optimization, leading to improved customer satisfaction, reduced expenses, and increased operational efficiency. In smart Factories 6.0, real-time tracking, automation, data-driven decision-making, and optimized logistics processes improve product delivery speed, precision, and cost-effectiveness.

- **Easy transportation in distribution:** By using technologies transportation of materials to the smart factories and the transportation of products to the customers will be more comfortable. The whole distribution process from the beginning point to the last point is performed as well as possible according to the next generation of smart factories. New technologies will update the whole participants of the supply chain.

- **Avoiding traffic rush:** In the context of a smart factory 6.0, the avoidance of traffic congestion holds importance as it plays a crucial role in maintaining seamless operations and reducing unnecessary delays. To tackle these obstacles, the implementation of advanced technologies and intelligent systems can be leveraged effectively.
- **On time delivery:** Factories can deliver the products in a rapid shape. As the delivery process of factories is quick in a high-quality way, the customers will be happier than ever they had. The factories in the new generation can perform their duty in a way that their target customer can have access to them better.

2.2.6. Sales and Marketing

After preparing products and goods the sales and marketing section plays one of the final roles of the story. In smart factories, the sixth generation of marketing can be effective. The important point is marketing 6.0 which as the next generation of marketing can help the factories to enhance their products and the quality of services after sales. Customers must receive their products as well as possible. There are two topics here that need to be stated.

- **Creating a feedback loop from the market:** The market and its members have their comments and suggestions. They are enthusiastic to express their feelings after they use the products. If consumers feel that there is a mechanism that is trying to understand their emotions, they will be very happy to be evaluated by that.
- **Impact on the supply chain cycle from the end to the change of raw materials supply:** In addition, whole members of the supply chain are trying to receive the best materials that they have ever had. The raw material can play a significant role in the finished products. It is like the recipe of the foods, if the ingredients are fine the output will be good too.

2.2.7. Artificial Intelligence of Everything (AIOE)

Artificial intelligence of everything (AIoE) integrates AI technologies into various aspects of our lives and industries. It envisions a future where AI can merge with our surroundings, including homes, workplaces, transportation, and healthcare. The goal is to use AI to augment and automate tasks, such as virtual assistants, smart homes, autonomous vehicles, and personalized healthcare. AIoE has the potential to revolutionize industries, improve efficiency, and enhance the human experience by providing personalized experiences, optimizing resource allocation, and offering valuable insights through data analysis.

2.2.8. Effect of AIOE on Smart Factory 6.0

The incorporation of AI into smart factory 6.0 brings consequences across multiple facets of the manufacturing process. It can increase the automation in the factories. Also, it can maintain predictively because forecasting as it is stated, is one of the key elements of the new generation of factories. Furthermore, the quality control will be intelligent and the supply chain management will be optimized in the smart factories. Also, data-driven management and human and machine collaboration can enhance the whole mechanism of smart factories. The most important effect is continuous improvement. It shows that factories always can improve their ways and can always be the best formats among other ones.

3. APPROACH AND FRAMEWORK

Indeed, the research approach for methodology includes a Focused group and a Conceptual framework. Authors of papers use the focus group to understand things in depth because practical and academic insight are mixed in this method. Also, through the conceptual framework, the content of papers is explained (Peltier et al., 2023).

3.1. Focus Group

The research's requirements determine utilizing a focus group as a qualitative research approach (Gurunathan, 2023). To highlight the significance of employing this method in the study, it is essential to present the outcomes of the focus group (Handayani & Ardini, 2023). A focus group discussion involved 12 participants with diverse ages, educational backgrounds, professions, research experience, and work experiences. After the pandemic situation, the online sharing of knowledge and experiences has become popular and universal. There is no exception for this research.

3.1.1. Descriptive Statistics

Descriptive statistics of the focus group are given in Table 1.

Table 1. Descriptive statistics

	Age	Academic Degree	Job Career	Research Experiences
1	62	Prof. in Industrial Production	Professor	A high h-index
2	60	Prof. in Industrial Technology	Professor	A high h-index
3	58	Ph.D. in Innovation and technology management	Assistant Professor	Several related papers
4	55	Ph.D. in Systems modeling	Assistant Professor	Several related papers
5	49	Ph.D. in logistic	Assistant Professor	Several related papers
6	48	Ph.D. in Supply chain	Assistant Professor	Several related papers
7	43	Ph.D. in Manufacturing management	Assistant Professor	Several related papers
8	40	Master of Engineering Management	Financial Manager	-
9	39	Master of Production systems	Supply chain analyst	-
10	35	Master of Planning and Systems Analysis	Production Supervisor	-
11	34	Master of Industrial Design	Industrial Designer	-
12	32	Master of Smart Industry	Quality Engineer	-

In certain studies, the participant count is restricted due to the recommendation of having fewer members in focus groups to manage the discussion effectively (Dupont et al., 2023). Utilizing the focus group approach is essential to optimize both time and cost for the readers.

3.2. Conceptual Framework

The conceptual framework for smart factory 6.0 A is shown in Fig. 2.

Figure 2. Smart Factory 6.0 framework

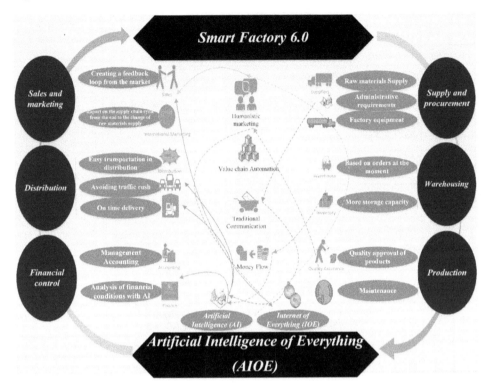

4. CONCLUSION

To summarize, the presented conceptual framework for Smart Factory 6.0 emphasizes the importance of embracing Industry 4.0 technologies in order to enhance efficiency and foster innovation in the manufacturing sector. By incorporating intelligent automation, data-driven decision-making, and interconnected cyber-physical systems, Smart Factory 6.0 enables a more flexible and adaptable industrial landscape. This framework guides organizations seeking to navigate the complexities of this transformative journey, promoting a comprehensive approach that maximizes the potential of emerging technologies.

Intelligent manufacturing holds a significant influence on the level of national development (Hongyan, 2024). Countries and cities can develop themselves when factories can make their mechanism smart. People, processes, and things are engaged in the smart factory 6.0 as it is stated before. The story of the smart factory 6.0 is comprehensive and long. The supplier will be found and dissected with the aid of AI. This process happens very quickly. Then, the raw materials will be put in the production lines automatically. Also, the whole process of quality control will be performed by IoT. Then, the raw material will be separated and the bill of material (BOM) will be standard. Also, there is a reliance on demand due to the BOM structure (Sereshti et al., 2024).

As the manufacturing industry continues to evolve, the adoption of Smart Factory 6.0 principles is not only a paradigm shift but also a strategic necessity for maintaining competitiveness in a constantly changing global marketplace. In the new generation of factories, it is very determined that society can adapt itself to the new circumstances.

REFERENCES

Aliahmadi, A., Bakhshi-Movahed, A., & Nozari, H. (2023). Collaboration analysis in supply chain 4.0 for smart businesses. In *Building Smart and Sustainable Businesses with Transformative Technologies* (pp. 103–122). IGI Global. doi:10.4018/979-8-3693-0210-1.ch007

Bakhshi-Movahed, A., Aliahmadi, A., Parsanejad, M., & Nozari, H. (2023). A systematic review of collaboration in supply chain 4.0 with meta-synthesis method. *Supply Chain Analytics*, 100052.

Bakhshi-Movahed, A., Bakhshi-Movahed, A., & Nozari, H. (2024). Opportunities and challenges of smart supply chain in Industry 5.0. *Information Logistics for Organizational Empowerment and Effective Supply Chain Management*, 108-138.

Bego, L. L., & Mattos, C. A. D. (2024). The interplay between agile manufacturing and the Internet of Things. *International Journal of Agile Systems and Management*, *17*(1), 106–128. doi:10.1504/IJASM.2024.135379

ElFar, O.A., Chang, C.K., Leong, H.Y., Peter, A.P., Chew, K.W., & Show, P.L., 2021. Prospects of Industry 5.0 in algae: Customization of production and new advanced technology for clean bioenergy generation. *Energy Conversion and Management*: X, 10, p.100048.

Gharaibeh, L., Eriksson, K. M., Lantz, B., Matarneh, S., & Elghaish, F. (2024). Toward digital construction supply chain-based Industry 4.0 solutions: Scientometric-thematic analysis. *Smart and Sustainable Built Environment*, *13*(1), 42–62. doi:10.1108/SASBE-12-2021-0224

Hongyan, J. (2024). Design and implementation of intelligent manufacturing system based on sensor networks and cloud computing technology. *Optical and Quantum Electronics*, *56*(3), 278. doi:10.1007/s11082-023-05923-1

Huang, L., Han, Y., Yuan, A., Xiao, T., Wang, L., Yu, Y., Zhang, X., Zhan, H., & Zhu, H. (2022). New business form of smart supply chain management based on "Internet of Things+ Blockchain". *Mobile Information Systems, 2022*, 2022. doi:10.1155/2022/1724029

Kannan, D., Khademolqorani, S., Janatyan, N., & Alavi, S. (2024). Smart waste management 4.0: The transition from a systematic review to an integrated framework. *Waste Management (New York, N.Y.), 174*, 1–14. doi:10.1016/j.wasman.2023.08.041 PMID:37742441

Nozari, H. (2024). Supply Chain 6.0 and Moving Towards Hyper-Intelligent Processes. In Information Logistics for Organizational Empowerment and Effective Supply Chain Management (pp. 1-13). IGI Global.

Peltier, J. W., Dahl, A. J., & Schibrowsky, J. A. (2023). Artificial intelligence in interactive marketing: A conceptual framework and research agenda. *Journal of Research in Interactive Marketing*, (ahead-of-print).

Sereshti, N., Adulyasak, Y., & Jans, R. (2024). Managing flexibility in stochastic multi-level lot-sizing problems with service level constraints. *Omega, 122*, 102957. doi:10.1016/j.omega.2023.102957

Singh, R., Tyagi, A. K., & Arumugam, S. K. (2024). Imagining the sustainable future with Industry 6.0: A smarter pathway for modern society and manufacturing industries. In *Machine Learning Algorithms Using Scikit and TensorFlow Environments* (pp. 318–331). IGI Global.

Tyagi, A. K., Mishra, A. K., Vedavathi, N., Kakulapati, V., & Sajidha, S. A. (2024). Futuristic technologies for smart manufacturing: Research statement and vision for the future. *Automated Secure Computing for Next-Generation Systems*, 415-441.

Wang, S., Zhang, J., Wang, P., Law, J., Calinescu, R., & Mihaylova, L. (2024). A deep learning-enhanced Digital Twin framework for improving safety and reliability in human–robot collaborative manufacturing. *Robotics and Computer-integrated Manufacturing, 85*, 102608. doi:10.1016/j.rcim.2023.102608

Chapter 2
Marketing 6.0 Conceptualization

Aminmasoud Bakhshi Movahed

https://orcid.org/0000-0003-3259-5419
Iran University of Science and Technology, Iran

Ali Bakhshi Movahed
Iran University of Science and Technology, Iran

Hamed Nozari

https://orcid.org/0000-0002-6500-6708
Azad University of the Emirates, UAE

ABSTRACT

Technologies are increasingly changing everything. The modern world needs modern concepts for sure. The concept of industry and business has rapidly changed in recent years. Industry 6.0 (I 6.0) includes many subjects like business and marketing. Marketing 6.0 (M 6.0) has its position in modern concepts in the modern world. Of course, the implementation of M 6.0 can be a sophisticated topic, but applying the sixth generation of marketing can widely make a more comfortable life for many people like participants in the supply chain, marketers, and customers. M 6.0 can rightfully be an effective version of marketing. This generation of marketing leads to some magnificent advantages which is demonstrated in this research. The advantages of M 6.0 lead to the evolution in sales and more convenience for people. The current people of the world live much easier than the previous ones, and it is definite that for people who will live in the future world, equipment, facilities, and modern science will position them in a more beautiful life according to the smart technologies.

DOI: 10.4018/979-8-3693-3108-8.ch002

1. INTRODUCTION

Industry 6.0 (I 6.0) is an ultra-advanced or hyper-advanced context with high security. This structure, by preserving privacy, not endangering the lives of future generations, and minimizing human manipulation, aligns most with the human intellectual foundation. The goal of I 6.0 is to create a synergy between humans and machines (Chourasia et al., 2023). It happens with the help of wealth that comes from business and productive companies. However, the types and applications of robots and machines are vital factors that need attention (Murugan & Prabadevi, 2023). From a practical view, the bases of I 6.0 can make smart, long-lasting, and ecologically sound structures (Almusaed et al., 2023). I 6.0 can based on a future insight (Kumar et al., 2023), and Learning I 6.0 needs a futuristic insight into the field of research (Singh, 2023).

In such an atmosphere, artificial intelligence (AI) strongly approaches natural intelligence, and calculations are performed with Quantum Computing; for this reason, the speed of data analysis will be several times the current situation, and with the possibility of timely analysis, the accuracy and transparency of data will increase along with the control of cyber-attacks. Of course, AI can improve itself by the companionship of human roles (Bryndin, 2023). As a practical insight, Quantum Computing is an art and can be applied to financial problems (Herman et al., 2023). In the economic progression of a company or even a country, the speed of data analysis plays an important role (Xu & Kuang, 2023).

As a result of such developments, the social, industrial, and commercial environment is expected to change. Nursing practice as a social development with the collaboration of AI can help the health care of humans more and more. Also, traditional occupation roles are certainly substituted by AI's progress. Autonomous systems and smart factories can increase productivity and efficiency from an industrial perspective. Also, the marketing field is influenced by many trends, encompassing technological advancements, socioeconomic changes, and geopolitical factors (Rust, 2020). Marketing is one of the most influential fields in this new structure. The most crucial goal of marketing is to create extraordinary value for the customer. In I 6.0, despite the previous periods, there is no myopic view of marketing, and there will be no product-oriented view. Customers' behavior changes daily, considering modern technologies and industry 4.0 and 5.0 technologies. On the other hand, the environment and atmosphere of consumers have changed according to modern technologies.

Indeed, when technologies are improved, people's demand level will also increase. They will not be satisfied as quickly as they would in the past. Marketing and its generation have hard work because of people's satisfaction level. Historically, marketing could be a key player in the field of industry. Data analysis means how customers behave. Data analysis gives insight to people. It helps companies use what they know and improve their marketing application in the marketplace (Park et al., 2023). Consequently, this newfound wealth of information empowers them to craft marketing campaigns that are highly personalized and precisely targeted to individual customers. Personalized marketing can target the vulnerability of users (Duivenvoorde, 2023). However, this type of marketing is one of the most effective ones. Because modern humans need more attention than their ancestors. So, if marketing can be customized optimally, people will be more satisfied.

Figure 1. From I 6.0 to Marketing 6.0

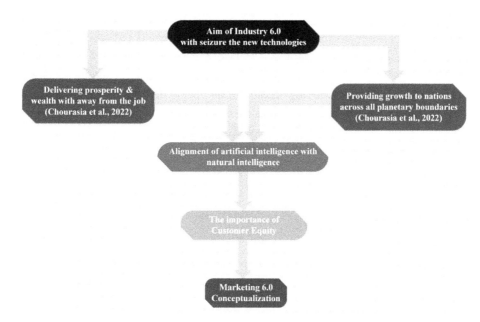

Marketing 6.0 (M 6.0) will be placed in a value chain that is fully automated. The required content is extracted with knowledge of data depth and based on performance. Also, maximum data transparency will be possible by overlapping data with blockchain. Increasing data extraction speed will lead to identifying customer preferences and the customer's unique value. With the proper perception and then analysis and refinement of this information, it becomes possible for supply chain components to master the processes. In continuing this cycle and after the transparency of people's acceptance and product preferences, retailers will get to know customers' actual and expected needs. For this purpose, new orders will be transferred to the distribution department after the inventory of retailers is empty

and then to the production department as a new framework so the suppliers can produce new products. Forming such a flow automates all stages of production and presentation of products and eliminates part of marketing methods such as word-of-mouth marketing. This cycle creates a customer-specific value chain throughout the supply chain.

Supply chain in various marketing types, like precision marketing, is essential (Xia et al., 2023). As stated in research, integrating advanced supply chain and marketing technologies has evaluated business operations, agile inventory management, customer-centric, and data-driven. Also, another dimension following this framework is the issue of advertising. Identifying tendencies by examining and analyzing the level of accuracy of people to various parameters such as web browsing, looking at a specific billboard, slowing down, or accelerating the speed of the car on the highway based on performance can lead to offering products based on customer interest. Such a process will provide the best and most optimal option to people. The M 6.0 process, using its concepts, offers the best and most appropriate choices to customers through advertising among all the available options. In social media, many marketers and influencers share their lifestyles and advertise products and services (Hazari & Sethna, 2023). According to the research, offering options in such a way is attractive to social media users and creates a delightful experience in the customers' lives.

2. LITERATURE REVIEW

This section will explain the sixth generation of industry and marketing. Historically, the generation of industry and marketing are connected. History shows that the Industrial Revolution has had magnificent transformation attempts until now. The marketing world has had the same history in its story. Scholars believe that with the current pace of technology, people will see many extraordinary titles in the future world. The elements of M 6.0, as stated in the conceptual framework, will be defined to better understand for M 6.0 concept.

2.1. Industry 6.0

Sustainability in I 6.0 is determined, and the transformation of Industrial Revolutions promotes people's quality of life (Chourasia et al., 2022). The connection between humanity and nature is demonstrated in this generation of industry. For this reason, renewable energy is one of the key elements of I 6.0 (Dovleac et al., 2023). From a historical point of view, the first industrial revelation happened many years ago. Industry 4.0 and 5.0 start to prepare the arena of the game for I 6.0. Surely, I 6.0

uses IoT, Quantum computing, Blockchain, Advanced robots, and AI to continue the way of the previous generation of the industry.

I 6.0 can generate and improve marketing strategies through AI-driven analytics, big data, machine learning (ML), and automation. Through the personalization of the customer experiences, marketers can prioritize, and people's feelings can predict their intentions in shopping and the exact product or service in their mind. Through hyper-targeted advertising, companies can create groups for their customers, send customized messages to them, and satisfy them. Also, leveraging emerging tech can optimize marketing campaigns and customer engagement.

2.2. Marketing 6.0

M 6.0 signifies the development of marketing strategies with the help of the framework of I 6.0. Cutting-edge technologies and digital platforms create some significant changes in the field of marketing. M 6.0 emphasizes personalized and focused marketing. Data analytics and AI are pivotal in finding the pattern of consumer behavior and trends which is important for companies and firms. The result of this subject will be seen in the customers' satisfaction. Additionally, the journey of marketing through the generations of the industry is very attractive to know because of the insight of history in fields like this. The current study will discuss the evolution of marketing concepts from M 1.0 to M 5.0. Initially, M 1.0 focused on the product itself, but with the introduction of M 2.0, the focus shifted to the customer. M 3.0 emphasized value and brand, while M 4.0 added brand interaction and experience. Also, M 5.0 incorporated relationships, authenticity, and co-creation. Finally, M 6.0 will be the most popular topic in the future of this field of research. In addition, if M 6.0 can be executed in the best way, everyone including founders of companies and customers will be satisfied for sure. It can be a prediction that will come true by a high percentage of sure. Thus, through this journey, M 6.0 will be presented in the far future. This transition is influenced by digitization, as shown in Figure 2.

Figure 2. Evolution of marketing and future picture of M 6.0

The researchers should be aware of M 6.0 emergence in the future. Especially, scholars in the marketing field must prepare themselves for some new megatrend. It can help people to be prepared for future trends and adapt themselves to them. Surely, people need to recognize M 6.0 because they will need to the outcomes of that.

2.2.1. Overlapping Data With Blockchain

Overlapping data with blockchain is defined as Integrating blockchain with existing data systems. This integration offers some advantages in data management, such as security improvement, increasing transparency, and efficiency. Transparency and security are the two factors that differentiate the M 6.0 from the previous generations. However, implementation is the key point and necessary to align with specific use cases and requirements. From a practical perspective, in the field of project management, blockchain and data mining have a close connection (Hammad, 2023). The correlation between them leads to many developments in managing projects and marketing processes.

2.2.2. Data Depth Extracting Speed

The extraction speed of data depth depends on various factors, such as data complexity, volume, system processing power, and algorithm efficiency. Surely, data complexity is calculated because of different sample ratios in classes, and the high dimensionality of the data (Dalal et al., 2023). Smart technologies, including AI and ML, can increase extraction speed by automating the process and utilizing parallel processing capabilities. Automaticity is one of the unfair advantages of M 6.0 and it can be used. However, it is crucial to understand that the speed of data depth extraction can vary based on the specific context and needs of tasks. So, it shows that M 6.0 considers the circumstances.

2.2.3. Data Transparency Maximization

Data transparency is very important in the new generation of supply chains to progress trust and collaboration among other partners (Hellani, 2021). Transparency is needed for companies and data transparency maximization assures them that data is comfortably accessible, available, and comprehensible. It encompasses meticulously providing concise and complete details and utilizing data. Considering details in analyzing helps companies to find out the deeper layer. By optimizing data transparency, M 6.0 can create more trust and responsibility. As a result, ethical issues can be more easily solved in M 6.0.

2.2.4. Value Chain Automation

Some autonomous companies signify the advancement in marketing and sales automation (Malio, 2022). Value chain automation utilizes technology and automation to improve the productivity of the various activities and processes within a value chain. The value chain encompasses all the duties and missions involved in the creation and delivery of a product or even service. This process starts from acquiring raw materials to the ultimate delivery to the customer.

2.2.5. Automatic Products Presentation

Automatic product presentation needs the application of smart technology, including AI and automation, to produce and distribute product presentations without anybody's involvement. Augmented reality can help businesses to improve product presentation (Aristantia & Liu, 2023). So, achieving a harmonious balance between automation and human participation is of the utmost importance to ensure the optimal presentation of products.

2.2.6. Offering the Most Appropriate Choices Through Advertising

Marketers can target their customer's precisely through digital advertising channels (Mohamed, 2023) and offer them the best items that customers can purchase. Advertising aims to steer consumers away from traditional paradigms and encourage them to adopt new paradigms for consumption (Yuan, 2023). So, it is a positive shift paradigm for the marketing era. This strategy cannot promote goods but rather focuses on managing consumers toward a shift in their mindset. By changing the shift paradigm, firms and companies can foster long-term progress.

2.2.7. Customer Equity Formation

Customer equity is the overall value of a company with a customer orientation, including all their interactions and transactions. Cultivating customer equity using strategies to attract, retain, and maximize the value from customers. Attracting people to the companies with the help of M 6.0 is the key element of M 6.0. So for sure, it can increase brand loyalty, revenue, and profitability. These strategies involve providing great user experiences, loyalty programs, and building sustainable relationships. So, M 6.0 can have various marketing strategies to increase the levels of customer satisfaction.

2.2.8. Highly Humanistic Marketing

Highly humanistic marketing can rank individuals by establishing genuine links, deep understanding of their desires, and crafting personalized experiences. Most of the time, customers are unaware of their needs, but companies must speculate on those. The focus on relationships, customer viewpoints, and ethical practices, with a commitment to social responsibility, can make a new way for companies to build their path.

3. APPROACH AND FRAMEWORK

Indeed, the research approach for methodology includes a Focused group, a Conceptual framework, and Causal relations. Authors of papers use the focus group to understand things in depth because practical and academic insight are mixed in this method. Also, through the conceptual framework, the content of papers is explained (Peltier et al., 2023), and there is no exception for this study. In addition, a causal relation is stated at the last step of the methodology process to demonstrate the relationship between factors.

3.1. Focus Group

The research's requirements determine utilizing a focus group as a qualitative research approach (Gurunathan, 2023). To highlight the significance of employing this method in the study, it is essential to present the outcomes of the focus group (Handayani & Ardini, 2023). A focus group discussion involved 12 participants with diverse ages, educational backgrounds, professions, research experience, and work experiences. After the pandemic situation, the online sharing of knowledge and experiences has become popular and universal. There is no exception for this research.

3.1.1. Descriptive Statistics

Descriptive statistics of the focus group are given in Table 1.

Table 1. Descriptive statistics

	Age	Academic Degree	Job Career	Research Experiences	Work Experiences
1	56	Prof. in Strategic Marketing	Professor	A high h-index	30 Years
2	54	Prof. in Marketing Management	Professor	A high h-index	28 Years
3	50	Ph.D. in Strategic policy	Assistant Professor	Several related papers	25 Years
4	49	Ph.D. in Strategic Marketing	Assistant Professor	Several related papers	20 Years
5	47	Ph.D. in Marketing Management	Product Manager	Several related papers	18 Years
6	47	Master of International Marketing	Market research analyst	Several related book chapter	15 Years
7	44	Master of Business Administration	Business Analyst	Several related book chapter	15 Years
	41	Master of Marketing Communications	Digital Marketing Strategist	-	12 Years
9	38	Master of Brand Management	Marketing Assistant	-	10 Years
10	35	Master of Business Administration	Social media Specialist	-	5 Years
11	31	Master of International Business	Event marketing Specialist	-	5 Years
12	31	Master of Business Administration	Chief marketing officer	-	5 Years

In certain studies, the participant count is restricted due to the recommendation of having fewer members in focus groups to manage the discussion effectively (Dupont et al., 2023). Utilizing the focus group approach is essential to optimize both time and cost for the readers.

3.2. Conceptual Framework

M 6.0 cycle is shown in Figure 3.

Figure 3. Highly humanistic marketing cycle in the M 6.0 platform

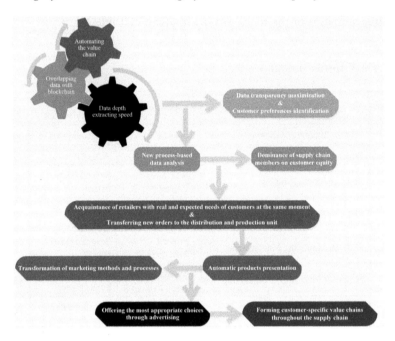

3.3. Causal Relations

Decision Making Trial and Evaluation Laboratory (DEMATEL) technique was applied to examine the causal relations of components to produce a causal relations map. DEMATEL is a comprehensive structural model analysis method considering probability environments (Seyed-Hosseini et al., 2006). An 8x8 non-negative matrix is established. Twenty matrices were obtained from experts' opinions, and their average was calculated using the initial matrix of direct relationships. Then, the matrix of total relations, the T matrix, is obtained (1).

$$\tilde{T} = \lim_{k \to \infty} \left(\tilde{x}^1 + \tilde{x}^2 + \ldots + \tilde{x}^k \right) \tag{1}$$

Then the values of (D+R) and (D-R) are obtained. D and R respectively are the sum of rows and columns for each element in the matrix T. As a result, $\left[\tilde{D}_{n\times1}\right], \left[\tilde{R}_{1\times n}\right]$ made with (2) and (3).

$$\tilde{D} = \left(\tilde{D}_i\right)_{n\times1} = \left[\sum_{j=1}^{n}\tilde{T}_{ij}\right]_{n\times1} \tag{2}$$

$$\tilde{R} = \left(\tilde{R}_i\right)_{1\times n} = \left[\sum_{i=1}^{n}\tilde{T}_{ij}\right]_{1\times n} \tag{3}$$

Then, the importance of the factors ($\tilde{D}_i + \tilde{R}_i$) and the relationship between them ($\tilde{D}_i - \tilde{R}_i$) are determined (Table 2).

Table 2. Influence of factors

Factors	Rank	D	R	D+R	D – R
Overlapping data with blockchain	5	0.8891	0.8377	1.7269	0.0514
Data depth extracting speed	4	1.0912	0.83175	1.9230	0.2595
Data transparency maximization	3	1.0663	0.5851	1.6514	0.4812
Value chain Automation	1	1.8371	0.9813	2.8185	0.8558
Automatic products presentation	2	1.4876	0.7178	2.2054	0.7698
Offering the most appropriate choices through advertising	6	0.5428	0.6636	1.2065	-0.1208
Customer Equity formation	7	0.5218	0.73075	1.2526	-0.2089
Highly humanistic marketing	8	-0.7287	-0.11635	-0.8451	-0.6124

The map of the factors' relationships is shown in Figure 4.

Figure 4. Relationships map

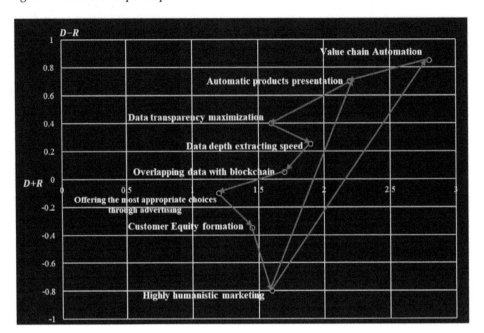

4. CONCLUSION

To sum up, there will be a new generation in marketing by considering technological development soon. In conclusion, the contrast between M 4.0, M 5.0, and M 6.0 at the first level will be explained. To better understand, the last part of the current study is delegated to defining the aspects of accuracy, automaticity, security, and privacy. Being aware of future trends is needed for everyone who lives in this world. M 6.0 is one of the megatrends of the future and we should be aware and prepare for that.

4.1. Comparing M 6.0 With Marketing 5.0 and 4.0

For sure, M 6.0 has some unfair advantages rather to the previous versions. Firstly, there is an explanation for M 4.0. Given the attractiveness and effectiveness of marketing in the realms of science and business, incorporating new technologies into marketing practices can enhance its appeal. These technologies, namely AI, IoT, and big data, are integral components of Industry 4.0. Applying these technologies in M 6.0 can make many changes in this world. Numerous companies are leveraging AI to develop their marketing strategies and enhance their sales performance (Cherukuri & Vududala, 2020). The primary objective of this research is to examine the impact of Industry 4.0 technologies on marketing. Marketing encompasses various aspects, including different types of marketing and corresponding strategies. Marketing strategies have a direct influence on the types of marketing employed (Sutaguna et al., 2023). Consequently, marketing strategies play a crucial role in shaping the landscape of marketing practices.

Secondly, there is an explanation for M 5.0. Smart enterprises are implementing the M 5.0 methodologies. In theory, the utilization of M 5.0 necessitates a reevaluation and redefinition of investment strategies in digital products and services (Petersen et al., 2022). Additionally, crucial decisions such as venturing into new markets and adopting innovative customer engagement approaches come into play (Verhoef et al., 2021). M 5.0 can be exemplified by the integration of cutting-edge technologies with marketing strategies, including big data analytics, AI, and IoT (Bakator et al., 2023). It is not surprising that M 5.0 can facilitate a transformation in the role of advanced technologies within advertising (Nowacki, 2023) and M 6.0 can perform better in this field.

4.1.1. The Difference in Accuracy

M 6.0 is widely regarded as a more sophisticated and refined version of M 5.0 and even M 4.0. It embraces modern technologies, data-centric techniques, and a customer-focused mindset. The excellence of M 6.0 lies in its capacity to harness AI, ML, and automation to scrutinize extensive data sets, enabling more accurate forecasts and informed decisions. As it is clear the automaticity influence on accuracy. Additionally, it is crucial to acknowledge that the productivity of any marketing strategy is ultimately contingent upon several factors, including data transparency, right execution, and alignment with the significant targets of the marketing campaign.

4.1.2. The Difference in Automaticity

M 6.0 introduces enhanced automation features in contrast to the previous versions like M 5.0 and M 4.0. By incorporating AI and ML, M 6.0 facilitates automated procedures for activities like data analysis, market segmentation, customized messaging, and campaign optimization. Automaticity streamlines marketing operations, making them more productive by minimizing manual labor and human mistakes, while simultaneously increasing speed and accuracy. So, it can be easily understood that automaticity, accuracy, and speed have a close connection.

4.1.3. The Difference in Security

M 6.0 demonstrates improved security measures in comparison to M 5.0. M 6.0 is the upgrade level of M 5.0. So, the features of M5.0 should be developed and reach the features of M6.0. With the progress in technology, M 6.0 integrates more powerful security practices to safeguard sensitive user data and prevent unauthorized access. M 6.0 often uses features that comply with data protection regulations, to be sure about privacy and security of the information of customers. Also, it is controversial for companies to perform in this way. However, it is obvious to recognize that no system is completely immune to security risks, and companies must continuously monitor and improve their security measures to proactively mitigate potential threats.

4.1.4. The Difference in Privacy

Privacy is always an important issue for people. Mentally, they need safety for their routine life. Also, privacy and security have a mutual connection. Data protection regulations and consumer demand for privacy made firms and enterprises to be sensitive to the privacy of customers. Finally, in M 6.0, applying the safe tool for customers takes a positive picture for people.

REFERENCES

Aliahmadi, Bakhshi Movahed, & Nozari. (2023). Collaboration Analysis in Supply Chain 4.0 for Smart Businesses. In Building Smart and Sustainable Businesses With Transformative Technologies (pp. 103-122). IGI Global.

Almusaed, A., Yitmen, I., & Almssad, A. (2023). Reviewing and integrating aec practices into industry 6.0: Strategies for smart and sustainable future-built environments. *Sustainability (Basel)*, *15*(18), 13464. doi:10.3390/su151813464

Aristantia, V., & Liu, A. Y. (2023, July). Study of the Influence of Augmented Reality Toward Consumer's Satisfaction and Repurchase Intention. In *3rd International Conference on Business and Engineering Management (ICONBEM 2022)* (pp. 51-63). Atlantis Press. 10.2991/978-94-6463-216-3_5

Badr Qorany Mohamed, H. (2023). Determinants of the formation of consumer attitudes towards advertisements via the TikTok and Instagram platforms in light of the advertising value model: A qualitative comparative study. *The Arab Journal of Media and Communication Research*, *2023*(42), 349–380.

Bakator, M., Vukoja, M., & Manestar, D. (2023). Achieving competitiveness with Marketing 5.0 in new business conditions. *UTMS Journal of Economics (Skopje)*, *14*(1).

Bryndin, E. (2023). Development of Artificial Intelligence of Ensembles of Software and Hardware Agents by Natural Intelligence on the Basis of Self-Organization. *Journal of Research in Engineering and Computer Sciences*, *1*(4), 93–105. doi:10.56397/JRSSH.2023.10.02

Cherukuri, P. A. A., Vududala, S. K., Saraswathi, N. R., & Sanda, J. (2020). *AI-based Strategic Marketing*. SMAI Model. In ICRMAT.

Chourasia, S., Pandey, S. M., & Keshri, A. K. (2023). Prospects and Challenges with Legal Informatics and Legal Metrology Framework in the Context of Industry 6.0. *MAPAN*, 1-26.

Chourasia, S., Tyagi, A., Pandey, S. M., Walia, R. S., & Murtaza, Q. (2022). Sustainability of Industry 6.0 in global perspective: Benefits and challenges. *MPAN. Journal of Metrology Society of India*, *37*(2), 443–452. doi:10.1007/s12647-022-00541-w

Dalal, A. A., Al-qaness, M. A., Cai, Z., & Alawamy, E. A. (2023). IDA: Improving distribution analysis for reducing data complexity and dimensionality in hyperspectral images. *Pattern Recognition*, *134*, 109096. doi:10.1016/j.patcog.2022.109096

Dovleac, L., Chiţu, I. B., Nichifor, E., & Brătucu, G. (2023). Shaping the Inclusivity in the New Society by Enhancing the Digitainability of Sustainable Development Goals with Education. *Sustainability (Basel)*, *15*(4), 3782. doi:10.3390/su15043782

Duivenvoorde, B. (2023). Consumer Protection in the Age of Personalised Marketing: Is EU Law Future-proof? *European Papers-A Journal on Law and Integration*, *2023*(2), 631–646.

Hammad, A. (2023). An improvement Of Blockchain and data mining in project Managemen. *International Journal of Computing and Digital Systems*, *14*(1), 1–xx.

Hazari, S., & Sethna, B. N. (2023). A Comparison of Lifestyle Marketing and Brand Influencer Advertising for Generation Z Instagram Users. *Journal of Promotion Management*, *29*(4), 491–534. doi:10.1080/10496491.2022.2163033

Hellani, H., Sliman, L., Samhat, A. E., & Exposito, E. (2021). On blockchain integration with supply chain: Overview on data transparency. *Logistics*, *5*(3), 46. doi:10.3390/logistics5030046

Herman, D., Googin, C., Liu, X., Sun, Y., Galda, A., Safro, I., ... Alexeev, Y. (2023). Quantum computing for finance. *Nature Reviews. Physics*, *5*(8), 450–465.

Kumar, R., Kariminejad, A., Antonov, M., Goljandin, D., Klimczyk, P., & Hussainova, I. (2023). Progress in Sustainable Recycling and Circular Economy of Tungsten Carbide Hard Metal Scraps for Industry 5.0 and Onwards. *Sustainability (Basel)*, *15*(16), 12249. doi:10.3390/su151612249

Malio, S. (2022). *Strengthening Humanitarian Disaster Response Value Chain Using Robotic Process Automation: a Case for World Food Programme* [Doctoral dissertation]. University of Nairobi.

Movahed, A. B., Aliahmadi, A., Parsanejad, M., & Nozari, H. (2023). A Systematic Review of Collaboration in Supply Chain 4.0 with Meta-Synthesis Method. Supply Chain Analytics, 100052.

Murugan, M., & Prabadevi, M. N. (2023). Impact of Industry 6.0 on MSME Entrepreneur's Performance and Entrepreneur's Emotional Intelligence in the Service Industry in India. *Revista de Gestão Social e Ambiental*, *17*(4), e03340–e03340. doi:10.24857/rgsa.v17n4-007

Oh, S., Park, M. J., Kim, T. Y., & Shin, J. (2023). Marketing strategies for fintech companies: Text data analysis of social media posts. *Management Decision*, *61*(1), 243–268. doi:10.1108/MD-09-2021-1183

Peltier, J. W., Dahl, A. J., & Schibrowsky, J. A. (2023). Artificial intelligence in interactive marketing: A conceptual framework and research agenda. *Journal of Research in Interactive Marketing*, (ahead-of-print).

Petersen, J. A., Paulich, B. J., Khodakarami, F., Spyropoulou, S., & Kumar, V. (2022). Customer-based execution strategy in a global digital economy. *International Journal of Research in Marketing*, *39*(2), 566–582. doi:10.1016/j.ijresmar.2021.09.010

Seyed-Hosseini, S. M., Safaei, N., & Asgharpour, M. J. (2006). Reprioritization of failures in a system failure mode and effects analysis by decision making trial and evaluation laboratory technique. *Reliability Engineering & System Safety*, *91*(8), 872–881. doi:10.1016/j.ress.2005.09.005

. Singh, K. (2023). Evaluation Planning for Artificial Intelligence-based Industry 6.0 Metaverse Integration. *Intelligent Human Systems Integration (IHSI 2023): Integrating People and Intelligent Systems, 69*(69).

Sutaguna, I. N. T., Achmad, G. N., Risdwiyanto, A., & Yusuf, M. (2023). Marketing strategy for increasing sales of cooking oil shoes in Barokah trading business. *International Journal of Economics and Management Research*, *2*(1), 132–152. doi:10.55606/ijemr.v2i1.73

Verhoef, P. C., Broekhuizen, T., Bart, Y., Bhattacharya, A., Dong, J. Q., Fabian, N., & Haenlein, M. (2021). Digital transformation: A multidisciplinary reflection and research agenda. *Journal of Business Research, 122*, 889–901. doi:10.1016/j.jbusres.2019.09.022

Xia, L., Li, K., Wang, J., Xia, Y., & Qin, J. (2023). Carbon emission reduction and precision marketing decisions of a platform supply chain. *International Journal of Production Economics*, 109104.

Xu, Z., & Kuang, D. (2023, July). Evaluation of Economic Development Data Management System Based on Particle Swarm Optimization Algorithm. In *2023 International Conference on Data Science and Network Security (ICDSNS)* (pp. 1-5). IEEE. 10.1109/ICDSNS58469.2023.10245900

Yuan, J. (2023). Application of micro film advertising communication under new media form. *The Frontiers of Society, Science and Technology, 5*(15).

Chapter 3
Green and Sustainable Supply Chain in Agriculture 6.0

Aminmasoud Bakhshi Movahed
https://orcid.org/0000-0003-3259-5419
Iran University of Science and Technology, Iran

Ali Bakhshi Movahed
Iran University of Science and Technology, Iran

Bentolhoda Aliahmadi
Islamic Azad University, Tehran, Iran

Hamed Nozari
https://orcid.org/0000-0002-6500-6708
Azad University of the Emirates, UAE

ABSTRACT

The agriculture industry has experienced new developments due to the world's population increasing and the lack of food. For this reason, farmland management is done by artificial intelligence and the internet of things with the aim of agriculture industry smartization. Quantity and quality product improvement, energy consumption optimization, reducing emissions, and reducing the number of workers in the production process are the results of advanced industrialization in agriculture. In this regard, the production of healthy and sustainable food seems vital, because nutritional health is one of the lofty goals of the modern industrial revolution. Supply chain cycle improvement of the agriculture industry to increase sustainability and environmental security is one of the concepts that will be important in Industry 6.0.

DOI: 10.4018/979-8-3693-3108-8.ch003

1. INTRODUCTION

With the advent of technology, every single industry can change itself through the modern tools of technology. The agriculture industry is not an exceptional item here. From the past until now, this industry has been the basic industry of every society. People need to grow their products and feed their families. Also, they could sell their products and earn money for their daily life.

The agriculture sector is crucial in guaranteeing food security, bolstering economies, promoting rural development, and tackling diverse environmental and social issues. It is a multifaceted industry that holds immense significance in enhancing the overall welfare of societies worldwide. Thus, the new generation of agriculture can facilitate the whole process of that.

Societies and people should be aware of the importance of the agriculture industry because if they are aware of this topic, they will attempt to improve the tools of that. From the past until now, mankind tried to invent tools and facilitate the whole process of agriculture. By this explanation, the reader can be aware of the necessity of the topic for various colonies.

On the other hand, technologies have been able to help all the industries. The agriculture industry is not an exception here. So, specialists and technicians must be able to provide a background for the implementation of the new generation of technologies. Also, the new generation of the industry can be a significant element in developing the agriculture industry.

In the ever-changing realm of Agriculture Industry 6.0, where the progress of technology intersects with environmental awareness, the necessity to establish an eco-friendly and enduring Supply Chain has taken on utmost importance. Furthermore, the agriculture industry 6.0 can be improved by human resource management. Generally, human resource management is important in Industry 6.0 (Pathak et al., 2024) because the investment in this concept is huge and needs risk management in an ideal way.

The advent of Agriculture Industry 6.0 signifies a fundamental change, marked by the assimilation of advanced technologies like the Internet of Things (IoT), artificial intelligence (AI), and data analytics into conventional farming methods. This revolutionary phase not only guarantees enhanced effectiveness, output, and financial gains but also calls for greater recognition of the industry's impact on the environment.

From the technology perspective, if things don't change, they will be replaced immediately. The development speed of the technology is transforming everything. So, the agriculture industry is under the effects of the speed rate of the technologies. AI plays a crucial role in the maintenance of the lands and farms. AI can monitor the crops by using drones. Drones fly over the whole field and take pictures. In this way, collecting data is feasible and easier. AI algorithms can analyze the collected images. It can analyze the trend of the growth in the plants. Machine learning algorithms also can be helpful in the process of analyzing.

In this paper, the introduction part is the first. Then the literature review exists. The Delphi method is in the next part. After that, the conceptual framework exists. The last part is the conclusion part.

2. LITERATURE REVIEW

The emergence of Agriculture Industry 6.0 signifies an important shift with the help of cutting-edge technologies. The scholarly literature sheds light on the progression of this sector, highlighting the incorporation of the IoT, AI, robotics, and precision agriculture.

The literature extensively examines the significance of technology in promoting a sustainable agricultural supply chain. Research studies emphasize the influence of the Internet of Things (IoT)-enabled sensors in effectively monitoring the health of crops, efficiently utilizing resources, and minimizing wastage. IoT agriculture can enhance food and farm technology (Jaiganesh et al., 2017).

Furthermore, the potential of AI-driven analytics is investigated in terms of predicting market demands, optimizing logistics, and reducing environmental impact. AI can realize the problems in the farms, and it is performed by deep learning (Xu et al., 2022). Thus, these technological interventions play a vital role in facilitating the shift towards a more environmentally friendly supply chain.

Scholars are actively exploring various approaches to minimize waste through the repurposing of by-products, the adoption of regenerative farming techniques, and the promotion of circular supply chain models. Through case studies, it has been demonstrated that waste reduction initiatives can be successfully implemented, thereby highlighting the potential of circular economy principles to improve sustainability within the realm of agriculture.

In this section, the literature review states that some elements are effective in the agriculture industry 6.0 which will be presented in the following.

2.1. Agriculture Internet of Things (AIOT)

The integration of internet-connected devices and sensors in agricultural practices is known as the Agriculture Internet of Things (AIOT). This innovative approach utilizes technology to gather, analyze, and leverage data to enhance and optimize agricultural operations.

2.2. Green Internet of Things (GIOT)

The Green Internet of Things (GIOT) places its emphasis on the utilization of IoT technologies in a manner that is environmentally sustainable. Its primary objective is to advocate for energy efficiency, monitor the environment, manage resources effectively, develop sustainable infrastructure, and make data-driven decisions to tackle environmental issues and foster sustainability.

2.3. Green Agriculture Internet of Things (GAIOT)

Green Agriculture Internet of Things (GAIOT) pertains to the utilization of Internet of Things (IoT) technology within the agricultural domain, emphasizing the principles of sustainability and environmental preservation. Additionally, The primary objective of GAIOT is to harness the potential of IoT devices, sensors, and data analytics to enhance agricultural methodologies, enhance the efficient utilization of resources, and mitigate the different effects on the whole environment.

2.3.1. Dimensions of GAIOT

In this section, the dimensions of the GAIOT are presented. Automatic planting and remote monitoring are at the first stage. Water, livestock, and product management by smart agriculture is the second element. Measurement of environmental temperature & humidity, soil moisture & PH by sensor data is the last element for the dimension of GAIOT.

- Automatic planting and remote monitoring

  Automatic planting and remote monitoring are two key factors that contribute to enhanced efficiency, cost reduction, and improved sustainability within the agriculture sector. By harnessing these technologies, farmers are empowered to make informed decisions based on data, thereby optimizing the allocation of resources, and minimizing negative environmental effects. Additionally, these advancements address the issue of labor shortages by automating repetitive tasks and enabling farmers to oversee and control their operations remotely. Consequently, the potential advantages of these innovations extend to increased productivity, efficiency, profitability, and sustainability within the agriculture industry.

- Water, livestock, and product management by smart agriculture

Through the utilization of intelligent agricultural technologies, farmers can enhance their water management techniques, improve the well-being of their livestock, and optimize the management of their products. These advancements play a crucial role in promoting sustainable farming practices, boosting productivity, facilitating farmer's work, and enhancing resource efficiency within the agriculture industry.

- Measurement of environmental temperature & humidity, soil moisture & PH by sensor data

Sensor data plays a crucial role in the agricultural sector as it enables the measurement of diverse environmental factors including temperature, humidity, soil moisture, and pH levels. These measurements offer significant insights that aid farmers in making well-informed decisions about crop management and resource allocation.

2.3.2. Applications of GAIOT

In this section, the application of GAIOT is presented in three items. Estimating the best harvesting time by the farmer is the first one. Assuring the best harvesting time by the farmer is the second one. The element is about alert email sending.

- Estimating the best harvesting time by the farmer

According to the many elements, farmers can estimate the harvesting time for themselves. Crop Monitoring Technologies is one of them. Contemporary agricultural practices have embraced the utilization of advanced technologies like satellite imagery, drones, and sensors to monitor the well-being and growth stage of crops effectively.

- Assuring the food mass production by farmer

One of the applications of the GAIOT is to guarantee food mass production for farmers. In this field, integrated pest management (IPM) can be effective. Utilize integrated pest management (IPM) techniques to regulate pests and diseases by employing a blend of biological, cultural, and chemical approaches.

- The most optimal actions based on farm parameter's variation by alert email sending

Implementing an email notification-based alert system, which is triggered by variations in farm parameters, represents a proactive strategy for effectively managing agricultural operations. It is undeniable that farmers must be ready for these fundamental changes. If they observe the results of technologies, they will be eager to use these types of technologies.

2.3.3. Advantages of GAIOT

In this section, the advantages of GAIOT are accurately presented. The two items of the benefits of GAIOT can be helpful for this topic. The first one is Sustainable agriculture with green nanotechnology in the supply chain and the second one is Precision agriculture (PA) by continuing soil/ plant monitoring.

- Sustainable agriculture with green nanotechnology in the supply chain

Sustainable agriculture in the supply chain can be achieved through the integration of green nanotechnology, which applies nanotechnology principles to improve agricultural practices while reducing negative environmental effects. The primary focus of green nanotechnology lies in the creation and utilization of nanomaterials and nanodevices that possess eco-friendly attributes. By incorporating these advancements, several crucial factors can be addressed, highlighting the significant role of green nanotechnology in promoting sustainable agriculture within the supply chain.

- Precision agriculture (PA) by continuing soil/ plant monitoring

Precision Agriculture (PA) encompasses the utilization of advanced technology and data-driven methodologies to enhance different facets of agricultural practices, such as soil and plant management. The continuous monitoring of soil and plants plays a pivotal role in precision agriculture, empowering farmers to make well-informed choices by leveraging real-time data.

2.4. Artificial Intelligence in Green Agriculture Internet of Things (AIGAIOT)

AI algorithms can examine data obtained from IoT sensors, including soil moisture sensors, weather stations, and satellite imagery. By doing so, they can furnish farmers with accurate details regarding the conditions of their crops. This, in turn, enables farmers to make targeted and optimized decisions regarding the utilization of resources such as water, fertilizers, and pesticides. Consequently, this approach aids in minimizing waste and mitigating the environmental impact.

3. DELPHI

Delphi is used to extract concept validation by influencing individual responses and feedback (Barrios et al., 2021). This method is a technique for reaching consensus by experts about specific issues when contentious empirical evidence is important (Barrios et al., 2021). Delphi is defined as an approach to presenting questionnaires and getting feedback from participants who are the research experts.

3.1. Delphi Statistics

The panel and team of Delphi are used to perform this method. Delphi team opinions were sent to Delphi panel members for aggregation on topics. Tables 1 and 2 show descriptive statistics of team and panel members.

Table 1. Delphi panel

	Gender	Job Career	Academic Degree	Experience
1	Man	Professor	Ph.D. in Food Industry	Scientific Researcher
2	Man	Professor	Ph.D. in Agricultural Engineering	Scientific Researcher
3	Woman	Associate Professor	Ph.D. in Supply Chain Management	Data analyst
4	Man	Production Engineer	Ph.D. in Industrial Engineering	Plants and industrial food
5	Man	Mechanization Engineer	Master of Agricultural Economics	Technological agricultural machines

Table 2. Delphi team

	Gender	Job Career	Academic Degree	Experience
1	Man	Assistant Professor	Ph.D. in Industrial Engineering	Scientific Researcher
2	Man	Assistant Professor	Ph.D. in Industrial Engineering	Agricultural Mechanization
3	Woman	Assistant Professor	Ph.D. in Technology Management	IT Security
4	Man	Researcher	Ph.D. in Supply Chain Management	Scientific Researcher
5	Man	Researcher	Ph.D. in Industrial Management	Supplier Manager
6	Woman	Quality Engineer	Ph.D. in Production Management	Product Manager
7	Woman	Animal Science Engineer	Ph.D. in Agricultural Engineering	Industrial Laboratory
8	Man	Supplier	Master of Production Management	Factory Production
9	Man	Mechanized Farmer	Master of Agriculture Biotechnology	Farming
10	Man	Plant Researcher	Master of Biosystem	Industrial Laboratory

3.2. Delphi Process

This process has been done in three rounds two of which are qualitative, and one of which is quantitative. Expert opinions were announced in qualitative rounds and the third round was quantitatively held because no new idea was received in the second round.

3.2.1. First Round

The expert's opinions are listed in Table 3 with the receiving questionnaire.

Table 3. First-round

	Factor	Viewpoint	Explanation
1	Agricultural Industry	Integration	Integration with 2
2	Internet of Things	Integration	Integration with 1
3	Green Internet of Things	Agreement	By all members of the Delphi team
4	Green Agriculture	Integration	Integration with 5
5	Industrial Internet of Things	Integration	Integration with 4
6	Industrial Farming Products	Remove	Suggestion By 8 members of the Delphi team
7	Automatic planting and monitoring	Correction	Correction to "Automatic planting and remote monitoring"
8	Agriculture based on sensor management	Correction	Correction to "Water, livestock and product management with smart agriculture"
9	Environmental temperature & humidity	Correction	Correction to "Measurement of environmental temperature & humidity, soil moisture & PH with sensor data"
10	Estimating the best harvesting time by the farmer	Agreement	9 members of the Delphi team
11	Assuring the food mass production by farmer	Agreement	8 members of the Delphi team
12	Optimal actions based on farm parameter's variation	Correction	Correction to "The most optimal actions based on farm parameter's variation by alert email sending"
13	Green nanotechnology creation for sustainable agriculture in the supply chain	Correction	Correction to "Sustainable agriculture with Green nanotechnology in the supply chain"
14	Continues soil and plant monitoring	Correction	Correction to "Precision agriculture (PA) by continues soil and plant monitoring"
15	Artificial Intelligence in Green Agriculture Internet of Things	Agreement	By all members of the Delphi team

Remove, integration, correction, or agreement are the expert viewpoints that are making the second round of the Delphi questionnaire.

3.2.2. Second Round

In this round, agreement or disagreement of experts collected with other viewpoints to show results in Table 4:

Table 4. Second round

	Factor	Explanation
1	Agriculture Internet of Things	10 people agreed
2	Green Internet of Things	10 people agreed
3	Green Agriculture Internet of Things	10 people agreed
4	Automatic planting and remote monitoring	9 people agreed without qualitative opinion
5	Water, livestock, and product management with smart agriculture	9 people agreed and one person disagreed
6	Measurement of environmental temperature & humidity, soil moisture & PH with sensor data	8 people agreed without qualitative opinion
7	Estimating the best harvesting time by the farmer	8 people agreed and 2 people did not answer
8	Assuring the food mass production by farmer	9 people agreed without qualitative opinion
9	The most optimal actions based on farm parameter's variation by alert email sending	10 people agreed
10	Sustainable agriculture with Green nanotechnology in the supply chain	9 people agreed and one person did not answer
11	Precision agriculture (PA) by continuing soil and plant monitoring	8 people agreed without qualitative opinion
12	Artificial Intelligence in Green Agriculture Internet of Things	10 people agreed

No new qualitative viewpoint was obtained, and 12 topics were confirmed.

3.2.3. Third Round

The range of 1 to 9 is used in this step for the quantitative questionnaire. Relative opinion consensus is reached when 75% of respondents mark in ranges of 1 to 3, 4 to 6, or 7 to 9. When 75% of the opinions are marked in the range of 7 to 9, the Factor has reached a consensus and is approved; but if 75% of opinion results are answered in the other ranges; the factor is rejected. Table 5 shows the results.

Table 5. Third round

	Topic	Average	Standard Deviation
1	Agriculture Internet of Things	2.42	0.61
2	Green Internet of Things	2.38	0.59
3	Green Agriculture Internet of Things	2.67	0.54
4	Automatic planting and remote monitoring	2.12	0.31
5	Water, livestock, and product management with smart agriculture	2.27	0.47
6	Measurement of environmental temperature & humidity, soil moisture & PH with sensor data	1.91	0.21
7	Estimating the best harvesting time by the farmer	1.74	0.14
8	Assuring the food mass production by farmer	2.04	0.41
9	The most optimal actions based on farm parameter's variation by alert email sending	2.34	0.67
10	Green nanotechnology creation for sustainable agriculture in the supply chain	2.17	0.56
11	Precision agriculture (PA) by continuing soil and plant monitoring	1.74	0.28
12	Artificial Intelligence in Green Agriculture Internet of Things	2.24	0.54

The experts approved all factors based on Table 5.

4. CONCEPTUAL FRAMEWORK

The presented conceptual framework should be explained in detail. AIOT and GIOT are at the top of Figure 1. They can cover all the context below.

Despite the advancements made in precision agriculture through AI and IoT technologies, the integration of these technologies in the form of AIOT is still in its nascent stages (Majeed et al., 2024). This integration poses several challenges, including data acquisition and connectivity, as well as the optimization of AI algorithms based on edge computing processing capabilities. So, using technologies is determining for industries and agriculture.

These challenges need to be addressed to fully harness the potential of AIOT in agriculture. The GIOT aims to optimize the advantages and minimize the negative effects of IoT on the environment, thereby addressing the demand for an intelligent and eco-friendly world (Albreem et al., 2023).

By mixing these two concepts, the GAIOT is created. It can explain the collaboration of AIOT and GIOT. Furthermore, the advantage of GIOT is described precisely. Also, the applications and the dimensions of the GIOT are explained properly. In addition, there are three elements for applications and dimensions. The advantages of the GAIOT were explained in two factors in the literature section.

In the last section of the conceptual model, the effects of using AI in agriculture are explained and the collaboration between AI and IoT can help the whole process of agriculture. In summary, the model presents the agriculture industry 6.0 which can define the modern concept of agriculture in the new generation.

Figure 1. Conceptual framework of chapter

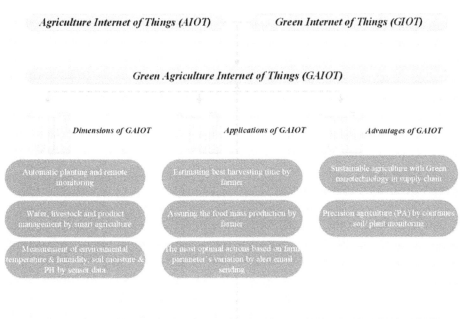

5. DISCUSSION

On one hand agriculture industry has always been a vital issue in the world and on the other hand, the Industrial Revolution developed all the industries. The agriculture industry has been developed too. Thus, society can use the developed version of agriculture.

In conclusion, the use of AI in green agriculture IoT can be the most important factor in this chapter. According to research the Agriculture Management Information System (AMIS), is an intelligent system, which utilizes an intelligent algorithm (Koshariya et al., 2023). So, it is understandable that by developing AI and IoT, the whole process of agriculture can thoroughly affect the agriculture industry.

In this chapter, the essence of applying technology is stated for readers. Also, the conceptual framework has shown that modern technologies can transform the whole process of the agriculture industry in the world. Farmers can harvest their products and earn their money in this way. For sure, the supply chain of this industry is affected by the new types of technology.

As a future study, the whole participants of the supply chain can be observed by using smart technologies. However, this chapter demonstrated the future trends of agriculture as an industrial insight.

REFERENCES

Albreem, M. A., Sheikh, A. M., Bashir, M. J., & El-Saleh, A. A. (2023). Towards green Internet of Things (IoT) for a sustainable future in Gulf Cooperation Council countries: Current practices, challenges and future prospective. *Wireless Networks*, *29*(2), 539–567. doi:10.1007/s11276-022-03133-3

Ali, T. A., Choksi, V., & Potdar, M. B. (2018, May). Precision agriculture monitoring system using green internet of things (g-iot). In *2018 2nd International Conference on Trends in Electronics and Informatics (ICOEI)* (pp. 481-487). IEEE.

Aliahmadi, A., Movahed, A. B., & Nozari, H. (2024). Collaboration Analysis in Supply Chain 4.0 for Smart Businesses. In Building Smart and Sustainable Businesses With Transformative Technologies (pp. 103-122). IGI Global.

Jaiganesh, S., Gunaseelan, K., & Ellappan, V. (2017, March). IOT agriculture to improve food and farming technology. In *2017 Conference on Emerging Devices and Smart Systems (ICEDSS)* (pp. 260-266). IEEE. 10.1109/ICEDSS.2017.8073690

Koshariya, A. K., Kalaiyarasi, D., Jovith, A. A., Sivakami, T., Hasan, D. S., & Boopathi, S. (2023). Ai-enabled IoT and wln-integrated smart agriculture system. In *Artificial Intelligence Tools and Technologies for Smart Farming and Agriculture Practices* (pp. 200–218). IGI Global. doi:10.4018/978-1-6684-8516-3.ch011

Madushanki, A. R., Halgamuge, M. N., Wirasagoda, W. S., & Syed, A. (2019). Adoption of the Internet of Things (IoT) in agriculture and smart farming towards urban greening: A review. *International Journal of Advanced Computer Science and Applications*, *10*(4), 11–28. doi:10.14569/IJACSA.2019.0100402

Majeed, Y., Fu, L., & He, L. (2024). Artificial intelligence-of-things (AIoT) in precision agriculture. *Frontiers in Plant Science*, *15*, 1369791. doi:10.3389/fpls.2024.1369791 PMID:38344185

Movahed, A. B., Movahed, A. B., & Nozari, H. (2024a). Opportunities and Challenges of Smart Supply Chain in Industry 5.0. Information Logistics for Organizational Empowerment and Effective Supply Chain Management, 108-138.

Movahed, A. B., Movahed, A. B., & Nozari, H. (2024b). Opportunities and Challenges of Marketing 5.0. *Smart and Sustainable Interactive Marketing*, 1-21.

Omanović-Mikličanin, E., & Maksimović, M. (2018). *Application of nanotechnology in agriculture and food production—Nanofood and nanoagriculture. IcETRAN. Palic*. Serbia.

Pathak, S., Arora, K., & Quraishi, S. J. (2024). Strategic Challenges of Human Resources Management in the Industry 6.0. In Futuristic e-Governance Security With Deep Learning Applications (pp. 169-190). IGI Global.

Tran, H. A. M., Ngo, H. Q. T., Nguyen, T. P., & Nguyen, H. (2018, November). Design of green agriculture system using the Internet of things and image processing techniques. In *2018 4th International Conference on Green Technology and Sustainable Development (GTSD)* (pp. 28-32). IEEE. 10.1109/GTSD.2018.8595663

Xu, B., Luo, C., & Xie, S. (2022). *Research and Design of "AI+ Agriculture" Disease Detection System Based on Deep Learning. In 3D Imaging—Multidimensional Signal Processing and Deep Learning: Multidimensional Signals, Images, Video Processing and Applications* (Vol. 2). Springer Nature Singapore.

Chapter 4
Hospital 6.0 Components and Dimensions

Mohammad Hadi Aliahmadi
ⓘ https://orcid.org/0000-0001-9588-2007
Iran University of Science and Technology, Iran

Aminmasoud Bakhshi Movahed
ⓘ https://orcid.org/0000-0003-3259-5419
Iran University of Science and Technology, Iran

Ali Bakhshi Movahed
Iran University of Science and Technology, Iran

Hamed Nozari
ⓘ https://orcid.org/0000-0002-6500-6708
Azad University of the Emirates, UAE

Mahmonir Bayanati
Islamic Azad University, Tehran, Iran

ABSTRACT

The processes and dimensions of the development of the health system are some of the most important parts of a healthy society. The positive vision formation for people toward a society's health system requires trust, honesty, specialization, and two-way interactions between people and the healthcare system. Hospitals as a physical environment symbolize society's health system. As much as this physical environment reflects a more efficient and developing image of society in appearance, process, logistics, and infrastructure, the physical and mental peace of people will be improved. For this purpose, health systems and hospitals must adapt to current industrial and technological conditions. The smart hospital is one of the concepts that is developed in this field. In this chapter, due to the importance of hospital smartization, Industry 6.0 has been integrated with the smart hospital, and Hospital 6.0 has been propounded.

DOI: 10.4018/979-8-3693-3108-8.ch004

1. INTRODUCTION

Throughout history, the concept of eternal life has captivated the minds of monarchs and the wealthy. Conversely, most individuals focused on mere survival. Consequently, both affluent and impoverished individuals shared anxieties about their existence. Since life is a gift, the preservation of this valuable gift has been the main issue of the human brain from the past until now. So, by facing this challenge, societies began to solve it by founding medical facilities. Communities established hospitals to prioritize the well-being and longevity of individuals. For the implementation of this goal, the industry had to play its part.

Industry 6.0 and Hospital 6.0 can be related to each other and can have many suitable results for society. There is some different research on Industry 6.0 explaining the technologies for better healthcare globally (Jeyaraman et al., 2022). Through the sixth generation of industry and hospitals, people can find a more comfortable healthcare system. According to the progress of technology and its tools, generations can transform the whole industry. In this research, industry and hospitals perform shoulder-by-shoulder and attempt to build a whole new generation in the new world as shown in Figure 1.

The concept of quality transformation in hospitals can be defined as the systematic endeavor of enhancing the quality of healthcare services. It encompasses the implementation of various strategies and initiatives aimed at augmenting patient safety, clinical outcomes, patient experience, and the overall delivery of healthcare. Additionally, Industry 5.0 effects and the technologies of Industry 4.0 transform the layer of quality in hospitals (Poornachandrika & Venkatasudhakar, 2020). Also, automation technologies can be an example of industry 5.0 effects (Movahed et al., 2024). In this way, quality transformation in life and industrial transformation can collaborate to evolve the healthcare system.

On the other hand, there is industrial transformation. Industrial transformation in healthcare facilities involves the utilization of industrial principles and methodologies to enhance the productivity and quality of healthcare services. This entails the incorporation of cutting-edge technologies and implementing data-driven strategies to elevate patient care, optimize operations, and ultimately achieve better outcomes (Nozari et al., 2021). The evolution of the healthcare system means that people can empty their minds of some obstacles like financial problems or level of service quality. The government can play a crucial role here. it needs to increase financial investments in the medical centers (Yang & Han, 2023).

Also, the whole process of accessing the healthcare system will be quick by applying new kinds of technologies. AI and Data analytics are some of the smart technologies that can facilitate the decision-making process in hospitals. AI, machine learning, and data analytics can address various concerns (Singha et al., 2023), especially in some dangerous cancers. Imagine a situation where the top management of an equipped hospital receives a poor circumstances report from the emergency room. For sure, the condition of the manager's mind will be tranquil for making decisions by having a strong tool of technologies.

In the sixth generation of hospitals, some of the processes will be done just in time. This issue helps employees and patients to manage their time better and better. However, in most countries, even the developed ones, the members of society are not satisfied with the healthcare system services, especially in imaging techniques. Magnetic resonance imaging (MRI) can be a good sample for this topic. MRI studies have high specificity in hospitals generally (Silva et al., 2023). Also, analyzing medical images is very determining in hospitals, especially in emergency cases. In addition, some applications are set up to play the role of a hospital in the house of patients. Huma is a proper example of this topic (Nozari., 2024). This new and popular application could attract and keep large numbers of customers. It can make a community with people who suffer from the same disease and connect them and increase the morality of patients.

In summary, Figure 1 tells the story of Industry 6.0 and Hospital 6.0 for those readers who tend to understand the power of science and technology in the new generation.

Figure 1. Industry 6.0 to Hospital 6.0

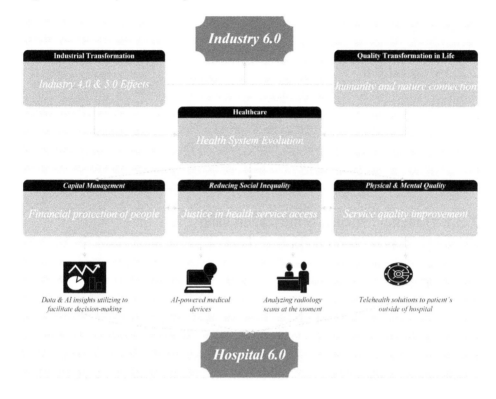

2. LITERATURE REVIEW

The important point of this section is the definition of Industry 6.0 and Hospital 6.0 and their significant elements that is explained in the following. Also, applying various types of technologies in the different sections of the healthcare systems will be defined.

2.1. Industry 6.0

Researchers are currently considering Industry 6.0, a groundbreaking concept that builds upon Industry 5.0 (Singh et al., 2024). One of the primary objectives of Industry 6.0 is to establish intelligent healthcare facilities. This emerging phase of industrialization is anticipated to yield significant advancements in sustainability. However, the ability to take care of the patients based on individual requirements is not limited. By helping Industry 6.0, hospitals can be more productive than ever. The agility of the process in them will be increased for sure. Industry 6.0 implies that all processes, individuals, and objects will undergo a transformative journey in the backdrop of technology (Nozari, 2024). The entire decision-making process within factories will undergo a metamorphosis, allowing people to experience tangible differences.

2.2. Hospital 6.0

In the process of establishing the sixth generation of hospitals in the global range, the technologies are determined as an important factor. Furthermore, the process in the hospitals and the operational instructions of the systems are signified by the performance of the new generation of healthcare systems. Some points in this field will be explained in the following.

2.2.1. Hospital Process Smartzation With Digital Network Infrastructure

The digitalization of hospital processes using a smart network infrastructure entails the utilization of advanced technologies and digital systems to enhance different operations within a hospital environment. It needs the integration of intelligent devices, data analysis, and network infrastructure to boost productivity, enhance patient care, and facilitate informed decision-making. Healthcare systems have a crucial role in facilitating the connection between patients (Zeadally & Bello, 2021). With the aid of digital network infrastructure, hospitals can establish connections between diverse devices and systems, including medical devices, and monitoring systems, via a secure and dependable network. This facilitates the smooth exchange of data, enables real-time monitoring, and grants remote access to patient information.

2.2.2. Digital Timing Design From the Beginning of the Patient's Pain

This title refers to the process of capturing and recording the timing and the duration of an ache experienced by an ill person using digital tools or technologies. The process of experiencing can be attained through various means, including electronic health records (EHRs), mobile applications, or wearable devices. By accurately documenting the timing of the patient's pain from its beginning, healthcare providers can gain valuable insights into the duration, frequency, and patterns of the ache. Medical diagnoses play a role in identifying patterns and creating patient profiles (Perry et al., 2020). Also, these types of information are practical in diagnosing and treating the underlying condition, monitoring the effectiveness of interventions, and making well-informed decisions regarding pain management strategies. Moreover, digital timing design can facilitate improved communication and collaboration between healthcare professionals and patients. It enables the sharing of real-time pain data, thereby allowing healthcare providers to offer timely interventions and make necessary adjustments to treatment plans. However, it is vital to emphasize that the use of digital timing design in pain management should always be accompanied by suitable clinical assessment and evaluation.

2.2.3. Automation of Healthcare Service Process

By implementing automation in the hospital's procedures, healthcare providers have the potential to minimize human errors and maximize patient satisfaction. Also, hospitals can allocate more time to patients. Automation is a core aspect of the hospitals' performance and aims to reduce manual errors (Muhammad & Munir, 2023) and enhance the enjoyment moments during sickness. Furthermore, automation can facilitate superior data management and analysis, resulting in well-informed decision-making.

2.2.4. Providing the Most Appropriate Suggestions According to the Patient's Problems With AI

There are some points in this title. AI can examine extensive volumes of patient data, including medical records and test outcomes, to detect patterns and potential risk elements. As it is stated, pattern recognition in medical science is the key element to progress. This ability aids healthcare providers in making well-informed decisions and tailoring treatment plans to individual patients. Also, AI remote monitoring can happen for patients. The monitoring and control process could be facilitated by the integration of remote sensing systems, supported by IoT and AI (Alshamrani, 2022).

2.2.5. Improving the Analytical Insight of Hospital Staff With Machine Learning

Implementing machine learning algorithms can augment analytical insights for healthcare professionals through the analysis of patient data. practical analysis of the facets of patients hospitalized can help the processes of data management (Ranzani et al., 2021). Also, machine learning can be applied in hospitals to diagnose diseases. By identifying patterns and predicting disease progression, these algorithms can optimize resource allocation. Moreover, they can aid in forecasting patient admission rates and identifying potential risks. Ultimately, the integration of machine learning algorithms can contribute to more efficient and informed healthcare practices.

2.2.6. Maximum Clarification of Patient's Condition for Medical Staff With IoT

The integration of the IoT framework within the healthcare sector can improve patient monitoring and furnish medical personnel with comprehensive information. By utilizing sensors, it becomes possible to track vital signs, including heart rate, blood pressure, and temperature, in real-time. Continuously wearable sensors can measure heart rate in the hospital (Peters et al., 2023) for patients who rely on this assessment more than the other. Furthermore, the incorporation of continuous glucose monitoring can be beneficial for diabetic patients (Asbaghi et al., 2023). To safeguard patient privacy, it is obligatory to establish secure data transmission protocols.

2.2.7. Health Worker Accompanying Discharged Patients Until Full Recovery With Smart Software

Implementing intelligent software to support discharged patients until complete recuperation is a highly encouraging concept. This could encompass the continuous monitoring of crucial health indicators, offering timely medication reminders, and facilitating seamless communication with healthcare practitioners. Smart software can help the process of discharge for patients. Such an approach probably can enhance patient care and mitigate the likelihood of complications arising after discharge (Nozari et al., 2024).

2.2.8. Predicting Other Possible Problems in the Patient's Future With Continued Controlling

Regularly evaluating and reevaluating the patient's well-being, imparting knowledge, and assistance, and adapting treatment strategies when necessary are imperative tasks for healthcare practitioners to mitigate the likelihood of potential issues. Nevertheless, predicting the future in such a fully possibility field is a difficult task to do but probably there will be more alternatives for controlling sick people in a way that will be continual.

3. APPROACH AND FRAMEWORK

H 5.0 needs a conceptual approach to submit its framework. The Delphi method was used to validate the extracted concepts. In Delphi, feedback influences individual responses and the achievement of consensus (Barrios et al., 2021).

3.1. Delphi Method

The Delphi method is considered in research as a technique for reaching consensus about specific titles when empirical evidence is contentious (Barrios et al., 2021). The Delphi technique is defined as a research approach to obtain consensus by using questionnaires and providing feedback to participants who have expertise in key areas. This technique is used to reach an agreement on the importance of indicators (Yousuf, 2019).

3.1.1. Delphi Statistics

A team and a panel contributed to performing the Delphi method. In a cycle process, the opinions of the Delphi team were provided to the Delphi panel for aggregation. Descriptive statistics of the Delphi team and panel are given in Tables 1 and 2.

Table 1. Delphi panel

	Academic Degree	Job Career	Work Experiences
1	Ph.D. in Biotechnology	Professor	25 Years
2	Ph.D. in Medical Science	Associate Professor	20 Years
3	Ph.D. in Information technology	Associate Professor	18 Years
4	Ph.D. in Industrial Engineering	Assistant Professor	10 Years
5	Ph.D. in Technology Management	Assistant Professor	10 Years

Table 2. Delphi team

	Academic Degree	Job Career	Work Experiences
1	Ph.D. in Medical Science	Associate Professor	20 Years
2	Ph.D. in Neurology	Associate Professor	18 Years
3	Ph.D. in Pharmaceutics	Pharmacist	18 Years
4	Ph.D. in Nursing	Hospital Supervisor	15 Years
5	Ph.D. in Information technology	System Admin	15 Years
6	Ph.D. in Information technology	Database Administrator	12 Years
7	Ph.D. in Technology Management	Supply chain Analytics	10 Years
8	Ph.D. in Industrial Engineering	Health and Safety manager	10 Years
9	Ph.D. in Industrial Engineering	Consultant of knowledge-based companies	8 Years
10	Master of Radiology	Hospital Radiologist	6 Years
11	Master of Pathology	Hospital Pathologist	5 Years
12	Master of Nursing	Hospital Nurse	5 Years

3.1.2. Delphi Results

The Delphi method was done in three rounds. In this process two rounds are qualitative, and one round is quantitative. In two qualitative rounds, expert's opinions were announced. Finally, the third round was held quantitatively, because no new qualitative opinion was obtained in the second round.

3.1.2.1 First Round

The questionnaire was sent to experts to express their opinions in this round. The opinions in the first round are listed in Table 3.

Table 3. First-round

	Components	Point of View	Explanation
1	Hospital process smartzation	Integration	Integration with 3
2	Hospital Digital timing design	Correction	Correction to "Digital timing design from the beginning of the patient pain"
3	Digital network infrastructure	Integration	Integration with 1
4	Service Automation	Integration	Integration with 5
5	Automation of the healthcare process	Integration	Integration with 4
6	Appropriate suggestions according to the patient's problems	Correction	Correction to "Providing the most appropriate suggestions according to the patient's problems with AI"
7	Improving the analytical insight of hospital staff	Correction	Correction to "Improving the analytical insight of hospital staff with machine learning"
8	Maximum clarification of patient's condition for medical staff with IoT	Agreement	Agreed by eleven experts of the Delphi team
9	Accompanying medical staff with discharged patients until full recovery	Correction	Correction to "Health worker accompanying discharged patients until full recovery with smart software"
10	Predicting other possible problems in the patient's future with continued controlling	Agreement	Agreed by twelve experts of the Delphi team

The expert's opinion includes integration, correction, or agreement. These opinions are the second round basis of the Delphi questionnaire.

3.1.2.2 Second Round

No new qualitative opinions were obtained in this step. Experts expressed their agreement and disagreement with the other's opinions of the previous round. The results are given in Table 4:

Table 4. Second-round

	Components	Explanation
1	Hospital process smartzation with digital network infrastructure	Eleven people agreed and one person did not answer
2	Digital timing design from the beginning of the patient's pain	Eleven people agreed without one people did not answer
3	Automation of the healthcare service process	Ten people agreed without declaring a qualitative opinion and Two people did not answer
4	Providing the most appropriate suggestions according to the patient's problems with AI	Twelve people agreed without declaring a qualitative opinion
5	Improving the analytical insight of hospital staff with machine learning	Eleven people agreed and one person disagreed without declaring a qualitative opinion
6	Maximum clarification of patient's condition for medical staff with IoT	Eleven people agreed without declaring a qualitative opinion and one person did not answer
7	Health workers accompanying discharged patients until full recovery with smart software	Ten people agreed without declaring a qualitative opinion and Two people did not answer
8	Predicting other possible problems in the patient's future with continued controlling	Twelve people agreed

In the end, components were confirmed because no new qualitative opinion was obtained.

3.1.2.3 Third Round of Delphi

A quantitative questionnaire was prepared in this step and the range of 1 to 9 is used. For reaching a relative opinion consensus, 75% of the respondents mark in one of the ranges 1 to 3, 4 to 6, or 7 to 9. If 75% of the opinions were in the range of 7 to 9, the component has reached a consensus and is approved; but if 75% of the results are answered in the other intervals; the component reaches consensus and is rejected. The results are given in Table 5.

Table 5. Third-round

	Components	Average	Standard Deviation	Interpretation
1	Hospital process smartzation with digital network infrastructure	2.38	0.41	Consensus and approval
2	Digital timing design from the beginning of the patient's pain	2.91	0.25	Consensus and approval
3	Automation of the healthcare service process	1.67	0.71	Consensus and approval
4	Providing the most appropriate suggestions according to the patient's problems with AI	2.09	0.43	Consensus and approval
5	Improving the analytical insight of hospital staff with machine learning	2.32	0.56	Consensus and approval
6	Maximum clarification of patient's condition for medical staff with IoT	2.14	0.68	Consensus and approval
7	Health workers accompanying discharged patients until full recovery with smart software	1.84	0.64	Consensus and approval
8	Predicting other possible problems in the patient's future with continued controlling	1.98	0.79	Consensus and approval

The experts approved all the components of H 6.0 according to Table 5.

3.2. Conceptual Framework

The basic elements of Figure 2 are defined in detail in the literature review for readers who tend to understand the concept of technology and the concept of health. For this reason, the conceptual framework states the connection between industry and hospital. Technology and industry are on one side of this research. Additionally, healthcare systems and hospitals are on the other side of the present research. It is important to state that innovation in this research can happen by the shadow of the sixth generation of the industry and hospital. Quick access and improving clinical experiences are the two factors that can occur by this innovation. Also, personal patient experiences can happen in a better way.

Figure 2. Conceptual framework of H 6.0

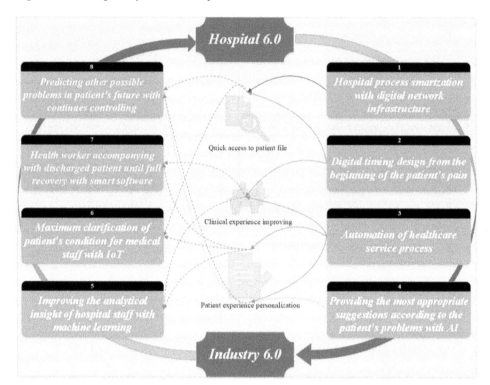

4. CONCLUSION

In conclusion, the significant concepts and outcomes of the research are explained. In this section, it is stated that by establishing a new generation of hospitals, people can live easier than in the past. They can use the technologies more and more. Thus, the quality of their life will be more and more too. In the history of humans, people asked scientists to investigate and discover new things. The elite part of society could invent many new tools for people. Hospitals could play their part in this story by caring for people and giving them the remedy. This generation of hospitals can create magic and miracles for patients. In the following, some of the advantages of Hospital 6.0 as an outcome of the research are demonstrated.

Quick access to the files and documentation of the patients in hospitals. Efficient retrieval of patient files and documentation is of utmost importance in hospitals. By incorporating a secure EHR system (Johnston et al., 2023), this process can be streamlined, guaranteeing swift access while upholding the integrity and confidentiality of data.

Clinical experience improvement in hospitals is another advantage. Structured training programs, the provision of diverse case exposure, and the facilitation of collaboration among healthcare practitioners probably can enhance the clinical experience within hospital settings. Paying attention to the clinical experience can probably enhance future procedures in hospitals. (Sartoretti et al., 2023). By integrating simulation exercises, fostering continuous professional development, and harnessing the power of technology, hospitals can establish a more all-encompassing and enriching clinical environment. Proving the appropriate circumstances for patients can significantly affect the recovery process in hospitals.

Applying customization and personalization is crucial as it caters to the preferences of the contemporary generation. So, to gain a deeper understanding of the present subject, a research study can explore it better (Wan & Xia, 2023). Personalizing the experiences of patients in hospitals entails customizing the care provided to meet their individual needs. This objective can be accomplished by developing comprehensive patient profiles, ensuring effective communication, and integrating patient preferences into treatment plans. The utilization of technology to gather real-time feedback, establish comfortable environments, and provide personalized support all contribute to fostering a more patient-centric approach within healthcare settings.

Thus, as a future insight, Hospital 6.0 is observed to be a player in the global healthcare system in the world for people who are eager to innovate and make a better society for the members. Physicians and doctors will be the people who can dedicate their lives more and more. So, if any type of doctor is reading the present chapter can realize that he or she must improve with the transformations of technology because it acts like a sea. If the swimmer is trying to resist the waves, he or she will not survive. Otherwise, the swimmer can swim over the water. Waves of the technologies in the context of the various Industrial Revolutions are those waves of the sea.

REFERENCES

Aliahmadi, A., Movahed, A. B., & Nozari, H. (2024). Collaboration Analysis in Supply Chain 4.0 for Smart Businesses. In Building Smart and Sustainable Businesses With Transformative Technologies (pp. 103-122). IGI Global.

Alshamrani, M. (2022). IoT and artificial intelligence implementations for remote healthcare monitoring systems: A survey. *Journal of King Saud University. Computer and Information Sciences*, *34*(8), 4687–4701. doi:10.1016/j.jksuci.2021.06.005

Asbaghi, O., Nazarian, B., Yousefi, M., Anjom-Shoae, J., Rasekhi, H., & Sadeghi, O. (2023). Effect of vitamin E intake on glycemic control and insulin resistance in diabetic patients: An updated systematic review and meta-analysis of randomized controlled trials. *Nutrition Journal, 22*(1), 1–22. doi:10.1186/s12937-023-00840-1 PMID:36800965

Barrios, M., Guilera, G., Nuño, L., & Gómez-Benito, J. (2021). Consensus in the Delphi method: What makes a decision change? *Technological Forecasting and Social Change, 163*, 120484. doi:10.1016/j.techfore.2020.120484

Forde-Johnston, C., Butcher, D., & Aveyard, H. (2023). An integrative review exploring the impact of Electronic Health Records (EHR) on the quality of nurse–patient interactions and communication. *Journal of Advanced Nursing, 79*(1), 48–67. doi:10.1111/jan.15484 PMID:36345050

Jeyaraman, M., Nallakumarasamy, A., & Jeyaraman, N. (2022). Industry 5.0 in orthopaedics. *Indian Journal of Orthopaedics, 56*(10), 1694–1702. doi:10.1007/s43465-022-00712-6 PMID:36187596

Movahed, A. B., Movahed, A. B., & Nozari, H. (2024). Opportunities and Challenges of Smart Supply Chain in Industry 5.0. *Information Logistics for Organizational Empowerment and Effective Supply Chain Management*, 108-138.

Muhammad, T., & Munir, M. (2023). Network Automation. *European Journal of Technology, 7*(2), 23–42. doi:10.47672/ejt.1547

Nozari, H. (2024). Supply Chain 6.0 and Moving Towards Hyper-Intelligent Processes. In Information Logistics for Organizational Empowerment and Effective Supply Chain Management (pp. 1-13). IGI Global.

Nozari, H., Fallah, M., Kazemipoor, H., & Najafi, S. E. (2021). Big data analysis of IoT-based supply chain management considering FMCG industries. *Бизнес-информатика, 15*(1, 1 (eng)), 78–96. doi:10.17323/2587-814X.2021.1.78.96

Nozari, H., & Szmelter-Jarosz, A. (2024). An Analytical Framework for Smart Supply Chains 5.0. In *Building Smart and Sustainable Businesses With Transformative Technologies* (pp. 1–15). IGI Global.

Perry, A., Lawrence, V., & Henderson, C. (2020). Stigmatization of those with mental health conditions in the acute general hospital setting. A qualitative framework synthesis. *Social Science & Medicine, 255*, 112974. doi:10.1016/j.socscimed.2020.112974 PMID:32388323

Peters, G. M., Peelen, R. V., Gilissen, V. J., Koning, M. V., van Harten, W. H., & Doggen, C. J. (2023). Detecting Patient Deterioration Early Using Continuous Heart rate and Respiratory rate Measurements in Hospitalized COVID-19 Patients. *Journal of Medical Systems*, *47*(1), 12. doi:10.1007/s10916-022-01898-w PMID:36692798

Poornachandrika, V., & Venkatasudhakar, M. (2020, September). Quality transformation to improve customer satisfaction: Using product, process, system, and behavior model. []. IOP Publishing.]. *IOP Conference Series. Materials Science and Engineering*, *923*(1), 012034. doi:10.1088/1757-899X/923/1/012034

Ranzani, O. T., Bastos, L. S., Gelli, J. G. M., Marchesi, J. F., Baião, F., Hamacher, S., & Bozza, F. A. (2021). Characterization of the first 250 000 hospital admissions for COVID-19 in Brazil: A retrospective analysis of nationwide data. *The Lancet. Respiratory Medicine*, *9*(4), 407–418. doi:10.1016/S2213-2600(20)30560-9 PMID:33460571

Sartoretti, T., Wildberger, J. E., Flohr, T., & Alkadhi, H. (2023). Photon-counting detector CT: Early clinical experience review. *The British Journal of Radiology*, *95*, 20220544. doi:10.1259/bjr.20220544 PMID:36744809

Silva, A. R., Almeida-Xavier, S., Lopes, M., Soares-Fernandes, J. P., Sousa, F., & Varanda, S. (2023). Is there a time window for an MRI in Wernicke encephalopathy—A decade of experience from a tertiary hospital? *Neurological Sciences*, *44*(2), 703–708. doi:10.1007/s10072-022-06477-y PMID:36335281

Singh, R., Tyagi, A. K., & Arumugam, S. K. (2024). Imagining the Sustainable Future With Industry 6.0: A Smarter Pathway for Modern Society and Manufacturing Industries. In Machine Learning Algorithms Using Scikit and TensorFlow Environments (pp. 318-331). IGI Global.

Singha, S., Arha, H., & Kar, A. K. (2023). Healthcare analytics: A techno-functional perspective. *Technological Forecasting and Social Change*, *197*, 122908. doi:10.1016/j.techfore.2023.122908

Wan, J., & Xia, H. (2023, March). How Advanced Practice Nurses Can Be Better Managed in Hospitals: A Multi-Case Study. *Health Care*, *11*(6), 780. PMID:36981438

Yang, F., Qi, W., & Han, J. (2023). Research on the mechanism of promoting coordinated development of ecological well-being in rural counties through industrial transformation. *PLoS One*, *18*(9), e0291232. doi:10.1371/journal.pone.0291232 PMID:37682965

Zeadally, S., & Bello, O. (2021). Harnessing the power of Internet of Things-based connectivity to improve healthcare. *Internet of Things : Engineering Cyber Physical Human Systems*, *14*, 100074. doi:10.1016/j.iot.2019.100074

Chapter 5
Security Criteria in Financial Systems in Industry 6.0

Ali Bakhshi Movahed
Iran University of Science and Technology, Iran

Aminmasoud Bakhshi Movahed
ⓘ https://orcid.org/0000-0003-3259-5419
Iran University of Science and Technology, Iran

Hamed Nozari
ⓘ https://orcid.org/0000-0002-6500-6708
Azad University of the Emirates, UAE

Maryam Rahmaty
Islamic Azad University, Chalous, Iran

ABSTRACT

The importance of the financial system in the industry is not only related to the organization itself but also depends on the industry's network. Technological developments, growth in industry, and increasing use of new technology in human life have changed the organization's financial system. One of the most important factors in the necessity of financial development is the issue of network security, monetary systems, banking systems, and privacy of customers and users. For this purpose, it will be considered to improve the quality level and speed of this process to pursue financial claims. Along with the industrial developments of different generations and the continuous and universal use of Industry 4.0 technologies, the financial and banking system also needs to be updated and mastered to reduce cybercrime and prevent financial fraud and bank stolen. This chapter examines the financial system by analyzing the financial security criteria and achieving Financial Security 6.0.

DOI: 10.4018/979-8-3693-3108-8.ch005

1. INTRODUCTION

In the dynamic landscape of Industry 6.0, the incorporation of smart technologies and digital transformation has brought forth unparalleled opportunities and efficiencies in the financial sector. Nevertheless, with the increasing interconnectivity and reliance on advanced technologies, the significance of robust security criteria cannot be overstated. Consequently, it becomes crucial to establish and adhere to comprehensive security criteria to protect the integrity, confidentiality, and availability of financial data and transactions.

Throughout history, ensuring security has consistently remained a paramount concern as individuals constantly seek to find themselves in a secure environment. Moreover, the utilization of various tools empowers individuals to safeguard their well-being. Therefore, the emergence of novel technologies can significantly impact their lives. As a result, the advancement of technology can greatly enhance the overall quality of life. Consequently, people will attain a sense of security while simultaneously experiencing increased ease in their daily lives.

Additionally, Security holds utmost significance in the financial sector, particularly within the context of Industry 6.0, where technological advancements have revolutionized the operations of financial systems. With the increasing dependence of financial institutions on digital platforms and applications and interconnected networks, the need for robust security measures becomes even more critical.

Industry 6.0 encompasses the integration of cutting-edge technologies such as AI, IoT, blockchain, and cloud computing, which bring numerous benefits but also introduce new security challenges. It always happens that the generations of the industrial revelation can change concepts and generate tools for the new world. So, the concept of security is always affected by the new generation of industry.

In this era of Industry 6.0, financial systems face a wide range of threats, including cyberattacks, data breaches, identity theft, and fraud. These threats not only jeopardize the integrity and confidentiality of sensitive financial information but also pose significant risks to the stability and trustworthiness of the entire financial ecosystem. Therefore, it is essential to establish comprehensive security criteria to safeguard financial systems, protect customer data, and maintain the integrity of transactions (Nozari et al., 2024).

Industry 6.0 is an advanced context focused on security, privacy, and reducing human manipulation. Its goal is to establish a harmonious relationship between humans and machines. Careful consideration of robots and machines is crucial. I 6.0 has the potential to create intelligent, durable, and environmentally sustainable structures. It is forward-thinking and draws upon future insights. To understand Learning I 6.0, a futuristic approach to research is necessary.

The security criteria in financial systems within Industry 6.0 encompass various aspects, including network security, data encryption, access controls, authentication mechanisms, and incident response protocols. Also, all these concepts can be measured for modern financial systems.

These criteria aim to ensure the confidentiality, integrity, and availability of financial data, as well as the resilience of the systems against potential threats. Additionally, compliance with regulatory frameworks and industry standards is crucial to meet legal requirements and maintain public trust (Nozari et al., 2023).

The Global Financial Crisis (GFC), also known as the financial crisis of 2008, had its origins in the United States when the housing bubble burst. Due to the interconnected nature of the international financial system, the crisis quickly spread globally. This led to major institutions facing insolvency, prompting government interventions and bailouts to prevent a systemic collapse. In response to its aftermath, regulatory reforms were implemented to enhance financial stability and prevent the recurrence of such a devastating economic downturn.

Following the global financial crisis that occurred in 2008, the financial system has adopted a formidable facade. Banks have become even more crucial than before, as the interconnectivity between nations has intensified. This enhanced global integration has undeniably facilitated international business for countries worldwide. Consequently, the emergence of new generations has given rise to novel forms of business across the globe.

This chapter provides an overview of the financial system, catering to individuals interested in staying informed about future trends in this field. Additionally, it delves into the key components that constitute the financial system.

2. LITERATURE REVIEW

Technological security involves implementing robust cybersecurity measures to protect financial systems from unauthorized access, data breaches, and other cyber threats. This includes deploying advanced encryption techniques, multi-factor authentication, and intrusion detection systems. Additionally, regular security audits and vulnerability assessments should be conducted to identify and address any potential weaknesses in the system.

2.1. Financial Systems

Financial systems are the key elements of the economy. The financial system assumes a pivotal role in bolstering economic growth and ensuring stability. However, this point should be considered a comprehensive analysis of the expanding range of scholarly works investigating the implications associated with the widespread impact of cybersecurity risk on the financial system (Bindseil, 2020).

The financial system is an intricate network consisting of various institutions, markets, and intermediaries that facilitate the movement of funds and financial services within an economy. It encompasses financial institutions like banks and non-banking financial entities, while financial markets include capital and money markets that deal with long-term and short-term financial instruments respectively (Aliahmadi et al., 2023).

These instruments, such as securities and derivatives, represent ownership or claims on assets and are traded within these markets. Regulatory bodies, such as central banks and financial regulatory authorities, have the responsibility of overseeing and regulating the system to ensure stability and safeguard the interests of investors. Payment and settlement systems are in place to ensure secure transfers of funds and securities.

Financial services, such as insurance and investment services, play crucial roles in the functioning of the system. Furthermore, technology and innovation, including fintech, are revolutionizing the landscape by improving efficiency and introducing new services. Despite challenges such as regulatory complexities and cybersecurity threats, the financial system plays a pivotal role in allocating resources, managing risk, and supporting economic activities.

2.2. Financial Security

Financial security is the condition of possessing a secure and safeguarded financial base that enables individuals, families, or institutions to fulfill their financial responsibilities, meet necessary expenses, strive for financial objectives, and endure unforeseen financial setbacks.

Attaining financial security necessitates a blend of careful financial strategizing, efficient risk mitigation, and the establishment of a robust financial standing. Additionally, the matter of financial security has gained significant importance at both domestic and global levels (Reznik et al., 2020).

Financial security is the state of being free from significant financial risk or instability. It is attained through a combination of prudent financial planning, wise investment choices, and a stable income. Both individuals and businesses strive for financial security to ensure their ability to meet current and future financial obligations, withstand unforeseen expenses, and accomplish long-term financial objectives (Nozari, 2024).

Several key components contribute to financial security, including the establishment of an emergency fund, the creation of a diversified investment portfolio, responsible debt management, and adequate insurance coverage. Additionally, planning for retirement and maintaining a budget are crucial aspects of attaining and sustaining financial security. By adopting sound financial habits and making well-informed decisions, individuals can strengthen their ability to withstand economic uncertainties and establish a solid foundation for a secure and prosperous financial future.

2.3. Financial Security Criteria

Attaining financial stability necessitates careful consideration of various factors. Key elements include establishing an emergency fund to cater for unforeseen expenses, maintaining a stable and diversified income, and effectively managing debt.

To ensure long-term stability, it is important to diversify investments across different asset classes, while adequate insurance coverage serves as a safeguard against unexpected financial setbacks.

Planning for retirement, which involves making contributions to retirement accounts, is crucial for securing a financially stable post-working life. Budgeting, financial literacy, and regular financial assessments are essential for effectively managing income, expenses, and savings.

Furthermore, addressing estate planning matters such as wills and trusts offers a comprehensive approach to safeguarding assets and providing financial security for beneficiaries (Nozari et al., 2023).

By incorporating these criteria into their financial planning, individuals and organizations can enhance their resilience against economic uncertainties and strive toward a stable and prosperous financial future.

Certainly, it is imperative to establish specific criteria for financial security as without them, assessing one's financial stability becomes impractical. In this section of the chapter, the criteria for financial security are determined properly.

Financial transaction verification at the highest level with AI and Maximizing financial claims pursuit are the two criteria for financial security. Also, there are two criteria including Minimizing financial fraud and bank stolen and Reducing cybercrime with ML which are necessary to state.

2.3.1. Financial Transaction Verification at the Highest Level With AI

Financial transaction verification at the most level utilizing AI entails harnessing cutting-edge AI technologies to guarantee the precision, safety, and effectiveness of financial transactions.

This procedure holds paramount importance in the financial sector as it serves to thwart fraudulent activities, bolster adherence to regulations, and uphold the soundness of financial systems. Fraudsters can use AI too (Ahmadi, 2023) and in a mutual path, financial systems can use new and modern types of technologies.

2.3.2. Maximizing Financial Claims Pursuit

Maximizing the pursuit of financial claims usually entails implementing strategic and methodical measures to guarantee the receipt of the utmost compensation or settlement within a legal or financial framework. In this way, the details should be recorded. Also, the necessary evidence should be gathered.

2.3.3. Minimizing Financial Fraud and Bank Stolen

Reducing the likelihood of financial fraud and safeguarding oneself against theft related to banking necessitates a blend of attentiveness, proactive actions, and understanding of possible risks.

According to the findings of the papers, it is revealed that the predominant form of cyber fraud within the banking system was accounting fraud committed by bank personnel (Ekong, 2023). So, it is important to use new technologies to monitor the banks' employees.

2.3.4. Reducing Cybercrime With ML

ML has the potential to significantly contribute to the mitigation of cybercrime by bolstering cybersecurity capabilities.

Through the utilization of ML algorithms, extensive datasets can be analyzed, enabling the identification of patterns and the detection of anomalies that could potentially signify cyber threats. AI and ML are utilized to achieve a decrease in downtime too (Khatoon et al., 2023).

2.4. Achieving Financial Security 6.0

In this section, four titles are explained to the readers who tend to be aware of the way that financial security 6.0 is achieved. Additionally, for title is explained according to the new generation of the industry.

Infrastructure network integration in the financial system and the Privacy importance of customers and beneficiaries are two of them. Also, controlling financial flows by smartphones and smart devices is another topic. The last one is related to the Automation of financial processes inside and outside the organization.

2.4.1. Infrastructure Networks Integration in the Financial System

The incorporation of infrastructure networks into the financial system entails utilizing technology and connectivity to improve the effectiveness, safety, and overall functionality of financial services. This integration encompasses a range of elements, such as communication networks, data centers, cloud computing, and emerging technologies.

2.4.2. Privacy Importance of Customers and Beneficiaries

The protection of personal and financial data holds immense significance for both clients and recipients within the financial industry. Also, ensuring the security of such information not only fosters trust but also guarantees adherence to legal and regulatory frameworks (Nissenbaum, 2020).

2.4.3. Controlling Financial Flows by Smartphones and Smart Devices

The management, monitoring, and execution of financial transactions can be seamlessly achieved by harnessing technology through smartphones and smart devices. The smartphone-enabled customer will have the capability to engage with banking and other institutions (Aripin and Paramarta, 2023).

2.4.4. Automation of Financial Processes Inside and Outside the Organization

The utilization of technology to enhance various financial tasks is integral to the automation of financial processes, both within and outside an organization. This not only leads to improved efficiency, but also mitigates errors, ensures compliance, and enables financial experts to dedicate their efforts towards more strategic endeavors.

3. APPROACH

This research approach includes a focused group, a conceptual framework, and causal relations.

Focus groups are used to understand concepts in depth to clarify the expert's insight. Also, the content of studies is explained by a conceptual framework and a causal relation is stated to demonstrate relations between factors. So, by this explanation, the third section of the chapter can easily explain the structure of the chapter.

3.1. Focus Group

A focus group is an approach to qualitative research wherein a small and diverse group of individuals is assembled to engage in discussions and exchange their viewpoints, perceptions, attitudes, and experiences regarding a specific subject or a series of subjects.

Typically, a skilled moderator leads these discussions by asking open-ended questions, thereby encouraging participants to express their thoughts and actively participate in a dynamic conversation. The primary objective of a focus group is to gather comprehensive insights and qualitative data that can offer a deeper comprehension of the participants' perspectives on the topic under investigation.

Focus group utilization as a qualitative approach highlighted the significance of opinions in this study. This focus group involved ten participants with diverse gender, career, and educational backgrounds.

3.1.1. Descriptive Statistics

Table 1 shows descriptive statistics of the focus group.

Table 1. Descriptive statistics

	Gender	Job Career	Academic Degree
1	Man	Professor	Ph.D. in Financial Management
2	Man	Assistant Professor	Ph.D. in Financial Technology
3	Man	Financial Manager	Ph.D. in Financial Management
4	Woman	Researcher	Ph.D. in Financial Engineering
5	Man	Financial Consultant	Ph.D. in Insurance Management
6	Man	Financial Analyst	Ph.D. in Technology Management
7	Man	Portfolio Manager	Ph.D. in Information Technology
8	Man	Bank Manager	Master of Banking Management
9	Woman	E-Banking Management	Master of Economics
10	Man	Fintech Manager	Master of Business Administration

Focus groups are essential to optimize time and cost for audiences and readers.

3.2. Conceptual Framework

Figure 1. Shows the chapter framework.

Figure 1. Chapter framework

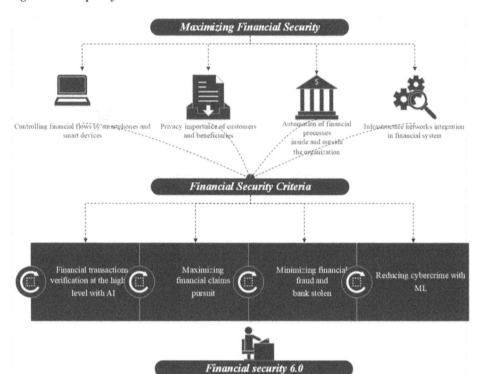

3.3. Causal Relations

DEMATEL technique (Decision Making Trial and Evaluation Laboratory) was applied to analyze the factor causal relations to make a causal map. This method is a comprehensive structural model that considers probability environments (Seyed-Hosseini et al., 2006). A 10x10 non-negative matrix was established and ten matrices were completed. Then, the average was calculated by the initial matrix of direct relationships. After that, the total relations matrix (T matrix) is obtained (1).

$$\tilde{T} = \lim_{k \to \infty} \left(\tilde{x}^1 + \tilde{x}^2 + \dots + \tilde{x}^k \right) \tag{1}$$

The values of (D+R) and (D-R) are obtained in the continuation of the DEMATEL process. The D and R respectively are the sum of rows and columns for matrix T factors. Then $\left[\tilde{D}_{n \times 1} \right], \left[\tilde{R}_{1 \times n} \right]$ is made with (2) and (3).

$$\tilde{D} = \left(\tilde{D}_i\right)_{n\times1} = \left[\sum_{j=1}^{n}\tilde{T}_{ij}\right]_{n\times1} \tag{2}$$

$$\tilde{R} = \left(\tilde{R}_i\right)_{1\times n} = \left[\sum_{i=1}^{n}\tilde{T}_{ij}\right]_{1\times n} \tag{3}$$

Table 2 shows the importance of factors ($\tilde{D}_i + \tilde{R}_i$) and the relationship between them ($\tilde{D}_i - \tilde{R}_i$).

Table 2. Influence of factors

Factor	Rank	D	R	D+R	D–R
Financial transaction verification at the highest level with AI	5	0.66	0.55	1.21	0.11
Maximizing financial claims pursuit	6	0.41	0.54	0.95	-0.13
Minimizing financial fraud and bank stolen	7	0.06	0.61	0.67	-0.55
Reducing cybercrime with ML	8	-0.095	0.665	0.57	-0.76
Infrastructure network integration in the financial system	2	1.2	0.55	1.75	0.65
Privacy importance of customers and beneficiaries	3	1.425	0.875	2.30	0.55
Controlling financial flows by smartphones and smart devices	4	0.825	0.615	1.44	0.21
Automation of financial processes inside and outside the organization	1	0.66	0.55	2.71	0.81

The relationship map is shown in Figure 2.

Figure 2. Relationships map

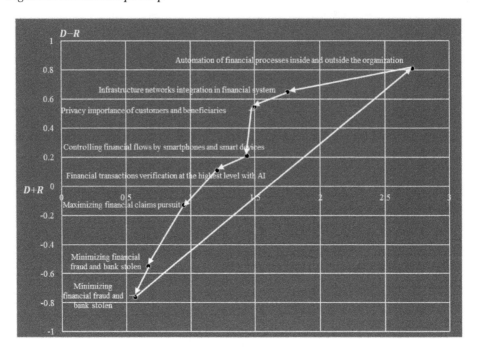

4. CONCLUSION

In the era of Industry 6.0, characterized by extensive interconnectivity and automation, the safeguarding of financial systems is not just a reactive obligation but an essential element of strategic decision-making. So, in this chapter, the necessity and importance of that is explained in detail.

The interdependent nature of technological advancements and security standards lays the groundwork for a robust, reliable, and forward-looking financial ecosystem. For sure the ecosystem in this field is designed to act in an optimum way. However, with the new generation of the financial system, everything in this field will be better than ever. So, the members in this field must collaborate in the shape that is needed.

As financial institutions navigate the intricate landscape of Industry 6.0, giving utmost importance to security standards guarantees not only the safeguarding of valuable assets and data but also the enduring confidence of customers, partners, and the global financial community. Furthermore, financial systems can develop themselves by using technologies.

As the research is explained, the topic of forecasting is improved with the help of modern technologies. Also, the financial systems can use these types of technologies to create and enhance the financial systems. It is also important to establish a new mechanism for financial systems. So, in this chapter as a futurology insight, many items are demonstrated.

REFERENCES

Ahmadi, S. (2023). Open AI and its Impact on Fraud Detection in Financial Industry. Academic Press.

Aliahmadi, A., Ghahremani-Nahr, J., & Nozari, H. (2023). Pricing decisions in the closed-loop supply chain network, taking into account the queuing system in production centers. *Expert Systems with Applications*, *212*, 118741. doi:10.1016/j.eswa.2022.118741

Aliahmadi, A., Movahed, A. B., & Nozari, H. (2024). Collaboration Analysis in Supply Chain 4.0 for Smart Businesses. In Building Smart and Sustainable Businesses With Transformative Technologies (pp. 103-122). IGI Global.

Aripin, Z., Paramarta, V., & Kosasih. (2023). Utilizing the Internet of Things (IoT)-based Design for Consumer Loyalty: A Digital System Integration. *Jurnal Penelitian Pendidikan IPA*, *9*(10), 8650–8655. doi:10.29303/jppipa.v9i10.4490

BindseilU. (2020). Tiered CBDC and the financial system. Available at SSRN 3513422.

Ekong Eyo, U. (2023). *Impact of Cyber-Security on Financial Fraud in Commercial Banks in Nigeria: A Case Study of Zenith Banks in Abuja* [Doctoral dissertation]. AUST.

Khatoon, N., Roy, S., & Narayan, R. Can ML Be Used in Cybersecurity? In Machine Learning in Healthcare and Security (pp. 174-183). CRC Press. doi:10.1201/9781003388845-15

Movahed, A. B., Movahed, A. B., & Nozari, H. (2024a). Opportunities and Challenges of Smart Supply Chain in Industry 5.0. Information Logistics for Organizational Empowerment and Effective Supply Chain Management, 108-138.

Movahed, A. B., Movahed, A. B., & Nozari, H. (2024b). Opportunities and Challenges of Marketing 5.0. Smart and Sustainable Interactive Marketing, 1-21.

Nissenbaum, H. (2020). Protecting privacy in an information age: The problem of privacy in public. In *The ethics of information technologies* (pp. 141–178). Routledge. doi:10.4324/9781003075011-12

Nozari, H. (2024). Supply Chain 6.0 and Moving Towards Hyper-Intelligent Processes. In Information Logistics for Organizational Empowerment and Effective Supply Chain Management (pp. 1-13). IGI Global.

Nozari, H., Ghahremani-Nahr, J., & Szmelter-Jarosz, A. (2023). A multi-stage stochastic inventory management model for transport companies including several different transport modes. *International Journal of Management Science and Engineering Management, 18*(2), 134–144. doi:10.1080/17509653.2022.2042747

Nozari, H., Szmelter-Jarosz, A., & Rahmaty, M. (2024). Smart Marketing Based on Artificial Intelligence of Things (AIoT) and Blockchain and Evaluating Critical Success Factors. In Smart and Sustainable Interactive Marketing (pp. 68-82). IGI Global.

Nozari, H., Tavakkoli-Moghaddam, R., Rohaninejad, M., & Hanzalek, Z. (2023, September). Artificial Intelligence of Things (AIoT) Strategies for a Smart Sustainable-Resilient Supply Chain. In *IFIP International Conference on Advances in Production Management Systems* (pp. 805-816). Cham: Springer Nature Switzerland. 10.1007/978-3-031-43670-3_56

Peltier, J. W., Dahl, A. J., & Schibrowsky, J. A. (2023). Artificial intelligence in interactive marketing: A conceptual framework and research agenda. Journal of Research in Interactive Marketing, (ahead-of-print).

Reznik, O. M., Hetmanets, O. P., Kovalchuk, A., Nastyuk, V., & Andriichenko, N. (2020). Financial security of the state. Academic Press.

Seyed-Hosseini, S. M., Safaei, N., & Asgharpour, M. J. (2006). Reprioritization of failures in a system failure mode and effects analysis by decision-making trial and evaluation laboratory technique. *Reliability Engineering & System Safety, 91*(8), 872–881. doi:10.1016/j.ress.2005.09.005

Uddin, M. H., Ali, M. H., & Hassan, M. K. (2020). Cybersecurity hazards and financial system vulnerability: A synthesis of the literature. *Risk Management, 22*(4), 239–309. doi:10.1057/s41283-020-00063-2

Chapter 6
The Dimensions and Components of Marketing 5.0:
Introduction to Marketing 6.0

Hamed Nozari
ID https://orcid.org/0000-0002-6500-6708
Azad University of the Emirates, UAE

Adel Pourghader Chobar
Department of Industrial Engineer, Islamic Azad University, Qazvin, Iran

ABSTRACT

In today's era, businesses are mixed with technologies. Industry 4.0 added the presence of roaming technologies with the power of extracting, analyzing, and fast data calculations to businesses. Therefore, the data with high transparency and accuracy increased the performance power of the marketing department and adopted powerful strategies. In the fifth generation of the emerging industry, in addition to analytical power, stability, resilience, and human-centeredness, the capabilities of transformative technologies have also been added. For this reason, marketing by refining the data that comes from the actions of humans, multiplied intelligence. Examining this ability in smart Marketing 5.0 will have tremendous effects on the entire supply chain and the value chain of organizations. Therefore, this research has tried to examine the dimensions and components of fifth-generation marketing. In this regard, an analytical framework is also provided for the smart marketing system. This framework has been approved by some active experts in the field of marketing.

DOI: 10.4018/979-8-3693-3108-8.ch006

1. INTRODUCTION

Smart marketing is defined as the process of collecting and implementing data-driven information to formulate effective marketing strategies for businesses in order to optimize the generated leads and conversions from target markets (Movahed et al., 2024).

Certainly, traditional marketing and smart marketing have many similarities, and the concepts of influencing customers and creating special customer value are common in all elements and types of marketing. In all types of marketing, we always seek to improve the basic capabilities of products and services. It gives a higher value to the customer to let him know. But the difference between intelligent marketing and intelligent marketing is in data extraction, refinement, and analysis. Undoubtedly, when we have more information about customers and their interests, we can reach a better understanding of creating value for them, because we can provide more desirable products and services (Nozari et al., 2021).

Smart marketing is focused on gathering general data from the market; hence it is focused solely on the company. While, on the other hand, the purpose of marketing research is to gain insight into customer preferences. It has a greater desire to learn key things about the research processes of buyers and the factors that influence their purchase decisions. Transformative technologies such as the Internet of Things are one of the most important sources of big data mining. Therefore, with their presence, deeper and more accurate customer data can be obtained. Artificial intelligence technology, as well as machine learning and deep learning, give high analytical power to the extracted data, and blockchain technology guarantees the transparency and accuracy of the data (Nozari et al., 2024).

It is important to pay attention to the fact that these technologies only increase the speed of data extraction and analysis, but in the new era, we must also look at the future of marketing development. Presenting value only to the current generation should not be considered, and in creating and developing value for customers, attention should also be paid to future generations. Therefore, the concept of marketing 5.0 can be defined as focusing on the characteristics of sustainability, resilience, and human-centeredness of marketing (Irani and Nozari, 2024). Therefore, by emphasizing technology in the new era, even though the depth of information can be achieved and the speed of calculations grows, the main goal is how to face security and privacy challenges. In other words, Marketing 5.0, which is an introduction to Marketing 6.0, means achieving the maximum power and analytical speed of market and customer information with an emphasis on maximum security in all marketing processes (Movahed et al., 2024).

This research has tried to investigate the dimensions, components, and key functional indicators of smart marketing systems in Industry 5.0, which is known as marketing 5.0, and explain this smart system. Also, a conceptual framework that shows the cause-and-effect relationships of all active actors in these systems is intended, which can provide insight into the implementation of Marketing 5.0.

2. LITERATURE REVIEW

The growth of the Internet, along with emerging technologies, has had a significant impact on traditional marketing. For example, advanced technologies, often referred to as big data analytics, have allowed companies to collect large and complex data sets and use sophisticated analytics to gain greater consumer insight. Advances in technology have facilitated the collection of consumer data (eg, purchasing patterns, transaction history, preferences) and the setting up of effective loyalty programs. The Internet has been a favorable environment for the growth of customer loyalty programs (Movahed et al., 2024). The emergence of these technologies has intensified consumer interest in and access to loyalty reward information, although acquiring loyal customers is still a challenge for brands. Most companies and marketing and sales teams in organizations are quickly adapting to smart technology solutions to improve their efficiency and customer experience. These smart solutions often come in the form of marketing and sales platforms based on artificial intelligence. Through these platforms, marketers can get a more accurate and comprehensive understanding of the target audience. The insights obtained from this process are used to convert the audience into buyers and reduce the workload of the marketing teams (Nozari, 2024).

Artificial intelligence plays a vital role in the communication between sellers, marketers, and consumers. Marketing solutions with artificial intelligence are superior solutions that bridge the gap between the huge amount of customer data and the practical steps of marketers in digital campaigns. The rise of digital media has led to an influx of "data overload" and opportunities for digital marketers to review their methods and carefully select valuable channels. This trend has also led to data oversaturation, and most marketers struggle to find data worth collecting. AI marketing can quickly analyze all that data and extract the essentials and not only analyze them, but also suggest the best ones for future digital marketing campaigns (Nozari & Szmelter-Jaros, 2024).

In marketing based on transformative technologies, artificial intelligence algorithms use facet clustering to identify and extract relevant details from social listening data. It enables businesses to gain a more accurate understanding of the customer's mind by analyzing millions of data points in real time. Through social media sentiment analysis, a deep understanding of customer attitudes and opinions can be gained. This makes it possible to predict the next moves of customers and take appropriate strategic actions to achieve the desired results. By using artificial intelligence in social marketing, it is possible to communicate more effectively with audiences, gain deeper insights about customers and improve marketing strategies (Aliahmadi et al., 2024). Artificial intelligence and machine learning are powerful tools that can provide critical insights about customers across a wide range of aspects to help make strategic marketing decisions.

In recent years, many researches have been done in the field of technology-based marketing. The researchers showed that the use of transformative technologies such as the Internet of Things, artificial intelligence, blockchain technology, and various hybrid technologies can have a significant impact on fifth generation marketing processes.

Diaz et al. (2022) analyzed the evolution of digital and smart technologies and their relationship with different topics in marketing journals. In addition, they considered the evolution of digital and smart technologies in the relevant International Marketing (IM)/International Business (IB) journals to describe the impact of technology on this particular field, which yielded interesting results. Reis et al. (2021) examined the effects and challenges of digital technologies on marketing. Jaiwant (2023) introduces the concept of Industry 5.0 in which robots and machines are intermingled with intelligence and human power instead of opponents. They examined various aspects of marketing in the face of Industry 5.0. In this research, challenges, trends and future methods in the field of marketing in the wake of Industry 5.0 are described as a way for companies to be sustainable and flexible.

Barbosa et al. (2023) presented a framework for content marketing. The aim of this study was to develop a theoretical framework related to content marketing and identify leading techniques and applications related to its development. In this research, an innovative data-based method including three stages was developed. In the first step, sentiment analysis powered by machine learning was performed with Textblob, and four experiments were conducted using support vector classifier, simple polynomial bays, logistic regression, and random forest classifier. In this research, the aim was to increase the accuracy of sentiment analysis (negative, neutral and positive) of a sample of user-generated content collected from the Twitter social network. Also, a mathematical topic modeling algorithm known as hidden Dirichlet allocation was used to divide the database into topics. Finally, a textual analysis was developed using the Python programming language.

Low et al. (2020) investigated the understanding of sustainable digital marketing principles and practices in the Malaysian property development industry by examining the adoption of digital marketing, barriers to its adoption, and strategies to improve digital capabilities for the local context. In this research, digital marketing theories, practices and models from other industries were used in the local real estate development industry to create the infrastructure of its smartness and sustainability.

This paper proposes a Marketing Technology Acceptance Model (MTAM) for digital marketing strategy and capability development.

Shuyi et al. (2024) conducted an online survey involving 347 Chinese consumers who used social media platforms managed by smartphone brands as part of their marketing activities during COVID-19. The data were analyzed using structural equation modeling using SmartPLS. The findings of this study can help smartphone brands in China develop the most effective strategies for SMMA, which can be designed for consumers to increase profits. to maximize, even during any crisis when physical business activities are considered difficult. In addition, the findings of this study can be useful for the government and policy makers in formulating and regulating e-commerce and social media commerce laws and regulations for all industries and fields.

Aripin et al. (2024) investigated the impacts and challenges facing the banking sector in adopting Internet of Things technology to improve services and transaction security. This study uses a descriptive qualitative approach, including literature analysis and case studies of IoT technology implementation in several leading banks. The research method includes collecting data from various sources including scientific journals, articles and related books. Also, data is collected through interviews with experts and specialists of the banking sector who have experience in implementing Internet of Things technology. The results of the research indicate that the implementation of Internet of Things technology in the banking sector has successfully improved the efficiency of transaction services. They demonstrated that the use of IoT sensors and connected devices enables banks to automate transaction processes and accelerate response to customer demands. In addition, blockchain technology has also brought significant improvements in transaction security by providing decentralized data structures that cannot be tampered with. Despite the success, this study also identifies several challenges in adopting IoT technology in the banking sector, including high implementation costs, complexity in integrating with existing infrastructure, and the need for a deep understanding of the technology. However, with strategic and planned actions, the banking sector can overcome these challenges and harness the full potential of IoT technology to create a better transaction experience for customers and society at large.

3. MARKETING IN INDUSTRY 5.0 AND INDUSTRY 6.0

Today, organizations and marketing teams are rapidly adapting to smart technology solutions to improve their efficiency and customer experience. These smart solutions often come in the form of marketing platforms based on transformative technologies. Through these platforms, marketers can get a more accurate and comprehensive understanding of the target audience. The insights obtained from this process are used to convert the audience into buyers and reduce the workload of the marketing teams (Nozari, 2023).

In fifth generation marketing, Internet of Things technologies, artificial intelligence, blockchain and hybrid technologies such as artificial intelligence of things play a fundamental role. By using these transformative technologies, it is possible to obtain and analyze data that has high transparency and accuracy. Therefore, they can provide marketers with a more accurate and clearer path (Rahmaty & Nozari, 2023).

For example, the Internet of Things is already affecting search engines, SEO, and web content. One of the emerging trends of the Internet of Things in SEO is to show personalized content to the intended audience on the Internet based on criteria such as geographic location. In general, the goal of smart technology is to move towards user comfort and efficiency. The presence of artificial intelligence along with the Internet of Things technology can add powerful analysis capabilities to the big data generated by the Internet of Things. The Internet of Things has brought many changes in digital marketing. These developments have led to the following:

1. *Real data collection*: IoT allows companies to collect accurate and real data about their products and customers. This data helps to make better decisions and optimize marketing campaigns.
2. *Better customer experience*: By using things connected to the Internet, companies can improve the experience of their customers. For example, AI objects can provide specific recommendations to customers or allow customers to interact with products remotely.
3. *Optimal allocation of resources*: IoT helps companies to optimize their resources. For example, by using sensors and collected data, traffic density in shopping centers can be adjusted or product inventory can be managed optimally.
4. *Marketing of artificial intelligence products*: Internet of Things allows businesses to market artificial intelligence products. These products often use big data analysis and artificial intelligence to make decisions and provide better services to customers.

Overall, IoT has improved digital marketing by interacting with Internet-connected objects and the data collected from them, allowing businesses to improve customer experience and optimize marketing processes (Nozari et al., 2023).

Artificial intelligence marketing uses artificial intelligence technology for automatic decision-making, which is based on collecting and analyzing data and examining audiences or economic trends. Artificial intelligence is often used in those digital marketing activities where speed is very important and plays a key role.

Artificial intelligence marketing tools use their data and profiles to best communicate with customers and then provide them with tailored messages at the right time without the involvement of marketing team members, resulting in maximum efficiency. Most digital marketers use AI to augment their marketing teams or perform more methodical tasks that require less human effort (Nozari & Aliahmadi, 2023).

Machine learning is driven by artificial intelligence and consists of computer algorithms that can analyze data and improve digital marketing campaigns automatically based on previous experience. Machine learning uses new information related to old data in any field. analyze and show digital marketing campaigns which ones have worked in the past and which ones have not (Ghahremani-Nahr et al., 2023).

The rise of digital media has led to an influx of "data overload" and opportunities for digital marketers to review their methods and carefully select valuable channels. This trend has also led to data oversaturation, and most digital marketers struggle to find data worth collecting.

Marketing based on transformative technologies can quickly analyze all that data and extract the essentials and not only analyze them, but also suggest the best ones for future digital marketing campaigns. In addition, the application of new technologies such as blockchain in marketing has changed traditional marketing methods. In addition, the application of new technologies such as blockchain in marketing has changed traditional marketing methods. This technology has provided new ways to increase productivity. Blockchain technology can provide exclusive benefits to consumers and brands by storing decentralized and distributed data (Nozari et al., 2023). In addition, with the help of blockchain technology in marketing, various security mechanisms such as access control, asymmetric encryption and digital signature can also be used. These security mechanisms can protect the storage, transmission and retrieval of large amounts of customer data. Blockchain technology can also help solve various privacy issues in digital marketing (Nozari et al., 2023). Transactions on the blockchain are not linked to real identities, and limiting the access of network members to blockchain information can help improve people's privacy. It is interesting to know that in blockchain, transactions are verified by the entire network and no one knows the details of the parties involved in the transaction. On the other hand, the history of transactions in the blockchain network can help better analyze information while protecting privacy (Aliahmadi et al., 2023). Figure 1 shows a conceptual framework for smart marketing systems in Industry 5.0 and Industry 6.0.

Figure 1. Conceptual framework for smart marketing systems

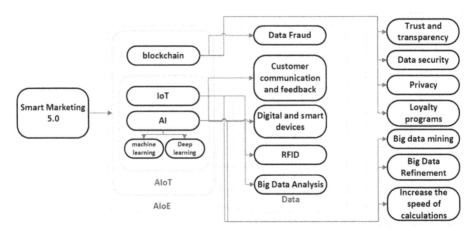

In modern marketing, you must deeply understand the needs and preferences of the customer and act quickly and effectively based on this knowledge. The ability to make immediate decisions based on data has made marketing solutions based on transformative technologies popular among marketers (Najafi et al., 2022). However, marketing teams should be vigilant in using the best smart strategies in their campaigns and operations. The development and use of smart marketing tools in the digital marketing strategy is still growing and has challenges that must always be taken into account (Aliahmadi & Nozari, 2023).

It should always be noted that organizations should collaborate with other organizations to implement smart marketing programs that can help in collecting and analyzing data to train their smart tools for optimal performance and make their maintenance easier (Nozari et al. 2023). As machine learning and AI marketing programs consume more data, they learn to make more accurate and effective decisions. However, if the data you feed your AI marketing program isn't standard and error-free, the resulting insights won't be useful and can actually lead to decisions that hurt your bottom line instead of improving it. Before implementing any AI marketing program, marketing teams must work with data management teams and other business departments to design processes for data cleansing and preservation. IoT-based tools accelerate this refining process (Nozari & Rahmary, 2023).

Artificial intelligence can analyze data faster than humans and make instant decisions based on the type of campaign and customers with the help of machine learning. As a result, team members have enough time to focus on strategic initiatives and strengthen AI campaigns. With AI marketing, digital marketers no longer have to wait until the end of the campaign to make decisions, but can use instant analytics and choose better media (Nozari et al., 2023).

Regardless of how big or small the marketing team is, smart marketing tools and machine learning programs and the practical use of IoT and blockchain technologies can help increase productivity, ROI, and efficiency.

4. CONCLUSION

Marketing based on transformational technologies with optimization capabilities is used in all types of digital marketing and in various industries including financial services, government, entertainment, healthcare, retail, etc. The use of smart marketing based on these technologies has different results in each case. These results include improving customer retention rates, improving campaign performance, improving customer experience, or making marketing operations more efficient.

If marketers properly use marketing based on these technologies, they can transform their entire marketing plan by extracting the most valuable insights from data and acting on them immediately. Smart platforms can quickly decide how much budget to allocate to each media channel or can determine the most effective advertising method to engage more with customers and get the most value from campaigns. Marketing based on transformative technologies such as the Internet of Things, artificial intelligence and blockchain can analyze data faster than humans and make immediate decisions based on the type of campaign and customers with the help of machine learning. As a result, team members have enough time to focus on strategic initiatives and strengthen smart campaigns. With smart analytics marketing, digital marketers no longer have to wait until the end of the campaign to make decisions, but can use instant analytics and choose better media. In addition to increasing efficiency in the supply chain, these technologies allow businesses to establish a closer and more effective relationship with customers. Finally, as a key element in the world of digital marketing, they help businesses take their marketing to a higher level of accuracy and effectiveness.

In this research, it has been tried to investigate the dimensions, features and key components of smart marketing systems based on transformative technologies in the era of Industry 5.0. Finally, a conceptual framework for these intelligent systems has been presented. Understanding this framework can provide deep insight for the proper implementation of these systems.

REFERENCES

Aliahmadi, A., Ghahremani-Nahr, J., & Nozari, H. (2023). Pricing decisions in the closed-loop supply chain network, taking into account the queuing system in production centers. *Expert Systems with Applications*, *212*, 118741. doi:10.1016/j.eswa.2022.118741

Aliahmadi, A., Movahed, A. B., & Nozari, H. (2024). Collaboration Analysis in Supply Chain 4.0 for Smart Businesses. In Building Smart and Sustainable Businesses With Transformative Technologies (pp. 103-122). IGI Global.

Aliahmadi, A., & Nozari, H. (2023, January). Evaluation of security metrics in AIoT and blockchain-based supply chain by Neutrosophic decision-making method. In *Supply Chain Forum* []. Taylor & Francis.]. *International Journal (Toronto, Ont.)*, *24*(1), 31–42.

Aripin, Z., Saepudin, D., & Yulianty, F. (2024, February). Transformation in the internet of things (iot) market in the banking sector: A case study of technology implementation for service improvement and transaction security. *Journal of Jabar Economic Society Networking Forum*, *1*(3), 17–32.

Barbosa, B., Saura, J. R., Zekan, S. B., & Ribeiro-Soriano, D. (2023). Defining content marketing and its influence on online user behavior: A data-driven prescriptive analytics method. *Annals of Operations Research*, 1–26. doi:10.1007/s10479-023-05261-1

Diaz, E., Esteban, Á., Carranza Vallejo, R., & Martin-Consuegra Navarro, D. (2022). Digital tools and smart technologies in marketing: A thematic evolution. *International Marketing Review*, *39*(5), 1122–1150. doi:10.1108/IMR-12-2020-0307

Ghahremani-Nahr, J., Nozari, H., Rahmaty, M., Zeraati Foukolaei, P., & Sherejsharifi, A. (2023). Development of a Novel Fuzzy Hierarchical Location-Routing Optimization Model Considering Reliability. *Logistics*, *7*(3), 64.

Irani, H. R., & Nozari, H. (Eds.). (2024). *Smart and Sustainable Interactive Marketing*. IGI Global. doi:10.4018/979-8-3693-1339-8

Jaiwant, S. V. (2023). The Changing Role of Marketing: Industry 5.0-the Game Changer. In Transformation for Sustainable Business and Management Practices: Exploring the Spectrum of Industry 5.0 (pp. 187-202). Emerald Publishing Limited.

Low, S., Ullah, F., Shirowzhan, S., Sepasgozar, S. M., & Lin Lee, C. (2020). Smart digital marketing capabilities for sustainable property development: A case of Malaysia. *Sustainability (Basel)*, *12*(13), 5402. doi:10.3390/su12135402

Movahed, A. B., Movahed, A. B., & Nozari, H. (2024a). Opportunities and Challenges of Marketing 5.0. *Smart and Sustainable Interactive Marketing*, 1-21.

Movahed, A. B., Movahed, A. B., & Nozari, H. (2024b). Opportunities and Challenges of Smart Supply Chain in Industry 5.0. *Information Logistics for Organizational Empowerment and Effective Supply Chain Management*, 108-138.

Najafi, Nozari, & Edalatpanah. (2022). Artificial Intelligence of Things (AIoT) and Industry 4.0–Based Supply Chain (FMCG Industry). *A Roadmap for Enabling Industry 4.0 by Artificial Intelligence*, 31-41.

Nozari, H. (Ed.). (2023). *Building Smart and Sustainable Businesses With Transformative Technologies*. IGI Global. doi:10.4018/979-8-3693-0210-1

Nozari, H. (2024). Supply Chain 6.0 and Moving Towards Hyper-Intelligent Processes. In Information Logistics for Organizational Empowerment and Effective Supply Chain Management (pp. 1-13). IGI Global.

Nozari, H., & Aliahmadi, A. (2023). Analysis of critical success factors in a food agile supply chain by a fuzzy hybrid decision-making method. [Formerly known as Iranian Journal of Management Studies]. *Interdisciplinary Journal of Management Studies*, *16*(4), 905–926.

Nozari, H., Ghahremani-Nahr, J., & Najafi, E. (2023). The Role of Internet of Things and Blockchain in the Development of Agile and Sustainable Supply Chains. In Digital Supply Chain, Disruptive Environments, and the Impact on Retailers (pp. 271-282). IGI Global. doi:10.4018/978-1-6684-7298-9.ch015

Nozari, H., Ghahremani-Nahr, J., & Szmelter-Jarosz, A. (2023). A multi-stage stochastic inventory management model for transport companies including several different transport modes. *International Journal of Management Science and Engineering Management*, *18*(2), 134–144. doi:10.1080/17509653.2022.2042747

Nozari, H., Ghahremani-Nahr, J., & Szmelter-Jarosz, A. (2023). AI and machine learning for real-world problems. *Advances In Computers*, (online first).

Nozari, H., & Rahmaty, M. (2023). Modeling the make-to-order problem considering the order queuing system under uncertainty. *International Journal of Industrial Engineering*, *34*(4), 1–20.

Nozari, H., & Szmelter-Jarosz, A. (2024). An Analytical Framework for Smart Supply Chains 5.0. In *Building Smart and Sustainable Businesses With Transformative Technologies* (pp. 1–15). IGI Global.

Nozari, H., Szmelter-Jarosz, A., & Ghahremani-Nahr, J. (2021). The Ideas of Sustainable and Green Marketing Based on the Internet of Everything—The Case of the Dairy Industry. *Future Internet*, *13*(10), 266. doi:10.3390/fi13100266

Nozari, H., Tavakkoli-Moghaddam, R., Ghahremani-Nahr, J., & Najafi, E. (2023). A conceptual framework for Artificial Intelligence of Medical Things (AIoMT). In Computational Intelligence for Medical Internet of Things (MIoT) Applications (pp. 175-189). Academic Press.

Nozari, H., Tavakkoli-Moghaddam, R., Rohaninejad, M., & Hanzalek, Z. (2023, September). Artificial Intelligence of Things (AIoT) Strategies for a Smart Sustainable-Resilient Supply Chain. In *IFIP International Conference on Advances in Production Management Systems* (pp. 805-816). Cham: Springer Nature Switzerland. 10.1007/978-3-031-43670-3_56

Rahmaty, M., & Nozari, H. (2023). Optimization of the hierarchical supply chain in the pharmaceutical industry. *Edelweiss Applied Science and Technology*, *7*(2), 104–123. doi:10.55214/25768484.v7i2.376

Reis, J. L., Peter, M. K., Cayolla, R., & Bogdanovic, Z. (2021). Marketing and smart technologies. *Proceedings of ICMarkTech, 1.*

Shuyi, J., Mamun, A. A., & Naznen, F. (2024). Social media marketing activities on brand equity and purchase intention among Chinese smartphone consumers during COVID-19. *Journal of Science and Technology Policy Management*, *15*(2), 331–352. doi:10.1108/JSTPM-02-2022-0038

Chapter 7

AI and Influencer Marketing:
Redefining the Future of Social Media Marketing in Industry 6.0

Manjit Kour
https://orcid.org/0000-0003-1043-3187
Chandigarh University, India

Rajinder Kour
CGC Technical College, India

ABSTRACT

Numerous sectors have been transformed by artificial intelligence (AI), and marketing is no exception. The rise of artificial intelligence (AI) influencers, or virtual people powered by cutting-edge AI algorithms, is one of the newest trends in marketing. These AI influencers are upending conventional marketing approaches and changing how firms interact with their target markets. AI influencers have developed into valuable marketing tools for companies looking to engage customers in a social environment thanks to their increased personalisation, expanded reach, and affordability. The world of social media marketing has been significantly altered by AI and influencer marketing, and this trend is expected to continue. This study examines how AI influencers are revolutionising brand promotion, reshaping the marketing environment, and creating a new industry in this chapter.

DOI: 10.4018/979-8-3693-3108-8.ch007

1. INTRODUCTION

With emerging disruptive technologies (such as blockchain technology, artificial intelligence, fintech, etc.) altering how business is conducted, the business world is changing at an astounding rate (Kour, 2023). One of the newest developments in the marketing industry is influencer marketing. Influencer marketing is a kind of advertising where a brand or service is promoted by using well-known social media users.(Lou & Yaun, 2019). Influencers are people who have a sizable social media following and are regarded as authorities in their industry. Influencers' followers are more inclined to follow their advice and act when they endorse a good or service (Kour and Kaur, 2020). As the number of individuals utilizing social media has increased, influencer marketing has grown in popularity.

Social media marketing has become a dominant force in the 21st-century fast-paced digital scene, completely changing the way brands communicate with their target customers. This dynamic ecosystem has gained a new dimension with the integration of Artificial Intelligence (AI) and influencer marketing, which presents intriguing potential and redefines the future of social media marketing.

Social networking sites are drawing billions of users worldwide and have evolved into virtual marketplaces. These platforms give brands a previously unheard-of level of reach and engagement, allowing them to communicate with customers in more genuine and tailored ways. Influencer marketing is a method that has shown to be very successful in building brand recognition, building trust, and motivating consumer actions on social media by utilizing the influence of content creators. Marketers are investigating AI-driven solutions more frequently as this type of advertising takes traction to maximize influencer campaigns and fully utilize social media.

Numerous opportunities arise from the combination of influencer marketing and artificial intelligence. Massive volumes of social media data may be combed through by AI algorithms to find the best influencers for certain businesses and campaigns. AI may tailor influencer-generated content to ensure that it resonates with the intended audience and encourages engagement by evaluating user behaviour and preferences. Additionally, AI-driven chatbots improve user experience and customer service by enabling smooth interactions between influencers and followers.

There is no doubt that influencers will continue to rule the digital sphere, and businesses will constantly come up with new strategies to utilize their extraordinary influencing powers. In this chapter, we discuss how AI influencers are influencing social media marketing and how they are fundamentally altering the digital landscape. This study is broken up into several pieces. The issue is introduced in the first section, which is followed by a review of the literature, an explanation of how AI is utilized in influencer marketing, a section on current AI influencer marketing status, followed by a section on the topic's future prospects, and a section on challenges in AI marketing. The research conclusion is provided in the final part.

2. REVIEW OF LITERATURE

Artificial intelligence influencers are fictional characters produced by deep learning and AI systems (Sookkaew & Saephoo, 2021). These social personas are created to look like actual people and have different personalities, which helps them connect with their target audience. An artificial intelligence (AI) influencer may interact with consumers on social media platforms, sharing content and endorsing brands thanks to its sophisticated picture and natural language processing abilities (Yang et al., 2019).

According to Nielsen's India Internet Report 2023, social networking has led to a revolution in social marketing, with over 700 million active internet users in India (Nielsen, 2023). In today's world, people use social media and the internet, and social marketing has taken over as the most popular form of advertising for companies. Organizations are now able to target their messages to a wider audience thanks to intelligence across numerous variables.

Influencer marketing is the modern buzzword and has completely altered the way social marketing is done (Lou & Yaun, 2019). In reality, in our socially dominated world, influencers have overtaken every area of interest. Influencer marketing has grown quickly because of technical advances that have made it possible for marketers to track KPIs and achieve their goals (Primasiwi, 2021). In this situation, artificial intelligence has proven beneficial in supporting brands across the value chain in areas like planning, discovery, negotiation, scheduling, publishing, and analysis, as well as the search for creators who are most similar to the brands in question.

Artificial intelligence has improved filtering even further while providing brands with accurate results (Wang et al., 2022). Millions of data points from an influencer's biography, content, audience, and prior performance are verified by AI-powered analytical algorithms to determine whether they are appropriate for a particular demographic. Based on the personas of the brands and campaigns, AI models are matched to the personas of the appropriate producers to maximize the success factors established by the brand (Haleem et al., 2022). In addition to AI, machine learning (ML) also enables them to identify problem areas, serve as the feedback loop, and choose the best course of action to aim for improved progress. Using the powerful mix of AI and data science, organizations can now easily undertake predictive research, create intent-based audiences, and target higher exposure and visibility.

3. RESEARCH METHODOLOGY

The chosen research design for this conceptual study on the relationship between AI and influencer marketing was essentially exploratory. It was decided that this design would be suitable for conducting a thorough analysis of the new trends, obstacles, and prospects in this ever-changing industry. A secondary data collecting approach was used to collect the data, with an emphasis on gathering information from pre-existing sources such as books, reliable web platforms, industry reports, and academic publications. A methodical approach to searching was adopted, employing terms such as "AI in influencer marketing" and "machine learning and influencers," to search databases such as PubMed, IEEE Xplore, Google Scholar, and platforms tailored to particular industries. The inclusion criterion comprised published works during the specified timeframe, with a particular emphasis on academic articles, whitepapers, and studies that addressed the convergence of AI and influencer marketing. The gathered data was then categorized and interpreted using a qualitative content analysis approach, which helped to uncover themes about the influence of AI on influencer marketing, the difficulties encountered, and the opportunities ahead.

4. INFLUENCER MARKETING: HOW AI IS CHANGING THE GAME

Influencer marketing via AI is the new thing in marketing. Its disruptive role is presented in figure 1.

Figure 1. AI in influencer marketing

4.1 Matchmaking

The biggest problem that brands and marketers face today is locating the right influencer De Veirman et al., 2017). The potential of an influencer cannot be assessed only based on the size of his or her subscriber base. It's critical to choose an influencer that complements your brand's offerings and has an appropriate following that appeals to your target market. Here, systems for influencer marketing powered by artificial intelligence are used. They carry out multiple integrations and create creator personas based on a range of factors, including location, genre, and content relevancy (Park & Kim, 2020). The brand persona is created together with the creator persona, and the two are then compared to see which one makes the best sense. Brands may target a larger audience and obtain the best reaction from the general public with the help of the proper influencer.

4.2 Predictive Analysis and Metrics Assessment

Thanks to artificial intelligence, brands can now assess the efficacy of their advertisements and perform real-time predictive assessments. By directly tying real-time data, such as brand mentions, traffic, and conversions, to an influencer's particular behaviour, artificial intelligence (AI)-powered analytics tools have enabled organisations to look beyond vanity metrics and analyse the impact of campaigns and influencer performance. According to a Deloitte survey, 45% of seasoned AI users and 26% of all respondents claimed that employing AI technologies has significantly increased their competitive edge (Deloitte, 2023). These technologies can also be used by marketers to do predictive research to forecast campaign success, anticipate future content needs, and apply data-driven decision-making based on insightful data (Sarker, 2021). Furthermore, since ML serves as the feedback loop, it is now simple to pinpoint issue areas and quantify the extent of adjustments to boost campaign success for longer-term outcomes.

4.3 Managing Multiple Campaigns Together

There are various moving parts to an influencer marketing strategy. However, as automation has taken control, it is now simpler for businesses to use AI systems to track every part of a campaign independently. In reality, these AI-driven analytical tools have given marketers the chance to perform creator persona sentiment research to determine the greatest fit with their product offers, assess campaign KPIs, and measure engagement rates (Chaffey & Smith, 2022). According to research by Influencer Marketing Hub, 61.4% of marketers allegedly use AI in their marketing campaigns. These technologies also provide end-to-end campaign lifecycle management, allowing brands to plan, execute, and monitor their campaigns from beginning to end. It is much simpler for marketers to examine the efficacy of their campaigns and gain from automated decision-making because AI compiles all the data points in one location to generate intelligent conclusions and increase transparency (Chaffey & Smith, 2022).

4.4 Scalability

Before AI technology was developed, managing campaigns of all sizes was thought to be a difficult task. However, owing to AI-powered analytical tools, brands are now able to conduct several campaigns, and influencers with a variety of follower numbers can successfully manage those campaigns (Dwivedi et al., 2021). Additionally, these systems do audience profiling, providing perspectives into the preferences and practises of the audiences and enabling content producers to more effectively target their audience with their work. As a result, more creator liquidity is generated, allowing influencers to take part in more projects and yet provide beneficial results. Furthermore, AI-enabled solutions find substitute lookalike producers for businesses to increase the catchment area (Garbuio & Lin, 2019).

4.5 Shift to B2B

With the top three categories being beauty, food, and fashion, influencer marketing is primarily a business-to-consumer (B2C) activity. However, it is gradually making its way into the B2B (business-to-business) market, which is growing in industries like financial services, pharmaceuticals, and technology and enabling companies to scale their operations widely. The association between superior thought leadership and proficiency, more valuable leads, targeted traffic, increased visibility and outreach, and increased return on investment has been advantageous for business-to-business marketers who have allocated funds to influencer marketing instead of more conventional channels.

4.6 Virtual Influencers

Finding the correct influencers has become increasingly difficult for marketers as influencer marketing has become more popular. The idea of "virtual influencers" has developed as a result of AI, giving marketers another way to express themselves in a unique way, have more control over the material, and aim for greater awareness (Gerlich, 2023). As of 2022, there were 200+ active virtual influencers on social media, according to a survey by VirtualHumans.org.

4.7 Expansion of the Creator Economy

The creative economy is altering marketing and commercial practices as more companies rely on trustworthy internet personas. The expansion of the creator economy has also been prompted by the fact that AI has become a crucial component of the industry (Kour & Rani, 2023). Given the significance of content in the creative economy, AI-powered solutions perform sentiment analysis on brand personas and content, allowing artists to base their strategies on the results in an effort to increase their exposure and attract more visitors.

Tools for creating visual material with AI are also becoming more popular. AI text-to-image models like Stable Diffusion, Midjourney, and DALL-E have been revolutionizing the production of visual material (Han & Cai, 2023). These systems utilize machine learning techniques to produce new versions of existing photographs or to produce images from text descriptions. While many artists have welcomed AI text-to-image generators as a fun tool for speeding up social art creation, others have viewed the introduction of this technology as contentious due to questions about the place of AI in visual art and difficulties with style appropriation.

Lensa AI is a developing trend in generative AI that merits consideration (Hutson & Cotroneo, 2023). Even though the software has been there for a long, its "magic avatars" function only lately become popular. Lensa develops stylized avatars that match embedded images and realistic images based on text input using the Stable Diffusion model (Hutson & Cotroneo, 2023). With the capacity to produce interesting material in a variety of categories, Lensa and other generative AI models have been making waves on social media.

4.8 Influencer Marketing

Selecting the right influencers may help a business become more well-known and is one of the most important aspects of any successful influencer marketing strategy (Lou & Yaun, 2019). Selecting the right influencer for a particular social media campaign may be challenging for marketers. It is vital that they comprehend their audience and evaluate their potential based on factors such as age, location, and level of engagement with their postings. By comparing data, AI may use natural language processing (NLP) to predict an influencer's level of alignment with a brand's objectives for each campaign. This helps marketers select the right social media influencers (Barbosa et al., 2023). AI is useful for a number of tasks, including determining which material is most successful for each campaign, identifying phoney influencers, and calculating campaign ROI.

4.9 Social Media Ad Management

Additional advantages that AI is bringing to social media platforms include optimization and ad management. AI-powered systems can find and segment audiences, design and test ads, improve speed and performance, and analyse hundreds or thousands of ad targeting and budget variants to get the best results (Roetzer & Kaput, 2022). Marketers may also optimise advertising for clicks and conversions because AI can predict which language would provide better results or what kind of content you should create based on the keywords your target audience uses to explore for products and services similar to yours.

4.10 Logo Detection for Monitoring Brand Campaigns

AI is using computer vision technology to advance visual search. Many businesses use logo detection to examine pictures of their items on social media networks. Brands may check how frequently their logos appear on social networks with the use of AI-powered logo detection tools (Hura, 2022). With visual material becoming a more and more popular format for social media platforms, it is crucial to examine how brand photos and videos are used, gather data on brand mentions on social media, and look for brand logos in the visual content.

5. CURRENT STATUS OF INFLUENCER MARKETING

Recent data suggests that AI market is increasing rapidly and is projected to increase in the future swiftly also (figure 1). Figure 2 also depicts the rapid increase in marketing revenue from AI is increasing at a rapid pace. This highlights the significance of AI in marketing.

Figure 2. AI market size worldwide actual and projections (in million US dollar)
Source: Statista (2023)

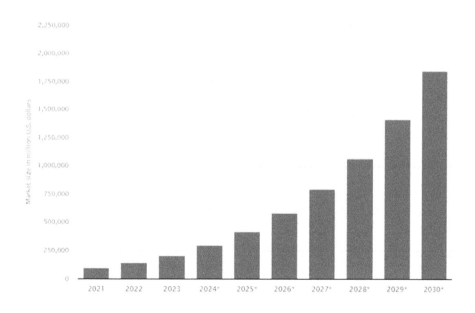

Figure 3. AI marketing revenue worldwide (in million US dollar)
Source: Statista (2023)

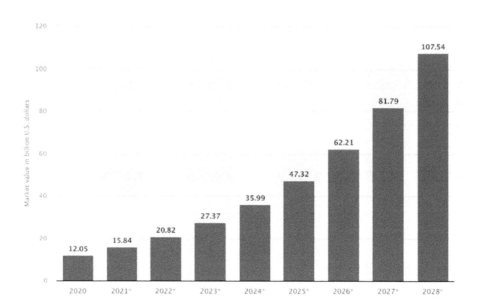

Over 4.62 billion people used social media as of 2022, and that number is projected to increase to 5.92 billion by 2025. Due to this expansion, firms now have access to a sizable pool of prospective influencers. By 2023, it is projected that 4.9 billion people will use social media globally. The number of people using social media has increased to 4.9 billion globally. Moreover, it is projected that this figure would rise to 5.85 billion users by 2027. In India, influencer marketing was projected to be worth about Rs 12 billion by 2022. Its estimated value by the end of 2026 is Rs 28 billion.

6. PROSPECTS OF AI INFLUENCER MARKETING

AI influencer marketing has a bright future ahead of it as new consumer-brand interactions are about to undergo a technological revolution. Precision audience targeting, mass personalization, and the upkeep of authenticity through data-driven insights are all made possible by AI. Chatbots improve engagement but predictive analytics and virtual influencers are changing the game. Real-time campaign evaluation, fraud detection, and regulatory compliance are all features of AI-driven metrics. Additionally, this technology helps cross-cultural communication and language hurdles. Influencer marketing will become more effective and data-driven as AI develops further, promoting deeper customer interactions and enhancing ROI for firms. The following section goes into greater depth on the potential of AI influencer marketing (Fig. 2):

6.1 Identifying the Right Influencers

Social media networks provide large volumes of data that AI technology may analyze to find influencers that share a brand's values and its target audience (Roetzer & Kaput, 2022). AI-powered technologies may identify the most appropriate influencers for a certain marketing campaign by taking into account elements like audience demographics, engagement rates, and content relevancy. This simplifies the procedure and guarantees that brands work with influencers who can produce superior outcomes.

6.2 Optimizing Content Strategy

Utilizing real-time data and user behaviour, AI enables social media marketers to optimize their content plans. AI systems can follow sentiment analyses, examine engagement trends, and determine which kinds of content work best on various platforms (Wu et al., 2022). Influencers and companies can adjust their content to appeal to their audience with the help of this data-driven methodology, creating campaigns that are more successful.

6.3 Personalization and Targeting

AI makes it easier to provide individualized content for various audience segments. It can do this to give highly tailored information that appeals to particular demographics by analyzing user preferences and behaviours (Wu et al., 2022). This degree of personalization raises the likelihood that a marketing campaign will be effective by making it more pertinent to and interesting to the target audience.

6.4 Automated Campaign Management

Influencer marketing campaign elements like performance tracking, reporting, and data analysis may all be automated with AI (Bharadiya, 2023). For marketers and influencers alike, this automation saves time and effort, allowing them to concentrate on creativity and strategy rather than manual tasks.

Figure 4. Future prospects of AI influencer marketing

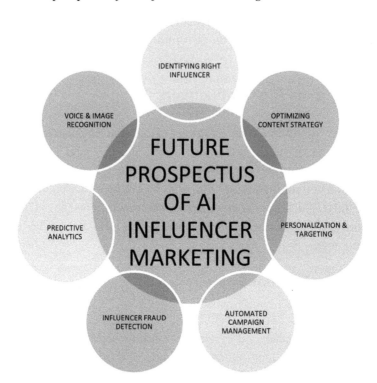

6.5 Influencer Fraud Detection

Artificial intelligence-powered techniques can be used to spot phoney influencers and unethical behaviour like the use of bot followers or engagement manipulation. This guarantees that companies spend their marketing funds properly and work with true influencers who can have a significant impact.

6.6 Predictive Analytics

Influencers and businesses may foresee forthcoming changes in the market by using AI, which can offer insightful data on audience behaviour and trends (Chaitanya et al., 2023). This enables them to maintain an advantage over the competition and change their strategy as necessary.

6.7 Voice and Image Recognition

Brands are now able to more efficiently monitor influencer-generated content thanks to advances in speech and picture recognition technologies driven by AI. They may make sure influencers adhere to brand requirements and steer clear of any problems or misrepresentations that might arise.

7. CHALLENGES AND LIMITATIONS

Although AI has improved social media user experiences, it still has some drawbacks. One of the key problems is the potential for algorithmic bias, which could lead to the unfair treatment of specific groups of people. Additionally, due to the slow adoption of ethical standards and regulatory frameworks, social media businesses and AI developers are left to deal with challenging moral and legal dilemmas on their own (Christodoulou & Iordanou, 2021). The future effects of AI on social media occupations are a second growing source of worry. Many functions that are currently performed by people could be automated with the advent of AI, changing the nature of labor. To address these issues, proactive steps must be taken to develop new training programs, support for workers in impacted industries, and regulations to ensure that the advantages of AI are shared more widely throughout society.

AI and social media combine to improve user experiences and marketing procedures. Through its ability to help with everything from influencer marketing and ad monitoring to content development and personalization, artificial intelligence (AI) has the potential to completely change the way brands market on social networks. As more sophisticated and cutting-edge solutions are created to enhance the social media experience, artificial intelligence will become more and more valuable in social media marketing.

8. DISCUSSION AND CONCLUSION

Artificial intelligence (AI) and other disruptive technologies have brought about a rapid shift in the ever-changing corporate landscape in recent times. This conceptual study examined the dynamics that form the digital marketing ecosystem by examining the intersection between influencer marketing and artificial intelligence. The survey emphasized how important influencers are to using their large social media followings to effectively promote brands.

The literature review emphasized the rise of artificial intelligence (AI) influencers—computer-generated characters with unique personalities—who interact with viewers by utilizing sophisticated picture and language processing skills. The impact of artificial intelligence (AI) on influencer marketing was demonstrated, along with its uses in metrics assessment, matchmaking, scalability, campaign administration, and the growth of the creative economy. The study focused on how artificial intelligence (AI) has changed the face of the creative economy by enabling the emergence of virtual influencers and streamlining influencer marketing procedures.

The present state of influencer marketing, as indicated by market size and revenue forecasts, demonstrated the noteworthy expansion and importance of artificial intelligence in molding the marketing environment. With more than 4.62 billion social media users worldwide, influencer marketing has grown to be a major force, greatly increasing the industry's projected value in India to Rs 12 billion by 2022. The study presented optimistic future prospects for artificial intelligence influencer marketing. Key areas where AI is expected to have a significant impact include fraud detection, mass personalization, precision audience targeting, and content strategy optimization. The potential for influencer marketing powered by AI to reach a larger audience is further highlighted by the projection that there will be 5.92 billion social media users by 2025. Notwithstanding the optimistic outlook, obstacles, and constraints were recognized. Regulation and ethics were brought up by algorithmic prejudice, ethical issues, and the possible automation of some work responsibilities. The necessity of proactive steps is emphasized in the conclusion, including training initiatives, assistance for impacted industries, and the creation of rules and ethical guidelines.

All things considered, this study has advanced our knowledge of artificial intelligence's revolutionary impact on influencer marketing by providing a thorough analysis of the technology's existing state, potential, and associated ethical issues. AI-powered influencer marketing is a dynamic force that is reshaping the future of consumer interaction and brand communication as the digital landscape continues to change. AI influencers are changing the marketing landscape by providing businesses with an innovative way to engage with their audience. As AI technology advances, we might expect AI influencers to have a greater influence on how marketing evolves. Using AI influencers opens up a world of opportunities for marketers to engage in personalized, authentic, and meaningful conversations with their target audience. AI will become more adept at recognizing user behaviour, preferences, and attitudes as it develops. This will make it possible for social media marketers to design highly tailored and successful programs, improving brand-consumer interactions and boosting ROI. In the future, artificial intelligence-generated material and virtual influencers may potentially gain popularity. These artificial intelligence (AI)-driven virtual personalities could provide distinctive and consistent marketing messaging without some of the drawbacks of using real influencers, like schedule issues or reputational problems.

But it's crucial to maintain a balance and make sure that human ingenuity and authenticity aren't completely replaced by AI. Genuine relationships and real storytelling—both of which human influencers are excellent at—remain the foundation of effective influencer marketing. In conclusion, the combination of AI with influencer marketing has the ability to completely reimagine social media marketing by making it more effective, data-driven, and personalized. More breakthroughs in this area are probably on the horizon, providing exciting chances for companies and influencers to engage audiences in fresh and significant ways.

REFERENCES

Barbosa, B., Saura, J. R., Zekan, S. B., & Ribeiro-Soriano, D. (2023). Defining content marketing and its influence on online user behavior: A data-driven prescriptive analytics method. *Annals of Operations Research*, 1–26. doi:10.1007/s10479-023-05261-1

Bharadiya, J. P. (2023). A Comparative Study of Business Intelligence and Artificial Intelligence with Big Data Analytics. *American Journal of Artificial Intelligence*, *7*(1), 24.

Chaffey, D., & Smith, P. R. (2022). *Digital marketing excellence: planning, optimizing and integrating online marketing*. Taylor & Francis. doi:10.4324/9781003009498

Chaitanya, K., Saha, G. C., Saha, H., Acharya, S., & Singla, M. (2023). The Impact of Artificial Intelligence and Machine Learning in Digital Marketing Strategies. *European Economic Letters*, *13*(3), 982–992.

Christodoulou, E., & Iordanou, K. (2021). Democracy under attack: Challenges of addressing ethical issues of AI and big data for more democratic digital media and societies. *Frontiers in Political Science*, *3*, 682945. doi:10.3389/fpos.2021.682945

De Veirman, M., Cauberghe, V., & Hudders, L. (2017). Marketing through Instagram influencers: The impact of number of followers and product divergence on brand attitude. *International Journal of Advertising*, *36*(5), 798–828. doi:10.1080/0265 0487.2017.1348035

Deloitte. (2023). Thriving in the area of pervasive AI. Retrieved from https://www2. deloitte.com/content/dam/Deloitte/cn/Documents/about-deloitte/deloitte-cn-dtt-thriving-in-the-era-of-persuasive-ai-en-200819.pdf

Dwivedi, Y. K., Ismagilova, E., Hughes, D. L., Carlson, J., Filieri, R., Jacobson, J., Jain, V., Karjaluoto, H., Kefi, H., Krishen, A. S., Kumar, V., Rahman, M. M., Raman, R., Rauschnabel, P. A., Rowley, J., Salo, J., Tran, G. A., & Wang, Y. (2021). Setting the future of digital and social media marketing research: Perspectives and research propositions. *International Journal of Information Management*, *59*, 102168. doi:10.1016/j.ijinfomgt.2020.102168

Garbuio, M., & Lin, N. (2019). Artificial intelligence as a growth engine for health care startups: Emerging business models. *California Management Review*, *61*(2), 59–83. doi:10.1177/0008125618811931

Gerlich, M. (2023). The Power of Virtual Influencers: Impact on Consumer Behaviour and Attitudes in the Age of AI. *Administrative Sciences*, *13*(8), 178. doi:10.3390/admsci13080178

Haleem, A., Javaid, M., Qadri, M. A., Singh, R. P., & Suman, R. (2022). Artificial intelligence (AI) applications for marketing: A literature-based study. International Journal of Intelligent Networks.

Han, A., & Cai, Z. (2023, June). Design implications of generative AI systems for visual storytelling for young learners. In *Proceedings of the 22nd Annual ACM Interaction Design and Children Conference* (pp. 470-474). 10.1145/3585088.3593867

Hura, A. (2022). Revealing consumer insights through visual analysis of social media images. *Journal of Digital & Social Media Marketing*, *10*(1), 69–75.

Hutson, J., & Cotroneo, P. (2023). Generative AI tools in art education: Exploring prompt engineering and iterative processes for enhanced creativity. Metaverse, 4(1).

Kour, M. (2023), Blockchain Technology Changing Landscape of Banking Industry. *2nd International Conference on Applied Artificial Intelligence and Computing (ICAAIC)*, Salem, India, 2023, pp. 1212-1216, 10.1109/ICAAIC56838.2023.10140854

Kour, M., & Kaur, R. (2020). Impact of Social Media Marketing on Consumer Buying Behaviour: An Empirical Study. *International Journal of Advanced Science and Technology*, *29*(11s), 975–984.

Kour, M., & Rani, K. (2023). Challenges and Opportunities to the Media and Entertainment Industry in Metaverse. Applications of Neuromarketing in the Metaverse, 88-102.

Lou, C., & Yuan, S. (2019). Influencer marketing: How message value and credibility affect consumer trust of branded content on social media. *Journal of Interactive Advertising*, *19*(1), 58–73. doi:10.1080/15252019.2018.1533501

Nielsen. (2023). State of the Media: The Social Media Report Q32023. Nielsen.

Park, S. M., & Kim, Y. G. (2022). A metaverse: Taxonomy, components, applications, and open challenges. *IEEE Access : Practical Innovations, Open Solutions*, *10*, 4209–4251. doi:10.1109/ACCESS.2021.3140175

Primasiwi, C., Irawan, M. I., & Ambarwati, R. (2021, May). Key Performance Indicators for Influencer Marketing on Instagram. In 2nd International Conference on Business and Management of Technology (iconbmt 2020) (pp. 154-163). Atlantis Press. Retrieved from https://www2.deloitte.com/content/dam/Deloitte/cn/Documents/about-deloitte/deloitte-cn-dtt-thriving-in-the-era-of-persuasive-ai-en-200819.pdf

Roetzer, P., & Kaput, M. (2022). *Marketing Artificial Intelligence: AI, Marketing, and the Future of Business*. BenBella Books.

Sarker, I. H. (2021). Data science and analytics: An overview from data-driven smart computing, decision-making and applications perspective. *SN Computer Science*, *2*(5), 377. doi:10.1007/s42979-021-00765-8 PMID:34278328

Sookkaew, J., & Saephoo, P. (2021). "Digital influencer": Development and coexistence with digital social groups. *International Journal of Advanced Computer Science and Applications*, *12*(12). Advance online publication. doi:10.14569/IJACSA.2021.0121243

Statista. (2023a). https://www.statista.com/statistics/1365145/artificial-intelligence-market-size/

Statista. (2023b). https://www.statista.com/statistics/1293758/ai-marketing-revenue-worldwide/#:~:text=In%202021%2C%20the%20market%20for,than%20107.5%20billion%20by%202028

Wang, Z., Li, M., Lu, J., & Cheng, X. (2022). Business Innovation based on artificial intelligence and Blockchain technology. *Information Processing & Management*, *59*(1), 102759. doi:10.1016/j.ipm.2021.102759

Wu, L., Dodoo, N. A., Wen, T. J., & Ke, L. (2022). Understanding Twitter conversations about artificial intelligence in advertising based on natural language processing. *International Journal of Advertising*, *41*(4), 685–702. doi:10.1080/02650487.2021.1920218

Yang, K. C., Varol, O., Davis, C. A., Ferrara, E., Flammini, A., & Menczer, F. (2019). Arming the public with artificial intelligence to counter social bots. *Human Behavior and Emerging Technologies*, *1*(1), 48–61. doi:10.1002/hbe2.115

Chapter 8
Assessing Digital Marketing Strategies in the Retail Sector Using Bayesian BWM and Fuzzy Topsis

Kevser Arman

https://orcid.org/0000-0002-4400-5976
Pamukkale University, Turkey

ABSTRACT

Digital marketing strategies play a crucial role in today's business world and have become an indispensable component of many sectors. The main objective of this study is to assess digital marketing strategies in the retail sector with multiple criteria decision making (MCDM) methods. Bayesian BWM (B-BWM) is utilized in the study to identify the weights of the criteria and fuzzy TOPSIS method is utilized to assess digital marketing strategies implemented in the retail sector. Based on the methodology used, customer satisfaction, customer loyalty, and competitive position in the market are the most important criteria that are taken into account in the selection of digital marketing strategies. Moreover, search engine optimisation and influencer marketing are the most suitable digital marketing strategies in the retail sector. The findings from this study could serve as a guide for evaluating digital marketing strategies in the retail sector.

DOI: 10.4018/979-8-3693-3108-8.ch008

1. INTRODUCTION

The pervasive influence and extensive utilization of the Internet have notably instigated significant changes. This situation has reshaped the business landscape and required companies and institutions to make adaptations (Mehta, 2022: 43). The internet and digital social networks have also begun to be widely used in the field of marketing, and thus new concepts have begun to appear in marketing literature (Dizman, 2022: 3867). Marketing is a discipline that is constantly changing and evolving over time. These improvement in marketing give rise to new insights and tools for practitioners to understand changing markets, customers, competitors, and collaborators (Durukal, 2019: 1616). Digital marketing is the integration of digital tools alongside traditional communication methods between customers and the company, employed to attain marketing goals. While traditional marketing and digital marketing may appear similar in the industry, its difference lies in the fact that digital marketing offers innovative approaches to communicating with customers and providing information (Nuseir et al., 2023: 24). The marketing sector underwent a shift from a conventional paradigm to a digital one, leading to the adoption of a more sophisticated approach in marketing. Considering the overarching global developmental it becomes evident that communication practices are undergoing a gradual transformation facilitated by technological advancements. This transformative shift plays a pivotal role in substantially increasing the promotional and sales endeavors of businesses (Trung and Thanh 2022: 1-2).

As stated by Leung and Mo (2019), the ascendancy of digital marketing has presented marketers with an array of marketing and promotional channels that were inconceivable a decade ago. Nevertheless, the escalating multitude of these options, each characterized by its distinctive features and limitations, renders the internal selection process of digital marketing tools, typically conducted by a cohort of professionals within a company, more intricate than ever before. Multi-Criteria Decision-Making (MCDM) emerges as a strong instrument extensively employed for addressing such complex problems. This study aimed to assess digital marketing strategies with Bayesian BWM (B-BWM) and fuzzy TOPSIS method. Within the scope of the purpose of the study, three main criteria and nine subcriteria have been used. These criteria have been introduced by Mukul et al. (2019). The criteria used in this study are as follows: customer satisfaction (R11), customer loyalty (R12), simultaneous accessibility of product/ service (R13), image (brand value) of company (R21), promotions (R22), utilization of social media (R23), competitive position in market (R31), market size (R32) and interaction with competitors (R33). The digital marketing strategies discussed in this study are social media marketing (S1), e-mail marketing (S2), search engine optimisation (S3), influencer marketing (S4), pay-per-click advertising (S5). These strategies have been presented by (Leung and Mo (2019).

This paper is based on three objectives as follows: (i) to assess the criteria affecting digital marketing strategies in terms of the retail sector; (ii) determining the most appropriate digital marketing strategies for the retail sector; and (iii) proposing a novel decision support model for digital marketing strategy selection. The existing body of literature encompasses various studies addressing digital marketing technologies or strategies with MCDM methods (Mukul et al., 2019; Leung and Mo 2019; Trung and Thanh, 2022; Korucuk et al., 2022; Gao et al., 2023). On the other hand, there are a limited number of papers that have handled digital marketing strategies within the context of particular sectors (Çalık, 2020; Esmaelnezhad et al., 2023). Additionally, since there was no study evaluating digital marketing strategies for the retail sector at the time the study was conducted, this study is expected to contribute to the literature. The remainder of this study is structured as follows. Section 2 presents the existing literature on digital marketing. Section 3 explains Bayesian BWM and fuzzy TOPSIS methods. Section 4 presents a case study. Section 5 offers conclusions, limitations, and some future research directions.

2. LITERATURE REVIEW

A digital marketing strategy is a plan that guides and optimizes a business's online presence. This strategy basically aims to increase sales by gaining a competitive advantage. Digital marketing utilizes mobile devices, the internet, social media, search engines, and various other channels to engage with consumers. Experts in the field view digital marketing as an innovative undertaking that requires a distinct approach to reaching consumers and understanding their behavior in contrast to conventional marketing methodologies (Nuseir et al., 2023: 24). While the rise of digital marketing offers many marketing and promotion channels, the increasing number of digital marketing tools every day complicates the selection process of digital marketing tools. Below, studies in the literature addressing digital marketing technology and/or strategy selection using various MCDM methods are summarized.

Mukul et al. (2019) was the first to use MCDM methods to assess digital marketing technologies. They applied Analytic Hierarchy Process (AHP) and COPRAS (Complex Proportional Assessment) method based on nine sub- criteria for all three aspects of digital marketing technologies. These three aspects of digital marketing technologies are customer, company, and market. Sub-criteria are customer satisfaction, customer loyalty, simultaneous accessibility of product/ service, image (brand value) of company, promotions, utilization of social media, competitive position in market, market size and interaction with competitors. They also identified five digital marketing strategies. These are artificial intelligence, big data, augmented/virtual reality, machine learning, and internet of things. As a result, artificial intelligence has been found to be the most suitable technology. Leung and Mo (2019) applied the Fuzzy-AHP method to digital marketing tool selection. They have utilized four criteria such as business fundamentals, trailing twelve month (TTM) active customer demographics, business acquisition performance and online exposure and commitment measure. Additionally, they evaluated three digital marketing strategies such as WOM advertising, e-mail marketing and search engine marketing. The findings show that social media marketing and influencer marketing have the highest weight. In a study by Trung and Thanh (2022), Spherical Fuzzy Analytic Hierarchy Process (SF-AHP) and TOPSIS methods have been used to assess and select digital marketing technologies. They used the criteria and alternatives presented by Mukul et al. (2019). The findings are similar to those of the study conducted by Mukul et al. (2019). The integrated Fermatean Fuzzy Step-wise Weight Assessment Ratio Analysis (FF–SWARA) and Fermatean Fuzzy Complex Proportional Assessment (FF–COPRAS) methods have been used by Korucuk et al. (2022) to assess digital marketing strategies by considering green approaches. In the study, five digital marketing strategies have been used: search engine optimization, search engine marketing, social media marketing, programmatic advertising, and influencer marketing. Findings show that the best digital marketing strategy is programmatic advertising. Gao et al. (2023) utilised the spherical fuzzy (SF)-MEREC–SWARA–ARAS approach to assess digital marketing technology. This study also used the criteria and alternatives introduced by Mukul et al. (2019). The most suitable strategy has been obtained as artificial intelligence. Esmaelnezhad et al. (2023) have presented a hybrid-MCDM method in a fuzzy environment to assess digital marketing strategies in the tourism industry according to nine criteria such as online loyalty, website traffic, online trust (e-trust), customer acquisition, word-of-mouth, sales prospect, returns on investments, cost, and brand awareness. They have determined ten digital marketing strategies such as search engine optimisation, search engine marketing, social media marketing, content marketing, app store optimisation, marketing automation, e-mail marketing, data-driven personalisation, in app advertising, and mobile marketing. The study has revealed that social media marketing, search engine optimisation and search engine marketing are suitable to be utilized as digital marketing strategies in the tourism industry.

A review of literature shows that evaluation of digital marketing strategies with MCDM method has been considered limited attention and generally studies have not examined digital marketing strategies/technologies from a sectoral perspective. It is thought that there is still a gap at this point. Moreover, Bayesian BWM and fuzzy TOPSIS has not been utilized to assess digital marketing strategies in the retail sector. It is expected that this study will contribute to the understanding of digital marketing strategies in the retail sector, which has an important place in the economy.

3. METHODOLOGY

In this study, the decision methodology of Bayesian BWM and fuzzy TOPSIS is used to assess digital marketing strategies. Firstly, Bayesian BWM is used to obtain the weights of the criteria. Then, F-TOPSIS is utilized with the Bayesian BWM weights to rank the digital marketing strategies in the retail sector.

3.1. Bayesian BWM (B-BWM)

The Best-Worst Method (BWM) introduced by Jafar Rezaei in 2015, involves the determination of optimal criteria through the identification of both the best and worst criteria. Through pairwise comparisons with other criteria, the method aims to ascertain the relative importance of each criterion. Subsequently, solving a min-max problem yields the optimal weights for these criteria. Notably, BWM operates under the assumption of one decision-maker's preferences. The study by Mohammadi and Rezaei (2020) shows that this method is not effective in cases where different best criteria are introduced by more than one decision maker (DM). Therefore, Mohammadi and Rezaei (2020) introduced Bayesian BWM (B-BWM), which is suitable for group decision-making models. When B-BWM is considered from a statistical perspective, the criteria are random events and criterion weights are seen as the probability of these random events occurring. For this reason, the data of the B-BWM is modeled with probability distributions. The advantage of the method is its ability to obtain criteria weights by combining pairwise comparisons of different DMs with probability distributions. (Tuş et al, 2023: 846-847). In this study, the B-BWM method is used to determine the criterion weights due to its superiority. B-BWM comprises the following steps (Mohammadi and Rezaei, 2020: 4-5; Hashemkhani Zolfani et al, 2022: 7-8).

Step 1: Determine the decision criteria set C= $\{c_1, c_2, \dots, c_n\}$.

Step 2: Select the best (C_B^k) and the worst (C_W^k) criterion for DM k.

Step 3: The best-to-others vector $\left(A_B^k\right)$ are acquired for each DM. The numbers 1 to 9 introduced by Saaty (1980) are used for comparison.

$$A_B^k = \left(A_{B1}^k, A_{B2}^k, A_{B3}^k, \dots, A_{Bm}^k\right), \; k=1,2,\dots,K. \tag{1}$$

108

Where K is the number of DMs, A_{Bi}^{k} denotes the pairwise comparison between the best and other criteria.

Step 4: The others-to-worst vector $\left(A_{W}^{k} \right)$ are acquired for each DM. The numbers 1 to 9 introduced by Saaty (1980) are used for comparison.

$$A_{W}^{k} = \left(A_{1W}^{k}, A_{2W}^{k}, A_{3W}^{k}, \ldots, A_{mW}^{k} \right)^{T}, k=1,2,\ldots,K. \tag{2}$$

Where K is the number of DMs, A_{jW}^{k} denotes the pairwise comparison between the the worst and other criteria.

Step 5: The input vectors for calculations from a probabilistic perspective include variables A_{B}^{k} and A_{W}^{k}. B-BWM shares similar computational procedures with BWM but distinguishes itself by aggregating criterion weights from multiple DMs through a probabilistic approach.

$$\left(A_{B}^{k_{H}} \# \ w^{k} \right) \sim \text{multinominal} \left(\frac{1}{w^{k}} \right), \forall k=1,\ldots,K. \tag{3}$$

$$\left(A_{W}^{k} \# \ w^{k} \right) \sim \text{multinominal} \left(w^{k} \right), \forall k=1,\ldots,K. \tag{4}$$

Here multinomial represent the multinomial distribution.

$$(w^{k} \mid w*) \sim \text{Dir}(\gamma \times w*), \tag{5}$$

$$\gamma \sim \text{Gamma}(0.1,0.1), \tag{6}$$

$$w* \sim \text{Dir}(1). \tag{7}$$

The aggregated weight matrix $\left(w^{*} = w_{1}^{*}, \ldots w_{n}^{*} \right)$ is obtained. Dir(1) is the Dirichlet distribution, and Gamma(0.1.0.1) is the Gamma distribution. B-BWM is calculated with JAGS, one of the Monte Carlo methods. Moreover, credal ordering is obtained by the procedure introduced by Mohammadi and Rezaei (2020).

3.2. Fuzzy TOPSIS (F-TOPSIS)

Despite TOPSIS' popularity, it has faced criticism for its limitations in capturing decision makers' perceptions and the ambiguity inherent in their opinions. Chen and Hwang (1992) were the first to use fuzzy numbers to fuzzy TOPSIS. Fuzzy TOPSIS, rooted in fuzzy logic as opposed to classical logic, addresses these shortcomings, and offers a more robust approach (Kazemi et al, 2024: 44). The basic concept of TOPSIS is to determine the distance of each alternative from the positive ideal solution (PIS) and negative ideal solution (NIS) by incorporating human-provided attribute information (Ertuğrul and Karakaşoğlu, 2008: 786; Nozari et al, 2012: 80). Consequently, an additional limitation of this approach lies in the reliance of TOPSIS results on the reliability of the human-based information, which necessitates that such information be deemed consistent. To address this limitation, fuzzy set theory is employed to reduce the inherent vagueness and subjectivity in human reasoning (Sadeghi et al, 2021: 250; Darzi, 2024: 6). Zadeh (1965) introduced fuzzy set theory as a pivotal method for addressing uncertainty, marking a significant advancement in this field. This theory encompasses various elements such as fuzzy sets, membership functions, linguistic variables, and fuzzy arithmetic rules, all developed within the framework of fuzzy logic theory and techniques. Among these, fuzzy sets and linguistic variables are particularly prominent for qualitative assessments. Linguistic variables are transformed into fuzzy numbers, facilitating their integration within fuzzy set theory (Sharma and Tripathy, 2023: 2392). In this study, Triangular Fuzzy Numbers (TFNs) have been used. The membership function of TFNs for the fuzzy number $\tilde{A}$ is defined as follow (Chen, 2000: 3).

$$\mu_{\tilde{A}}(x) = \begin{cases} 0, x < l \\ \dfrac{(x-l)}{(m-l)}, l \leq x < m \\ \dfrac{(u-x)}{(u-m)}, m \leq x \leq u \\ 0, otherwise \end{cases} \tag{8}$$

The operational laws of the two positive TFNs $\tilde{A}_1 = (l_1, m_1, u_1)$, and $\tilde{A}_2 = (l_2, m_2, u_2)$, are calculated as follow (Sun, 2010: 7746):

$$\tilde{A}_1 \oplus \tilde{A}_2 = (l_1 + l_2, m_1 + m_2, u_1 + u_2) \tag{9}$$

$$\tilde{A}_1 \ominus \tilde{A}_2 = (l_1 - u_2, m_1 - m_2, u_1 - l_2) \tag{10}$$

$$\tilde{A}_1 \otimes \tilde{A}_2 = (l_1.l_2, m_1.m_2, u_1.u_2) \tag{11}$$

$$\tilde{A}_1 \oslash \tilde{A}_2 = (l_1 / u_2, m_1 / m_2, u_1 / l_2) \tag{12}$$

$$d_v\left(\tilde{A}_1, \tilde{A}_2\right) = \sqrt{\frac{1}{3}\left[\left(l_1 - l_2\right)^2 + \left(m_1 - m_2\right)^2 + \left(u_1 - u_2\right)^2\right]} \tag{13}$$

The calculation steps of F-TOPSIS are as follows (Han and Trimi 2018: 11-12 ; Darzi, 2024: 6-7):

Step 1: DMs assess alternatives according to Table 1 which was introduced by Han and Trimi (2018) and fuzzy decision matrix is constructed by Eq. (14).

Table 1. Linguistic variables and TFNs

Linguistic variables	Abbreviation	TFNs
Very Good	5	(7, 9, 9)
Good	4	(5, 7, 9)
Fair	3	(3, 5, 7)
Poor	2	(1, 3, 5)
Very Poor	1	(1, 1, 3)

$$\tilde{D} = \begin{array}{c} A_1 \\ A_2 \\ \vdots \\ A_m \end{array}\begin{bmatrix} \tilde{x}_{11} & \tilde{x}_{12} & \cdots & \tilde{x}_{1n} \\ \tilde{x}_{21} & \tilde{x}_{22} & \cdots & \tilde{x}_{2n} \\ \vdots & \vdots & \ddots & \vdots \\ \tilde{x}_{m1} & \tilde{x}_{m2} & \cdots & \tilde{x}_{mn} \end{bmatrix} \tag{14}$$

Here $a=1,2,\ldots,m$; $b=1,2,\ldots,n$.

Step 2: Aggregated fuzzy decision matrix is constructed. The aggregated importance of TFN $\tilde{A}_k = \left(l_k, m_k, u_k\right)$ is calculated as follows.

$$l = \min\{l_K\}, m = \frac{1}{k}\sum_{K=1}^{k} m_K, u = \max\{u_K\} \tag{15}$$

Here K is the number of DMs and $K=1,2,\ldots,k$.

Step 3: Calculate the normalized fuzzy decision matrix $\left(\tilde{R}\right)$. Eq. (16) is used for benefit criteria and Eq. (17) is used for cost criteria.

$$\tilde{R} = \left[\tilde{r}_{ab}\right]_{m\times n}, a=1,2,3,\ldots,m; b=1,2,3,\ldots,n.$$

$$\tilde{r}_{ab} = \left(\frac{l_{ab}}{u_b^+}, \frac{m_{ab}}{u_b^+}, \frac{u_{ab}}{u_b^+}\right), \quad u_b^+ = \max_a\{u_{ab} \mid a = 1,2,\ldots,n\} \tag{16}$$

$$\tilde{r}_{ab} = \left(\frac{l_b^-}{u_{ab}}, \frac{l_b^-}{u_{ab}}, \frac{l_b^-}{u_{ab}}\right), \quad l_b^- = \min_a\{l_{ab}\# a = 1,2,\ldots,n\} \tag{17}$$

Step 4: Calculate the weighted fuzzy normalized decision matrix $(\tilde{V})$.

$$\tilde{V} = \left[\tilde{v}_{ab}\right]_{m\times n}, a=1,2,3,\ldots,m; b=1,2,3,\ldots,n.$$

Here $\tilde{v}_{ab} = \tilde{r}_{ab} \times \tilde{w}_b$. (18)

Step 5: Determine the fuzzy positive ideal solution $\left(A_b^+\right)$ and the fuzzy negative ideal solution $\left(A_b^-\right)$ considering the type of criterion.

$$A^+ = \left(\tilde{v}_1^+, \tilde{v}_2^+, \tilde{v}_3^+, \cdots, \tilde{v}_n^+\right) \tag{19}$$

$b = 1,2,3,\ldots,n$ and $\tilde{v}_n^+ = \max v_{av}$ if $(b \in B)$; $\min v_{ab}$ if $(b \in C)$

$$A^- = \left(\tilde{v}_1^-, \tilde{v}_2^-, \tilde{v}, \cdots, \tilde{v}_n^-\right) \tag{20}$$

$b = 1,2,3,\ldots,n$ and $\tilde{v}_n^- = \min v_{ab}$ if $(b \in B)$; $\max v_{ab}(b \in C)$

Step 6:   Calculate the distance of each alternative from the fuzzy positive ideal solution $(\tilde{d}_a^+)$ and fuzzy negative ideal solution $(\tilde{d}_a^-)$.

$$\tilde{d}_a^+ = \sum_{b=1}^{n} d\left(\tilde{v}_{ab} - \tilde{v}_b^+\right), \ a=1,2,3,\ldots,m; \ b=1,2,3,\ldots,n \tag{21}$$

$$\tilde{d}_a^- = \sum_{b=1}^{n} d\left(\tilde{v}_{ab} - \tilde{v}_b^-\right), \ a=1,2,3,\ldots,m; \ b=1,2,3,\ldots,n \tag{22}$$

Step 7:   Calculate the closeness coefficient $\left(\widetilde{CC}_a\right)$ of each alternative.

$$\widetilde{CC}_a = \frac{\tilde{d}_a^-}{\tilde{d}_a^+ + \tilde{d}_a^-} \ a = 1,2,3,\ldots,m. \tag{23}$$

Step 8:   Ranking the alternative according to $\widetilde{CC}_a$ values; the highest value of $\widetilde{CC}_a$ presents the best alternative.

4. CASE STUDY

The retail sector, which is an integral part of economies, holds significant importance due to its contribution to economic growth and employment generation, ensuring the healthy functioning of supply chains, and shaping the consumption habits of society among sectors. The digital transformation brought about by the era has also significantly impacted the retail sector, leading to an increase in online retail sales. The integration of digital transformation with the retail sector necessitates a proper understanding of digital marketing strategies employed within this sector. For this reason, the main objective of this study is to assess digital marketing strategies in the retail sector with B-BWM and fuzzy TOPSIS method. In this study, three main criteria and nine subcriteria have been proposed by Mukul et al. (2019). The criteria used in this study are as follows: customer satisfaction (R11), customer loyalty (R12), simultaneous accessibility of product/ service (R13), image (brand value) of company (R21), promotions (R22), utilization of social media (R23), competitive position in market (R31), market size (R32) and interaction with competitors (R33). Moreover, the digital marketing strategies handled in this study are social media marketing (S1), e-mail marketing (S2), search engine optimisation (S3), influencer marketing (S4), pay-per-click advertising (S5). These strategies have been introduced by (Leung and

Mo (2019). According to DMs' opinions and literature reviews, hierarchy of digital marketing strategy selection in the retail sector is presented in Figure 1.

Figure 1. Hierarchy of digital marketing strategy selection

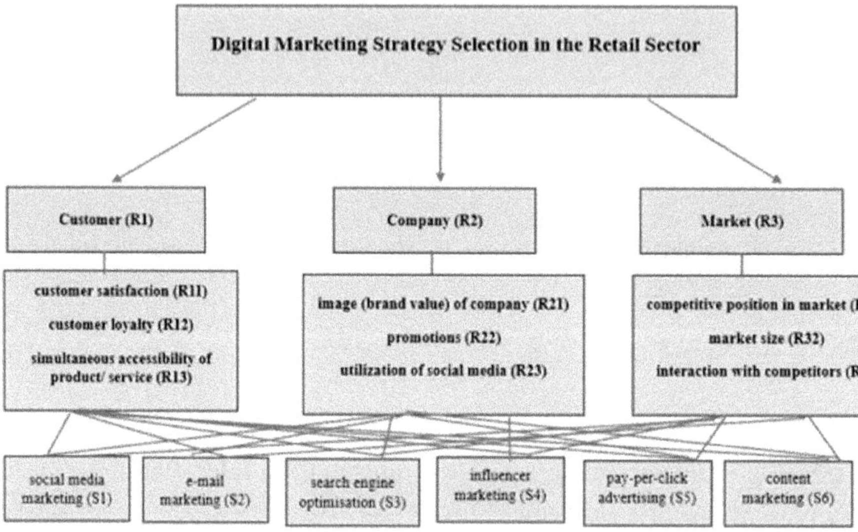

Considering Figure 1, the flow of the study can be summarized as follows.

1. Identify the digital marketing strategy selection problem.
2. Define the criteria that should be satisfied to fulfill all objectives.
3. Define digital marketing strategies for the retail sector.
4. Calculate criteria weights with B-BWM.
5. Identify the most appropriate digital marketing strategies in the retail sector with fuzzy TOPSIS.

4.1. Analysis Results

In the study, five DMs are included in the evaluation of digital marketing strategies in the retail sector. The decision committee includes marketing manager, marketing expert, professor, assistant professor, and research assistant in the field of marketing. The main criteria evaluation results made by DMs are shown in Table 2.

Table 2. Best-to-others and others-to-worst vectors for main criteria

	Vector	R1	R2	R3
DM1	Best-to-others	1	3	5
	others-to-worst	5	4	1
DM2	Best-to-others	1	4	3
	others-to-worst	5	1	4
DM3	Best-to-others	1	3	2
	others-to-worst	6	1	4
DM4	Best-to-others	1	4	3
	others-to-worst	7	2	1
DM5	Best-to-others	2	2	1
	others-to-worst	1	1	2

Figure 2. Main criteria weights of digital marketing strategy assessment

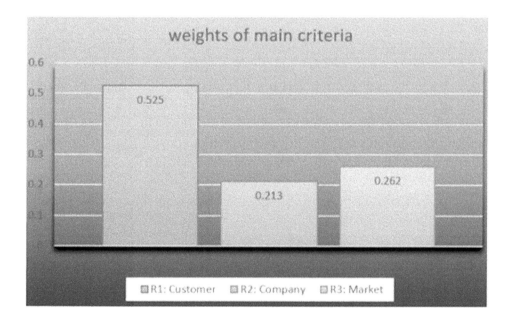

Then the weights for the subcriteria are obtained. Table 3 shows the evaluations made by DM 1 from the decision committee for the sub-criteria.

Table 3. Best-to-others and others-to-worst vectors for sub-criteria (sample evaluation for DM 1)

	Vector	R11	R12	R13		R21	R22	R23		R31	R32	R33
DM1	best-to-others	1	2	4	best-to-others	1	5	3	best-to-others	1	6	5
	others-to-worst	4	3	1	others-to-worst	5	1	4	others-to-worst	6	1	4

The same process is repeated for each DM. Then B-BWM calculation steps are applied. Table 4 denotes the local weights and global weights of all criteria. The global weights are calculated by multiplying the local weights with the respective main criteria local weight.

Table 4. Weights of main and sub-criteria with B-BWM

Main Criteria	Local Weight	Sub-Criteria	Local Weight	Global Weight	Rank
R1	0.525	R11	0.510	0.268	1
		R12	0.341	0.179	2
		R13	0.148	0.078	5
R2	0.213	R21	0.526	0.112	4
		R22	0.143	0.030	9
		R23	0.330	0.070	7
R3	0.262	R31	0.578	0.151	3
		R32	0.150	0.039	8
		R33	0.272	0.071	6

Figure 3. Sub-criteria weights of digital marketing strategy assessment

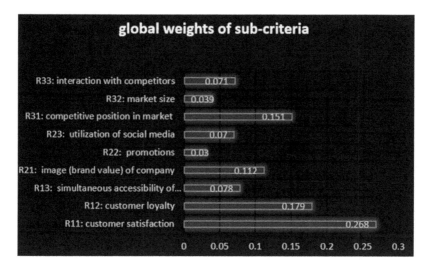

Based on Table 4, customer satisfaction (R11) has the highest weight (0.268) and becomes the first criterion that is taken into account in the selection of digital marketing strategies. The second and third important criteria are customer loyalty (R12) and competitive position in the market (R31) with a weight of 0.341 and 0.151 respectively.

Then, with fuzzy TOPSIS, the ranking of digital marketing strategies in the retail sector was obtained as follows. The DMs used linguistic terms (see Table 1), to define their opinions about the rating of every digital marketing strategies regarding each criteria. Aggregated fuzzy decision matrix is obtained by Eq. (14). It can be seen in Table 5.

Table 5. Fuzzy decision matrix

		DM1			DM2			DM3			DM4			DM5		
R11	S1	3	5	7	3	5	7	3	5	7	3	5	7	3	5	7
	S2	5	7	9	5	7	9	5	7	9	5	7	9	5	7	9
	S3	7	9	9	5	7	9	7	9	9	7	9	9	7	9	9
	S4	5	7	9	5	7	9	5	7	9	5	7	9	5	7	9
	S5	1	1	3	7	9	9	7	9	9	5	7	9	7	9	9
R12	S1	7	9	9	7	9	9	5	7	9	7	9	9	7	9	9
	S2	5	7	9	5	7	9	5	7	9	5	7	9	5	7	9
	S3	5	7	9	3	5	7	5	7	9	5	7	9	5	7	9
	S4	3	5	7	3	5	7	3	5	7	3	5	7	5	7	9
	S5	1	1	3	5	7	9	5	7	9	5	7	9	5	7	9
R13	S1	3	5	7	3	5	7	3	5	7	3	5	7	5	7	9
	S2	1	3	5	1	3	5	1	3	5	1	3	5	1	3	5
	S3	7	9	9	7	9	9	5	7	9	7	9	9	7	9	9
	S4	1	3	5	1	3	5	1	3	5	1	3	5	1	3	5
	S5	7	9	9	7	9	9	7	9	9	7	9	9	7	9	9
R21	S1	7	9	9	7	9	9	7	9	9	7	9	9	7	9	9
	S2	3	5	7	3	5	7	3	5	7	3	5	7	3	5	7
	S3	5	7	9	3	5	7	5	7	9	5	7	9	5	7	9
	S4	7	9	9	7	9	9	7	9	9	7	9	9	7	9	9
	S5	3	5	7	3	5	7	3	5	7	3	5	7	3	5	7
R22	S1	3	5	7	3	5	7	3	5	7	3	5	7	5	7	9
	S2	5	7	9	5	7	9	5	7	9	5	7	9	5	7	9
	S3	3	5	7	3	5	7	3	5	7	3	5	7	3	5	7
	S4	3	5	7	3	5	7	3	5	7	3	5	7	3	5	7
	S5	1	1	3	7	9	9	7	9	9	7	9	9	7	9	9
R23	S1	3	5	7	3	5	7	3	5	7	3	5	7	3	5	7
	S2	3	5	7	3	5	7	3	5	7	3	5	7	3	5	7
	S3	1	3	5	1	3	5	1	3	5	1	3	5	1	3	5
	S4	5	7	9	5	7	9	5	7	9	5	7	9	5	7	9
	S5	3	5	7	3	5	7	3	5	7	3	5	7	5	7	9
R31	S1	5	7	9	5	7	9	5	7	9	5	7	9	5	7	9
	S2	3	5	7	3	5	7	3	5	7	3	5	7	3	5	7
	S3	7	9	9	7	9	9	7	9	9	7	9	9	7	9	9
	S4	7	9	9	7	9	9	5	7	9	7	9	9	7	9	9
	S5	5	7	9	5	7	9	5	7	9	5	7	9	5	7	9

Continued on following page

Table 5. Continued

		DM1			DM2			DM3			DM4			DM5		
R32	S1	3	5	7	3	5	7	3	5	7	3	5	7	3	5	7
	S2	5	7	9	3	5	7	5	7	9	5	7	9	5	7	9
	S3	5	7	9	5	7	9	5	7	9	5	7	9	5	7	9
	S4	1	1	3	5	7	9	5	1	1	3	7	9	1	1	3
	S5	3	5	7	3	5	7	3	5	7	3	5	7	3	5	7
R33	S1	3	5	7	3	5	7	3	5	7	3	5	7	3	5	7
	S2	5	7	9	5	7	9	5	7	9	5	7	9	5	7	9
	S3	5	7	9	3	5	7	5	7	9	1	3	5	3	5	7
	S4	7	9	9	7	9	9	7	9	9	5	7	9	7	9	9
	S5	5	7	9	5	7	9	5	7	9	3	5	7	7	9	9

Using Eq. (15), aggregated fuzzy decision matrix is calculated as Table 6.

Table 6. Aggregated fuzzy decision matrix of digital marketing strategies under subjective criteria

	R11			R12			R13			R21			R22		
S1	3	5	7	5	8.60	9	3	5.40	9	7	9	9	3	5.40	9
S2	5	7	9	5	7	9	1	3	5	3	5	7	5	7	9
S3	5	8.60	9	3	6.60	9	5	8.60	9	3	6.60	9	3	5	7
S4	5	7	9	3	5.40	9	1	3	5	7	9	9	3	5	7
S5	1	7	9	1	5.80	9	7	9	9	3	5	7	1	7.40	9

	R23			R31			R32			R33		
S1	3	5	7	5	7	9	3	5	7	3	5	7
S2	3	5	7	3	5	7	3	6.6	9	5	7	9
S3	1	3	5	7	9	9	5	7	9	1	5.4	9
S4	5	7	9	5	8.6	9	1	3.4	9	5	8.6	9
S5	3	5.4	9	5	7	9	3	5	7	3	7	9

Using Eq. (16), normalized fuzzy decision matrix is calculated. The resulting normalized fuzzy decision matrix is shown as Table 7.

Table 7. Normalized fuzzy decision matrix

	R11			R12			R13			R21			R22		
S1	0.333	0.556	0.778	0.556	0.956	1	0.333	0.600	1	0.778	1	1	0.333	0.600	1
S2	0.556	0.778	1	0.556	0.778	1	0.111	0.333	0.556	0.333	0.556	0.778	0.556	0.778	1
S3	0.556	0.956	1	0.333	0.733	1	0.556	0.956	1	0.333	0.733	1	0.333	0.556	0.778
S4	0.556	0.778	1	0.333	0.600	1	0.111	0.333	0.556	0.778	1	1	0.333	0.556	0.778
S5	0.111	0.778	1	0.111	0.644	1	0.778	1	1	0.333	0.556	0.778	0.111	0.822	1

	R23			R31			R32			R33		
S1	0.333	0.556	0.778	0.556	0.778	1	0.333	0.556	0.778	0.333	0.556	0.778
S2	0.333	0.556	0.778	0.333	0.556	0.778	0.333	0.733	1	0.556	0.778	1
S3	0.111	0.333	0.556	0.778	1	1	0.556	0.778	1	0.111	0.600	1
S4	0.556	0.778	1	0.556	0.956	1	0.111	0.378	1	0.556	0.956	1
S5	0.333	0.600	1	0.556	0.778	1	0.333	0.556	0.778	0.333	0.778	1

Using Eq. (18), the weighted normalized fuzzy-decision matrix is calculated as Table 8. At this stage, the weights obtained by B-BWM are used.

Table 8. Weighted normalized fuzzy-decision matrix

	R11			R12			R13			R21			R22		
S1	0.089	0.149	0.208	0.099	0.171	0.179	0.026	0.047	0.078	0.087	0.112	0.112	0.010	0.018	0.030
S2	0.149	0.208	0.268	0.099	0.139	0.179	0.009	0.026	0.043	0.037	0.062	0.087	0.017	0.023	0.030
S3	0.149	0.256	0.268	0.060	0.131	0.179	0.043	0.075	0.078	0.037	0.082	0.112	0.010	0.017	0.023
S4	0.149	0.208	0.268	0.060	0.107	0.179	0.009	0.026	0.043	0.087	0.112	0.112	0.010	0.017	0.023
S5	0.030	0.208	0.268	0.020	0.115	0.179	0.061	0.078	0.078	0.037	0.062	0.087	0.003	0.025	0.030

	R23			R31			R32			R33		
S1	0.023	0.039	0.054	0.084	0.117	0.151	0.013	0.022	0.030	0.024	0.039	0.055
S2	0.023	0.039	0.054	0.050	0.084	0.117	0.013	0.029	0.039	0.039	0.055	0.071
S3	0.008	0.023	0.039	0.117	0.151	0.151	0.022	0.030	0.039	0.008	0.043	0.071
S4	0.039	0.054	0.070	0.084	0.144	0.151	0.004	0.015	0.039	0.039	0.068	0.071
S5	0.023	0.042	0.070	0.084	0.117	0.151	0.013	0.022	0.030	0.024	0.055	0.071

Using Eq. (19-20), The fuzzy positive ideal solution $\left(A_b^+ \right)$ and the fuzzy negative ideal solution $\left(A_b^- \right)$ are calculated as follows.

$$A^+ = \left(\tilde{v}_1^+, \tilde{v}_2^+, \tilde{v}_3^+, \cdots, \tilde{v}_n^+ \right) = (0.268, 0.179, 0.078, 0.112, 0.03, 0.07, 0.151, 0.039, 0.071)$$

$A^- = \left(\tilde{v}_1^-, \tilde{v}_2^-, \tilde{v}, \cdots, \tilde{v}_n^- \right) =$ (0.03, 0.02, 0.009, 0.037, 0.003, 0.008, 0.05, 0.004, 0.008)

Using Eq. (21-22), the distance of each alternative from the fuzzy positive ideal solution $(\tilde{d}_a^+)$ and fuzzy negative ideal solution $\tilde{d}_a^-$ are calculated and then the closeness coefficient $\left(\widetilde{CC}_a \right)$ of each strategies using by Eq. (23) is obtained as Table 9.

Table 9. The distance for digital marketing strategies

	$\tilde{d}_a^+$	$\tilde{d}_a^-$	$\widetilde{CC}_a$	Rank
S1	0.37	0.55	0.60	3
S2	0.39	0.53	0.58	4
S3	0.34	0.62	0.64	1
S4	0.34	0.60	0.64	1
S5	0.44	0.57	0.56	5

According to Table 9, the ranking order of the digital marketing strategies in the retail sector is S3: search engine optimisation, S4: influencer marketing, S1: social media marketing, S2:e-mail marketing and S5: pay-per-click advertising. According to the results obtained from this study, it was determined that the most suitable digital marketing strategies in the retail industry are search engine optimisation, influencer marketing and social media marketing.

CONCLUSION

Digital marketing has become a significant component of the many sector's to adapt to changing consumer behaviors and drive sustainable business growth in today's digital-first economy. The aim of this study is to construct a B-BWM and fuzzy TOPSIS model to assess digital marketing strategies in the retail sector. The importance of the determined criteria is evaluated by DMs and the uncertainty of human decision-making is taken into consideration in fuzzy environment. From the applied method, B-BWM and fuzzy TOPSIS, we have revealed the first three important criteria for digital marketing strategies in the retail sector are customer satisfaction, customer loyalty and competitive position in the market. Furthermore, promotions rank last priority. This study revealed that the most suitable digital marketing strategies for the retail industry were search engine optimisation and influencer marketing as of the period in which the study was conducted. The most important contributions in this paper as follows:

- The introduced B-BWM and fuzzy TOPSIS model is the first to assess digital marketing strategies in the retail sector.
- The findings of this study can be guidance in the digital marketing strategies assessment in the retail sector.

The main limitation of this study is the presence of a limited number of DMs and the lack of quantitative data. Future research should focus on a more detailed examination of search engine optimization and influencer marketing strategies, which have been determined as the most appropriate digital marketing strategies in the retail sector. In addition, the digital marketing strategies used in this study could be assessed in terms of different sectors and the results are comparable. Moreover, the robustness of the introduced model should be tested by sensitivity analysis.

REFERENCES

Çalık, A. (2020). Evaluation of social media platforms using Best-Worst method and fuzzy VIKOR methods: A Case Study of Travel Agency. *Iranian Journal of Management Studies*, *13*(4), 645–672.

Chen, C. T. (2000). Extensions of the TOPSIS for group decision-making under fuzzy environment. *Fuzzy Sets and Systems*, *114*(1), 1–9. doi:10.1016/S0165-0114(97)00377-1

Chen, S. J., & Hwang, C. L. (1992). Fuzzy multiple attribute decision making methods. In *Fuzzy multiple attribute decision making: Methods and applications* (pp. 289–486). Springer Berlin Heidelberg. doi:10.1007/978-3-642-46768-4_5

Darzi, M. A. (2024). Overcoming barriers to integrated management systems via developing guiding principles using G-AHP and F-TOPSIS. *Expert Systems with Applications*, *239*, 122305. doi:10.1016/j.eswa.2023.122305

Dizman, H. (2022). A Historical Review From Marketing 1.0 to Marketing 5.0. *Social Sciences Studies Journal (Sssjournal)*, *7*(87), 3866–3871. doi:10.26449/sssj.3412

Durukal, E. (2019). Change from Marketing 1.0 to Marketing 4.0. *İnsan ve Toplum Bilimleri Araştırmaları Dergisi*, *8*(3), 1613-1633.

Ertuğrul, İ., & Karakaşoğlu, N. (2008). Comparison of fuzzy AHP and fuzzy TOPSIS methods for facility location selection. *International Journal of Advanced Manufacturing Technology*, *39*(7-8), 783–795. doi:10.1007/s00170-007-1249-8

Esmaelnezhad, D., Bahmani, J., Babgohari, A. Z., Taghizadeh-Yazdi, M., & Nazari-Shirkouhi, S. (2023). A fuzzy hybrid approach to analyse digital marketing strategies towards tourism industry. *International Journal of Tourism Policy*, *13*(5), 463–480. doi:10.1504/IJTP.2023.133201

Gao, K., Liu, T., Yue, D., Simic, V., Rong, Y., & Garg, H. (2023). An Integrated Spherical Fuzzy Multi-criterion Group Decision-Making Approach and Its Application in Digital Marketing Technology Assessment. *International Journal of Computational Intelligence Systems*, *16*(1), 125. doi:10.1007/s44196-023-00298-3

Han, H., & Trimi, S. (2018). A fuzzy TOPSIS method for performance evaluation of reverse logistics in social commerce platforms. *Expert Systems with Applications*, *103*, 133–145. doi:10.1016/j.eswa.2018.03.003

Hashemkhani Zolfani, S., Bazrafshan, R., Ecer, F., & Karamaşa, Ç. (2022). The suitability-feasibility-acceptability strategy integrated with Bayesian BWM-MARCOS methods to determine the optimal lithium battery plant located in South America. *Mathematics*, *10*(14), 2401. doi:10.3390/math10142401

Kazemi, A., Kazemi, Z., Heshmat, H., Nazarian-Jashnabadi, J., & Tomášková, H. (2024). Ranking factors affecting sustainable competitive advantage from the business intelligence perspective: Using content analysis and F-TOPSIS. *Journal of Soft Computing and Decision Analytics*, *2*(1), 39–53. doi:10.31181/jscda21202430

Korucuk, S., Aytekin, A., Ecer, F., Karamaşa, Ç., & Zavadskas, E. K. (2022). Assessing green approaches and digital marketing strategies for twin transition via fermatean fuzzy SWARA-COPRAS. *Axioms*, *11*(12), 709. doi:10.3390/axioms11120709

Leung, K. H., & Mo, D. Y. (2019, December). A fuzzy-AHP approach for strategic evaluation and selection of digital marketing tools. In 2019 IEEE international conference on industrial engineering and engineering management (IEEM) (pp. 1422-1426). IEEE. doi:10.1109/IEEM44572.2019.8978797

Mehta, S. (2022). The Evolution of Marketing 1.0 to Marketing 5.0. *Issue 4 Int'l JL Mgmt. &. Human.*, *5*, 469.

Mohammadi, M., & Rezaei, J. (2020). Bayesian best-worst method: A probabilistic group decision making model. *Omega*, *96*, 102075. doi:10.1016/j.omega.2019.06.001

Mukul, E., Büyüközkan, G., & Güler, M. (2019, April). Evaluation of digital marketing technologies with MCDM methods. In *Proceedings of the 6th International Conference on New Ideas in Management Economics and Accounting*, France, Paris (pp. 19-21). 10.33422/6th.imea.2019.04.1070

Nozari, H., Sadeghi, M. E., Eskandari, J., & Ghorbani, E. (2012). Using integrated fuzzy AHP and fuzzy TOPSIS methods to explore the impact of knowledge management tools in staff empowerment (Case study in knowledge-based companies located on science and technology parks in Iran). *International Journal of Information, Business and Management*, *4*(2), 75–92.

Nuseir, M. T., El Refae, G. A., Aljumah, A., Alshurideh, M., Urabi, S., & Kurdi, B. A. (2023). Digital Marketing Strategies and the Impact on Customer Experience: A Systematic Review. *The Effect of Information Technology on Business and Marketing Intelligence Systems*, 21-44.

Rezaei, J. (2015). Best-worst multi-criteria decision-making method. *Omega*, *53*, 49–57. doi:10.1016/j.omega.2014.11.009

Saaty, T. L. (1980). *The analytical hierarchy process, planning, priority. Resource allocation.* RWS publications.

Sadeghi, M. E., Nozari, H., Dezfoli, H. K., & Khajezadeh, M. (2021). Ranking of different of investment risk in high-tech projects using TOPSIS method in fuzzy environment based on linguistic variables. *arXiv preprint arXiv:2111.14665*.

Sharma, J., & Tripathy, B. B. (2023). An integrated QFD and fuzzy TOPSIS approach for supplier evaluation and selection. *The TQM Journal*, *35*(8), 2387–2412. doi:10.1108/TQM-09-2022-0295

Sun, C. C. (2010). A performance evaluation model by integrating fuzzy AHP and fuzzy TOPSIS methods. *Expert Systems with Applications*, *37*(12), 7745–7754. doi:10.1016/j.eswa.2010.04.066

Trung, N. Q., & Thanh, N. V. (2022). Evaluation of digital marketing technologies with fuzzy linguistic MCDM methods. *Axioms*, *11*(5), 230. doi:10.3390/axioms11050230

Tuş, A., Öztaş, G. Z., Öztaş, T., Özçil, A., & Aytaç Adalı, E. (2023). *An alternative approach for calculating Turkey's digital transformation index: Bayesian BWM*. Pamukkale University Journal of Engineering Sciences-Pamukkale Universitesi Muhendislik Bilimleri Dergisi.

Zadeh, L. A. (1965). Fuzzy sets. *Information and Control*, *8*(3), 338–353. doi:10.1016/S0019-9958(65)90241-X

Chapter 9
Competitive Advantage in the Supply Chain With an Emphasis on Blockchain Technology

Masoud Vaseei
(iD) https://orcid.org/0000-0002-9221-2128
Islamic Azad University of Lahijan, Iran

Mohammadreza Nasiri Jan Agha
Islamic Azad University of Lahijan, Iran

ABSTRACT

With regard to the increasing number of international industries and integrated industries and the vertical and horizontal globalization of industries and the challenges that exist in this direction on the way of world trade, a lot of motivation has been created to share the different dimensions of the two fields of information technology and chain management. In this direction, steps should be taken to meet industrial needs and industrial technologies. Blockchain technology has been able to gain a high position in this regard in the opinion of industry managers and researchers in the world. Therefore, suitable opportunities for research and identification of operational applications have been provided. In this research, the development of blockchain-based global supply chains has been investigated and evaluated. Investing in blockchain is one of the most important tools for growing competitive advantage in process-oriented businesses with large financial flows in today's era.

DOI: 10.4018/979-8-3693-3108-8.ch009

1. INTRODUCTION

Supply chain, as its name suggests, is a network of all people, organizations, resources, activities and technologies involved in creating and selling a product. A supply chain includes everything from the delivery of raw materials from the supplier to the manufacturer to its final delivery to the end user. One of the challenges of supply chain globalization is its management and control. Today, blockchain technology, as a transparent digital technology that ensures traceability and security throughout the supply chain, promises to reduce a significant portion of the management problems of this global supply chain (Nozari et al., 2023).

Blockchain technology is a distributed database of public/private records of all processes that are shared on a secure platform. In a private blockchain, the supply chain network is made up of known individuals who work to produce or distribute products. But in the public blockchain, it is designed for the use of many anonymous users, and encryption methods are used to maintain their trust, so that users can enter the network and register their information (movahed et al., 2024).

Using blockchain technology, businesses can see the movement of goods throughout the supply chain in real time. This enables data sharing among all parties involved, providing a source of truth and fostering trust among stakeholders. The immutable nature of blockchain ensures that the data stored in the ledger cannot be altered or manipulated. This improves auditability and can help businesses meet regulatory requirements for transparency and traceability. Blockchain technology can help automate and streamline supply chain processes, including procurement, inventory management, and procurement. This can lead to cost savings and increased operational efficiency (Nozari, 2024).

By providing a single, transparent source of data, blockchain can help eliminate the errors and inconsistencies that often result from manual processes and hidden information in traditional supply chains. Blockchain's ability to securely store data and provide end-to-end traceability can It helps businesses ensure the authenticity of their products, reduces the risk of counterfeiting and protects brand reputation. With the increased transparency provided by blockchain, businesses can easily identify gray market activities such as unauthorized sales of goods and Blockchain technology can be combined with IoT devices and sensors to monitor and record information about product conditions, such as temperature and humidity, throughout the supply chain. This can help ensure product quality and safety, especially for perishable goods. In the event of a product recall or quality issue, blockchain traceability features can allow businesses to quickly identify damaged products and their origin, enabling resolution. It becomes faster and minimizes potential harm to consumers. By incorporating blockchain-based solutions, consumers can verify the authenticity of the products they purchase and ensure that they are receiving the original goods (Nozari & Szmelter-Jarosz, 2024).

All the mentioned cases show that blockchain technology is effective from supply and procurement to sales and distribution, i.e., all supply chain processes, and this can create the biggest competitive advantage for businesses. Therefore, in this research, it is tried to examine and evaluate the competitive advantage of this technology by examining the effects of blockchain technology.

2. THEORETICAL LITERATURE

The basic purpose of supply chain management is to exchange information related to market requirements, develop new products, reduce the number of suppliers for manufacturers, and activate and free management resources in order to develop long-term and important relationships, which are based on the trust of these members from the beginning. This definition includes: the set of elements of suppliers, logistics service providers, manufacturers, distributors and sellers, where there are flows related to raw materials, products and information flow among these supply chain elements. Blockchain can be used to develop the ledger. Blockchain can be used to develop digital ledgers and all stakeholders can access and share data with greater reliability. In a traditional supply chain, it is very difficult to piggyback all the purchases of the supply chain members, but with the blockchain 5 tracker, it is easy because of the existence of a shared digital ledger (Aliahmadi et al., 2024).

With the investment and application of blockchain, this payment gap can be reduced with digital trust between the parties to the contract. Due to features such as irreversibility and traceability, these contracts greatly reduce the possibility of breaching the contract by any of the parties. In addition, smart contracts will reduce transaction costs due to the elimination of intermediaries and third parties. Blockchain also improves traceability and brings transparency to logistics, leading to improved delivery cycles. In the traditional supply chain, if the supply chain is widely expanded, the possibility of inconsistency increases, and blockchain technology can be very useful in this case to overcome such inconsistencies (Nozari, 2023).

The blockchain platform has the ability to store and perform transactions with high security due to its technology and data encryption, and it also has the feature of transparency in order to present these transactions for public viewing. Blockchain is useful in more accurate forecasting of demand, inventory management and backup as the market situation changes. Blockchain empowers the organization to quickly change suppliers, designs, etc. In addition, all quality documents can be standardized and shared with all members of the supply chain improving decision making (Rahmaty and Nozari, 2023).

Agility is the supply chain's ability to meet unexpected changes in market demand and turn them into business opportunities. Blockchain enables business partners to share documents, plans, quality documents and transaction data with greater speed, accuracy and confidence. Such data sharing improves demand forecasting, better inventory management, and backups. Therefore, companies must constantly look for new opportunities, and such features can lead companies to improve performance. Dynamic management capabilities enable businesses to create, allocate and protect intangible assets that support superior long-term business performance.

In this regard, many researches have been conducted in this field in recent years. In a study, Ali Ahmadi et al. (2022) addressed the topic of "critical success factors of blockchain for a sustainable supply chain". The analysis has been done with the help of Fuzzy DEMATEL method. The researchers show the important role of some of the causes that lead to the integration of blockchain with the supply chain and ultimately, achieving sustainability. Data security and non-centralization, accessibility, rules and policies, documents and documents, data management and quality, are the things that help to develop strategy with blockchain. Nozari and Ali Ahmadi (2023) in a study investigated and explained the implementation of blockchain technology in the delivery system of the egg production and supply chain from the farm to consumption by the end user by a company based in the Midwest of the United States. Researchers show that for stakeholders in the food supply chain, having traceability and transparency creates better relationships with customers, increases efficiency and reduces the risk and costs of food recalls, fraud and product loss. Ali Ahmadi and Nozari (2023) have investigated the traceability and observation of agricultural products based on blockchain: a decentralized method to ensure food safety. They state that due to globalization, the food supply chain industry and food safety from farm to consumption and quality certification have become much more important than in the past. In this case, a basic proposed solution is to use the capacity of the emerging blockchain technology. It eliminates the need for a centralized secure structure and follows a strong level of safety and integrity.

Nozari et al. (2021) investigated the role of blockchain in achieving the key goals of supply chain management. This study shows various mechanisms by which blockchain can help to achieve goals in the supply chain. Ghahremani-Nahar et al. (2022), during a study, investigated blockchain technology from the perspective of operations and supply chain management, identifying potential application areas and providing plans for future research. In this research, countless ways that blockchain can change actions and methods have been identified, including: increasing product safety and security; improving quality management; reducing illegal fraud; improving sustainable supply chain management; Accelerating inventory management and restocking, reducing the need for intermediaries; impact on new product design and development; and reducing supply chain transaction costs. Bathaee et al.

(2023) with the aim of investigating the role of using this technology in improving collaborative interactions and the performance of the defense industry supply chain, structural equation modeling was used to check the research hypotheses. The results showed that the use of blockchain technology has a positive and significant effect. It is based on collaborative interactions and chain performance, and the creation of collaborative interactions also leads to the improvement of defense industry supply chain performance.

Nozari et al. (2019) investigated the role of blockchain technology in improving the supply chain performance of Iran's postmodern businesses. The research method is descriptive-analytical and of an applied type. There is a positive and meaningful relationship with the application of blockchain technology in improving supply chain performance. In addition, among all the independent variables included in the regression equation, 5 variables (social networks, improvement of banking services, financial transparency, ambiguity tolerance) explain about 72% of the changes in the supply chain performance of internet businesses. The results of the path analysis also show that the variables of the legal, political and managerial fields, social networks, financial transparency, improvement of banking services, the ability to tolerate ambiguity explain the most direct and indirect effects of blockchain technology on the supply chain performance of Iranian businesses.

In a study, Tezel et al. (2021) investigated the effect of factors affecting the acceptance of financial technology by bank customers. The purpose of their research was to investigate and better understand the effect of perceived usefulness, perceived ease, customer experience, word of mouth, and reliability on acceptance. The results show that the variable of perceived ease has a negative effect on the trust of data customers and other variables have a positive effect on the reliability and therefore the acceptance of financial technology. In a study, Ronaghi (2021) investigated the relationships between the effective indicators of blockchain to improve the competitiveness of the food industry. Based on this, basic indicators in the food industry are identified based on blockchain technology, then structural and cause-and-effect relationships between the eight identified indicators are determined based on the opinions of experts using the fuzzy DEMATEL method. The findings of the research showed that the index of traceability and prevention of fraud is the most effective index. Also, the food waste prevention index has the most interaction with other indices and the smart contract index is the most effective index. In a study, Jamil et al. (2019) studied the design of the integrated management model of the electronic supply chain of goods and its effect on the company's financial performance.

Casino (2019), in a study investigated the role of blockchain technology in improving the performance of the supply chain of the defense industry. First, by using the Delphi technique, the key performance criteria of the defense industry supply chain were identified, and then by applying the qualitative research method of content analysis and using semi-structured and in-depth interviews, the role of blockchain technology in each of the key criteria of the defense industry supply chain was investigated. The results indicate that the proper application of this new technology can be effective in improving the performance of the defense industry supply chain. In a research, Wang et al. (2021) examined the structural capacity of blockchain in the context of the Internet of Things to promote the trust and accessibility of information and knowledge to the stakeholders of the supply chain. The results showed that blockchain has the capacity to respond to the serious challenges of information management in the supply chain. Structural improvement of information security will reduce cumbersome controls and facilitate access to information. Also, having data and information with high reliability will provide more reliable knowledge.

3. BENEFITS OF BLOCKCHAIN IN SUPPLY CHAIN

The traditional model of the supply chain is based on trust and causes people to be unaware of important parts of the supply chain stages, which has caused many problems. Creating a blockchain structure and infrastructure can solve these problems.

Blockchain technology allows companies to track all types of transactions with greater security and transparency. By using blockchain in the supply chain, companies can trace the history of a product right from its point of origin to where it currently is. With the help of this powerful technology, parties collaborating on a common platform can dramatically reduce the time delays, overhead, and human error often associated with transactions. Reducing intermediaries in the supply chain also reduces the risks of fraud.

In the event of any breach or fraud in the supply chain, comprehensive records recorded on the blockchain enable organizations to easily pinpoint the source of the problem. A shared blockchain ledger between key actors in a supply chain provides a reliable, tamper-free audit trail of the flow of information, inventory, and finances in a supply chain. Using a shared blockchain, companies can synchronize logistics data, track shipments and automate payments. Blockchain efficiency makes global supply chains more efficient by allowing companies to complete and confirm transactions directly. Integrated payment solutions reduce the time between order and payment processing and ensure proper and timely movement of products. Additionally, blockchain and smart contracts help companies increase compliance, reduce legal costs and late tax penalties, and curb fraud. Organizations can integrate blockchain with radio frequency identification (RFID) tags that use electromagnetic fields to identify and track items. Blockchain is used to store product information and verify when ownership is transferred, increasing supply chain automation. A smart contract is executed when a shipment arrives at its destination tagged with RFID codes, which are automatically scanned. Since the records on the blockchain cannot be erased, the blockchain brings transparency to the supply chain.

Using blockchain, logistics issues can be easily traced back to their source. The same applies to the supply of parts or raw materials, which can be traced with the help of blockchain. Increasing accountability and transparency, and reducing illegal activities are also other solutions that blockchain does in the supply chain for the prosperity of this industry. The characteristics of the blockchain-based supply chain are shown in Figure 1.

Figure 1. Blockchain-based supply chain features

Despite all these strengths, the use of this technology in the supply chain faces a series of challenges and limitations that must be taken into account. The general change of the infrastructure of a company and business requires a huge responsibility and may cause a lot of interference in the executive work and financial resources of that company. For this reason, companies may be hesitant to invest in blockchain before it becomes widespread and used by competitors. When the blockchain system is implemented on the supply chain of a product or service, many companies must use new systems and technologies and update themselves in some way. A change management program should define what blockchain is and what changes it will bring to their job duties, while also teaching them how to work with the new system. For all these cases, a continuous and detailed training program is needed so that all partners are familiar with the potential and benefits of blockchain, which requires a lot of time and financial resources.

4. CONCLUSION

With the increasing development of blockchain technology, due to the specific features of blockchain in the supply chain, such as: creating information transparency, maintaining data security and high speed of information transfer, we will soon witness the presence of this technology in various industries. This will improve the supply chain and speed up the transfer of products, resulting in a higher quality experience in product presentation. Considering the scope of supply chain activity in various industries, there is a significant space for the growth of blockchain technology in the supply chain. By enabling end-to-end traceability along the supply chain, the speed of product delivery, coordination and financing, blockchain can revolutionize a lot. Blockchain can be a powerful tool to eliminate defects. In today's era, managers of various industries should evaluate the potential of blockchain in the supply chain for their business. They should join efforts to develop new rules, experiment with different technologies, run trials with different blockchain platforms, and build an ecosystem with other companies. Because the future industry needs technology development along with security and blockchain can be a useful tool in this direction.

REFERENCES

Aliahmadi, A., Movahed, A. B., & Nozari, H. (2024). Collaboration Analysis in Supply Chain 4.0 for Smart Businesses. In Building Smart and Sustainable Businesses With Transformative Technologies (pp. 103-122). IGI Global.

Aliahmadi, A., & Nozari, H. (2023, January). Evaluation of security metrics in AIoT and blockchain-based supply chain by Neutrosophic decision-making method. In *Supply Chain Forum* []. Taylor & Francis.]. *International Journal (Toronto, Ont.)*, *24*(1), 31–42.

Aliahmadi, A., Nozari, H., Ghahremani-Nahr, J., & Szmelter-Jarosz, A. (2022). Evaluation of key impression of resilient supply chain based on artificial intelligence of things (AIoT). *arXiv preprint arXiv:2207.13174.*

Bathaee, M., Nozari, H., & Szmelter-Jarosz, A. (2023). Designing a new location-allocation and routing model with simultaneous pick-up and delivery in a closed-loop supply chain network under uncertainty. *Logistics*, *7*(1), 3. doi:10.3390/logistics7010003

Casino, F., Kanakaris, V., Dasaklis, T. K., Moschuris, S., & Rachaniotis, N. P. (2019). Modeling food supply chain traceability based on blockchain technology. *IFAC-PapersOnLine*, *52*(13), 2728–2733. doi:10.1016/j.ifacol.2019.11.620

Ghahremani-Nahr, J., Najafi, S. E., & Nozari, H. (2022). A combined transportation model for the fruit and vegetable supply chain network. *Journal of Optimization in Industrial Engineering*, *15*(2), 131–145.

Jamil, F., Hang, L., Kim, K., & Kim, D. (2019). A novel medical blockchain model for drug supply chain integrity management in a smart hospital. *Electronics (Basel)*, *8*(5), 505. doi:10.3390/electronics8050505

Movahed, A. B., Movahed, A. B., & Nozari, H. (2024). Opportunities and Challenges of Smart Supply Chain in Industry 5.0. *Information Logistics for Organizational Empowerment and Effective Supply Chain Management*, 108-138.

Nozari, H. (Ed.). (2023). *Building Smart and Sustainable Businesses With Transformative Technologies*. IGI Global. doi:10.4018/979-8-3693-0210-1

Nozari, H. (2024). Supply Chain 6.0 and Moving Towards Hyper-Intelligent Processes. In Information Logistics for Organizational Empowerment and Effective Supply Chain Management (pp. 1-13). IGI Global.

Nozari, H., & Aliahmadi, A. (2023). Analysis of critical success factors in a food agile supply chain by a fuzzy hybrid decision-making method. [Formerly known as Iranian Journal of Management Studies]. *Interdisciplinary Journal of Management Studies*, *16*(4), 905–926.

Nozari, H., Fallah, M., Kazemipoor, H., & Najafi, S. E. (2021). Big data analysis of IoT-based supply chain management considering FMCG industries. *Бизнес-информатика*, *15*(1, 1 (eng)), 78–96. doi:10.17323/2587-814X.2021.1.78.96

Nozari, H., Najafi, E., Fallah, M., & Hosseinzadeh Lotfi, F. (2019). Quantitative analysis of key performance indicators of green supply chain in FMCG industries using non-linear fuzzy method. *Mathematics*, *7*(11), 1020. doi:10.3390/math7111020

Nozari, H., & Szmelter-Jarosz, A. (2024). An Analytical Framework for Smart Supply Chains 5.0. In *Building Smart and Sustainable Businesses With Transformative Technologies* (pp. 1–15). IGI Global.

Nozari, H., Tavakkoli-Moghaddam, R., Rohaninejad, M., & Hanzalek, Z. (2023, September). Artificial Intelligence of Things (AIoT) Strategies for a Smart Sustainable-Resilient Supply Chain. In *IFIP International Conference on Advances in Production Management Systems* (pp. 805-816). Cham: Springer Nature Switzerland. 10.1007/978-3-031-43670-3_56

Rahmaty, M., & Nozari, H. (2023). Optimization of the hierarchical supply chain in the pharmaceutical industry. *Edelweiss Applied Science and Technology*, 7(2), 104–123. doi:10.55214/25768484.v7i2.376

Ronaghi, M. H. (2021). A blockchain maturity model in agricultural supply chain. *Information Processing in Agriculture*, 8(3), 398–408. doi:10.1016/j.inpa.2020.10.004

Tezel, A., Febrero, P., Papadonikolaki, E., & Yitmen, I. (2021). Insights into blockchain implementation in construction: Models for supply chain management. *Journal of Management Engineering*, 37(4), 04021038. doi:10.1061/(ASCE) ME.1943-5479.0000939

Wang, Z., Zheng, Z., Jiang, W., & Tang, S. (2021). Blockchain-enabled data sharing in supply chains: Model, operationalization, and tutorial. *Production and Operations Management*, 30(7), 1965–1985. doi:10.1111/poms.13356

Chapter 10
Blockchain and Its Financial Impact

Aditya Kumar

ⓘD https://orcid.org/0009-0005-6532-0624
Central University of South Bihar, India

Jainath Yadav
Central University of South Bihar, India

ABSTRACT

This chapter investigates the commercial applications of blockchain technology and how it affects the banking industry and other industries through the use of cryptocurrencies. It first examines the functioning of blockchain technology and identifies its benefits for business and economic transactions. It then explores the impact of this technology on financial operations and beyond. Through synthesizing knowledge from various fields such as technology, economics, finance, and politics, the chapter establishes four scenarios for the future of blockchain technology. The results of the study show that blockchain technology is still in the early stages of altering many businesses, but it has already had a significant impact on the financial industry. The chapter finds that blockchain technology's benefits in terms of security, efficiency, transparency, and accountability are undeniable, and it has the capacity to completely transform the way we conduct transactions and interact with organizations.

DOI: 10.4018/979-8-3693-3108-8.ch010

1. INTRODUCTION

Blockchain technology is a type of distributed ledger technology that facilitates secure and transparent transactions between parties without the need for a central authority or intermediary. It operates through a decentralized network of nodes that validate and record transactions in a tamper-proof manner. The fundamental concept is a digital ledger, where each block in the chain contains a set of transactions and is cryptographically linked to the previous block, ensuring the immutability and integrity of the ledger. One notable characteristic is decentralization, as the validation of transactions relies on a network of nodes rather than a central authority, promoting a more inclusive and democratic system. Additionally, the security of blockchain technology stems from the cryptographic linkage between blocks, making it challenging to modify or tamper with the ledger. Furthermore, the distribution of the ledger across multiple nodes enhances security by preventing any single party from controlling the entire blockchain (AlShamsi et al., 2022; Bashir, 2017).

Blockchain technology holds immense potential across various sectors, including finance, supply chain management, healthcare, and voting systems (Ahmed, 2022; Rajasekaran et al., 2022). In finance, it has the capacity to redefine transaction processes by eliminating intermediaries, enhancing transaction speed, and ensuring security. Supply chain management can benefit from blockchain's ability to establish a transparent and secure record of the entire supply chain, enabling efficient tracking and tracing of goods (Peres et al., 2022). However, along with its potential, blockchain technology also faces challenges that must be addressed. Scalability remains a significant hurdle, as current blockchains have limitations on the number of transactions they can handle per second. Additionally, concerns exist regarding the energy consumption associated with blockchain networks due to the computational power required for transaction validation. Despite these challenges, the transformative possibilities of blockchain technology generate enthusiasm. As the technology advances and matures, we can anticipate further innovative applications across various industries in the future.

1.1 Working of Blockchain

Blockchain technology is a decentralized system that facilitates secure and transparent recording of transactions. It operates through a distributed ledger, eliminating the need for a central authority. Rather than relying on a single entity, it utilizes a network of computers, known as nodes, to maintain the ledger. The functioning of blockchain technology can be described through the following steps (also shown in Figure 1 and Figure 2):

Figure 1. Components in blockchain

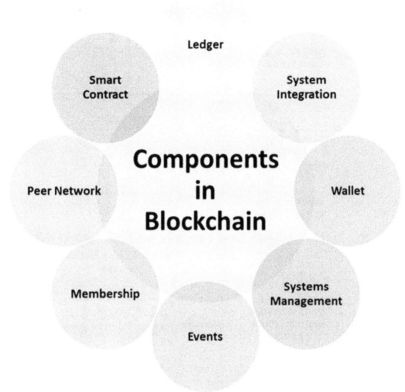

Figure 2. Working of blockchain

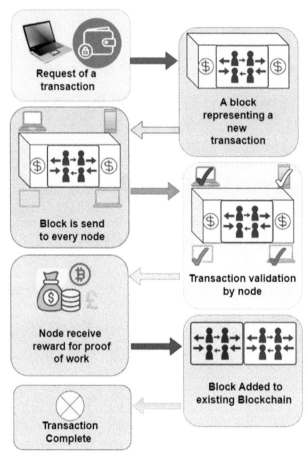

1. *Participants in the Network:* There are many participants in a blockchain network, including nodes, miners, and users. Nodes are the computers that uphold and verify the blockchain ledger. The nodes designated as miners carry out difficult calculations to validate and add new transactions to the network. Users are people or organisations that take part in the blockchain network by conducting transactions with one another.

2. *Transactions:* A transaction is broadcast to the network of nodes when a user starts it. The transaction includes information on the sender, the recipient, and the amount of currency that is being exchanged. A transaction is included to a block once it has been examined and approved by the nodes.

3. *Blocks:* A group of verified transactions are added to the blockchain as a block. It has a list of transactions and a heading. The hash of the block, the timestamp, and the hash of the preceding block are all included in the header's metadata.

A chain is created by connecting the current block to the preceding one using the hash of the earlier block.

4. *Mining:* Miners in the blockchain network use their computing power to solve difficult mathematical calculations to examine and add transactions to the blockchain. Cryptocurrency is awarded to the first miner who finds the solution. This process is known as mining.

5. *Consensus:* A block will be replicated and saved on each network node as soon as it is added to the blockchain. As a result, the ledger is resistant to tampering and there is no single point of failure. The network's nodes must concur on the blockchain's contents in order to preserve its integrity. This is accomplished using an establishing consensus technique. In blockchain networks, a variety of procedures for consensus are employed, including Proof of Work (PoW), Proof of Stake (PoS), Delegated Proof of Stake (DPoS), and Byzantine Fault Tolerance (BFT). Miners utilise their processing power to solve difficult mathematical issues in order to validate and add transactions to the blockchain in a PoW consensus mechanism. Bitcoin is awarded to the first miner who finds the solution. Validators in a PoS consensus mechanism are chosen based on the amount of bitcoin they own and are obligated to stake their cryptocurrency in order to approve transactions.

6. *Security:* Blockchain technology is meant to be safe and unchangeable. An entry on the blockchain cannot be changed or removed once it has been made. Attackers would need to alter all the blocks on the blockchain, which is virtually impossible, in order to change a transaction. The blockchain network is also resistant to cyberattacks due to its decentralised structure.

7. *Smart Contracts:* Smart contracts, which are self-executing contracts, directly encode the terms of the agreement between the buyer and seller into lines of code. They make it possible to automate transactions and get rid of middlemen. Complex transactions, like the sale of real estate or the transfer of ownership of assets, can be made easier with the use of smart contracts.

1.2 Objective and Motivation

The chapter aims to analyze the effects of blockchain technology on the financial sector, specifically focusing on cryptocurrencies and its commercial applications. It begins by exploring the functioning of blockchain technology and its benefits for business and economic transactions. The study also examines the implications of blockchain on financial operations and its potential to revolutionize buying, selling, and ownership verification processes. By combining knowledge from various fields, the chapter presents four scenarios for the future of blockchain, using a scenario-based approach and trend analysis for reliable predictions. The research findings indicate that blockchain has already had a significant impact on finance and is poised to transform numerous industries in the coming years. Businesses are increasingly recognizing its potential to leverage the benefits of the Fourth Industrial Revolution. Most significant white papers and articles on blockchain technology emphasize primarily technical as well as legal issues to give readers a thorough grasp of how the technology operates and how it might be used (Castro & Liskov, 1999; Greenspan, 2015; Nakamoto, 2008; Schwartz et al., 2014). The goal of this chapter is to look beyond technical and legal issues and examine how Blockchain technology might affect several sectors, particularly finance. Ultimately, it aims to answer the question of whether Blockchain is only a promising technological advancement or a seismic shift that will alter the face of business.

2. CURRENCIES USING BLOCKCHAIN TECHNOLOGY

Over the past 40 years, the Internet has introduced a multitude of positive developments, such as the World Wide Web, email, social media platforms, cloud computing, the Internet of Things, mobile applications, and big data. These innovations have significantly impacted the ways in which we work, consume, and interact with one another, leading to improvements in commerce, culture, and organizational management. However, despite its positive influence, recent technological advancements have also brought about negative social and political effects. For instance, the Internet has exacerbated issues related to privacy, security, and inclusion. Today, numerous intermediary parties, many of which are untrustworthy, collect sensitive data that pertains to both private individuals and businesses, thereby infringing on our right to privacy for their own benefit. In an effort to combat these limitations, numerous attempts have been made to establish new protocols and technologies that aim to improve privacy, security, and inclusion on the Internet.

David Chaum, a brilliant mathematician, created eCash in 1993 - a digital payment system that was perfectly designed to send electronic money securely and anonymously (eCash, n.d.). However, the system failed to take off as online shoppers didn't value their privacy and security at the time. Despite being technically sound, eCash didn't receive enough attention from the public and hence, couldn't gain traction. As a result, the project was eventually abandoned. It is worth noting that eCash was a precursor to modern cryptocurrency and blockchain technology. The concepts of digital currencies and secure, anonymous transactions were ahead of their time, and the world wasn't quite ready for them yet. Nonetheless, eCash laid the foundation for later developments in this field, and its ideas were eventually realized through the advent of bitcoin and other cryptocurrencies. Today, the importance of privacy and security in online transactions is widely recognized, and digital currencies have become an important part of the global financial landscape. Under the pseudonym Satoshi Nakamoto, an unknown individual or group unveiled a ground-breaking new protocol for a peer-to-peer electronic cash system in 2008 that utilised a kind of digital currency named Bitcoin. This was a substantial achievement since cryptocurrencies provide a decentralised alternative to conventional fiat currencies that are neither generated nor controlled by governments. The protocol introduced a new concept of a distributed network, where data exchange between various devices can occur without any trusted third party. The Bitcoin protocol enabled distributed computations and introduced a set of rules that allowed for secure and anonymous electronic transactions. This protocol was the foundation for the development of blockchain technology, which is now being widely used for various purposes beyond digital currencies. The capacity of blockchain technology to facilitate direct money transactions between individuals without the need for intermediaries like banks or financial organisations is one of its key advantages. Bitcoin remains the most well-known and popular cryptocurrency, but there are now many other digital currencies using blockchain technology. These currencies are often designed to serve different purposes, and some have even been developed specifically for use in certain industries. For example, some cryptocurrencies are used in supply chain management, while others are used for gaming or social media platforms. Blockchain technology has the potential to revolutionise a wide range of industries, including finance, healthcare, and real estate because of its decentralised nature. By eliminating intermediaries and reducing transaction costs, blockchain technology can enable faster, more secure, and more efficient transactions. However, there are also challenges and limitations to the technology, including issues around scalability, regulation, and energy consumption. As such, the future of blockchain technology remains uncertain, but it is clear that it has the potential to be a disruptive force in many industries for years to come.

The combination of Peer-to-Peer (P2P) network and distributed servers has enabled the creation of an autonomous and shared database among all participants in the network. This decentralized database eliminates the need for a central authority and ensures transparency. Instead of individuals maintaining separate transaction records, there is a single public ledger that is collectively owned by everyone in the network. Whenever a Bitcoin transaction occurs, it is recorded and timestamped by all participants in the system. The security of this system lies in its immutability and synchronization. Any attempt to send an asset that is not owned or manipulate the records would be immediately detected by other participants in the network, rendering fraudulent transactions impossible. Furthermore, the system's rules are initially defined and implemented through program code, ensuring that they cannot be altered without the unanimous consent of all network participants. Satoshi Nakamoto's innovation in creating Bitcoin was a solution to the problem of double spending on digital goods, which had previously required a trusted third-party intermediary to prevent fraud. The solution involved creating a decentralized network in which participants can make direct, secure exchanges of digital goods without intermediaries. By creating a distributed ledger that records all transactions in a shared, public database, the system ensures that no one can spend the same digital good twice. This is achieved through a consensus mechanism that requires multiple participants to verify each transaction and record it in the shared ledger. Thus, a person or organization can safely and anonymously exchange digital value, whether it be money or other types of digital assets, without having to trust a third party. This not only improves security and privacy but also reduces transaction costs and enables a faster and more efficient exchange of value between parties.

Every participant in the decentralised network on which blockchain technology runs has a copy of every transaction that has ever occurred on the network. This means that the records are preserved and shared by all network participants, and each record must match the ones stored on the other devices. Additionally, a predetermined number of network nodes must validate each transaction that occurs within the network. This validation process is crucial for ensuring the accuracy and legitimacy of the transaction. Once the transaction is validated, it is permanently encrypted, or cryptographically locked, making it impossible for anyone to alter or tamper with the transaction. This process ensures the transparency, security, and immutability of the network and its transactions.

According to Chung and Kim (2016), the development of the steam engine, electricity, and information technology are all regarded to be pillars of the fourth industrial revolution, which also includes blockchain technology. However, when it first emerged, it did not receive much attention. R. Collins (2016) has pointed out that the technology's potential was not fully recognized in the beginning. Nevertheless, as long as Bitcoin has operated reliably and securely, society has gradually learned about the enormous potential of blockchain technology not limited to cryptocurrencies. This technology can be applied in various other areas and has thus gained more attention and importance. Its impact is likely to continue growing in the future.

3. BENEFITS OF USING BLOCKCHAIN TECHNOLOGY

Many researchers have highlighted the immense benefits that blockchain technology can bring to various sectors, including finance and industry. In fact, some experts believe that the technology has the potential to revolutionize how business is conducted on a global scale. For instance, S. Underwood (2016) emphasized that blockchain has the potential to drastically change how business, industry, and education are conducted. It may also accelerate the emergence of a knowledge-based economy.

The immutable and transparent record of all transactions made within a network that blockchain provides is one of its main benefits since it builds participant confidence. Due to these characteristics, blockchain technology is thought to have a wide range of potential uses outside of the financial sector.

The "Internet of Information Sharing" has undergone an incredible change as a result of the development of blockchain technology, becoming the "Internet of Value Exchange". As a result of its innovative features, blockchain has attracted a great deal of interest from various organizations, institutions, nations, and scholars, making it a popular and trending topic. The technology's capacity to facilitate secure, decentralized, and transparent value exchange has spurred its adoption in diverse domains, including finance, healthcare, supply chain management, and more. This has led to a growing body of research exploring the potential applications and implications of blockchain technology in different domains.

Several researchers (Beck et al., 2016; Jang & Lee, 2017; Szetela et al., 2016), have noted that blockchain technology has found its applications in various fields. One of the most prominent areas of use is the financial sector, where it has given rise to popular cryptocurrencies like Bitcoin, Ethereum, Zcash, and others. However, the potential of blockchain extends beyond just financial transactions, and it has been applied to other fields like supply chain management, healthcare, real estate, and more. The distributed ledger technology of blockchain provides a secure and transparent method of recording transactions, which can increase efficiency and reduce costs in various industries.

There are many organizations and companies that are working on developing platforms based on blockchain technology. Some examples of these organizations are provided by authors (Zheng et al., 2017) who mention "Arcade City" which is a ride-sharing company that has integrated its business model into Ethereum, including identity and reputation systems. Another example is "Ubitquity", which is a digital property management company that provides secure recording and tracking of records using a blockchain platform. These are just a couple of the numerous instances of businesses and institutions utilising blockchain technology to its fullest potential in their respective industries.

The banking industry benefits greatly from the use of blockchain technology. One significant benefit is that it streamlines processes by automatically matching positions to accounts, resulting in quicker clearing and settlement avoiding having to wait for subsequent approval. Additionally, blockchain technology provides increased transparency, which helps financial institutions to better fulfill regulatory requirements. Another advantage is the fixed and transparent conditions for every transaction, reducing risks as the conditions are not subject to change. Decentralised registers prevent data centralization by storing all relevant information about transactions as well as the provenance of traded assets. Finally, blockchain technology eliminates interim steps, saving time and resources. To sum up, the benefits of blockchain technology are numerous in the banking industry. It simplifies processes, increases transparency, reduces risks, avoids centralization of data, and eliminates interim steps. By embracing blockchain technology, financial institutions can improve efficiency and offer better services to their clients.

The effectiveness of financial markets can be increased by the usage of blockchain technology. Although trades are executed in a matter of seconds, the actual settlement and exchange of assets may take several days and involve multiple parties, such as banks and clearinghouses. This process can result in errors, delays, and additional costs, which can create unnecessary risks. However, by using blockchain technology, the settlement and exchange process can be streamlined, reducing the need for intermediaries and decreasing the likelihood of errors or delays. Furthermore, the use of blockchain technology can increase transparency and trust in the market, which can further enhance market efficiency.

Smart contracts (Adam, 2022), which are self-executing agreements with the conditions of the agreement directly put into lines of code, are made possible by blockchain technology. This makes it possible to automate transactional operations, which decreases the need for middlemen and boosts the effectiveness and speed of transactions. Smart contracts are linked to specific blockchains and can track and transfer various assets and goods as needed for a transaction. For instance, a broker can purchase shares on behalf of a client using a smart contract. The smart contract includes private keys for the buyer and seller, which are then linked to multiple blockchains to confirm buying and selling power before executing the transaction between the two parties.

In addition to tracking financial transactions, blockchain technology can be used to store sensitive data, particularly that produced and maintained by governmental organisations. A digital identification system using blockchain technology could potentially provide a safer and more secure method for identification verification (Ansar et al., 2022). An international blockchain-based ID system would allow individuals to easily prove their identity, connect with family members, and even conduct peer-to-peer financial transactions without the need for intermediary banks. This might make financial transactions more streamlined and efficient while also lowering the possibility of fraud and identity theft.

The process of verifying a person's identity can be simplified and secured through the use of blockchain technology. By linking a person's fingerprint with other personal information, such as their name, gender, and nationality, a unique digital identity can be created and stored on the blockchain. This digital ID can then be used for a variety of purposes, such as accessing services, making transactions, or proving one's identity. The benefit of this method is that it does not require identity verification by intermediaries like banks or governmental organisations. Instead, the person's digital ID can be verified instantly and securely through the blockchain network. This not only saves time and money but also increases privacy and security by ensuring that personal information is not stored in a centralized database that can be hacked or misused.

4. TRANSFORMING THE FINANCIAL INDUSTRY

Blockchain technology has the potential to fundamentally alter the global financial system, which supports an economy worth more than $100 trillion and moves trillions of dollars every day. The conventional paper-based paradigm has continued to predominate despite the introduction of Internet banking and other technical improvements in the financial sector. According to Vikram Pandit, a former CEO of Citigroup, technology has transformed paper-based processes into semi-automated, semi-electronic processes, the basic theory is still grounded on the paper model. Blockchain technology promises to change this by offering a new paradigm that is secure, efficient, and transparent. By using blockchain, financial institutions can automate processes, reduce costs, increase transparency, and streamline operations. Moreover, it can also enable new business models, such as peer-to-peer lending and microfinance, which were not possible before. The potential of blockchain technology in the financial sector is enormous, and it is expected to have a profound impact on the industry in the years to come.

The intermediaries who hold significant power can often hinder progress and innovation by creating monopolies that benefit themselves and slow down the system. These intermediaries often have a monopoly over certain services or products, leading to higher prices and a lack of innovation. Additionally, outdated technology can also be a barrier to progress. This implies that the use of blockchain technology could potentially eliminate the need for powerful intermediaries and their monopolistic practices, resulting in a more efficient and consumer-friendly system. By utilizing decentralized technology, blockchain allows for greater transparency, security, and efficiency in transactions, reducing the need for intermediaries and increasing competition in the market. This could lead to better products and services for consumers, as well as a more dynamic and innovative industry overall.

Table 1. Transformation of Financial Services through Blockchain

Financial Services	Description
Increased Security	Blockchain technology provides enhanced security for financial transactions through its decentralized and tamper-evident nature. By doing away with middlemen, it lowers the possibility of fraud, data breaches, and unauthorised access.
Improved Efficiency	Blockchain makes financial transactions quicker and more efficient by doing away with the need to perform manual reconciliation and documentation. Smart contracts automate processes, reducing the time and effort required for executing and verifying transactions.
Enhanced Transparency	Blockchain's transparency makes it possible to see and track financial transactions more easily. Every transaction is recorded on the blockchain, providing an auditable trail of activities and minimizing the possibility of financial misconduct.
Cost Reduction	By removing intermediaries and streamlining processes, blockchain reduces transaction costs associated with traditional financial services. It saves businesses and consumers money by doing away with the need for third-party verification, clearinghouses, and reconciliation.
Financial Inclusion	By enabling access to financial services for those who are underbanked and unbanked, blockchain has the capability to increase financial inclusion. With blockchain-based solutions, individuals can have secure and direct control over their financial transactions, enabling participation in the global economy.
Cross-Border Payments	By removing the need for additional middlemen and lowering transaction costs, blockchain technology enables quicker and more affordable cross-border payments. It enables near-instantaneous settlement and reduces currency exchange complexities.
Tokenization and Asset Management	Blockchain allows for the tokenization of assets, enabling fractional ownership and easier transferability of traditionally illiquid assets such as real estate or artwork. It opens up new opportunities for asset management, investment, and liquidity.
Regulatory Compliance	Blockchain provides a transparent and immutable ledger, which can aid in regulatory compliance for financial institutions. It makes it possible to report in real-time, be auditable, and follow Know Your Customer (KYC) and Anti-Money Laundering (AML) laws.
Smart Contracts and Automation	Smart contracts on the blockchain automate contract execution, eliminating the need for manual processing and reducing the risk of errors. They enable self-executing agreements, automatic payments, and conditional transactions based on predefined rules.
Data Privacy and Ownership	Blockchain's decentralised and permissioned access model gives users more control over their personal data. Users can choose to share data, protecting their privacy while keeping the accuracy and control of their personal data.

Blockchain technology provides both individuals and institutions with the opportunity to create and manage value in a new way. It offers several benefits, such as attestation, lower costs, faster transactions, reduced risks, and increased innovation. Beyond payments, these advantages could revolutionise a number of other sectors, including investment banking, accountancy, venture capital, insurance, securities, enterprise risk management, and retail banking. Table 1 summarizes the impact of blockchain on financial services. This technology can provide a real choice for users by eliminating the need for powerful intermediaries and reducing their monopolistic positions. Blockchain's decentralized structure also enables faster and more transparent transactions, reducing the risks associated with centralization. These benefits can bring about significant improvements in product quality, efficiency, and consumer experience.

5. CASE STUDIES

The author (Knezevic, 2018) has identified four potential possible scenarios for the future of blockchain technology that can be discussed:

Case 1: The first scenario examines the potential failure of the blockchain technology platform, which was highlighted by Mike Hearn, a prominent developer of bitcoin core, in 2015. Hearn expressed concerns about unresolved technical standards, discord within the community, and the potential downfall of bitcoin. Several challenges, including the issue of multi-stakeholder governance, remain unanswered. Additionally, questions about scalability without environmental consequences and resolving controversial standard matters without resorting to hierarchy still persist. Despite these challenges, potential solutions exist. It is crucial to recognize that code is merely a tool and human leadership is essential. Research suggests that global solution networks (GSNs) can facilitate cooperation, drive societal change, and manage underlying technologies. D. Tappsocott and S. Undervood have proposed this approach as a potential solution.

Figure 3. Approximate market price in USD of Bitcoin over the last 13 years

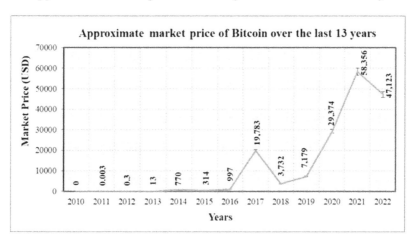

147

Case 2: As indicated by the second scenario, blockchain technology has a big impact on the financial industry but less potential in other sectors. The release of Bitcoin in 2009 marked the beginning of blockchain technology, and since then, it has gained massive popularity (Chiu & Thorsten, 2022). As of March 2017, cryptocurrencies had a combined market capitalization of over $24 billion, with Bitcoin accounting for over $16 billion of this value. Additionally, more than 200 million Bitcoin transactions have been made, and over 12 million wallets have been created. The value of Bitcoin has significantly increased, with 1 BTC being worth 8,667.50 euros in February 2018. Despite its success in the financial sector, blockchain technology has not yet shown the same potential in other industries. Figure 3 represents the approximate market price in USD of Bitcoin over the last 13 years. Note that these prices are approximate and can vary depending on the specific timeframe and data source used. Additionally, Bitcoin was not traded on exchanges until 2010, so the price before 2010 can be considered as $0.

Case 3: Scenario third involves a rapid transformation of the financial system while other industries such as education and healthcare undergo a slower transformation. The financial sector has been significantly impacted by blockchain technology, with the existence of numerous blockchain platforms evident in cryptocurrency market data. Various studies show that many of these platforms are still in the development phase (Yadav et al., 2022). The top 10 platforms in terms of cryptocurrency value and ownership are presented in Figure 4, with Bitcoin and Ethereum being the top two platforms with tokens available for trading on the marketplace.

Figure 4. The top 10 platforms in terms of cryptocurrency value (Tretina, 2023)

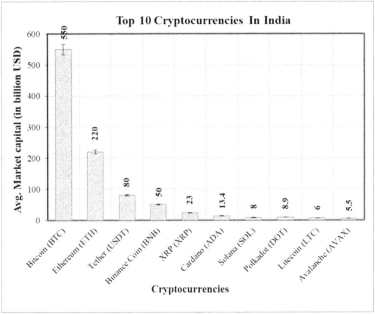

One of the main challenges to achieving this scenario is the issue of governance. While blockchain technology has made significant strides in the financial sector, the development of effective governance structures has proven to be a major hurdle. According to experts in the field, the success of blockchain platforms will depend on their ability to meet operational and governance requirements across a range of applications. Capital markets regulators, for instance, are unlikely to adopt blockchain-based solutions that do not meet their disclosure requirements. To ensure the scalability and interoperability of blockchain platforms, the industry needs to focus on efforts to enhance these capabilities. Despite the challenges in governance, blockchain technology has had a significant influence on the financial industry. Bitcoin, originally an experiment in monetary theory, has emerged as the leading cryptocurrency and platform in terms of value, volume, and hashing rate. Ethereum, another notable public blockchain platform, has gained attention for its potential to transform peer-to-peer contracting through smart contracts. The impact of blockchain extends beyond finance, with major companies like IBM, Deloitte, and Microsoft, as well as influential figures like Richard Branson, contributing to its rapid advancement. In fact, PwC's executive highlighted that $1.4 billion was invested in blockchain start-ups globally within the first nine months of 2016.

As blockchain technology progresses, it is anticipated to bring about substantial changes across multiple industries in the near future. The financial sector, in particular, is poised to reap significant benefits from the transparency, security, and accuracy offered by blockchain. These advantages have the potential to generate substantial cost savings for financial institutions, potentially amounting to billions of dollars. Despite initial skepticism towards Bitcoin as a speculative tool, many institutions are now making substantial investments in blockchain technology. The growing interest is evident even in academia, with esteemed universities such as Stanford, Duke, New York University, and Princeton offering courses on blockchain, bitcoin, and cryptocurrencies.

According to researchers and experts from diverse industries, the disruptive potential of blockchain technology extends beyond the financial sector. Various industries can reap benefits from this technology, including supply chain management, asset tracking, trade finance, digital rights management, insurance, corporate filings databases, personal identity verification, patent filings, forensic evidence, sports merchandising, and more. The broad range of applications highlights the versatility and transformative nature of blockchain technology across different sectors. Many researchers have provided evidence of industries that have already been disrupted by blockchain technology, as shown in Figure 5. It is expected that many more industries will be disrupted in the next 5 to 10 years as technology continues to evolve and mature. Blockchain technology has the ability to completely transform a variety of businesses by enhancing process efficiency, security, and transparency. Blockchain technology, for instance, can assist to promote transparency in supply chain management by tracing the flow of commodities from one party to another. This can help to lower fraud and increase responsibility. It has the capability to enhance fraud detection and automate the processing of insurance claims.

Figure 5. Impact of blockchain technology in industry

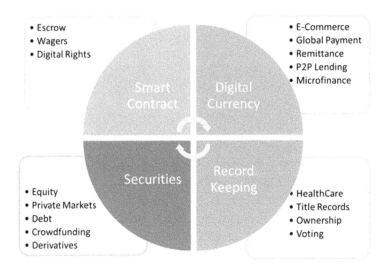

- Escrow
- Wagers
- Digital Rights

- E-Commerce
- Global Payment
- Remittance
- P2P Lending
- Microfinance

Smart Contract

Digital Currency

Securities

Record Keeping

- Equity
- Private Markets
- Debt
- Crowdfunding
- Derivatives

- HealthCare
- Title Records
- Ownership
- Voting

Case 4: Forth Scenario suggests that there could be radical and fast changes in both the financial sector as well as in the majority of industries within the next five years (Chen et al., 2022). Some experts, such as Nobel laureate Robert Shiller from Yale University, have analyzed the impact of underlying technologies on central banking and the financial system as a whole. However, there may be the possibility that this scenario is not likely to occur, and the following paragraph provides reasons why.

One reason for this skepticism is the fact that radical and fast change requires a significant shift in the underlying infrastructure and institutions that support the financial system. This would require a massive overhaul of existing systems and a high degree of coordination among different stakeholders, including governments, central banks, and financial institutions. Achieving such a degree of consensus and collaboration is unlikely within the next five years. Moreover, the financial sector is heavily regulated, and any significant changes would require the cooperation of regulators and policymakers. These stakeholders are unlikely to support rapid and radical changes that could potentially destabilize the financial system and have negative consequences for the broader economy. Another challenge to this scenario is the fact that most industries are deeply interconnected and interdependent. Changes in one industry can have ripple effects throughout the entire economy. Thus, it is unlikely that one sector, such as finance, would undergo a radical transformation without affecting other industries as well. Finally, it is important to note that technological change, while important, is only one factor that shapes the evolution of industries and economies. Social, political, and economic factors also perform an important part in determining the direction and pace of change. Therefore, it is unlikely that technology alone would drive a radical and fast transformation of the financial sector and all industries within the next five years.

5.1 Issues in Blockchain

In the financial sector (Sedlmeir et al., 2022; Zheng et al., 2018), blockchain suffers from several issues:

- *Scalability:* Blockchain technology currently has a limited capacity to process transactions. This makes it difficult for the technology to handle large volumes of transactions that are typical in financial markets.
- *Regulation:* Blockchain technology is still largely unregulated, and there is a lack of clarity on how financial regulators will approach the use of blockchain in financial markets. This creates uncertainty for financial institutions and their clients.
- *Interoperability:* There are numerous blockchain platforms, and they do not always work seamlessly with one another. This can create issues when financial institutions want to transfer assets between different platforms.
- *Security:* While blockchain technology is designed to be secure, there have been instances of hacks and thefts. This is a concern for financial institutions, as any loss of assets or data can have significant financial and reputational consequences.
- *Governance:* Blockchain networks require governance mechanisms to ensure their ongoing operation. However, the decentralized nature of blockchain can make it difficult to establish effective governance structures.
- *Adoption:* The development of blockchain technology is still quite recent, and adoption in the financial sector is not yet widespread. This creates challenges for financial institutions that want to use blockchain but are limited by the lack of supporting infrastructure.
- *Cost:* Even if blockchain technology could help financial organisations cut expenses, the initial investment required to implement it can be significant. This may be a barrier for smaller institutions or those with limited resources.

6. CONCLUSION

Blockchain technology has emerged as a disruptive innovation with significant potential to transform the financial sector and other industries. This technology has already proven to be a secure, transparent, and efficient way to conduct transactions and is expected to bring more benefits as it matures. By creating a tamper-evident and decentralized ledger, blockchain technology does not require intermediaries, reduces costs, and increases accountability. The potential of blockchain technology to revolutionize industries beyond finance, such as supply chain management and identity verification, cannot be underestimated. Looking to the future, businesses and policymakers need to be aware of the transformative impact of blockchain technology and the opportunities it presents. With blockchain technology still in its infancy, its potential uses are far-reaching and likely to transform multiple industries. The financial sector, in particular, is expected to continue to benefit from blockchain technology, with more efficient and cost-effective transactions. However, there are also challenges that must be addressed, such as regulatory issues, scalability, and interoperability. To fully harness the potential of blockchain technology, businesses and policymakers need to collaborate on developing appropriate regulations and standards, investing in research and development, and fostering innovation. Blockchain technology is anticipated to have a significant impact on how the world's economy and society develop during the coming years.

REFERENCES

Adam, P. (2022). Blockchain technology and smart contracts in decentralized governance systems. *Administrative Sciences*, *12*(3), 96.

Ahmed, G. (2022). Emerging trends in blockchain technology and applications: A review and outlook. *Journal of King Saud University. Computer and Information Sciences*, *34*(9), 6719–6742. doi:10.1016/j.jksuci.2022.03.007

AlShamsi, M., Al-Emran, M., & Shaalan, K. (2022). A systematic review on blockchain adoption. *Applied Sciences (Basel, Switzerland)*, *12*(9), 4245. doi:10.3390/app12094245

Ansar, S. A., Arya, S., Aggrawal, S., Yadav, J., & Pathak, P. C. (2022). Bitcoin-blockchain technology: Security perspective. In *2022 3rd International Conference on Intelligent Engineering and Management (ICIEM)*. IEEE.

Bashir, I. (2017). *Mastering blockchain*. Packt Publishing Ltd.

Beck, R., Czepluch, J. S., Lollike, N., & Malone, S. (2016). Blockchain–the gateway to trust-free cryptographic transactions. In *Twenty-Fourth European Conference on Information Systems (ECIS), I`stanbul, Turkey, 2016*. Springer Publishing Company.

Castro, M., & Liskov, B. (1999). Practical byzantine fault tolerance. OsDI, 99, 173–186.

Chen, Y., Lu, Y., Bulysheva, L., & Kataev, M. Y. (2022). Applications of blockchain in industry 4.0: A review. *Information Systems Frontiers*, 1–15. doi:10.1007/s10796-022-10248-7

Chiu, J., & Thorsten, V. (2022). The economics of cryptocurrency: Bitcoin and beyond. *The Canadian Journal of Economics. Revue Canadienne d'Economique*, *55*(4), 1762–1798. doi:10.1111/caje.12625

Chung, M., & Kim, J. (2016). The internet information and technology research directions based on the fourth industrial revolution. *KSII Transactions on Internet and Information Systems*, *10*(3), 1311–1320.

Collins, R. (2016). Blockchain: A new architecture for digital content. *EContent (Wilton, Conn.)*, *39*(8), 22–23.

eCash. (n.d.). Wealth Redefined. https://e.cash/

Greenspan, G. (2015). Multichain private blockchain-white paper. http://www. multichain. com/download/MultiChain-White-Paper. pdf

Jang, H., & Lee, J. (2017). An empirical study on modeling and prediction of bitcoin prices with bayesian neural networks based on blockchain information. *IEEE Access : Practical Innovations, Open Solutions*, *6*, 5427–5437. doi:10.1109/ACCESS.2017.2779181

Knezevic, D. (2018). Impact of blockchain technology platform in changing the financial sector and other industries. *Montenegrin Journal of Economics*, *14*(1), 109–120. doi:10.14254/1800-5845/2018.14-1.8

Nakamoto. (2008). Bitcoin: A peer-to-peer electronic cash system. *Decentralized Business Review*, 21260.

Peres, Schreier, Schweidel, & Sorescu. (2022). Blockchain meets marketing: Opportunities, threats, and avenues for future research. Academic Press.

Rajasekaran, A. S., Azees, M., & Al-Turjman, F. (2022). A comprehensive survey on blockchain technology. *Sustainable Energy Technologies and Assessments*, *52*, 102039. doi:10.1016/j.seta.2022.102039

Schwartz, D., Youngs, N., & Britto, A. (2014). The ripple protocol consensus algorithm. *Ripple Labs Inc White Paper*, *5*(8), 151.

Sedlmeir, J., Lautenschlager, J., Fridgen, G., & Urbach, N. (2022). The transparency challenge of blockchain in organizations. *Electronic Markets*, *32*(3), 1–16. doi:10.1007/s12525-022-00536-0 PMID:35602109

Szetela, Mentel, & Stanis-Law. (2016). Dependency analysis between bitcoin and selected global currencies. *Dynamic Econometric Models*, 16, 133–144.

Tretina, K. (2023). Top 10 Cryptocurrencies In India. https://www.forbes.com/ advisor/in/investing/ cryptocurrency/top-10-cryptocurrencies/

Underwood, S. (2016). Blockchain beyond bitcoin. *Communications of the ACM*, *59*(11), 15–17. doi:10.1145/2994581

Yadav, S. P., Agrawal, K. K., Bhati, B. S., Al-Turjman, F., & Mostarda, L. (2022). Blockchain-based cryptocurrency regulation: An overview. *Computational Economics*, *59*(4), 1659–1675. doi:10.1007/s10614-020-10050-0

Zheng, Z., Xie, S., Dai, H., Chen, X., & Wang, H. (2017). *An overview of blockchain technology: Architecture, consensus, and future trends. In 2017 IEEE international congress on big data (BigData congress).* IEEE.

Zheng, Z., Xie, S., Dai, H.-N., Chen, X., & Wang, H. (2018). Blockchain challenges and opportunities: A survey. *International Journal of Web and Grid Services*, *14*(4), 352–375. doi:10.1504/IJWGS.2018.095647

Chapter 11

Artificial Intelligence and Data Mining Techniques:
Applications in Financial Fraud Detection

Jaber Dehghani
Department of Management, Economics, and Progress Engineering, Iran University of Science and Technology, Iran

Hossein Mohammadi Dolat-Abadi
iD https://orcid.org/0000-0002-0526-0157
Department of Industrial Engineering, College of Farabi, University of Tehran, Iran

Saeed Karimi
Department of Industrial Engineering, Iran University of Science and Technology, Iran

ABSTRACT

Modern services like e-commerce, which emerged from the technological revolution, are some of the many domains that greatly contributed to business thriving by reducing costs, saving time, and increasing productivity by enabling companies and individuals to execute their financial transactions electronically. However, the remarkable rise of financial transactions due to the massive adoption of internet bank services, FinTech innovation, and e-commerce has increased the risk of malicious attacks aiming to perform fraudulent activities. Data mining and artificial intelligence are approaches that have widely been used as fraud detection techniques. Researchers have taken advantage of such methods to discover abnormal activities through which fraudsters intend to violate the law. In this research, the authors first introduce different types of financial fraud in e-commerce systems, then review various data mining methods to deal with them. Finally, the most efficient techniques regarding different types of fraud that can be applied to detect anomalies have been identified.

DOI: 10.4018/979-8-3693-3108-8.ch011

1. INTRODUCTION

Industry 6.0 is defined as digital transformation of Industrial processes including production, manufacturing, value creation, etc. It is a revolutionized vision of human-free business processes that promote machine-to-machine communication and networking (Golovianko et al., 2023). Industry 4.0 does not merely refer to the integration of value chain component in the automation systems, rather it also encompasses their assimilation with each other (Machkour and Abriane, 2020). Hence, this concept offers faster, more efficient and better industrial transformation through intelligence and autonomous machine interactions, which resulted in unavoidable changes in the way people live, work, and think. The financial sector, which constitutes an integral part of our everyday life, is not immune to these changes. The intervention of FinTech and Blockchain technologies plays a profound role in restructuring the financial sector. To remain competitive and avoid disappearing due to the cutting-throat competition and ever-increasing intricacies of the market, businesses and organizations are required to adapt to digital payment systems and other technologies that offer services in the various areas including personal finance, retail investment, corporate investments, asset management, money transfer, etc. Hence, the transition of company's services and activities to the era of Information and Communication Technologies (ICTs) is imperative and offers them a great opportunity to achieve considerable gains in performance and efficiency.

It is crystal clear that new emerging technologies transformed the way economy and society work, reshaping applicable models by allowing favorable interaction and flexibility among different parties. Nonetheless, financial fraud is a negative but essential part of such changes that influence both finance sector and everyday life. Financial abuse also has an adverse impact on integrities and confidences in financial sector along with individuals' life. It is an illegal or wrongful action committed by either individual or organization in an unethical or illegal way to gain beneficial (Barman et al., 2016). Since any E-commerce system involving internet-based transactions like financial services is prone to be targeted by fraudsters, anti-fraud has become a heated debate among scientists to explore the effective solution in this field. Over the past few years, various approaches has been introduced in dealing with financial frauds, however, none of them are a permanent, solid solution due to the constant evolution and development of methods by fraudulent parties or introduction of new technologies such as cryptocurrencies. Thus, financial fraud detection has turned out to be an important issue, motivating researchers to develop detection methods and estimate fraud risk.

Knowledge discovery objective is obtaining useful knowledge from data stored in large repositories. It is a fundamental necessity in various field, specifically those related to business (M. Delgado, 2003). Data mining is an effective approach that implemented in the field of data to extract meaningful information from large databases by taking advantage of one or more methods including Machine Learning, Statistical, Mathematical, or Artificial Intelligence techniques. Such approaches can be used for financial fraud detection, especially methods using Support Vector Machine (SVM), Logistic Regression (LR), and Naïve Bayes. The aim of this research is to introduce the latest practical data mining techniques in the area of financial fraud detection. These techniques contribute to fraud detection by exploring the underlying patterns in large datasets and differentiating between normal and suspicious transactions.

The remainder of this study is structured as follows. Section 2 provides a detailed review of common financial fraud types in various financial sectors. It highlights the vulnerable sectors targeted by fraudsters and refers to most used methods applied by fraudulent parties. Section 3 introduces data mining techniques in dealing with financial fraud and its application in financial domains. Section 4 discusses the pros and cons of each technique and identifies the best practical method for each sector, and finally, section 5 concludes the study and highlights its contribution.

2. FINANCIAL FRAUD TYPES

Fraud is an illegal and offensive activity carried out by an unauthorized organization or person by cheating innocents. According to studies, fraudulent activities vary based on the industry sector. Researchers in literature (Barman et al., 2016, Hilal, 2022, Nikkel, 2020) classify financial fraud into multiple categories including corporate fraud, bank fraud, and insurance fraud. In whatever way, the-cutting-edge technologies such as Blockchain, with all advantages, has introduce new breeding ground for emergence of cybercrime and fraud. Therefore, this study has also augmented cryptocurrency fraud to financial fraud domain. Figure 1 illustrate common area of financial frauds and their subcategories. The following subsections describe each of these categories in details.

2.1. Credit Card Fraud

In recent years, the fast paced growing technologies have encouraged businesses and individuals to perform money transactions electronically independent of presence of physical money. Almost all of the enterprises, ranging from small to large industries, are taking advantage of credit cards as a mean of payment. It has led to widespread use of credit cards, a small piece of plastic card that store personal and financial information of cardholders. The application of credit cards is significantly extending rapidly as they are widely used in E-commerce systems and internet baking. Such fast growth in their application by people and businesses was a main source of inspiration for fraudsters to consider them as a suitable tool for committing illegitimate transactions that resulted in a huge losses to card owners and banks.

Fake or suspicious transaction happens when fraudsters strive to illegally access the system that makes it face intermittent errors due to the conduction of suspicious action (Al-Hashedi and Magalingam, 2021). Credit card fraud can be classified into two main categories: online and offline frauds. Online fraud refers to fraudulent transactions that carried out through Internet, Cell phone, or via web browsers. In contrast, fraudsters use a stolen card or its information to perform their activities in offline fraud. The classifications of credit card frauds are as follows (RB and KR, 2021):

- Application fraud: Fraudster gets access to the application, steals customer's credentials, creates a fake account, and performs the transactions.
- Electronic/Manuel card imprints: Fraudster skims the information from the magnetic strip on the card, take advantage of the credentials for performing fraud.

Figure 1. Different types of financial fraud and their related sectors

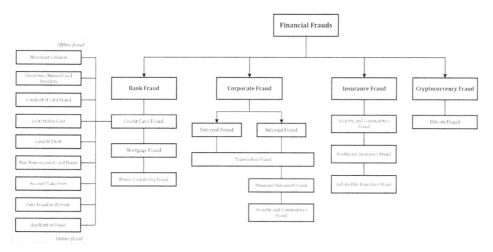

- Counterfeit card: Fraudsters stills all the data from original card through magnetic strip and uses them in a counterfeit card so that it looks and works as the original one.
- Lost/Stolen card: Loosing the card by or stealing the card from cardholder.
- Card id theft: the id of cardholder is stolen and used for fraud.

- Mail non-received card: Defrauding the mail or phishing the mail that has sent to recipient when credit card has issued.
- Account takeover: Fraudster takes the complete control of the account holder and makes fraud.
- Fake fraud in website: Introducing a fake code through which fraudster does their work in the website.
- Merchant collision: Card owners' information is shared with third party or the fraudster by merchants without cardholder authorization.

Based on credit card fraud data, credit card issuers, retailers, and consumers collectively lost $32.34 billion to credit card fraud in 2021, with authorities currently addressing less than 1% of daily fraudulent activity. The increasing prevalence of credit card fraud is having a remarkable impact on financial institutions, affecting their service quality, costs, and reputation. Hence, using effective models for credit card fraud detection is indispensable for regulators, banks, and costumers.

2.2. Mortgage Fraud

This type of fraud deals with mortgage documents. Mortgage fraud is defined as "material misstatement, misrepresentation, or omission relating to the property or potential mortgage relied on by an underwriter or lender to fund, purchase, or insure a loan". Fraudsters modify or remove information in the process of mortgage loan application. The real estate fraud misinforms about original value of the property with the intention of gaining more benefit or influence the financier to finance its lend (Ngai et al., 2011a).

2.3. Money Laundering

Money laundering is the illicit procedure in which criminals attempt to conceal or alter the origin of their illegal gains by either disguising them or converting them into goods and services. In this type of fraud, fraudsters deliberately exchange financial transitions related to legal activities and businesses with income earned through illicit activities to cover the original source of the money in order to make it appear legitimate. It is a way that lawbreakers employ to hide the main source of dirty money and legalize it (Makki et al., 2017). Money laundering enables criminals to Inject illegal money into the stream of commerce, thereby corrupting financial institutions and giving criminals unwarranted economic power. Thus, it has a deep adverse impact on society as, over the years, many organized crimes like terrorism activities and weapon trading has been financed through the money laundering.

2.4. Financial Statement Fraud

It is a part of internal section of corporate frauds. Corporate fraud refers to different kind of illegal activities such as misleading statements, stock price manipulation, and unauthorized changes in capital usage. In general, financial statement fraud is defined as *"the intentional misstatement of certain financial values to enhance the appearance of profitability and deceive shareholders or creditors"* (Singleton et al., 2006). Financial statement presents a universal picture of the company's situation that helps shareholders to figure out how successful the company is and whether it is bankable. A company is required to file its financial statements with government. While companies cannot control the leakage of statement fraud uncovered by government, they can control the information aspect on statement fraud. Managers abuse their position to alter financial statements to avoid representing a true and valid view of their company. They manipulate financial statement users by altering misstatements, thereby enabling the organization to look successful. However, the stockholders' faith on the company plummets when stories about financial statement fraud leak. Increasing share prices, getting bank loans, decreasing tax liabilities, and attracting investors are some motivations for performing financial statement fraud (West and Bhattacharya, 2016).

Financial statement fraud is the least frequent but most expensive (with a median loss of approximately $1 million) forms of corporate fraud. It typically costs businesses 5% of their annual revenues. Early detection of this type of fraud can prevent its exorbitant financial consequences. Therefore, financial fraud detection in time would prevent devastation of an economy.

2.5. Transaction Fraud

Transaction fraud is the subcategory of both internal and external section of corporate fraud. Corporate fraud consists of four factors including greed, opportunity, need, and exposure. These factors interact with each other and codetermine the risk of corporate fraud commitment. As opposed to internal fraud, external fraud is performed by individuals or organizations that externally related to the company. The main aim of transaction fraud is to steal or embezzle organizational assets through asset misappropriation, corruption over pilferage and petty theft, false invoices, using personal benefit to payroll and sick time abuse (Wells, 2014). Just as internal fraud, files on external fraud are also classified meticulously for the same goal. The fundamental difference between transaction and statement fraud is in no theft of assets involving financial statement fraud.

2.6. Securities and Commodities Fraud

Another type of fraud encountered in financial domain is securities and commodities fraud. It is a misleading practice to deceive individuals who are pursuing to invest in an organization via providing fake information. The most common ways of committing securities and commodities fraud are market manipulation, Ponzi schemes, pyramid schemes, prime bank schemes, foreign currency exchange fraud. In another definition, securities fraud includes theft from manipulation of market, securities accounts, and wire fraud.

As capital markets continue to integrate, businesses have unprecedented opportunities to raise or access capital, and investors have new options to diversify their portfolios. The growing range of opportunities also brings a corresponding increase in the risk of fraud, highlighting the need for research to identify and prevent these fraudulent activities.

2.7. Insurance Fraud

In financial territory, insurance is an instrument to protect assets and businesses against financial losses. Insurance fraud is the act of performing illegitimate action with unethical intention to misuse insurance policies in order to gain unlawful profit from insurance companies. It can occur throughout insurance procedure, from application and eligibility to rating, billing, and claims, and be committed by anyone, clients, agents and brokers, insurance company employees, healthcare providers and others. Some of the most prevalence types of insurance fraud happens when people in purpose committee a fake car accident or report lost assets and claim an exaggerated costs for compensation.

Insurance fraud can include a wide range of insurance sector such as healthcare, automobile, crop, and so on. In healthcare system, fraud can be carried out in various segments using different methods like billing for services not rendered, up-coding of services and items, duplicate claims, etc. (Ngai et al., 2011b) Automobile insurance fraud includes a set of illegal activities such as staged accidents, superfluous repairs, and fake personal injuries. Fraudsters may report a fake document that overstates bills of a fabricated accident. In crop insurance fraud, fraudsters exaggerate or fake their loss of crops due to natural catastrophe or their loss of revenue due to market price fluctuations.

It is worth noting that the main focus of data mining applications for insurance fraud have most often been on automobile insurance fraud. Over all, the insurance fraud along with credit card fraud are the most prominent area for application of data mining.

2.8. Cryptocurrency Fraud

Cryptocurrencies are classified as a digital currency with some distinguishing features. In contrast to traditional fiat, cryptocurrencies take advantage of blockchain technology to record transactions, so they bypass a central authority as mediators. The decentralized concept leverage blockchain to verify transaction permanently, organizing them into separate blocks. Hence, it prevents cryptocurrencies to be spent more than once, negating the problem of double-spending. The emergence of cryptocurrencies, and on top of them Bitcoin, introduce a new definition of decentralization, flexibility, and transparency in E-commerce and online transitions, which can be a decent alternative to fiat currency.

The decentralized nature of cryptocurrencies twined with advent of state-of-the-art technologies have become an attractive frontier for fraudsters. Crypto fraud is a new type of financial fraud targeted naïve client by offering them fake investments or services. The main goal of crypto scammers is to deceive innocent users, who are lack of adequate knowledge in online investments, with the promise of fast reaching profit in return to their investments. One of the prominent investment frauds that is unauthorized in traditional market but still unregulated in crypto world is "pump-and-dump" scheme. Scammers persuade unsuspecting clients to buy a cryptocurrency at an artificially high price, then quickly sell their previous holdings to make profit.

Further, the absence of regulation in cryptocurrencies domain has turn it to be a mean for criminals to carry out their illegal activities. Many illegal organizations and individuals around the world use cryptocurrencies to finance their illegitimate and organized activities. So, cryptocurrencies services can be fraudulent by design, attempting to lure numerous victims and generate revenues worth of millions of dollars. Besides, it helps fraudsters in their cyber and organized crimes in various ways.

3. DATA MINING TECHNIQUES

Industry 4.0 is the virtualization and interconnection of intelligent industrial objects that has make a new and deeper transformation in world. Financial sector like other sectors has been influenced by the development of information technologies, widespread use of computers, and internet and mobile phones. There is a growing studies by academic and industrial research on financial fraud, which implies its importance in diverse critical industries. In the last few years, scientists have been trying to develop financial fraud detection approaches and methods to find some efficient solution techniques. Data mining is one of the most used approaches in dealing with financial frauds that enabled researchers to explore underlying patterns in large data repositories and discern suspicious transactions from normal transactions. Practically, data mining approaches are based on either statistical or computational models. Statistical models involves mathematical computations such as Naïve Bayesian theorem and Logistic Regression. On the other side, computational methods are based on modern techniques like Neural Network and Decision Tree. The computational methods are more suitable and adaptive to the problems as they can learn from problem domain while the statistical methods are more rigid and considered inflexible to some problems in financial domain. All in all, both approaches are useful in various financial sectors.

In general, data mining techniques used in financial fraud detection can be classified in six categories: clustering, classification, prediction, outlier detection, regression, and visualization (Figure 2). Clustering is an unsupervised learning mainly used in multivariate datasets and results in separating data into similar and non-similar to each other groups. Classification is employed to predict categorical labels out of unknown objects in order to differentiate among objects of different classes. Its prevalence application is in detecting fraud in credit cards, healthcare and automobile insurance, and corporate. Prediction models such as neural networks and logistic regression can predict continuous valued function and unknown or missing values. The characteristics of the object in prediction models needs to be continuous instead of being categorical or discrete valued.

Outlier detection is a commonly utilized data mining model employed to distinguish data objects which behaviors are not in accordance with common behavior or data model. The detection of anomalies in dataset has always been of great interest. Grubbs (Grubbs, 1969) defined outlier detection as "An outlying observation, or outlier, is one that appears to deviate markedly from other members of the sample in which it occurs". The motivation for detecting outliers significantly change over time as, back then, the main goal of outlier detection was removing them from datasets, also known as data cleansing, since they had an adverse impact on algorithms performance. Now, however, its function has changed when researchers started to get interested in anomalies itself. The scientist figured out that outliers associated with some specific events or suspicious activities. So, many new algorithms have been developed in context of anomaly and outlier detection. Outlier detection algorithms are classified in three categories: Supervised, semi-supervised, and unsupervised anomaly detection. In supervised methods, the setup comprises of fully labeled training and test datasets while unsupervised algorithms does not require any labels. Semi-supervised outlier detection algorithms use training and test datasets, which training datasets contains only normal data without any anomalies. Outlier detection algorithms have many application in various areas including intrusion detection, data leakage prevention, medical application and fraud detection. In particular, financial log data analyzed in outlier detection algorithms to detect suspicious events indicating fraud.

Regression models are classified as statistical methods used for explaining the relationship among discrete valued dependent/independent variables. These models have excellent performance for detection of fraud in credit cards, crop and automobile insurance, corporate. Many of very common and popular models use visualization to present data. It helps to extract clear patterns and relationship between data in hand to make their understanding easy for users, enabling them to discuss and briefly explain the logic behind the model. Other approached developed around these six classes. The most used data mining techniques utilized in fraud detection has been reviewed in the following subsections.

Figure 2. Six categories of data mining techniques used in financial fraud detection problem and their derived approaches

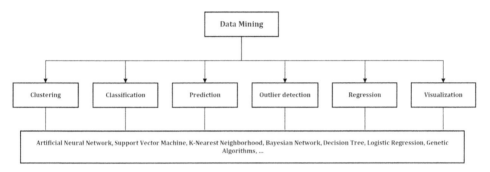

3.1. Support Vector Machine (SVM)

The SVM is a statistical learning techniques that have successfully been used in a variety of classification tasks. Some unique characteristics makes SVM a suitable method for binary classification problems like fraud detection. SVM works in a high dimensional feature space that is a non-linear mapping of the input space of the problem as a linear classifier. In general, the non-linear classification task in input space turns to a linear classification task in the high-dimensional feature space. SVM is able to work in a high dimensional feature space while do not incorporate any extra computational complexity. Typically, highly unbalanced nature of data makes it difficult to extract meaningful features from dataset, which is critical to detect fraudulent transaction. SVM capability of working in a feature-rich space and the simplicity of linear classifier make it an attractive tools in fraud detection problems.

Recently, plenty of companies, institutions, and researchers have employed SVM for different purposes from quantitative trading analysis and trading strategy selection to portfolio optimization and fraud detection. Since company financial data is extremely complex, and due to the non-linear relationship between financial variables and fraud, SVM with its non-linear characteristic is able to handle the imbalanced datasets. The strength of SVM in minimizing the risk of overfitting the training data through determining the classification function with maximal separation margin between two classes provides it a powerful generalization capability in classification suitable for dealing with financial datasets. Furthermore, kernel function allows SVM to map data points to a high dimension feature space and learn classification task in that space without adding any additional computational complexity. Hence, SVM takes advantage of learning the classification task in a high dimension feature space while explicit mapping of data to that space does not happen.

3.2. Artificial Neural Network (ANN)

The artificial Neural Network was first presented by Warren S. McCulloch and Walter Pitts for classification and prediction problem (McCulloch and Pitts, 1943). ANN refers to a set of nonlinear, statistical modeling techniques inspired and derived from human brain structure. It works in identical way to human thoughts and provide a good performance in examining large datasets. The fundamental concept of neural networks is the neuron that is structured into layers of computing units. The number of neurons, the number of layers, and the connection between nodes determine the topology of a neural network. In a brief, a neuron in a neural network accepts many inputs, sums them up, applies a transformative function that usually is nonlinear, and generates the result. The output of a neuron can be either a model prediction or an input to other neuron. A neural network is made of many such neurons that is connected in a systematic way. The ANN can be applied in modeling any complex transaction patterns, which makes it a suitable method for financial fraud detection problems. Multilayer perceptron also known as feed-forward neural network is the most well suited neural networks used in fraud detection.

3.3. K-Nearest Neighborhood (KNN) Algorithm

The KNN is a supervised learning technique that has widely been used in detection problems. This method was first applied by Aha, Albert, and Kibler in 1991. It is categorized into non-parametric methods well-developed for classification and regression. The KNN methodology is finding the closets, similar neighborhoods in a given dataset, then generate a new sample point according to the distance between two data samples. So, its results depends on the following factors:

- The distance metric applied to measure the nearest neighbors.
- The distance rule used for classification of K-nearest neighbor.

- The number of neighbors (K) considered to classify the new sample.

The distance and the similarity of two data sample are two major parameters in KNN algorithm. The larger the number of K, the lower noise in the dataset. Besides, different methods can be used for measuring the distance between two data instances. For example, Euclidean distance is applied in continuous attribute while an easy matching coefficient is used in categorical attributes. The K-nearest algorithm has proven to have a high performance in transaction fraud detection problems.

3.4. Bayesian Network (BN)

One of the graphical models that is used to represent conditional dependencies and independent relationships among random variables is Bayesian Network. This model is based on directed acyclic graph between nodes and edges. The BN models are applicable in finding unknown probabilities given known probabilities in the presence of uncertainty. In other words, Bayesian networks plays a profound role in modeling situations where some basic information are available but incoming data is uncertain or partially unavailable. Its applications include a wide range of areas including pattern recognition, fault diagnosis, and forecast. In addition, these networks have a prevalence use in anomaly and fraud detection in financial transactions.

3.5. Decision Tree (DT)

Decision Tree is a supervised learning technique producing a classification or regression tree that depicts every possible occurrence of decisions consequence. Decision tree uses a top-down recursive approach to build branches representing binary options over the features and dependencies that implies the result of this selection. It creates a tree that recursively splits the training dataset into subsets according to single attribute. Therefore, the algorithm requires the best split and best choice of attribute to be used for splitting. The process of dividing the dataset continues while at the same time decision tree at incremental stages is built. Each node in a decision tree represent either a decision node or a leaf node. A decision node includes branches whilst leaf nodes possess labels.

The decision tree algorithm can deal with both numerical and categorical data. It is an easy to use methods that can be readily understand and display. Long training time and deficiency in limited available memory when dealing with large datasets are some of its drawbacks. Yet, it stands out as an acceptable tool in detecting fraud activities.

3.6. Logistic Regression (LR)

The LR is a statistical linear model applied to analyze datasets. The main concept of this method is based on executing regression on a set of variables. In general, this method can be applied to describe patterns and explain relationships among single or multiple dependent binary variables. Logistic regression is a commonly used method for pattern prediction in data with unambiguous or numeric attributes. It employs a series of input vectors and a dependent response variable and make use of natural logarithm to the probability of a specific category in which the result lies.

Logistic Regression is a well-established and popular model used as a control method by which other techniques can be tested. Initial financial fraud detection studies had a great focus on statistical methods such as Logistic Regression as a prediction technique. This model is most commonly used in detecting fraud in credit cards, crop and automobile insurance, and corporate fraud.

3.7. Genetic Algorithm (GA)

The GA inspired from natural evolution is an algorithms that first introduce by John Holland (Sampson, 1976). This algorithm searches for optimum solution with a set of candidate solution represented in the form of binary strings called chromosomes. GA is based on the idea that stronger members of population have more chance to survive and reproduce. It is a parametric solution procedure that needs to be fine-tuned well for the given problem to provide a better performance.

This algorithm is used in data mining problems mainly for feature selection, parameter tuning, and optimization. Although, time consuming and high memory usage is some of GA deficiencies in its implantation in different areas, it also have various application in data mining and fraud detection as classification tool. Genetic algorithm code are prevalence in different programming languages, making it a popular and strong algorithm for credit card fraud and other fraud detection problems. GA is considered an expensive algorithm in consuming time and using memory.

4. APPLICATION OF DATA MINING TECHNIQUES

In financial world, data mining-based approaches are extensively used to detect small deviation in large datasets and clarify suspicious activities. Data mining can be referred to as core element of data science. So, establishing and executing a data mining-based technique needs an implied commitment to scientific approach. In financial fraud domain, blindly applying data mining techniques to dataset without attention to the nature of data, strength and weaknesses of techniques, appropriate assessment, and deployment desires will lead the model to inadequately address the problem. The better modeling practices, the better business decisions.

Devising data mining application encompasses various phases including data preparation, training, and deployment. Data preparation is the significant phase of an effective data mining model. It is about appropriately transforming and cleaning existing data as well as good understanding of the features in the first place. Approximately 80% of the time spent in devising a successful technique would be dedicated to data preparation. The process of training models is the next phase in using data mining algorithms to discover patterns in dataset. As with data preparation, the training phase should be done carefully in order to reach a proper understanding of the algorithm concept and applying them appropriately. Selecting the data mining technique is the most difficult part in financial fraud detection problem. The decision of selecting the most suitable technique depends of answering questions about the size and nature of data, accuracy of the model, time needed for process of data, and interpretability of the results.

There are three most commonly used standards to determine data mining algorithm performance, namely accuracy, sensitivity, and specificity. Accuracy is the ratio of successfully classified samples to unsuccessful tries. It provides the best basis for comparing data mining algorithms with each other. Sensitivity measures the amount of items that correctly listed as fraud to the ones that incorrectly identified as fraud. It represents the ratio of true positives to false positives. In contrast to sensitivity, specificity measures the ratio of correctly and incorrectly identified legitimate transactions. In other words, this standard compares the true negative to false negative. In literature, there exists considerable differences in data mining methods' sensitivity and specificity results. Some studies (Bhattacharyya et al., 2011, Ravisankar et al., 2011) showed that support vector machine, genetic algorithm, and neural networks have a better performance in detecting legitimate transactions, implying their higher specificity rate rather than sensitivity while Bayesian Network and Decision Tree enjoy higher sensitivity.

Among introduced technique, the SVM, due to its efficiency in solving non-linear classification problem and relatively easy-to-use training process, has prevalence application in fraud detection in financial statement fraud (Deng, 2009, Li and Ying, 2010), credit card fraud (Deng, 2009, Li and Ying, 2010, Xu and Liu, 2012), auto insurance fraud and health insurance fraud (Nwagor and Offor) . Yet, SVM does show a good performance in applying directly to the large datasets and often needs preprocessing and combination with other algorithms, which implies its time consuming nature. Further, it has a low speed of detection, medium accuracy, and lack of transparency in results.

Bayesian networks is another most used data mining technique that employed in bank fraud and insurance fraud detection. This method has the privilege of working with binary classification and non-algorithmic problems. The need of comprehensive knowledge about the behavior of fraud type is its main drawback.

The neural network and genetic algorithm has also been used in different area of financial fraud (A. A. Rizki et al., 2017, Peng and You, 2016) due to its advantage of working with binary classification and non-algorithmic problems. ANN also have the ability to learn from past, extract rules and predict future activities based on the current situation, providing this algorithm high accuracy, portability, high speed in detection and adaptability. However, artificial neural network requires high computational power for data training. ANN is sensitive to data format as it needs non-numerical data to be converted and normalized.

The Logistic regression has the advantage of high accuracy in detection and easy-to-use procedure in fraud detection problems. Its application ranges from credit card fraud detection (J. O. Awoyemi et al., 2017) and financial statement fraud detection (D. Yue, 2009) to health fraud (Bauder and Khoshgoftaar, 2017) and auto insurance frauds (Roy and George, 2017). Logistic regression has a low performance and high computational process.

Outlier detection is another data mining technique that has been extensively used in health insurance fraud (J. Peng et al., 2018), cryptocurrency fraud (P. Monamo et al., 2016), and credit card fraud (J. O. Awoyemi et al., 2017). This method has developed to work with unlabeled data and is able to work with non-standard data types. Inefficiency in working with collective outliers and high false positive rate is some disadvantages of this technique. In the Table 1, the advantages and disadvantages of these approaches are reviewed and the most suited sectors for their application are summarized.

Out of the data mining techniques used in the field of financial fraud detection, the literature shows that SVM is the most applied one followed by Naïve Bayes and random forest. Other techniques such as Neural Network and Logistic Regression have fewer application due to their limitations. These results show that support vector machine is the leading DM technique in financial fraud detection domain. Further, the supervised learning techniques such as Bayesian Network, Neural Network, and Decision Tree have been widely used compared to unsupervised learning models due to their better performance. It can be attributed to their abilities in using labeled data while unsupervised models suffer from lack of labeled data in the process of identifying fraud in datasets.

The result of reviewing literature demonstrates that credit card fraud detection constitutes the largest portion of DM technique application followed by insurance fraud detection. However, there are a distinct lack of studies that discusses the application of data mining in mortgage fraud, money laundering fraud, and commodities and securities fraud. It can be due to difficulty of collecting related data for analysis. Besides, the highly sensitive nature of topic may result in the prohibition of publishing results

Table 1. The most used data mining techniques and their advantages, disadvantages, and application

Method	Advantages	Disadvantages	Main Application
Support Vector machine (SVM)	Efficiency in solving non-linear classification problems, quite easy-to-use training process for accuracy sensitive financial fraud detection	Low performance in processing large datasets, low speed of detection, medium accuracy, expensive, lack of transparency of results	Bankruptcy prediction, insurance fraud, credit cards
Bayesian Network	Efficiency in working with binary classification and non-algorithmic problems	Need a comprehensive knowledge of fraud type behavior	Financial statement fraud
Neural Networks	Efficiency in working with binary classification and non-algorithmic problems,	Need high computational power for data training, sensitivity to data format	Credit card rating
K-Nearest Neighborhood (KNN)	Easy-to-Implement, Efficiency in working with datasets	Accuracy sensitive to value of K, need high computational power	Money laundering analysis
Decision Tree (DT)	Simple and easy-to-Implement, capability of processing real-time data with low computational process	Need high computational power in initial steps	Stock market prediction, financial statement fraud
Logistic Regression	Easy-to-implement, high accuracy in detection	Low performance with high computational process	Credit cards failure in marketing
Outlier Detection	Well-suited for unlabeled data, ability of working with non-standard data types	Inefficiency in working with collective outliers, high false-positive rate	Credit card fraud, Marketing analysis, money laundering

5. CONCLUSION

In the present world, technology improvements has extended its application in various field. It has provided businesses and companies a great opportunity to improve their efficiency by lowering the costs, saving time, and enhancing productivity. While E-commerce systems, online banking, Blockchain technology, and FinTech innovations remarkably transformed the businesses, they have also prepared the ground for fraudsters to perform fraudulent activities. In this study, we pointed out that researchers have classified financial fraud into three groups including bank fraud, insurance fraud, and corporate fraud. Recently, cryptocurrencies as a new type of currency based on blockchain technology has introduced a new way of financial transactions. Some of the cryptocurrencies features like decentralization has also attracted fraudsters and criminals. So, in our study, we added cryptocurrency fraud as the fourth category of financial fraud. Fig. 1 illustrated a brief summary of different types of financial fraud and their subcategories.

Technology advancements and new introduced type of financial fraud has motivated scientists and researchers to introduce and develop a wide variety of fraud detections methods using different approaches and techniques. In this research, some of the most used methods of financial fraud detection based on data mining and artificial intelligence techniques has been reviewed. We explored their advantages, disadvantages, and well-suited applications in different sectors. The result showed that some of the introduced methods including SVM and ANN have wide application in specific sectors like bank fraud detection such as credit card and transaction fraud while other methods are suitable for detecting financial fraud in Health and insurance sectors. Besides, there are few studies reporting the application of data mining techniques in money laundering, mortgage, and securities and commodities fraud. However, fraudulent activities in these sectors needs more attention and deserve more research.

Table 1 summarized these methods and described their advantages, disadvantages, and their application area. In sum, this study provided academic and industrial researchers useful information about various kind of financial fraud and practical solutions in dealing with them. Further, it helps researchers to have fast access to proper techniques employed in fraud detections fields and make comparison among them in their application area.

REFERENCES

Al-Hashedi, K. G., & Magalingam, P. (2021). Financial fraud detection applying data mining techniques: A comprehensive review from 2009 to 2019. *Computer Science Review*, *40*, 40. doi:10.1016/j.cosrev.2021.100402

Awoyemi, J. O., Adetunmbi, A. O., & Oluwadare, S. A. (2017). Credit card fraud detection using machine learning techniques: A comparative analysis. *International Conference on Computing Networking and Informatics (ICCNI)*. 10.1109/ICCNI.2017.8123782

Barman, S., Pal, U., Sarfaraj, M. A., Biswas, B., Mahata, A., & Mandal, P. (2016). A complete literature review on financial fraud detection applying data mining techniques. *International Journal of Trust Management in Computing and Communications*, *3*(4), 336–359. doi:10.1504/IJTMCC.2016.084561

Bauder, R. A., & Khoshgoftaar, T. M. (2017). Medicare Fraud Detection Using Machine Learning Methods. *16th IEEE International Conference on Machine Learning and Applications*, 8. 10.1109/ICMLA.2017.00-48

Bhattacharyya, S., Jha, S., Tharakunnel, K., & Westland, J. C. (2011). Data mining for credit card fraud: A comparative study. *Decision Support Systems*, *50*(3), 602–613. doi:10.1016/j.dss.2010.08.008

Delgado, M., Marin, N., Sanchez, D., & Vila, M.-A. (2003). N.M., D. Sanchez, M. -A. Vila, *Fuzzy association rules: General model and applications. IEEE Transactions on Fuzzy Systems*, *11*(2), 11. doi:10.1109/TFUZZ.2003.809896

Deng, Q. (2009). *Application of support vector machine in the detection of fraudulent financial statements. 2009 4th International Conference on Computer Science & Education*.

Golovianko, M., Terziyan, V., Branytskyi, V., & Malyk, D. (2023). Industry 4.0 vs. Industry 5.0: Co-existence, Transition, or a Hybrid. *Procedia Computer Science*, *217*, 102–113. doi:10.1016/j.procs.2022.12.206

Grubbs, F. E. (1969). Procedures for Detecting Outlying Observations in Samples. *Technometrics*, *11*(1), 21. doi:10.1080/00401706.1969.10490657

Hilal, W., Gadsden, S. A., & Yawney, J. (2022). Financial Fraud: A Review of Anomaly Detection Techniques and Recent Advances. *Expert Systems with Applications*, *193*, 193. doi:10.1016/j.eswa.2021.116429

Li, X., & Ying, S. (2010). *Lib-SVMs Detection Model of Regulating-Profits Financial Statement Fraud Using Data of Chinese Listed Companies*. International Conference on E-Product E-Service and E-Entertainment, 4. 10.1109/ICEEE.2010.5660371

Machkour, B., & Abriane, A. (2020). Industry 4.0 and its Implications for the Financial Sector. *Procedia Computer Science*, *177*, 496–502. doi:10.1016/j.procs.2020.10.068

Makki, S. (2017). *Fraud Analysis Approaches in the Age of Big Data-A Review of State of the Art*. 2017 IEEE 2nd International Workshops on Foundations and Applications of Self* Systems, 17.

McCulloch, W. S., & Pitts, W. (1943). A logical calculus of the ideas immanent in nervous activity. *The Bulletin of Mathematical Biophysics*, *5*(4), 19. doi:10.1007/BF02478259

Monamo, Marivate, & Twala. (2016). *Unsupervised learning for robust Bitcoin fraud detection*. Information Security for South Africa (ISSA), 6.

Ngai, E., Hu, Y., Wong, Y. H., Chen, Y., & Sun, X. (2011a). The application of data mining techniques in financial fraud detection: A classification framework and an academic review of literature. *Decision Support Systems*, *50*(3), 10. doi:10.1016/j. dss.2010.08.006

Ngai, E., Hu, Y., Wong, Y. H., Chen, Y., & Sun, X. (2011b). The application of data mining techniques in financial fraud detection: A classification framework and an academic review of literature. *Decision Support Systems*, *50*(3), 11. doi:10.1016/j. dss.2010.08.006

Nikkel, B. (2020). Fintech forensics: Criminal investigation and digital evidence in financial technologies. *Forensic Science International Digital Investigation*, *33*, 33. doi:10.1016/j.fsidi.2020.200908

Nwagor Offor. (n.d.).*Simulation of Oil Production with Simultaneous Inclusion of a Hydrocarbon Constituent Driven Random Environmental Perturbation Value of 0.08.*

Peng & You. (2016). *The Health Care Fraud Detection Using the Pharmacopoeia Spectrum Tree and Neural Network Analytic Contribution Hierarchy Process.* IEEE Trustcom/BigDataSE/ISPA, 6.

Peng, J. (2018). *Fraud Detection of Medical Insurance Employing Outlier Analysis.* IEEE 22nd International Conference on Computer Supported Cooperative Work in Design (CSCWD), 6. 10.1109/CSCWD.2018.8465273

Ravisankar, P., Ravi, V., Raghava Rao, G., & Bose, I. (2011). Detection of financial statement fraud and feature selection using data mining techniques. *Decision Support Systems*, *50*(2), 491–500. doi:10.1016/j.dss.2010.11.006

RB. (2021). Credit card fraud detection using artificial neural network. *Global Transitions Proceedings*, *2*(1), 6.

Rizki, A. A., Surjandari, I., & Wayasti, R. A. (2017). Data mining application to detect financial fraud in Indonesia's public companies. *3rd International Conference on Science in Information Technology*, 5. 10.1109/ICSITech.2017.8257111

Roy, R., & George, K. T. (2017). Detecting insurance claims fraud using machine learning techniques. *International Conference on Circuit, Power and Computing Technologies*, 6. 10.1109/ICCPCT.2017.8074258

Sampson, J. R. (1976). Adaptation in natural and artificial systems (John H. Holland). Society for Industrial and Applied Mathematics.

Singleton, T. W. (2006). *Fraud auditing and forensic accounting.* John Wiley & Sons.

Wells, J. T. (2014). *Principles of fraud examination*. John Wiley & Sons.

West, J., & Bhattacharya, M. (2016). Intelligent financial fraud detection: A comprehensive review. *Computers & Security*, *57*, 47–66. doi:10.1016/j. cose.2015.09.005

Xu, W., & Liu, Y. (2012). *An optimized SVM model for detection of fraudulent online credit card transactions*. In *2012 International Conference on Management of e-Commerce and e-Government*. IEEE. 10.1109/ICMeCG.2012.39

Yue, D. (2009). *Logistic Regression for Detecting Fraudulent Financial Statement of Listed Companies in China. International Conference on Artificial Intelligence and Computational Intelligence*, 5.

Chapter 12

Navigating the Future:
Harnessing Artificial Intelligence and Robotics for Economic Growth While Safeguarding Societal Well-being

D. Renuka Devi
https://orcid.org/0000-0002-6525-1172
Stella Maris College (Autonomous), India

T. A. Swetha Margaret
Stella Maris College (Autonomous), India

K. Avanthika
Stella Maris College (Autonomous), India

ABSTRACT

AI and robotics are tremendously growing in the industry. It is going to affect the human labor in the coming decades. Artificial intelligence and robotics are rapidly being adapted by the industry. So, there is a need for humans to be competitive to survive in the growing industry. Due to the enormous demand for intelligent robots across all industries globally, employment in the field of artificial intelligence is growing along with this technology. The ample opportunity to understand the impact of these technology and preempt their negative effect is closing rapidly. In order to cope with these technological changes, humans are expected to be proactive rather than being reactive. So, this chapter discusses the technological aspects as well as the societal norms it's affecting. The aim is to increase awareness in understanding and rapidly adapting the significance of these technologies to help in formation of policies and regulation that maximize the uses and benefits of this technological evolution and minimize the possible danger it could do to the society.

DOI: 10.4018/979-8-3693-3108-8.ch012

1. INTRODUCTION

Industry 6.0, called as the sixth revolution wherein advanced technologies such as quantum and Nano technology replaces the existing in industry 5.0. Here, advanced production techniques merge seamlessly with brilliant and intuitive systems that collaborate with individuals and businesses alike. According to the World Economic Forum, "The Fourth Industrial Revolution ushers in an era where digital and physical manufacturing entities work harmoniously on a global scale" (Khan et al., 2021). But Industry 6.0 goes beyond just the development of clever technology. Its impact reaches far and wide, reaching ground-breaking achievements in gene sequencing, nanotechnology, quantum computing, and beyond.

Although Industry 6.0, is the start of a new revolution, paving the way for the discovery and development of many advanced technologies, Artificial Intelligence and robotics are some important technologies which have the capability of transforming the economy, labor market, and society (Peres et al., 2020). While the growing trend of automation and digitalization continues to prevail in developed countries, the question is whether it is same for the developed countries. There is always a threat to human society, with the growing development of automation. In one way this growth is important as it is going to increase the productivity in the organizations and on the other side, its growth might lead to unemployment in the coming years. Therefore, it is essential to be competitive and sustain in the "new economy".

At present, the investment in the autonomous system is excessive compared to the cost of human labor. Additionally, businesses based in developing markets need to market their proper systems to increase their production and allure compared to rivals and maintain their competitiveness over time. At the same time, every year, the cost of (production) robots decreases. In nations with low labor costs, replacing human manual labor with robots is economical, when the price of human labor is 15% more expensive than the price of robotic labour. This would happen in countries like Mexico by 2025, based on a study by the Boston Consulting Group. Already, Chinese companies started to build factory robots which are expected to replace 90% of human labour.

It can be forecasted that emerging markets will progressively embrace autonomous IT systems in the next few years. Familiar systems will be integrated by global corporations in all of their production sites worldwide, making them the key players driving this development. In the coming years, businesses will strategically position themselves where they can find the best-suited and highly skilled workforce for overseeing and producing AI. As a result, developing nations may reap the rewards of technological advancements if they can supply proficient workers in the technological sphere.

The industry 6.0 technologies will pave the way for robotics in the field of security and manufacturing process. In addition, the industry can leverage the block chain technology for enhanced data communication and sharing in creating new economic models. All things considered, the implementation of Industry 6.0 will continue to change the way that we produce, manage, and use products, services, and data. But like every technical advancement, Industry 6.0 can also have certain drawbacks or unfavourable outcomes. In order to secure a sustainable and inclusive future for all, this chapter emphasizes the significance of accepting AI and robots as potent instruments for economic growth while proactively addressing ethical, social, and governance concerns.

2. BACKGROUND STUDY

The changes in the industry, the way the goods are manufactured, and delivered to the consumers, and how they provide employment opportunities have been a lot of changes which are categorized as industry revolution from 1.0 to 6.0. These changes have adverse effects on the economic growth of the country and are attributed to the living standards of the people. In this section the deep background analysis of how the industry had transformed from 1.0 to 6.0.

Industry 1.0, where the beginning of the revolution like the use of mechanized production started in the nineteenth century. The energy sources were used for manufacturing products. The coal and steaming process was majorly used in this process. The viability of mass production was made possible by this upheaval, which also saw the creation of the first industrial titans, such as ironworks and cotton mills (Ellitan, 2020).

Industry 2.0, so called as mass production year. It was the era of usage of electricity and assembly line. Along with the rise of new industries like the automobile industry, the revolution led to increased productivity, efficiency, and quality in the manufacture of commodities (van Agtmael, 2007). The huge leap in computer technology eventually changed the industry as well. The digital revolution and computer-based automation processes have enhanced and elevated the levels of production processes with precision. So, Industry 3.0 is the era of digital transformation (Yadav et al., 2022). In fourth industry transformation, is affected by a huge number of advanced technologies such as AI, Machine Learning, and IoT. It began in the 21st Century and supported complete automation and enhanced data management. The driving forces are more precise data processing, enhanced decision-making, and problem-solving (Yadav et al., 2022).

The further advancement in the industry revolution towards advanced technologies such as machine learning, AI, Quantum computing, and block chain. The processing capability and enhanced accuracy of these system changes the industry as more of revolutionize the entire process of manufacture, delivery, consume goods and services (Groumpos, 2021). To summarize, the Industrial Revolution introduced notable obstacles such as worker exploitation, urban overpopulation, and social inequality, but it also ushered in an era of technological advancement and economic development. These effects still have an impact on contemporary industrial countries, which emphasizes how crucial it is to keep addressing problems with social fairness, labor rights, and fair economic growth.

3. IMPACTS OF AI AND ROBOTICS

Robotics technology has expanded beyond just production and is now utilized in industries such as service robotics and self-driving cars. The presence of robots in factories has grown rapidly. Despite this progress, experts in robotics recognize that there is still much to be done before robots can entirely replace human labour. One particular issue is the limited movement and manipulation abilities of robots in non-structured environments, such as factory assembly lines. Even existing factory robots require significant reprogramming when faced with a slightly different task. They are far from being able to learn new skills independently or through instruction from humans.

3.1 Impact of AI and Robotics in Tourism Sector

With an increase in demand for advanced robots that can handle dangerous tasks, the loss of low-paid labourers in industries like agriculture and mining has become a pressing issue. Studies have revealed that customers tend to hold human employees responsible for service failures, while organizations bear the brunt of criticism when a robot makes a mistake. The rise of automation and robotics has undoubtedly led to a decline in job opportunities, as these machines are known for their precise and error-free work, potentially reducing the need for human labour. In fact, over 700 speakers have acknowledged that the technological revolution has rendered redundant low-paying and low-skilled jobs.

As interaction between humans and robots becomes more prevalent, there is a concern for potential harm to humans. However, this issue can currently be addressed by limiting the sharing of workspaces between human and robot employees. Factory settings, particularly those that produce automobiles, have already adopted the use of robots. The development of self-driving transportation systems has also spurred the creation of autonomous robots. Humanoid robots, which have been in the works since 1975, are being continuously improved. The MIT-AI-Lab has been developing their humanoid robot, 'Cog', since 1994 (From, n.d.). Despite their abilities, robots still require direction from humans to perform tasks. While the increased use of robotics has led to a decline in employment opportunities, it also has the potential to reduce workplace discrimination.

The integration of AI and robotics is rapidly expanding within the tourism industry (McCartney & McCartney, 2020). From automating tasks to enhancing the overall travel experience, the use of technology is transforming the way we travel. Through intelligent automation, tourists can now access a plethora of services and assistance throughout their trip. This is especially valuable during the pre-trip planning stage, where AI can inspire travellers and streamline the process of information gathering, booking, and pre-arrival preparations. Moreover, AI is proving to be a valuable tool for tackling challenges associated with navigation, transportation, and overall transit experience. As with any technological advancement, it's important to consider the potential benefits and risks for both tourists and destinations alike.

Intelligent automation is a powerful tool for enhancing the travel experience, offering tourists travel inspiration and assistance throughout their journey. Through the use of artificial intelligence, service providers can effectively reach a global market, customize offers to individual clients, and streamline the booking process. The integration of advanced 'analytical AI' systems, which can quickly and efficiently process large amounts of client data, has become a dominant feature in the travel industry. These smart interfaces can support travelers at every stage of their trip, from planning and booking to remembering and sharing their experiences, ultimately enhancing the overall travel experience. In a world where travel is becoming increasingly complex, intelligent automation offers a simpler and more convenient way for travelers to explore and navigate their journeys.

Right now, it is of utmost importance for service providers and authorities to address security issues and find a middle ground between making travel convenient and ensuring proper verification when tourists cross borders. To streamline air travel, many airlines have introduced self-service check-ins and baggage systems. This phase has also paved the way for "embodied AI", which incorporates robotics to enhance mobility and customer service. The past decade has witnessed significant advancements in autonomous mobility technologies, including drones and people-moving pods. At airports, travelers are now assisted by interactive robots, such as KLM's Care-E and Munich Airport's Josie Pepper, which possess both mobility and customer service features. These robots have real-time question-answering and self-learning abilities.

Airports are bustling hubs of activity, housing a variety of retail and hospitality establishments. What's even more intriguing is the use of both mechanical and interactive robots to cater to the needs of travelers. Keeping pace with the ever-evolving digital landscape, smartphones have become the primary source of information for navigation and wayfinding, with digital travel companions and Chatbots taking the lead. Delivery of items to hotel rooms has also been taken over by intelligent mobile robots, equipped to self-navigate even in crowded and confined spaces, seamlessly blending in with people and objects. Guests are now greeted by in-room robot companions and pervasive agents, operating on voice commands to create the perfect room ambiance, handle laundry services, make reservations, and more. While receptionist front-desk robots may not have advanced interaction capabilities just yet, their presence alone adds a touch of futurism and convenience.

Their presence serves mainly to enhance the self-service check-in and check-out processes. They can be found in various industries, such as automated locker and storage systems, restaurants, cafes, and bars, as stationary industrial robots. In places like museums and galleries, humanoid robots are utilized as interactive tour guides for a more engaging visitor experience. In Kyoto, Japan, miniature humanoid robots equipped with AI and proficient in multiple languages have been introduced in taxis to cater to the growing trend of sightseeing by taxi. Furthermore, the use of user-friendly human-machine interfaces with humanoid robots allows for immediate customer assistance and ultimately leads to improved customer experiences and satisfaction. These robots can also accompany and guide tourists throughout their journey, creating a seamless and enjoyable trip.

4. POSSIBLE LOSERS OF THE INDUSTRY 6.0

BRIC nations (Brazil, Russia, India, and China) were considered to be seen as the world economy's spark of optimism (O'Neill, 2011). Investors anticipate long-term returns as a result of increased raw material extraction and the offshore outsourcing of many Western industrial sectors to nations with low labor costs. However, there is a low demand for raw materials right now, therefore Brazil and Russia are losing attractiveness. With the technical development of production robots, many industries that currently produce in nations with low labor costs will move their manufacturing to countries where the robots are being produced. The fourth industrial revolution trend will not benefit the developing nations in Central and South America either. Due to the lack of investment in digital infrastructure, the lack of education among a large portion of the population, and the absence of a legal framework, it is feared that these nations, like those in North Africa and Indonesia, are ill-prepared to deal with automation and digitalization.

In these nations, a mere 40% of the younger generation is employed and the majority of these positions in the third sector offer low wages and no safety net. It's no wonder then that a significant number of educated young people feel compelled to leave their homeland and seek opportunities in Western industrialized countries.

To stem this trend, these nations must address issues of corruption, provide greater social security, and bolster their infrastructure. Additionally, enhancing access to higher education and training, particularly for women, is essential to boost their competitiveness.

5. POSSIBLE WINNERS OF THE INDUSTRY 6.0

On the other hand, the highly developed Asian nations with strong educational institutions, like Singapore, Hong Kong, Taiwan, and South Korea, are expected to emerge as the digital revolution's winners. These nations have long been conducting research and attempting to develop digital solutions for challenging problems, together with the Scandinavian nations. People in these nations are also extremely well connected via digital means. In these nations, 6% of the population is considered to be at risk of unemployment.

China and India show a promising trend in participating in the digital revolution due to their high proficiency in both English and IT. In these nations, IT skills are prioritized and taught in schools as critical skills. As a result, it comes as no surprise that experts from India and China possess more advanced computer knowledge compared to their counterparts in countries like France or England. According to a report by Forrester Research, it is estimated that the UK will outsource 25,000 IT jobs to India. This is because not only are salaries and wages lower in India, but there is also a larger pool of highly qualified professionals available. Similarly, India is shifting from being solely known for its low labor costs to a society with a growing focus on Western culture, where the majority of the population has a strong aptitude for IT. With their substantial populations, these two nations boast a robust consumer base. However, to truly elevate the standard of living for urban inhabitants in the long term, these emerging economies need cutting-edge logistical and environmental technologies, like the innovative concept of a smart city.

In just six years, the market value of Uber skyrocketed from $0 to an impressive US$40 billion. This serves as a remarkable example of how artificial intelligence (AI) is continuously advancing, particularly in the ever-growing gig economy within the service industry (Balakrishnan, 2022). While the majority of robots are typically utilized in Germany, the US, Japan, South Korea, and other countries to streamline operations in the manufacturing sector, recent developments in service-based business models will undoubtedly shape the future. The flourishing growth of this sector has the added benefit of making the US more resilient in times of economic turmoil. It's therefore no surprise that the World Economic Forum has recognized the United States, Japan, Switzerland, and Germany as leading countries in innovation, as evident in their ranking in the Global Competitiveness Index. To conclude, the prevalence of automation and digitalization is a pressing international concern, exacerbated by the lack of economic resources in various developing countries. Specifically, up-and-coming Asian nations, as well as established Western powers, will likely emerge as the frontrunners of Industry 6.0 due to their technological prowess and forward-thinking approach to service models.

6. CREATION OF NEW JOBS AND EMPLOYMENT DEMAND

About 47% of total US employment is at risk, as per the report by Frey/Osborne. Regarding the severe effects of the changes in job arrangements, experts have wildly divergent views. Others assert that despite technological advancements making a replacement possible, many individuals whose jobs are highly at risk won't be entirely replaced. While it's true that the rise of machines may not result in the complete replacement of all occupations, certain specialized tasks will inevitably be automated. Take for example the role of a bartender, with an estimated 87% chance of being filled by a robot. Already, we see robotic systems being utilized to expertly mix drinks, relay orders directly to the kitchen, handle customer complaints, and process payments. However, while efficiency may improve, the atmosphere at the pub or restaurant will undoubtedly suffer. Not all bartenders will certainly be at risk of losing their jobs shortly, as the high cost and possible lack of appeal to potential customers serve as a major barrier.

Data Scientist

The position of data scientist, which has only just become available, will become more significant in the coming years (Zhang et al., 2020). This new occupational group will create forecasts based on statistical computations and probability theories. For this challenging task, in-depth IT knowledge is essential. Writing sophisticated computer routines and using the appropriate programming languages fall under this category. A data scientist also needs to be conversant with the organization's business procedures to make reasonable connections. Therefore, it is crucial to have a foundational understanding of marketing, economics, stochastics, and business administration. Additionally, to this extensive information, interpersonal skills are needed. A data scientist needs to be able to communicate and adjust their services to the needs of clients or employers.

Crowd Worker

The use of crowd workers is a growingly important field of work. Freelancers who use their computers to offer their services on Internet marketplaces are known as crowd workers. Crowdworking is a representation of how the gig economy is transforming the nature of employment for white-collar workers. In today's world, we can all participate in a wide range of tasks, from the straightforward task of writing a product review or finding phone numbers to more complex endeavors such as software testing, legal consulting, ghostwriting, and website creation. These larger and more impactful projects fall under the term "crowdsourcing." While in developed Western countries working may only yield a small amount of extra income, in the coming years, there will likely be an increased need for freelancers to offer their skills beyond traditional employment. Additionally, the Internet can also be utilized for marketing efforts. Crowdworking can be used to get first legal opinions or even package deals for legal concerns at affordable pricing, especially in the context of legal services.

7. JOBS THAT ARE AT RISK

High-Routine Occupations

Shortly, positions like accountant, court clerk, and desk officer at fiscal authorities will primarily exist in the past tense. This is due to the increasing autonomy of software in completing these tasks, as their performance is highly routine. Nearly all roles that involve processing and analyzing data on a computer screen are at a high risk of being replaced by software.

Manual Work

Shortly, basic tasks that have traditionally relied on manual labor will gradually be taken over by machines. However, there will always be a need for human involvement, as the level of repetition remains a critical factor. Only when a process can be automated and performed regularly can a machine be effectively utilized instead of a human worker. As a result, numerous companies in the supply industry have been strategizing ways to replace industrial jobs with robots. Additionally, the use of robots may be seen as justifiable in industries where minimum wages are typically lower.

Job Loss Due to Digitalization

Companies and organization, initially retrain their employees to cope with the new technologies. If the employee is not ready to take up the training, he will lose his job due to the lack of the needed skills.

Restriction on the Usage of Intelligent System

Robots and AI systems will not replace human labor shortly but they may in a few decades, which should not happen. Science and technological advancement are there to make people's lives easier, not to become slaves of intelligent systems. There should always be restrictions on the usage of AI systems, to prevent humans from being sabotaged by intelligent systems.

Should Not Make Independent Decision

At this point, the capabilities of robots are limited to fulfilling their assigned tasks. They play a vital role in assisting humans in the production of goods and services, providing answers to employee inquiries, and even serving as competent workplace aides rather than mere chatbots. Interestingly enough, the profound human intellect of IT pioneers like Bill Gates, Elon Musk, and Stephan Hawking may soon be overshadowed by the advancement of artificial intelligence in a mere decade. This begs the question, will robots, equipped with AI, soon be responsible for making critical decisions rather than humans? If current trends continue, the widespread positive perception of Industry 6.0 may likely shift, as robots potentially surpass humans in their occupations. However, in the current state of progress, particularly in the processing business, humans still hold the upper hand. The question at hand is whether leveraging machines to make decisions would have a positive impact. Unlike humans, who often rely on intuition, autonomous systems rely solely on objective criteria when making choices. Furthermore, having a robot announce the decision removes the potential for miscommunication caused by emotions. However, there is a strong argument for entrusting decision-making to humans, as it contributes to the acceptance of systems within society. Ultimately, it is the reasoning behind the decision that holds the greatest significance.

Should Not Make Killing Robots

Current laws in the field of artificial intelligence strictly prohibit research on intelligent weapons that operate without human decision-making. It is important to note the distinction between current remote-controlled weapons, such as the drones employed by the US military, and intelligent systems equipped with sensors to assist in target selection and acquisition. The potential consequences of any malfunction in these machines are significant, making it imperative for both the US and the United Nations to engage in discussions about banning autonomous weapon systems.

Inequality in the New Economy

Furthermore, as the gap between rich and poor increases, social unrest will unavoidably result, which will be "dangerous for the progress of the economy." Even though many nations, like the US, Germany, France, and the UK, have set minimum wages, wage disparities will therefore be more pronounced than ever. There will be fewer opportunities for well-paid labor in the low- and medium-wage sectors as a result of increased digitalization and the job streamlining that this involves. Many individuals will become unemployed, but highly skilled, innovative, and wealthy professionals will become richer.

8. PROPOSED SOLUTIONS

The rapid growth of AI and robotics lead to the elimination of various jobs, in different domains (Vrontis et al., 2022). Different job elimination will be evident, at least by a decade from now, if not shortly. Most of the workers will lose their jobs to the robots and the employees who are retained will experience physical and psychological pressure. The World Economic Forum lists some skills that are needed now. The skills listed in the World Economic Forum deal with cognitive and emotional capabilities (Miao & Holmes, 2021). There is no mention of physical labour or physical abilities. The skill sets are given in Table 1.

Table 1. Top ten skills required

SKILLS	DESCRIPTION
Complex problem solving	It basically has to do with having the psychological flexibility to deal with problems we've never seen and understanding them in a situation that is always changing and becoming more unpredictable.
Critical thinking	Investigating a topic or issue using logic and reasoning, considering alternative solutions, and weighing the benefits and drawbacks of each strategy are all instances of critical thinking.
Creativity	In order to benefit from the creation of new goods, technologies, and working methods, people must develop their creativity.
People management	Business team leaders and managers are skilled at leading their teams, increasing their productivity, and responding to their needs.
Coordinating with others	Social skill entered the list at number 5, highlighting the trend of businesses emphasising strong interpersonal skills and employees who can work well with others. Cooperation is crucial in any business, and fortunately, humans are still better at it than robots are.
Emotional intelligence	Each cooperation we have is literally illuminated by emotional intelligence. According to Bradberry's explanation in a Forbes article," It influences how we behave, explore social complexities, and make smart decisions that give positive outcomes"
Judgement and Decision making	This is hardly surprising given the enormous amount of data that businesses own and the rising demand for individuals who can sort through the data, identify important events, and use a variety of data to advise on corporate strategies and decisions.
Service Orientation	A strong service orientation competence is linked to providing excellent customer service and anticipating future demands. Service orientation is the capacity to "successfully look for alternatives to serve consumers."
Negotiation	Social skills will be more important than they were previously, as machines are expected to increasingly replace humans in the workforce.
Cognitive flexibility	Cognitive flexibility is the ability to switch between different modes of cognition quickly (and efficiently).

The growth of such abilities could be said to be created by individuals through experience, education/training, and naturally occurring intellectual prowess. This implies that it is important that this generation should be given a good quality education, which concentrates more on cognitive and IT skills and is also a necessity to learn more human things (like creativity, complex communication skills, emotional intelligence, etc.). A good education makes them competitive in the competitive world. To sustain in the market, one has to continue learning new things, and keep themselves updated. Those who are unfit to train themselves with the coming advancement, are destined to lose their jobs (Charles, 2023).

In the upcoming years, the challenge of incorporating untrained workers into the workforce will become increasingly pressing. This is due to a growing number of university graduates, as well as those without a degree from an established institution of higher education. At the same time, we can expect a surge in immigration to developed, industrialized countries in the West. While currently there is a reliance on untrained employees, students, and apprentices in low-skill roles, the trend is expected to shift in technologically advanced businesses. These jobs will see a sharp decline in demand as automation and robotics become more prevalent. As a result, it will become increasingly difficult to integrate these workers into the evolving digital job market. Furthermore, the implementation of robots will also lead to a reduction in the number of employees handling basic auxiliary tasks.

As technology rapidly progresses, a pressing issue arises - the potential loss of jobs for countless individuals and the resulting financial struggles that may ensue. The looming question is who will shoulder the burden and how will societal safety nets cope with the fallout? Companies will surely have to contribute to the costs through measures like funding retraining programs and offering severance packages to those affected by layoffs. Unfortunately, not everyone will have the ability to adapt and retrain, whether due to cognitive or physical limitations. This will lead to prolonged unemployment and a greater demand for government aid. Undoubtedly, one of the most concerning repercussions will be the strain on social welfare systems as they try to manage the significant financial strain.

The government should make sure that these employees get their basic needs satisfied. One way to see through is by enforcing Universal Basic Income or the Unconditional Basic income. The idea of universal basic income (UBI) has also been put out to unemployment due to technical advancements, with all individuals or residents of a nation receiving unconditionally sufficient regular sums of money to support their daily needs. Additionally, neither working nor looking for jobs would be necessary. There are numerous variations of UBI, each with a different recommended benefit level and funding source. The positive aspects of UBI are that it will maintain social peace whereas unemployment due to automation might lead to frustration and social disobedience and it will also lead to the deregulation of the legal aspects of labor and social laws. Another solution to address the possible unemployment caused by automation has been the idea of robot taxes. The fundamental notion, according to Bill Gates, is to tax businesses and organizations that utilize robots to eliminate jobs. The tax revenue could then be applied to workers who have been laid off to help offset their financial hardships or to retrain them so they can rejoin the workforce.

9. CONCLUSION

Technology has brought about enormous changes that people need to be aware of and adapt to. First, we predict that the role of humans in the production of products and services will diminish over time. Human labor will continue to be an aspect of production, but it is no longer the main driver of production. The ability to create, interpret, and collaborate with others will continue to be the qualities that a human worker possesses and contribute to the factors of production. The ability of humans to physically perform tasks that many robots struggle to do well and quickly (such as opening doors, walking, and other physical activities) will also be highly valued shortly. Humans will continue to be excellent multipurpose tools capable of navigating the layout of a home or workplace. However, these physical tasks will be overtaken by workers who are being replaced by robots and artificial intelligence, overwhelming the labor markets. People lacking the abilities necessary to compete in the new economy will be pitted against one another in the human race. Many workers will need to gain skills that are currently only human-specific to remain relevant. People will be able to stay relevant in the new economy if they have problem-solving, emotional intelligence, interpersonal communication, and other talents that are within their grasp. However, the old institutions that educate people will need to change to meet the needs of the new economy and the needs of workers. Moreover, the new economy must be considered in the political and judicial framework. Governments and taxation systems must adapt to the new economic reality as labor becomes more flexible and focused on gigs and contracts.

The government will be less likely to tax workers conventionally, and because the gig and sharing economies are here to stay, taxation policies will need to be modified to be effective in a modernized economy. Taxation will alter, and maintaining the new economy's stability and health will require new approaches. As there are many unneeded workers, it is crucial to ensure that people have a stable means of subsistence, particularly if they are not needed in the labor force. The guarantee of a minimal income for everybody, a concept that may appear radical but has a long history and has gained considerable popularity in recent years, is one simple method to account for this. Even though a large portion of the labor force is not needed for the political economy to function, it will be competing for jobs that require less expertise and with workers who have lost their employment owing to the rising robotization of the workplace. The notion that humans can function effectively in the new economy is the subject of the greatest worry. While the World Economic Forum (2018) can define the skills required in the workplace, it is debatable if all people can acquire those abilities. While some people might disagree that intelligence is a useful notion (Gould, 1996), most people believe that there is variety in each person's capacity to take in, remember, and process information. It seems that many people would be excluded from the new economy due to their inability to acquire the necessary abilities unless it is discovered that all humans have about the same intellectual potential to do so. The inability to acquire the abilities required to participate in the economy as a human could, therefore, result in a sizable portion of mankind being excluded from the new one. To conclude, a new era of mechanical reproduction, unimaginable in the past, is beginning for humans. Humans may still be a factor in production, but their importance may be diminishing in terms of the physical demands of the job and increasing in terms of the intellectual demands. In any case, humans will play a different role. To remain relevant and in line with the requirements of a society with an increasingly automated production base, many economic institutions, including the government and education, will need to alter.

Declaration of Conflicting Interests: The Author(s) declare(s) that there is no conflict of interest
Funding: NA

REFERENCES

Balakrishnan, J. (2022). Building capabilities for future of work in the gig economy. *NHRD Network Journal, 15*(1), 56–70. doi:10.1177/26314541211064726

Charles, S. (2023). *Blueprint.* Academic Press.

Ellitan, L. (2020). Competing in the era of industrial revolution 4.0 and society 5.0. *Jurnal Maksipreneur: Manajemen, Koperasi, dan Entrepreneurship, 10*(1), 1-12.

From, A. (n.d.). Humanoid Robots: A New Kind of Tool. Academic Press.

Groumpos, P. P. (2021). A critical historical and scientific overview of all industrial revolutions. *IFAC-PapersOnLine, 54*(13), 464–471. doi:10.1016/j.ifacol.2021.10.492 PMID:38620687

Khan, I. S., Ahmad, M. O., & Majava, J. (2021). Industry 4.0 and sustainable development: A systematic mapping of triple bottom line, Circular Economy and Sustainable Business Models perspectives. *Journal of Cleaner Production, 297,* 126655. doi:10.1016/j.jclepro.2021.126655

McCartney, G., & McCartney, A. (2020). Rise of the machines: Towards a conceptual service-robot research framework for the hospitality and tourism industry. *International Journal of Contemporary Hospitality Management, 32*(12), 3835–3851. doi:10.1108/IJCHM-05-2020-0450

Miao, F., & Holmes, W. (2021). International Forum on AI and the Futures of Education, developing competencies for the AI Era, 7-8 December 2020: synthesis report. Academic Press.

O'Neill, J. (2011). The growth map: Economic opportunity in the BRICs and beyond. Penguin UK.

Peres, R. S., Jia, X., Lee, J., Sun, K., Colombo, A. W., & Barata, J. (2020). Industrial artificial intelligence in industry 4.0-systematic review, challenges and outlook. *IEEE Access : Practical Innovations, Open Solutions*, 8, 220121–220139. doi:10.1109/ACCESS.2020.3042874

van Agtmael, A. (2007). Industrial Revolution 2.0. *Foreign Policy*, *158*, 40.

Vrontis, D., Christofi, M., Pereira, V., Tarba, S., Makrides, A., & Trichina, E. (2022). Artificial intelligence, robotics, advanced technologies and human resource management: A systematic review. *International Journal of Human Resource Management*, *33*(6), 1237–1266. doi:10.1080/09585192.2020.1871398

Yadav, R., Arora, S., & Dhull, S. (2022). A path way to Industrial Revolution 6.0. *Int. J. Mech. Eng*, *7*, 1452–1459.

Zhang, A. X., Muller, M., & Wang, D. (2020). How do data science workers collaborate? roles, workflows, and tools. Proceedings of the ACM on Human-Computer Interaction, 4, 1-23. 10.1145/3392826

Chapter 13

Customer–Centric Excellence in the Marketing 6.0 Era:
Industry 6.0

S. C. Vetrivel

https://orcid.org/0000-0003-3050-8211
Kongu Engineering College, India

T. Gomathi
Gnanamani College of Technology, India

K. C. Sowmiya
Sri Vasavi College, India

V. Sabareeshwari
Amrita School of Agricultural Sciences, India

ABSTRACT

This chapter examines the evolving landscape of marketing in the contemporary business environment, with a particular focus on the sixth wave of marketing (Marketing 6.0). This wave represents a paradigm shift towards unprecedented customer-centricity, where businesses are compelled to align their strategies with the ever-changing expectations and preferences of the modern consumer. The chapter begins by providing a comprehensive overview of the historical progression of marketing, from its inception to the current era, highlighting the pivotal shifts that have shaped each phase. It then meticulously explores the core principles and characteristics that define the Marketing 6.0 era, emphasizing the pivotal role of technology, data analytics, and artificial intelligence in reshaping the marketing landscape. Furthermore, the chapter addresses the key challenges and opportunities faced by businesses as they strive to adopt customer-centric excellence in Marketing 6.0.

DOI: 10.4018/979-8-3693-3108-8.ch013

1. INTRODUCTION

1.1. Setting the Stage for the Evolution of Marketing

Customer-Centric Excellence in Marketing 6.0 Era involves a comprehensive understanding of the dynamic shifts in consumer behavior, technological advancements, and the emergence of new business models. In this era, the focus is squarely on the customer, with marketing strategies designed to meet their needs and expectations. Firstly, the digital revolution has significantly altered how consumers interact with brands. The prevalence of smartphones, social media, and e-commerce platforms has created a hyper-connected world where customers have instant access to information and can voice their opinions globally. This necessitates a shift in marketing strategies towards personalized, real-time engagement (Anderson & Jacobson, 2000). Brands need to leverage data analytics and artificial intelligence to gain insights into customer preferences, behaviors, and journeys. Secondly, the Marketing 6.0 Era emphasizes the importance of creating a seamless and integrated customer experience across multiple touchpoints. This involves breaking down silos within organizations to ensure that marketing, sales, customer service, and other departments work cohesively to deliver a consistent brand experience. Companies are adopting omnichannel approaches to meet customers wherever they are, providing a unified and personalized experience across online and offline channels. Moreover, the rise of social responsibility and ethical consumerism is another key factor in Customer-Centric Excellence in Marketing 6.0 Era. Customers are increasingly valuing brands that demonstrate a commitment to sustainability, social justice, and ethical practices. Companies must align their marketing strategies with these values, transparently communicating their efforts to build trust and loyalty among socially conscious consumers. Furthermore, advancements in technology, such as augmented reality (AR), virtual reality (VR), and the Internet of Things (IoT), are reshaping the way products and services are marketed. These technologies enable immersive and interactive experiences that can enhance customer engagement and create memorable brand interactions. Marketers need to stay abreast of these technological trends and incorporate them into their strategies to stay competitive in Marketing 6.0.

1.2. Overview of the Customer-Centric Approach

The customer-centric approach is a business strategy that places the customer at the center of all decision-making processes, aiming to meet their needs and exceed their expectations. This approach recognizes that a satisfied and loyal customer base is crucial for the long-term success of any business. Unlike traditional product-centric models, where the focus is primarily on the features and benefits of the product or service, the customer-centric approach shifts the focus towards understanding and fulfilling the unique needs and preferences of individual customers. One of the key elements of the customer-centric approach is a deep understanding of customer behavior and preferences. Businesses employ various methods such as data analytics, customer surveys, and market research to gather insights into customer needs and expectations. This information is then used to tailor products, services, and experiences to meet and exceed customer expectations. This approach recognizes that customer needs are dynamic and can change over time, requiring continuous monitoring and adaptation. Another crucial aspect of a customer-centric approach is personalized communication and engagement (Consoli & Musso, 2010). Businesses strive to build meaningful relationships with their customers by delivering personalized interactions across various touch points, such as social media, email, and in-store experiences. This personalization goes beyond addressing customers by their names; it involves understanding their purchase history, preferences, and providing relevant recommendations and offers. Customer feedback is highly valued in a customer-centric approach. Businesses actively seek and welcome customer feedback to understand their pain points and areas of improvement. This feedback loop is essential for continuous refinement of products and services. Companies often leverage technology to facilitate feedback collection, using online surveys, social media monitoring, and customer reviews to gain valuable insights. In addition to being customer-focused, a customer-centric approach involves creating a customer-centric culture within the organization. This requires aligning the entire workforce with the goal of providing exceptional customer experiences. Training programs, clear communication of customer-centric values, and employee empowerment are common strategies employed to embed this culture. When employees understand the importance of customer satisfaction and are empowered to make decisions that benefit the customer, it leads to a more responsive and customer-oriented organization. The customer-centric approach also recognizes the importance of customer lifetime value (CLV). Instead of focusing solely on individual transactions, businesses look at the long-term value of a customer relationship. This involves not only acquiring new customers but also retaining existing ones through loyalty programs, personalized offerings, and exceptional customer service. Ultimately, adopting a customer-centric approach is a strategic shift that goes beyond superficial customer service initiatives (DeTienne et al., 2021). It requires a fundamental change in mindset and organizational culture to prioritize the customer at every stage of the business process. Companies that successfully implement this approach can build strong customer loyalty, increase customer retention, and gain a competitive advantage in the marketplace.

2. THE CHANGING LANDSCAPE OF CONSUMER BEHAVIOR

2.1. Understanding the Modern Consumer

The changing landscape of consumer behavior in the modern era is marked by a multitude of factors that have collectively altered how individuals approach, evaluate, and make purchasing decisions. One fundamental aspect is the influence of technology. With the widespread use of smartphones, tablets, and the internet, consumers now have unprecedented access to information. This easy access has empowered them to research products, compare prices, and read reviews before making a purchase. As a result, the modern consumer is more informed, discerning, and often seeks value for their money (Erragcha & Romdhane, 2014). Social media also plays a pivotal role in shaping contemporary consumer behavior. Platforms like Facebook, Instagram, and Twitter have become integral to people's lives, providing a space for individuals to share opinions, experiences, and recommendations. This peer-to-peer influence has a significant impact on purchasing decisions, as consumers tend to trust the opinions of their peers more than traditional advertising. Businesses have had to adapt to this trend by actively engaging with consumers on social media, managing online reviews, and building positive brand perception through these platforms. Moreover, the rise of e-commerce has transformed the way people shop. Online marketplaces offer convenience, a vast selection, and the ability to shop from anywhere at any time. The modern consumer values these aspects and often opts for online transactions over traditional brick-and-mortar stores. The convenience of doorstep delivery, hassle-free return policies, and personalized recommendations based on browsing history contribute to the appeal of e-commerce (Fornell et al., 2020). In the changing landscape of consumer behavior, sustainability and ethical considerations are increasingly important factors influencing purchasing decisions. Consumers are more conscious of the environmental and social impact of their choices. They prefer products and brands that demonstrate a commitment to eco-friendly practices, fair labor conditions, and overall ethical business conduct. As a result, companies are under pressure to adopt sustainable practices, transparent supply chains, and socially responsible initiatives to attract and retain consumers. The evolution of consumer behavior is also shaped by the desire for personalized experiences. Advances in data analytics and artificial intelligence enable businesses to analyze consumer preferences and behaviors, allowing for the customization of marketing strategies and product offerings. Personalized recommendations, targeted advertising, and tailored promotions contribute to a more engaging and satisfying consumer experience.

2.2. Impact of Technology on Consumer Expectations

The changing landscape of consumer behavior is heavily influenced by the rapid advancements in technology. One of the most significant impacts is on consumer expectations. With the advent of smartphones, high-speed internet, and smart devices, consumers now expect seamless and personalized experiences across all touchpoints. Technology has made information readily accessible, enabling consumers to research products, read reviews, and compare prices before making a purchase decision. E-commerce platforms have revolutionized the retail industry, allowing consumers to shop online from the comfort of their homes. This shift has heightened expectations for convenience, speed, and reliability. Consumers now expect quick and hassle-free online transactions, easy returns, and personalized recommendations based on their previous purchases. Retailers who fail to meet these expectations risk losing customers to competitors who leverage technology to enhance the shopping experience. Moreover, social media and digital marketing have played a pivotal role in shaping consumer expectations. Consumers are constantly bombarded with targeted advertisements and personalized content based on their online behavior (Kartajaya et al., 2019). This has led to an increased demand for personalized communication and offerings from brands. Consumers expect businesses to understand their preferences and deliver relevant content, products, and services, creating a more personalized and engaging experience. The rise of artificial intelligence (AI) and machine learning has further elevated consumer expectations. Chatbots and virtual assistants powered by AI provide instant and efficient customer support, raising the bar for responsiveness in the business-customer relationship. Consumers now expect quick resolutions to their queries, and businesses that implement AI-driven solutions can meet these expectations while also optimizing operational efficiency. In the era of the Internet of Things (IoT), connected devices have become an integral part of consumers' lives. Smart homes, wearable devices, and connected cars contribute to a more interconnected consumer experience. As a result, consumers expect seamless integration between their devices and services. Businesses that can offer a cohesive and integrated experience across various touch points are more likely to meet the evolving expectations of tech-savvy consumers.

3. DATA-DRIVEN MARKETING STRATEGIES

3.1. Leveraging Data for Customer Insights

Leveraging data for customer insights is a fundamental aspect of data-driven marketing strategies. In today's highly competitive business landscape, organizations are increasingly relying on data to understand customer behavior, preferences, and trends. By harnessing the power of data, businesses can create targeted and personalized marketing campaigns that resonate with their audience, ultimately leading to improved customer engagement and loyalty. One of the primary ways to leverage data for customer insights is through customer segmentation (Kotler, 2007). This involves dividing the customer base into distinct groups based on shared characteristics, such as demographics, purchasing behavior, or psychographics. Analyzing these segments allows marketers to tailor their messaging and offerings to specific customer needs, enhancing the relevance of their campaigns. This segmentation can be achieved by employing advanced analytics tools, machine learning algorithms, and customer relationship management (CRM) systems.

Furthermore, businesses can leverage historical and real-time data to create customer personas. These detailed representations of target customers help marketers understand the motivations, pain points, and preferences of different customer segments. By developing accurate personas, organizations can craft highly targeted and personalized content that resonates with specific customer groups, increasing the likelihood of conversion. Another crucial aspect of leveraging data for customer insights is analyzing customer journey data. This involves tracking and understanding the various touchpoints a customer has with a brand throughout their buying process. By mapping the customer journey, businesses can identify key moments and opportunities for engagement. This information enables marketers to optimize the customer experience by delivering timely and relevant content, thus increasing the chances of conversion and customer satisfaction. Data-driven marketing strategies also involve predictive analytics to anticipate future customer behavior (Lommeruda & Sørgard, 2003; Martin-Consuegra et al., 2007). By analyzing historical data and identifying patterns, businesses can make data-driven predictions about potential customer actions, such as purchasing decisions or churn likelihood. This foresight allows organizations to proactively tailor marketing strategies and offerings to meet the evolving needs of their customer base. To effectively leverage data for customer insights, businesses must invest in robust data infrastructure and analytics capabilities. This includes implementing data management platforms, ensuring data quality and accuracy, and employing data visualization tools to make insights easily understandable for marketing teams. Additionally, organizations should prioritize data privacy and security to build and maintain customer trust while adhering to relevant regulations.

3.2. Personalization and Customization in Marketing

Personalization and customization are integral components of data-driven marketing strategies that aim to enhance customer engagement and satisfaction. These concepts involve tailoring marketing messages, products, and experiences to meet the unique preferences and needs of individual consumers. By leveraging data analytics and customer insights, businesses can create more relevant and targeted marketing campaigns, ultimately driving better results and fostering stronger customer relationships. One key aspect of personalization in marketing is the use of customer data to understand individual behaviors, preferences, and demographics. This information can be gathered through various channels, such as online interactions, purchase history, social media activities, and surveys. Analyzing this data allows marketers to segment their audience effectively and deliver personalized content that resonates with specific customer segments. For example, an e-commerce platform might use browsing history and purchase patterns to recommend products that align with a customer's preferences.

Customization in marketing takes personalization to the next level by offering customers the ability to tailor products or services according to their unique preferences. This can include personalized product configurations, design choices, or even personalized pricing models. For instance, a sportswear brand might allow customers to customize the color, size, and design of their shoes, providing a unique and personalized product that caters to individual tastes. The implementation of personalization and customization in marketing relies heavily on advanced data analytics and machine learning algorithms. These technologies enable marketers to process vast amounts of customer data quickly and derive meaningful insights. Machine learning algorithms can predict customer behavior, identify patterns, and recommend personalized content or product suggestions based on historical data. This level of automation not only improves the efficiency of marketing campaigns but also ensures that personalized experiences are delivered at scale. One of the benefits of personalization and customization in marketing is the ability to enhance customer loyalty and retention (Oliver, 1997; Patterson & Spreng, 1997). When customers receive personalized and relevant offers, they are more likely to feel valued and understood by the brand. This, in turn, fosters a stronger emotional connection, leading to increased customer loyalty. Additionally, personalized marketing can contribute to higher conversion rates, as customers are more likely to engage with content that aligns with their interests and needs. However, it is crucial for businesses to navigate the ethical considerations surrounding the use of customer data in personalization efforts. Striking the right balance between delivering tailored experiences and respecting customer privacy is essential to build trust and maintain a positive brand image. Clear communication about data usage policies, obtaining consent, and ensuring data security are essential components of a responsible data-driven marketing strategy.

4. BUILDING CUSTOMER PERSONAS IN THE 6.0 ERA

4.1. Creating Detailed Customer Profiles

Creating detailed customer profiles, often referred to as building customer personas, is a crucial step in understanding and targeting the audience effectively. In the 6.0 era, the focus is not only on collecting data but on interpreting and acting upon it. By creating detailed customer profiles, businesses can craft personalized and targeted strategies that resonate with their audience, leading to improved customer satisfaction and loyalty. Here are detailed steps and considerations for creating customer profiles:

- **Define Your Target Audience:** Identify your primary and secondary target markets. Consider demographics, geographic location, and psychographics.
- **Gather Data:** Utilize data analytics tools, CRM systems, and customer surveys. Collect information on age, gender, income, education, job title, interests, and behavior.
- **Segmentation:** Group your audience based on shared characteristics or behaviors. Consider factors like customer needs, preferences, and purchasing behavior.
- **Create Personas:** Develop detailed fictional characters that represent specific segments. Give each persona a name, background, and a set of traits. Include personal and professional details to make them relatable.
- **Customer Journey Mapping:** Understand the stages a customer goes through in their interaction with your brand. Identify touch points, pain points, and opportunities for engagement.
- **Behavioral Insights:** Analyze customer interactions with your brand. Understand how they engage with your website, social media, and other channels.
- **Feedback and Reviews:** Leverage customer feedback, reviews, and testimonials. Identify common themes and sentiments to refine your personas.
- **Competitor Analysis:** Analyze your competitors' customer base. Understand what attracts customers to them and how you can differentiate.
- **Technology Integration:** Leverage AI and machine learning for more accurate predictions. Use tools to track customer behavior across multiple channels.
- **Dynamic Personas:** Regularly update personas based on evolving market trends. Be adaptable to changes in customer behavior and preferences.
- **Empathy and Understanding:** Develop a deep understanding of your customers' needs and challenges. Create personas that reflect real-world scenarios.

- **Cross-Functional Collaboration:** Involve teams across departments in persona creation. Ensure that marketing, sales, and product development have a shared understanding.
- **Personalization:** Tailor your marketing messages and product offerings to align with each persona. Use personalization technologies to enhance the customer experience.
- **Privacy Considerations:** Respect customer privacy and adhere to data protection regulations. Use anonymized data where possible and ensure transparency in data collection.
- **Regular Review and Optimization:** Periodically review and update customer personas. Stay attuned to changes in market dynamics and consumer behavior.

4.2. Tailoring Marketing Strategies to Different Personas

In the 6.0 era, tailoring marketing strategies to different personas has become a crucial aspect of successful business operations. Building customer personas involves creating detailed profiles of various customer segments based on demographics, behaviors, preferences, and other relevant data. Once these personas are established, it's essential to customize marketing strategies to effectively engage each group. This tailored approach allows businesses to connect with their audience on a more personal level, increasing the chances of conversion and brand loyalty. One key aspect of tailoring marketing strategies to different personas is understanding the unique needs and preferences of each group. For example, a tech-savvy millennial may respond better to social media campaigns and influencer marketing, while an older demographic might prefer traditional advertising methods like print or television. By identifying these preferences, businesses can allocate their marketing budget more effectively and generate a higher return on investment (Perreault et al., 2000). Moreover, tailoring content is paramount in the 6.0 era. Content marketing has evolved to cater to specific personas with personalized messaging. For instance, a persona interested in environmental sustainability might respond well to content highlighting a company's eco-friendly practices, while a budget-conscious persona may be more swayed by promotions and discounts. Crafting content that resonates with each persona's values and interests strengthens the brand-customer relationship. In the 6.0 era, advanced analytics and AI-driven tools play a pivotal role in tailoring marketing strategies. These technologies can analyze vast amounts of data to identify patterns and trends within different personas. By leveraging predictive analytics, businesses can anticipate customer needs and behaviors, allowing for more targeted and proactive marketing efforts. This data-driven approach enables companies to stay ahead of market trends and adapt their strategies accordingly. Additionally, the rise of omnichannel marketing in the 6.0 era has made it crucial to tailor strategies across various platforms. Different personas may engage with brands through multiple channels such as social media, email, or in-store experiences. Therefore, marketers need to ensure a seamless and consistent brand experience across these channels. This includes adapting the tone, style, and content to suit each platform and persona, creating a cohesive brand image.

5. OMNI-CHANNEL MARKETING

5.1. Integration of Online and Offline Channels

The integration of online and offline channels is a fundamental aspect of omni-channel marketing, a strategy designed to provide a seamless and consistent customer experience across various touchpoints. In the modern business landscape, consumers often move between online and offline channels during their purchasing journey, and a successful omni-channel approach recognizes and accommodates this behavior. Online channels, such as e-commerce websites, social media platforms, and mobile apps, have become integral components of retail operations. These platforms offer convenience, accessibility, and the ability to reach a global audience. The integration of these online channels with offline ones, like brick-and-mortar stores, creates a cohesive brand presence. For instance, customers might browse products online and then make a purchase in-store, or vice versa. An omni-channel strategy ensures that the transition between these channels is smooth and enhances the overall customer experience. One critical element of integrating online and offline channels is having a centralized customer data system. This enables businesses to have a unified view of customer interactions, irrespective of the channel. Customer profiles, purchase history, and preferences can be accessed by both online and offline teams, allowing for a personalized and consistent experience. This integration minimizes the chances of disjointed communication, ensuring that customers receive relevant and targeted messages regardless of the channel through which they engage with the brand. Moreover, an integrated inventory management system is vital for omni-channel success. When online and offline channels share real-time inventory information, it prevents issues like over-selling or stockouts. Customers can confidently shop across various channels, knowing that product availability is accurate (Reichheld et al., 2000; Schnatz et al., 2022). This integration is particularly crucial for businesses offering services like buy online, pick up in-store (BOPIS) or same-day delivery, enhancing the convenience and flexibility of the customer experience. Retailers embracing omni-channel marketing often implement strategies such as click-and-collect, where customers can order online and pick up in-store, or showrooming, where they browse products in-store and make the final purchase online. This convergence of channels caters to different customer preferences, providing a holistic shopping experience that aligns with the diverse ways consumers prefer to engage with brands.

5.2. Providing a Seamless Customer Experience

Providing a seamless customer experience is a core objective of omni-channel marketing, focusing on creating consistency and cohesion across various customer touchpoints. A seamless experience ensures that customers can interact with a brand effortlessly, regardless of the channels they choose, leading to enhanced satisfaction and loyalty. One key aspect of achieving a seamless customer experience under omni-channel marketing is maintaining consistent branding. From the website and mobile app to physical stores and social media platforms, the brand's identity, messaging, and visuals should remain uniform. This consistency helps in reinforcing brand recall and building trust, as customers encounter a cohesive image, irrespective of the channel they engage with. Additionally, the integration of customer communication channels is crucial (Sheth et al., 1999). Whether a customer reaches out via social media, email, live chat, or phone, their interactions should be connected. This means that customer service representatives have access to the customer's history and context, allowing for more personalized and efficient support. By providing a seamless flow of communication, brands can demonstrate a commitment to understanding and meeting customer needs. Another vital element is the synchronization of inventory and pricing information across all channels. Customers should encounter the same product availability and pricing whether they are shopping online or in-store. Real-time updates prevent discrepancies and disappointments, ensuring that customers have accurate information, regardless of the channel they choose for their purchasing journey. Mobile optimization is also critical for a seamless customer experience. With the increasing use of smartphones, customers often switch between devices during their buying process. An effective omni-channel strategy ensures that websites and apps are optimized for various devices, offering a consistent and user-friendly experience. This consistency in the user interface and functionality enhances customer satisfaction and encourages engagement. Furthermore, omni-channel marketing leverages data analytics to gain insights into customer behavior (Thomas & Shivani, 2020). By analyzing customer interactions across channels, businesses can better understand preferences, anticipate needs, and tailor their marketing efforts accordingly. This data-driven approach enables brands to provide highly personalized experiences, creating a sense of individualized attention for each customer.

6. CONTENT MARKETING IN THE DIGITAL AGE

6.1. Creating Engaging and Relevant Content

Creating engaging and relevant content is paramount in the digital age, where information overload is a common challenge. In the realm of content marketing, the goal is not only to produce material but to captivate the audience, providing value and resonating with their needs and interests. To achieve this, content creators must understand their target audience thoroughly. This involves researching demographics, understanding behaviors, and identifying pain points, ensuring that the content is tailored to address the specific needs and preferences of the audience.

The digital age has ushered in various content formats, and creating diverse, multimedia content is essential for engagement. This includes not only well-crafted written articles but also visually appealing graphics, videos, podcasts, and interactive elements. Different audience segments may prefer different types of content, so a multi-format approach ensures broader reach and increased engagement. Utilizing storytelling techniques can also be highly effective, allowing brands to connect with their audience on a more emotional level, making the content more memorable and shareable. Relevance is a key factor in the success of content marketing. Understanding the current trends, industry news, and customer concerns helps in crafting timely and pertinent content. This may involve staying updated on industry developments, monitoring social media for trending topics, and actively engaging with the target audience to understand their evolving needs. Content that aligns with the current zeitgeist and provides solutions or insights is more likely to capture the audience's attention and maintain their interest. Moreover, personalization is a powerful tool in content marketing (Treviño et al., 2014). By leveraging data analytics, brands can tailor content based on individual user preferences, behaviors, and interactions. Personalized content creates a sense of exclusivity and relevance, strengthening the relationship between the brand and the audience. This might include personalized emails, content recommendations, or targeted advertising, ensuring that the content speaks directly to the individual, making it more impactful. In the digital age, the importance of search engine optimization (SEO) cannot be overstated. Creating content that is not only engaging but also optimized for search engines enhances discoverability (Westberg & Jason, 2004). Keyword research, strategic placement of relevant terms, and a user-friendly website structure all contribute to improved visibility. This ensures that the content reaches a broader audience, driving organic traffic and establishing the brand as an authoritative source in its industry.

6.2. Utilizing Storytelling for Brand Connection

In the digital age, where consumers are constantly bombarded with information, utilizing storytelling has emerged as a powerful strategy for creating a meaningful brand connection. Storytelling goes beyond presenting facts and figures; it enables brands to convey their identity, values, and mission in a compelling and relatable manner. By weaving narratives, brands can engage emotionally with their audience, fostering a deeper connection that goes beyond a transactional relationship. Storytelling allows brands to humanize themselves, making them more approachable and relatable. Instead of a faceless entity, a brand becomes a character in a story, with a unique personality and a journey that the audience can understand and connect with. This connection builds trust and loyalty as consumers feel they are engaging with a brand that shares their values and understands their experiences. One crucial element of effective storytelling is authenticity. In the digital age, where consumers are highly discerning, authenticity is paramount. Brands that share genuine stories about their origin, challenges, and triumphs resonate more with the audience. Authentic storytelling helps in building credibility and transparency, creating a narrative that consumers can trust and feel a genuine connection with. Moreover, storytelling enables brands to differentiate themselves in a crowded market. When products or services are similar, the brand story becomes a unique selling proposition. A well-crafted narrative sets a brand apart, creating a memorable and distinctive identity that resonates with the audience (Xia et al., 2004). This distinctiveness not only attracts new customers but also helps in retaining existing ones, as the brand story becomes a part of the customer's own narrative. Digital platforms provide an ideal medium for storytelling. Social media, blogs, videos, and podcasts offer diverse channels for brands to share their stories. Visual content, in particular, is highly effective in conveying emotions and creating a lasting impact. Platforms like Instagram and YouTube allow brands to visually narrate their stories, providing a dynamic and immersive experience for the audience. In the digital age, where consumers are not just passive receivers but active participants, storytelling encourages user-generated content. Brands can invite their audience to share their experiences, creating a collective narrative. User-generated content not only adds authenticity but also amplifies the brand story, turning customers into brand advocates.

7. SOCIAL MEDIA MASTERY

7.1. Harnessing the Power of Social Platforms

Harnessing the power of social platforms is an essential component of social media mastery in the digital age. Social media has become a ubiquitous part of people's lives, offering unparalleled opportunities for businesses to connect with their audience, build brand awareness, and foster engagement. The mastery of social platforms involves strategic utilization of various channels to effectively communicate a brand's message, connect with the target audience, and drive meaningful interactions. Firstly, understanding the unique features and dynamics of each social platform is crucial. Different platforms cater to diverse demographics and content preferences. For instance, Instagram may be more visual and lifestyle-oriented, while Twitter emphasizes concise and real-time updates. By tailoring content to match the nuances of each platform, businesses can ensure that their message resonates with the specific audience present on that platform. Consistency in branding across social platforms is key. From profile pictures to the tone of voice in captions, maintaining a cohesive brand identity reinforces recognition and trust. A consistent visual and messaging approach helps in creating a unified brand presence, irrespective of the social channel. This consistency contributes to a seamless and recognizable brand experience for the audience across various platforms. Engagement is a central focus when harnessing the power of social platforms. Successful social media mastery involves actively participating in conversations, responding to comments, and initiating dialogues with the audience (Kudeshia & Mittal, 2015). This not only helps in building a sense of community but also enhances the visibility of the brand's personality. Social platforms are not just broadcasting tools; they are interactive spaces where brands can connect with their audience on a more personal level. Utilizing multimedia content is another crucial aspect of social media mastery. Visuals, videos, and interactive content tend to perform exceptionally well on platforms like Facebook, Instagram, and TikTok. Leveraging these formats helps capture the audience's attention in a crowded digital landscape. Additionally, the use of compelling visuals and storytelling techniques contributes to making the content more shareable, extending its reach beyond the immediate follower base. Paid social media advertising plays a significant role in social media mastery. Platforms like Facebook and Instagram offer targeted advertising options, allowing businesses to reach specific demographics based on interests, behaviors, and other criteria. This precision targeting ensures that the content is presented to individuals most likely to be interested in the brand, optimizing advertising spend and improving overall ROI. Analytics and data-driven insights are integral to social media mastery. Monitoring performance metrics such as engagement rates, click-through rates, and follower growth provides valuable insights into the effectiveness of social media strategies. Utilizing these metrics allows businesses to adapt and refine their approach, ensuring that the content resonates with the audience and aligns with overarching business goals.

7.2. Building and Managing Online Communities

Building and managing online communities is a crucial facet of social media mastery in the contemporary digital landscape. Online communities provide a platform for businesses to cultivate a loyal audience, foster engagement, and create a sense of belonging among their followers. The first step in this process involves identifying the target audience and understanding their preferences, interests, and pain points. By tailoring content to resonate with the community's needs, brands can establish a strong foundation for connection and interaction. A key element in community-building is the establishment of a consistent brand voice and personality (Kudeshia & Mittal, 2016; Lemon & Verhoef, 2016). This helps in creating a recognizable and relatable identity, fostering a sense of community among the followers. Whether through humor, inspiration, or informational content, maintaining a cohesive tone across social media platforms builds trust and contributes to the formation of a dedicated community that identifies with the brand on a personal level. Facilitating meaningful conversations within the community is pivotal for engagement and sustained interest. This involves responding to comments, encouraging discussions, and actively participating in conversations. By acknowledging and valuing the contributions of community members, businesses can strengthen the bond between the brand and its audience. Hosting regular Q&A sessions, polls, or live events further enhances the interactive nature of the community, making members feel heard and appreciated. In the context of social media mastery, the use of user-generated content (UGC) plays a vital role in building and managing online communities. Encouraging followers to share their experiences, testimonials, and creative content not only adds authenticity but also fosters a sense of ownership within the community. Brands can leverage UGC to showcase the diversity and enthusiasm of their community members, creating a dynamic and inclusive online space. The establishment of clear guidelines and community standards is essential for maintaining a positive and respectful environment. By setting expectations for behavior and content, businesses can ensure that their online community remains a safe and welcoming space for all members. This involves actively moderating discussions, addressing inappropriate behavior promptly, and promoting constructive dialogue within the community. Strategic use of exclusive content and perks contributes to community loyalty. Providing members with access to special promotions, early product releases, or behind-the-scenes content incentivizes their continued engagement. Loyalty programs and incentives can further motivate community members to actively participate and contribute to the growth of the community (Li & Hitt, 2018). Effective community management also requires the monitoring of analytics and metrics to assess community health and engagement levels. Tracking metrics such as active members, post reach, and engagement rates provides insights into the community's dynamics. By analyzing these metrics, businesses can refine their strategies, ensuring that the content and community management approach align with the evolving needs and preferences of the audience.

8. CUSTOMER RETENTION STRATEGIES

8.1. Loyalty Programs and Retention Initiatives

Loyalty programs and retention initiatives are critical components of customer retention strategies, particularly in the 6.0 era, where customer loyalty plays a pivotal role in sustaining business success. Loyalty programs are structured schemes designed to reward and incentivize repeat business, fostering a sense of allegiance between the brand and its customers. These initiatives go beyond mere transactions, aiming to build lasting relationships and encourage customers to choose a particular brand consistently. One key element of successful loyalty programs is offering tangible and appealing rewards. These incentives can include discounts, exclusive access to products or services, cashback, or loyalty points that customers can accumulate and redeem. The attractiveness of the rewards directly influences customer participation and engagement with the loyalty program. The rewards should align with the interests and preferences of the target audience, ensuring that they perceive value in their loyalty. Personalization is increasingly becoming integral to loyalty programs and retention initiatives. Tailoring rewards and promotions based on individual customer behavior and preferences enhances the relevance of the incentives offered. Advanced data analytics and customer relationship management (CRM) systems play a crucial role in gathering and utilizing the necessary information to create personalized experiences, making customers feel appreciated and understood. Building a seamless and user-friendly loyalty program interface is essential for customer retention. A straightforward process for earning and redeeming rewards contributes to a positive customer experience. Mobile apps, online platforms, or physical loyalty cards should be easily accessible and intuitive, allowing customers to track their rewards, access exclusive offers, and participate effortlessly. The convenience of engagement enhances customer satisfaction and encourages continued participation.

Incorporating tiered loyalty structures adds an additional layer of motivation for customers to stay loyal to the brand. As customers progress through different tiers, they can unlock progressively more significant benefits (Malthouse & Hofacker, 2018; Nair et al., 2022). This tiered approach not only provides a sense of achievement for customers but also incentivizes them to maintain and advance their loyalty status. It creates a gamified aspect to the loyalty program, enhancing customer engagement. Retention initiatives go beyond formal loyalty programs and encompass various strategies aimed at keeping customers satisfied and committed to the brand. These initiatives may include proactive customer support, personalized communication, and targeted promotions for existing customers. Proactively addressing customer concerns, acknowledging their feedback, and making them feel valued contributes significantly to retention efforts. The utilization of predictive analytics is an emerging trend in loyalty programs and retention initiatives. By analyzing customer data, businesses can anticipate customer needs, identify potential churn risks, and implement targeted interventions. Predictive analytics enable proactive strategies, such as sending personalized offers to customers who exhibit signs of decreased engagement or providing tailored recommendations based on their purchase history.

8.2. Nurturing Long-Term Customer Relationships

Nurturing long-term customer relationships is a critical aspect of effective customer retention strategies. In the 6.0 era, where customer expectations are high and competition is fierce, building lasting connections with customers goes beyond mere transactions. It involves a holistic approach that prioritizes customer satisfaction, engagement, and loyalty throughout the entire customer journey. The foundation of nurturing long-term customer relationships lies in delivering exceptional customer experiences. From the first interaction to post-purchase support, every touch point should be optimized to exceed customer expectations. This entails providing prompt and personalized service, anticipating customer needs, and addressing issues with empathy and efficiency. Consistently positive experiences contribute to the development of trust and a positive brand perception, fostering a sense of loyalty. Effective communication is key to nurturing long-term relationships. Regularly engaging with customers through various channels, such as email newsletters, social media, or personalized messages, helps in staying top-of-mind. Communication should extend beyond transactional updates to include valuable content, special offers, and relevant information that adds value to the customer's experience. This ongoing dialogue contributes to the development of a deeper connection and ensures that customers feel appreciated and informed. Building a loyalty program is a tangible way to reward and incentivize repeat business. Loyalty programs offer perks, discounts, or exclusive access to loyal customers, encouraging them to continue choosing the brand. These programs can be tailored to match customer preferences and behaviors, providing a personalized touch. By demonstrating appreciation for loyalty, businesses create a reciprocal relationship where customers are more likely to stick with the brand in the long run. Implementing customer feedback mechanisms is crucial for nurturing long-term relationships (Pansari & Kumar, 2018). Actively seeking and listening to customer feedback, whether through surveys, reviews, or direct interactions, shows a commitment to improvement and customer satisfaction. Analyzing feedback helps identify areas for enhancement and allows businesses to demonstrate responsiveness to customer concerns, fostering a sense of partnership and mutual growth. Personalization is a cornerstone of effective long-term relationship building. Utilizing customer data to tailor product recommendations, communications, and offers demonstrates a deep understanding of individual preferences. Whether through personalized emails, targeted advertising, or custom product suggestions, businesses can create a more intimate and relevant experience, strengthening the emotional connection with customers (Parasuraman et al., 2018; Payne et al., 2013). Strategic customer retention initiatives involve proactively addressing potential issues before they escalate. This includes predictive customer service, where businesses use data and analytics to anticipate customer needs and resolve problems before customers even reach out. By taking a proactive stance, businesses not only prevent potential churn but also showcase their commitment to customer satisfaction.

9. THE ROLE OF ARTIFICIAL INTELLIGENCE IN MARKETING 6.0

9.1. AI-Driven Marketing Automation

AI-driven marketing automation has emerged as a transformative force in the realm of marketing, playing a pivotal role in shaping the landscape of Marketing 6.0. This advanced technology leverages artificial intelligence algorithms to automate various marketing processes, allowing for enhanced efficiency, precision, and personalization. One key area where AI-driven marketing automation excels is in analyzing vast datasets to extract actionable insights. Through machine learning algorithms, marketers can gain a deep understanding of customer behaviors, preferences, and trends, facilitating data-driven decision-making. Personalization is a cornerstone of Marketing 6.0, and AI-driven marketing automation takes this to a new level. By analyzing individual customer data, AI algorithms can dynamically tailor content, recommendations, and interactions based on unique preferences and behaviors. This level of personalization goes beyond traditional segmentation, creating highly targeted and relevant experiences for each customer (Pine & Gilmore, 2013; Rai & Srivastava, 2018). From personalized emails to website content customization, AI-driven marketing automation ensures that every customer interaction is optimized for individual engagement. The efficiency gains provided by AI-driven marketing automation are substantial. Repetitive and time-consuming tasks, such as email campaigns, social media posting schedules, and lead scoring, can be automated with precision. This not only frees up valuable human resources but also ensures a level of consistency and accuracy that manual processes may struggle to maintain. Marketers can then focus on more strategic and creative aspects of their roles, while AI handles the routine tasks seamlessly. Lead nurturing and customer journey mapping are areas where AI-driven marketing automation excels. By analyzing past interactions and predicting future behaviors, AI algorithms can guide customers through a personalized journey, delivering content and offers at the most opportune moments. This level of sophistication ensures that each touchpoint contributes to the overall customer experience, maximizing the chances of conversion and retention. Predictive analytics is another powerful application of AI in marketing automation. By analyzing historical data and patterns, AI algorithms can predict future trends, behaviors, and market shifts. This foresight enables marketers to proactively adjust their strategies, ensuring they stay ahead in a rapidly evolving landscape. From predicting customer churn to forecasting product demand, AI-driven marketing automation empowers businesses with actionable intelligence (Nozari et al., 2024). Moreover, AI-driven marketing automation contributes to dynamic pricing strategies. Algorithms can analyze market conditions, competitor pricing, and customer behavior to determine optimal pricing structures in real-time. This agility allows businesses to remain competitive, maximize revenue, and respond swiftly to market changes. The result is a more adaptive and responsive pricing model that aligns with the dynamic nature of Marketing 6.0.

9.2. Chatbots and Virtual Assistants for Customer Engagement

In the era of Marketing 6.0, chatbots and virtual assistants have emerged as indispensable tools for customer engagement, demonstrating the transformative influence of artificial intelligence (AI) on marketing strategies. These AI-powered conversational agents offer businesses the ability to provide instantaneous and personalized interactions with customers across various touchpoints. Chatbots, often integrated into websites or messaging platforms, act as the first line of customer support, offering quick responses to queries, guiding users through product information, and even facilitating transactions. Virtual assistants, on the other hand, take customer engagement a step further, embodying a more sophisticated level of AI that understands natural language and context, allowing for more complex interactions.

One of the primary advantages of chatbots and virtual assistants is their availability 24/7, providing customers with instant responses and assistance irrespective of the time zone or business hours. This immediate accessibility contributes to enhanced customer satisfaction, as users can obtain information or resolve issues promptly, fostering a positive perception of the brand. Moreover, the scalability of these AI-driven solutions allows businesses to handle a high volume of inquiries simultaneously, ensuring efficiency in customer interactions even during peak periods. The personalization capabilities of chatbots and virtual assistants significantly contribute to improved customer engagement. These AI tools can analyze user data, preferences, and behaviors to deliver tailored recommendations, responses, and offers. By understanding individual customer needs, chatbots and virtual assistants create a more personalized and relevant experience, thereby strengthening the customer-brand relationship. Personalized interactions foster a sense of understanding and appreciation, increasing the likelihood of customer loyalty and retention. Additionally, chatbots and virtual assistants play a crucial role in streamlining customer journeys. From guiding users through product selection to assisting with the purchase process, these AI-driven tools provide a seamless and efficient experience. Integration with e-commerce platforms allows customers to make purchases, track orders, and receive support within the same conversational interface. This cohesive journey contributes to a positive customer experience and influences the overall perception of the brand. The continuous learning capabilities of chatbots and virtual assistants further enhance their effectiveness in customer engagement. Through machine learning algorithms, these AI solutions evolve over time, learning from interactions, customer feedback, and data trends. This iterative learning process enables them to continuously improve their responses and recommendations, ensuring relevance and accuracy in addressing customer inquiries.

10. MEASURING CUSTOMER-CENTRIC SUCCESS

Measuring customer-centric success is a multifaceted process that goes beyond traditional key performance indicators (KPIs) and requires a comprehensive understanding of customer satisfaction, loyalty, and overall experience (Reinartz & Ulaga, 2016). In the era of customer-centricity, businesses are increasingly recognizing the need to focus on metrics that directly reflect their commitment to meeting customer needs and delivering exceptional experiences. Several key metrics and methodologies are employed to gauge customer-centric success:

Net Promoter Score (NPS): NPS is a widely used metric that measures customer loyalty and satisfaction by asking customers a simple question: "How likely is it that you would recommend our company/product/service to a friend or colleague?" Responses are categorized into promoters, passives, and detractors. A high NPS indicates a strong customer-centric approach, as it reflects a higher likelihood of customers recommending the brand.

Customer Satisfaction (CSAT) Score: CSAT measures overall customer satisfaction with a product, service, or interaction. Customers are asked to rate their satisfaction on a numerical scale. Monitoring CSAT scores provides a snapshot of customer sentiment and helps businesses identify areas for improvement.

Customer Effort Score (CES): CES measures the ease with which customers can accomplish a task, such as making a purchase or resolving an issue. Lowering customer effort is a key aspect of a customer-centric approach, as it indicates a commitment to delivering a seamless and convenient experience.

Customer Lifetime Value (CLV): CLV assesses the total revenue a business can reasonably expect from a customer throughout their entire relationship. A customer-centric strategy aims to not only acquire customers but also maximize their long-term value through loyalty and repeat business.

Retention Rate: A high customer retention rate is indicative of a customer-centric strategy. It measures the percentage of customers that a business retains over a specific period, highlighting the effectiveness of efforts to keep customers engaged and satisfied.

Churn Rate: Conversely, the churn rate reflects the percentage of customers who stop doing business with a company within a given period. A lower churn rate signifies successful customer-centric initiatives, as it indicates that customers are less likely to abandon the brand.

Customer Feedback and Reviews: Monitoring customer feedback on various platforms and analyzing reviews provides qualitative insights into customer satisfaction. Positive reviews and constructive feedback signal that the business is meeting customer expectations.

Customer Journey Analytics: Analyzing the entire customer journey helps identify pain points, areas for improvement, and moments that contribute positively to the customer experience. Understanding the customer journey enables businesses to align their strategies with customer expectations.

Social Media Mentions and Sentiment Analysis: Tracking mentions on social media platforms and employing sentiment analysis tools allows businesses to gauge how customers perceive their brand online. Positive sentiment and active engagement reflect a customer-centric approach.

Employee Satisfaction: Recognizing the link between employee satisfaction and customer satisfaction is essential. Satisfied employees are more likely to deliver better customer service, creating a positive feedback loop that contributes to customer-centric success.

11. ADAPTING TO FUTURE TRENDS

11.1. Emerging Technologies and Trends in Marketing

Adapting to future trends in marketing requires a keen awareness of emerging technologies that shape consumer behaviors and expectations. One significant trend is the rise of Artificial Intelligence (AI) and machine learning, which empowers marketers to analyze vast datasets, predict customer preferences, and deliver highly personalized experiences. Chatbots and virtual assistants, powered by AI, are becoming increasingly sophisticated, enhancing customer interactions and automating various facets of customer service. Augmented Reality (AR) and Virtual Reality (VR) are gaining prominence, allowing businesses to create immersive and engaging experiences for consumers, especially in the e-commerce sector where AR enables virtual try-ons and product visualization (Sheth & Sisodia, 2018). Voice search optimization is becoming crucial as more users rely on voice-activated devices like smart speakers and virtual assistants, altering traditional SEO practices. Influencer marketing continues to evolve, with nano and micro-influencers gaining significance for their highly engaged, niche audiences. Data privacy and ethical considerations in marketing practices are also emerging trends, emphasizing the importance of transparent and responsible data usage. Embracing these emerging technologies and trends positions businesses to stay ahead of the curve, connect with their audience in innovative ways, and adapt to the dynamic landscape of future marketing.

11.2. Staying Ahead in the Ever-Evolving Marketing Landscape

Staying ahead in the ever-evolving marketing landscape necessitates a proactive and adaptive approach that embraces emerging trends and technologies. One key strategy involves keeping a pulse on consumer behavior and preferences through data analytics and market research. Understanding the shifts in customer expectations allows marketers to tailor their strategies accordingly. Embracing technological advancements, such as Artificial Intelligence (AI), machine learning, and automation, enables businesses to streamline operations, personalize customer experiences, and optimize marketing efforts. Additionally, staying agile in content creation and distribution is vital as trends in video content, interactive experiences, and virtual engagement methods continue to evolve. Building a robust online presence and maintaining an active social media strategy helps businesses stay connected with their audience and react promptly to changing trends (Tariq & Syed, 2018). Investing in continuous learning and professional development keeps marketing teams equipped with the skills needed to navigate the latest tools and strategies. Collaboration with industry leaders, attending conferences, and networking further provide insights into upcoming trends and best practices. Overall, staying ahead requires a combination of strategic foresight, technological adoption, and a commitment to ongoing learning and innovation in the ever-changing marketing landscape.

12. EXAMPLES IN CUSTOMER-CENTRIC EXCELLENCE

Customer-centric excellence is exemplified by businesses that prioritize customer satisfaction, anticipate needs, and create exceptional experiences. A prominent example is Amazon, known for its relentless focus on customer-centricity. The company excels in providing a seamless online shopping experience, offering personalized recommendations based on previous purchases and user behavior. Their customer-centric approach extends to quick and reliable delivery services, hassle-free return policies, and responsive customer support. By prioritizing customer satisfaction, Amazon has built a loyal customer base. Another exemplar is Zappos, an online shoe and clothing retailer. Zappos is renowned for its outstanding customer service, which goes beyond traditional norms. The company encourages its representatives to engage with customers genuinely, aiming not just to resolve issues but also to build positive, lasting relationships. They empower their customer service team to spend ample time on calls, providing a human touch and ensuring customers feel heard and valued. In the airline industry, Southwest Airlines stands out for its customer-centric practices. They prioritize transparency and simplicity in their policies, offering features like no change fees and baggage fees. Southwest consistently ranks high in customer satisfaction, emphasizing a people-centric approach both in serving customers and treating employees well. This dedication to a positive experience contributes to their strong brand loyalty. Starbucks is another notable example of customer-centric excellence. The coffee giant not only focuses on delivering a quality product but also on creating a welcoming and personalized environment (Nozari, 2024). Their mobile app allows customers to order ahead, earn rewards, and receive personalized offers based on previous purchases. This approach extends to in-store interactions, where baristas often remember and use customers' names, fostering a sense of connection. In the tech industry, Apple is recognized for its commitment to user experience. From the sleek design of their products to the user-friendly interfaces, Apple prioritizes creating an enjoyable and intuitive experience for customers. Their customer-centric approach is evident in features like the Apple Genius Bar, where customers can receive personalized technical support and assistance. These examples showcase that customer-centric excellence spans various industries and manifests in different ways. Whether through personalized services, transparent policies, outstanding customer support, or a focus on creating delightful experiences, businesses that prioritize their customers tend to foster loyalty, positive word-of-mouth, and long-term success in the ever-evolving marketplace.

13. CHALLENGES AND SOLUTIONS IN THE 6.0 ERA

- **Data Privacy Concerns:** As businesses gather more customer data for personalized marketing, there's a growing concern about data privacy. Customers are becoming more conscious of how their data is collected, stored, and utilized.
- **Information Overload:** The digital age inundates consumers with an abundance of information, making it challenging for businesses to capture and retain their audience's attention amidst the noise.
- **Rapid Technological Changes:** The speed at which technology evolves in Marketing 6.0 poses a challenge for businesses to adapt quickly. Staying abreast of emerging technologies and incorporating them into marketing strategies can be demanding.
- **Fragmented Customer Journey:** With customers interacting with brands across various touch points, creating a cohesive and seamless customer journey is challenging. Maintaining consistency and relevance across channels is crucial but often difficult to achieve.
- **Increasing Competition:** The ease of entry into digital spaces has led to a surge in competition. Businesses must find innovative ways to differentiate themselves and stand out amid a crowded marketplace.

Solutions in the Marketing 6.0 Era:

- **Transparent Data Practices:** Addressing data privacy concerns involves being transparent about how customer data is collected and used. Implementing stringent security measures and complying with data protection regulations builds trust with consumers.
- **Content Personalization:** To combat information overload, businesses can leverage AI to personalize content delivery. Tailoring messages to individual preferences ensures that customers receive relevant and engaging content, cutting through the noise.
- **Agile Marketing Strategies:** Rapid technological changes require businesses to adopt agile marketing strategies. This involves staying informed about industry trends, investing in employee training, and being ready to pivot strategies based on emerging technologies.

- **Unified Customer Experience:** Creating a seamless customer journey involves integrating various channels. Utilizing tools like Customer Relationship Management (CRM) systems helps businesses track interactions across platforms, providing a unified view of the customer.
- **Unique Value Proposition:** Facing increased competition, businesses need to articulate a unique value proposition. This involves identifying what sets them apart and communicating it effectively to their target audience. Differentiation can come from innovative products, exceptional customer service, or sustainable business practices.

14. CONCLUSION

Achieving customer-centric excellence in the Marketing 6.0 era is not merely a strategy but a fundamental necessity for sustained success. As businesses navigate the dynamic landscape characterized by rapid technological advancements, data-driven insights, and heightened customer expectations, prioritizing the customer becomes a guiding principle. The examples of customer-centric leaders such as Amazon, Zappos, Southwest Airlines, Starbucks, and Apple underscore the significance of aligning marketing practices with customer needs and preferences. By embracing personalization, delivering exceptional experiences, and fostering genuine connections, businesses can build enduring relationships that go beyond transactions. In this era of heightened competition and evolving consumer behaviors, customer-centric excellence emerges not only as a differentiator but as an imperative for businesses aiming to thrive and prosper in the Marketing 6.0 era.

REFERENCES

Anderson, H., & Jacobson, P. (2000). Creating loyalty: Its strategic importance in your customer strategy. *Customer Relationship Management, 55*.

Consoli, D., & Musso, F. (2010). Marketing 2.0: A new marketing strategy. *Journal of International Scientific Publications: Economy & Business*, *4*, 315–325.

DeTienne, K. B., Ellertson, C. F., Ingerson, M. C., & Dudley, W. R. (2021). Moral development in business ethics: An examination and critique. *Journal of Business Ethics*, *170*(3), 429–448. doi:10.1007/s10551-019-04351-0

Erragcha, N., & Romdhane, R. (2014). New faces of marketing in the era of the web: From marketing 1.0 to marketing 3.0. *Journal of Research in Marketing*, *2*(2), 137–142. doi:10.17722/jorm.v2i2.46

Fornell, C., Morgeson, F. V. III, Hult, G. T. M., & VanAmburg, D. (2020). *The Reign of the Customer: Customer-Centric Approaches to Improving Satisfaction.* Springer Nature. doi:10.1007/978-3-030-13562-1

Kartajaya, H., Kotler, P., & Hooi, D. H. (2019). Marketing 4.0: Moving from traditional to digital. World Scientific Book Chapters, 99-123.

Kotler, P. (2007). *Marketing Management* (11th ed.). Pearson Education Asia LTD and Tsinghua University Press.

Kudeshia, C., & Mittal, A. (2015). The journey of Chumbak: From mail to mall – leveraging social media networks for on-going dialogue with customers. *Emerald Emerging Markets Case Studies*, *5*(4), 1–20. doi:10.1108/EEMCS-09-2014-0209

Kudeshia, C., & Mittal, A. (2016). The effect of eWOM on brand attitude and purchase intention of consumers: A cross-sectional study on consumer electronics. *International Journal of Internet Marketing and Advertising*, *10*(3), 131–151. doi:10.1504/IJIMA.2016.080162

Lemon, K. N., & Verhoef, P. C. (2016). Understanding customer experience throughout the customer journey. *Journal of Marketing*, *80*(6), 69–96. doi:10.1509/jm.15.0420

Li, X., & Hitt, L. M. (2018). How social media and big data analytics generate marketing insights. *Journal of Advertising Research*, *58*(1), 81–85.

Lommeruda, K. E., & Sørgard, L. (2003). Entry in telecommunication: Customer loyalty, price-sensitive and access prices. *Information Economics and Policy*, *15*(1), 55–72. doi:10.1016/S0167-6245(02)00086-0

Malthouse, E. C., & Hofacker, C. F. (2018). Looking back and looking forward on the twenty-fifth anniversary of "Integrated Marketing Communications: Putting it together and making it work". *Journal of Advertising*, *47*(1), 3–12.

Martin-Consuegra, D., Molina, A., & Esteban, A. (2007). An integrated model of price, satisfaction, and loyalty: An empirical analysis in the service sector. *Journal of Product and Brand Management*, *16*(7), 459–468.

Nair, N., Jayachandran, S., & Park, M. (2022). Digital customer engagement, customer satisfaction, and loyalty: Evidence from US retail industry. *Journal of Retailing and Consumer Services*, *66*, 102895.

Nozari, H. (2024). Supply Chain 6.0 and Moving Towards Hyper-Intelligent Processes. In Information Logistics for Organizational Empowerment and Effective Supply Chain Management (pp. 1-13). IGI Global.

Nozari, H., Szmelter-Jarosz, A., & Rahmaty, M. (2024). Smart Marketing Based on Artificial Intelligence of Things (AIoT) and Blockchain and Evaluating Critical Success Factors. In Smart and Sustainable Interactive Marketing (pp. 68-82). IGI Global.

Oliver, R. L. (1997). *Satisfaction: A Behavioral Perspective on the Consumer.* McGraw Hill.

Pansari, A., & Kumar, V. (2018). Customer engagement: The construct, antecedents, and consequences. *Journal of the Academy of Marketing Science, 46*(2), 252–270.

Parasuraman, A., Zeithaml, V. A., & Berry, L. L. (2018). A conceptual model of service quality and its implications for future research. *Journal of Marketing, 49*(4), 41–50. doi:10.1177/002224298504900403

Patterson, P. G., & Spreng, R. A. (1997). Modelling the relationship between perceived value, satisfaction, and repurchase intentions in a business-to-business, services context: An empirical examination. *International Journal of Service Industry Management, 8*(5), 414–434. doi:10.1108/09564239710189835

Payne, A., Storbacka, K., & Frow, P. (2013). Managing the co-creation of value. *Journal of the Academy of Marketing Science, 41*(2), 133–150.

Perreault, J., McCarthy, E. J., Parkinsen, S., & Stewda, K. (2000). *Basic Marketing.* McGraw Hill.

Pine, B. J., & Gilmore, J. H. (2013). *The experience economy: Work is theatre & every business a stage.* Harvard Business Press.

Rai, A. K., & Srivastava, R. K. (2018). Role of social media engagement in creating brand experience and loyalty. Vision. *The Journal of Business Perspective, 22*(3), 311–322.

Reichheld, F., Markey, R. G. J., & Hopton, C. (2000). The loyalty effect: The relationship between loyalty and profits. *European Business Journal, 12*, 134–139.

Reinartz, W. J., & Ulaga, W. (2016). How to sell services more profitably. *Harvard Business Review, 94*(3), 90–97. PMID:18543811

Schnatz, J., Guerrero-Ruiz, A., & Sachin, K. (2022). *Aligning development co-operation to the SDGs in lower middle-income countries: A case study of Bangladesh (No. 105)*. OECD Publishing.

Sheth, J. N., Mittal, B., & Newman, B. I. (1999). *Customer Behaviour: Consumer Behaviour and Beyond*. Dryden.

Sheth, J. N., & Sisodia, R. S. (2018). The future of marketing is human. *Journal of Business Research*, *86*, 374–376.

Tariq, S., & Syed, J. (2018). Impact of customer-centric marketing on customer loyalty: Moderating role of customer involvement. *Journal of Marketing and Consumer Research*, *46*, 10–18.

Thomas, M. R., & Shivani, M. P. (2020). Customer profiling of alpha: The next generation marketing. *Ushus Journal of Business Management*, *19*(1), 75–86.

Treviño, L. K., Den Nieuwenboer, N. A., & Kish-Gephart, J. J. (2014). (Un)ethical behavior in organizations. *Annual Review of Psychology*, *65*(1), 635–660. doi:10.1146/annurev-psych-113011-143745 PMID:23834354

Westberg, J., & Jason, H. (2004). *Fostering Learning in Small Groups: A Practical Guide*. Springer Publishing Company.

Xia, L., Monroe, K., & Cox, J. (2004). The price is unfair! A conceptual framework of price fairness perceptions. *Journal of Marketing*, *68*(4), 1–15. doi:10.1509/jmkg.68.4.1.42733

Compilation of References

. Singh, K. (2023). Evaluation Planning for Artificial Intelligence-based Industry 6.0 Metaverse Integration. *Intelligent Human Systems Integration (IHSI 2023): Integrating People and Intelligent Systems, 69*(69).

Adam, P. (2022). Blockchain technology and smart contracts in decentralized governance systems. *Administrative Sciences, 12*(3), 96.

Ahmadi, S. (2023). Open AI and its Impact on Fraud Detection in Financial Industry. Academic Press.

Ahmed, G. (2022). Emerging trends in blockchain technology and applications: A review and outlook. *Journal of King Saud University. Computer and Information Sciences, 34*(9), 6719–6742. doi:10.1016/j.jksuci.2022.03.007

Albreem, M. A., Sheikh, A. M., Bashir, M. J., & El-Saleh, A. A. (2023). Towards green Internet of Things (IoT) for a sustainable future in Gulf Cooperation Council countries: Current practices, challenges and future prospective. *Wireless Networks, 29*(2), 539–567. doi:10.1007/s11276-022-03133-3

Al-Hashedi, K. G., & Magalingam, P. (2021). Financial fraud detection applying data mining techniques: A comprehensive review from 2009 to 2019. *Computer Science Review, 40*, 40. doi:10.1016/j.cosrev.2021.100402

Ali, T. A., Choksi, V., & Potdar, M. B. (2018, May). Precision agriculture monitoring system using green internet of things (g-iot). In *2018 2nd International Conference on Trends in Electronics and Informatics (ICOEI)* (pp. 481-487). IEEE.

Aliahmadi, A., Movahed, A. B., & Nozari, H. (2024). Collaboration Analysis in Supply Chain 4.0 for Smart Businesses. In Building Smart and Sustainable Businesses With Transformative Technologies (pp. 103-122). IGI Global.

Aliahmadi, A., Nozari, H., Ghahremani-Nahr, J., & Szmelter-Jarosz, A. (2022). Evaluation of key impression of resilient supply chain based on artificial intelligence of things (AIoT). *arXiv preprint arXiv:2207.13174.*

Aliahmadi, Bakhshi Movahed, & Nozari. (2023). Collaboration Analysis in Supply Chain 4.0 for Smart Businesses. In Building Smart and Sustainable Businesses With Transformative Technologies (pp. 103-122). IGI Global.

Aliahmadi, A., Bakhshi-Movahed, A., & Nozari, H. (2023). Collaboration analysis in supply chain 4.0 for smart businesses. In *Building Smart and Sustainable Businesses with Transformative Technologies* (pp. 103–122). IGI Global. doi:10.4018/979-8-3693-0210-1.ch007

Aliahmadi, A., Ghahremani-Nahr, J., & Nozari, H. (2023). Pricing decisions in the closed-loop supply chain network, taking into account the queuing system in production centers. *Expert Systems with Applications, 212*, 118741. doi:10.1016/j.eswa.2022.118741

Aliahmadi, A., & Nozari, H. (2023, January). Evaluation of security metrics in AIoT and blockchain-based supply chain by Neutrosophic decision-making method. In *Supply Chain Forum* []. Taylor & Francis.]. *International Journal (Toronto, Ont.), 24*(1), 31–42.

Almusaed, A., Yitmen, I., & Almssad, A. (2023). Reviewing and integrating aec practices into industry 6.0: Strategies for smart and sustainable future-built environments. *Sustainability (Basel), 15*(18), 13464. doi:10.3390/su151813464

Alshamrani, M. (2022). IoT and artificial intelligence implementations for remote healthcare monitoring systems: A survey. *Journal of King Saud University. Computer and Information Sciences, 34*(8), 4687–4701. doi:10.1016/j.jksuci.2021.06.005

AlShamsi, M., Al-Emran, M., & Shaalan, K. (2022). A systematic review on blockchain adoption. *Applied Sciences (Basel, Switzerland), 12*(9), 4245. doi:10.3390/app12094245

Anderson, H., & Jacobson, P. (2000). Creating loyalty: Its strategic importance in your customer strategy. *Customer Relationship Management, 55.*

Ansar, S. A., Arya, S., Aggrawal, S., Yadav, J., & Pathak, P. C. (2022). Bitcoin-blockchain technology: Security perspective. In *2022 3rd International Conference on Intelligent Engineering and Management (ICIEM)*. IEEE.

Aripin, Z., Paramarta, V., & Kosasih. (2023). Utilizing the Internet of Things (IoT)-based Design for Consumer Loyalty: A Digital System Integration. *Jurnal Penelitian Pendidikan IPA, 9*(10), 8650–8655. doi:10.29303/jppipa.v9i10.4490

Aripin, Z., Saepudin, D., & Yulianty, F. (2024, February). Transformation in the internet of things (iot) market in the banking sector: A case study of technology implementation for service improvement and transaction security. *Journal of Jabar Economic Society Networking Forum, 1*(3), 17–32.

Aristantia, V., & Liu, A. Y. (2023, July). Study of the Influence of Augmented Reality Toward Consumer's Satisfaction and Repurchase Intention. In *3rd International Conference on Business and Engineering Management (ICONBEM 2022)* (pp. 51-63). Atlantis Press. 10.2991/978-94-6463-216-3_5

Asbaghi, O., Nazarian, B., Yousefi, M., Anjom-Shoae, J., Rasekhi, H., & Sadeghi, O. (2023). Effect of vitamin E intake on glycemic control and insulin resistance in diabetic patients: An updated systematic review and meta-analysis of randomized controlled trials. *Nutrition Journal*, *22*(1), 1–22. doi:10.1186/s12937-023-00840-1 PMID:36800965

Awoyemi, J. O., Adetunmbi, A. O., & Oluwadare, S. A. (2017). Credit card fraud detection using machine learning techniques: A comparative analysis. *International Conference on Computing Networking and Informatics (ICCNI)*. 10.1109/ICCNI.2017.8123782

Badr Qorany Mohamed, H. (2023). Determinants of the formation of consumer attitudes towards advertisements via the TikTok and Instagram platforms in light of the advertising value model: A qualitative comparative study. *The Arab Journal of Media and Communication Research*, *2023*(42), 349–380.

Bakator, M., Vukoja, M., & Manestar, D. (2023). Achieving competitiveness with Marketing 5.0 in new business conditions. *UTMS Journal of Economics (Skopje)*, *14*(1).

Bakhshi-Movahed, A., Aliahmadi, A., Parsanejad, M., & Nozari, H. (2023). A systematic review of collaboration in supply chain 4.0 with meta-synthesis method. *Supply Chain Analytics*, 100052.

Bakhshi-Movahed, A., Bakhshi-Movahed, A., & Nozari, H. (2024). Opportunities and challenges of smart supply chain in Industry 5.0. *Information Logistics for Organizational Empowerment and Effective Supply Chain Management*, 108-138.

Balakrishnan, J. (2022). Building capabilities for future of work in the gig economy. *NHRD Network Journal*, *15*(1), 56–70. doi:10.1177/26314541211064726

Barbosa, B., Saura, J. R., Zekan, S. B., & Ribeiro-Soriano, D. (2023). Defining content marketing and its influence on online user behavior: A data-driven prescriptive analytics method. *Annals of Operations Research*, 1–26. doi:10.1007/s10479-023-05261-1

Barman, S., Pal, U., Sarfaraj, M. A., Biswas, B., Mahata, A., & Mandal, P. (2016). A complete literature review on financial fraud detection applying data mining techniques. *International Journal of Trust Management in Computing and Communications*, *3*(4), 336–359. doi:10.1504/IJTMCC.2016.084561

Barrios, M., Guilera, G., Nuño, L., & Gómez-Benito, J. (2021). Consensus in the Delphi method: What makes a decision change? *Technological Forecasting and Social Change*, *163*, 120484. doi:10.1016/j.techfore.2020.120484

Bashir, I. (2017). *Mastering blockchain*. Packt Publishing Ltd.

Bathaee, M., Nozari, H., & Szmelter-Jarosz, A. (2023). Designing a new location-allocation and routing model with simultaneous pick-up and delivery in a closed-loop supply chain network under uncertainty. *Logistics*, *7*(1), 3. doi:10.3390/logistics7010003

Bauder, R. A., & Khoshgoftaar, T. M. (2017). Medicare Fraud Detection Using Machine Learning Methods. *16th IEEE International Conference on Machine Learning and Applications*, 8. 10.1109/ICMLA.2017.00-48

Beck, R., Czepluch, J. S., Lollike, N., & Malone, S. (2016). Blockchain–the gateway to trust-free cryptographic transactions. In *Twenty-Fourth European Conference on Information Systems (ECIS), I˙stanbul, Turkey, 2016*. Springer Publishing Company.

Bego, L. L., & Mattos, C. A. D. (2024). The interplay between agile manufacturing and the Internet of Things. *International Journal of Agile Systems and Management*, *17*(1), 106–128. doi:10.1504/IJASM.2024.135379

Bharadiya, J. P. (2023). A Comparative Study of Business Intelligence and Artificial Intelligence with Big Data Analytics. *American Journal of Artificial Intelligence*, *7*(1), 24.

Bhattacharyya, S., Jha, S., Tharakunnel, K., & Westland, J. C. (2011). Data mining for credit card fraud: A comparative study. *Decision Support Systems*, *50*(3), 602–613. doi:10.1016/j.dss.2010.08.008

BindseilU. (2020). Tiered CBDC and the financial system. Available at SSRN 3513422.

Bryndin, E. (2023). Development of Artificial Intelligence of Ensembles of Software and Hardware Agents by Natural Intelligence on the Basis of Self-Organization. *Journal of Research in Engineering and Computer Sciences*, *1*(4), 93–105. doi:10.56397/JRSSH.2023.10.02

Çalık, A. (2020). Evaluation of social media platforms using Best-Worst method and fuzzy VIKOR methods: A Case Study of Travel Agency. *Iranian Journal of Management Studies*, *13*(4), 645–672.

Casino, F., Kanakaris, V., Dasaklis, T. K., Moschuris, S., & Rachaniotis, N. P. (2019). Modeling food supply chain traceability based on blockchain technology. *IFAC-PapersOnLine*, *52*(13), 2728–2733. doi:10.1016/j.ifacol.2019.11.620

Castro, M., & Liskov, B. (1999). Practical byzantine fault tolerance. OsDI, 99, 173–186.

Chaffey, D., & Smith, P. R. (2022). *Digital marketing excellence: planning, optimizing and integrating online marketing*. Taylor & Francis. doi:10.4324/9781003009498

Chaitanya, K., Saha, G. C., Saha, H., Acharya, S., & Singla, M. (2023). The Impact of Artificial Intelligence and Machine Learning in Digital Marketing Strategies. *European Economic Letters*, *13*(3), 982–992.

Charles, S. (2023). *Blueprint*. Academic Press.

Chen, C. T. (2000). Extensions of the TOPSIS for group decision-making under fuzzy environment. *Fuzzy Sets and Systems*, *114*(1), 1–9. doi:10.1016/S0165-0114(97)00377-1

Chen, S. J., & Hwang, C. L. (1992). Fuzzy multiple attribute decision making methods. In *Fuzzy multiple attribute decision making: Methods and applications* (pp. 289–486). Springer Berlin Heidelberg. doi:10.1007/978-3-642-46768-4_5

Chen, Y., Lu, Y., Bulysheva, L., & Kataev, M. Y. (2022). Applications of blockchain in industry 4.0: A review. *Information Systems Frontiers*, 1–15. doi:10.1007/s10796-022-10248-7

Cherukuri, P. A. A., Vududala, S. K., Saraswathi, N. R., & Sanda, J. (2020). *AI-based Strategic Marketing*. SMAI Model. In ICRMAT.

Chiu, J., & Thorsten, V. (2022). The economics of cryptocurrency: Bitcoin and beyond. *The Canadian Journal of Economics. Revue Canadienne d'Economique*, *55*(4), 1762–1798. doi:10.1111/caje.12625

Chourasia, S., Pandey, S. M., & Keshri, A. K. (2023). Prospects and Challenges with Legal Informatics and Legal Metrology Framework in the Context of Industry 6.0. *MAPAN*, 1-26.

Chourasia, S., Tyagi, A., Pandey, S. M., Walia, R. S., & Murtaza, Q. (2022). Sustainability of Industry 6.0 in global perspective: Benefits and challenges. *MPAN. Journal of Metrology Society of India*, *37*(2), 443–452. doi:10.1007/s12647-022-00541-w

Christodoulou, E., & Iordanou, K. (2021). Democracy under attack: Challenges of addressing ethical issues of AI and big data for more democratic digital media and societies. *Frontiers in Political Science*, *3*, 682945. doi:10.3389/fpos.2021.682945

Chung, M., & Kim, J. (2016). The internet information and technology research directions based on the fourth industrial revolution. *KSII Transactions on Internet and Information Systems*, *10*(3), 1311–1320.

Collins, R. (2016). Blockchain: A new architecture for digital content. *EContent (Wilton, Conn.)*, *39*(8), 22–23.

Consoli, D., & Musso, F. (2010). Marketing 2.0: A new marketing strategy. *Journal of International Scientific Publications: Economy & Business*, *4*, 315–325.

Dalal, A. A., Al-qaness, M. A., Cai, Z., & Alawamy, E. A. (2023). IDA: Improving distribution analysis for reducing data complexity and dimensionality in hyperspectral images. *Pattern Recognition*, *134*, 109096. doi:10.1016/j.patcog.2022.109096

Darzi, M. A. (2024). Overcoming barriers to integrated management systems via developing guiding principles using G-AHP and F-TOPSIS. *Expert Systems with Applications*, *239*, 122305. doi:10.1016/j.eswa.2023.122305

De Veirman, M., Cauberghe, V., & Hudders, L. (2017). Marketing through Instagram influencers: The impact of number of followers and product divergence on brand attitude. *International Journal of Advertising*, *36*(5), 798–828. doi:10.1080/02650487.2017.1348035

Delgado, M., Marin, N., Sanchez, D., & Vila, M.-A. (2003). N.M., D. Sanchez, M. -A. Vila, *Fuzzy association rules: General model and applications. IEEE Transactions on Fuzzy Systems*, *11*(2), 11. doi:10.1109/TFUZZ.2003.809896

Deloitte. (2023). Thriving in the area of pervasive AI. Retrieved from https://www2.deloitte.com/content/dam/Deloitte/cn/Documents/about-deloitte/deloitte-cn-dtt-thriving-in-the-era-of-persuasive-ai-en-200819.pdf

Deng, Q. (2009). *Application of support vector machine in the detection of fraudulent financial statements. 2009 4th International Conference on Computer Science & Education.*

DeTienne, K. B., Ellertson, C. F., Ingerson, M. C., & Dudley, W. R. (2021). Moral development in business ethics: An examination and critique. *Journal of Business Ethics*, *170*(3), 429–448. doi:10.1007/s10551-019-04351-0

Diaz, E., Esteban, Á., Carranza Vallejo, R., & Martin-Consuegra Navarro, D. (2022). Digital tools and smart technologies in marketing: A thematic evolution. *International Marketing Review*, *39*(5), 1122–1150. doi:10.1108/IMR-12-2020-0307

Dizman, H. (2022). A Historical Review From Marketing 1.0 to Marketing 5.0. *Social Sciences Studies Journal (Sssjournal)*, *7*(87), 3866–3871. doi:10.26449/sssj.3412

Dovleac, L., Chiţu, I. B., Nichifor, E., & Brătucu, G. (2023). Shaping the Inclusivity in the New Society by Enhancing the Digitainability of Sustainable Development Goals with Education. *Sustainability (Basel)*, *15*(4), 3782. doi:10.3390/su15043782

Duivenvoorde, B. (2023). Consumer Protection in the Age of Personalised Marketing: Is EU Law Future-proof? *European Papers-A Journal on Law and Integration*, *2023*(2), 631–646.

Durukal, E. (2019). Change from Marketing 1.0 to Marketing 4.0. *İnsan ve Toplum Bilimleri Araştırmaları Dergisi*, 8(3), 1613-1633.

Dwivedi, Y. K., Ismagilova, E., Hughes, D. L., Carlson, J., Filieri, R., Jacobson, J., Jain, V., Karjaluoto, H., Kefi, H., Krishen, A. S., Kumar, V., Rahman, M. M., Raman, R., Rauschnabel, P. A., Rowley, J., Salo, J., Tran, G. A., & Wang, Y. (2021). Setting the future of digital and social media marketing research: Perspectives and research propositions. *International Journal of Information Management*, *59*, 102168. doi:10.1016/j.ijinfomgt.2020.102168

eCash. (n.d.). Wealth Redefined. https://e.cash/

Ekong Eyo, U. (2023). *Impact of Cyber-Security on Financial Fraud in Commercial Banks in Nigeria: A Case Study of Zenith Banks in Abuja* [Doctoral dissertation]. AUST.

ElFar, O.A., Chang, C.K., Leong, H.Y., Peter, A.P., Chew, K.W., & Show, P.L., 2021. Prospects of Industry 5.0 in algae: Customization of production and new advanced technology for clean bioenergy generation. *Energy Conversion and Management*: X, 10, p.100048.

Ellitan, L. (2020). Competing in the era of industrial revolution 4.0 and society 5.0. *Jurnal Maksipreneur: Manajemen, Koperasi, dan Entrepreneurship, 10*(1), 1-12.

Erragcha, N., & Romdhane, R. (2014). New faces of marketing in the era of the web: From marketing 1.0 to marketing 3.0. *Journal of Research in Marketing*, *2*(2), 137–142. doi:10.17722/jorm.v2i2.46

Ertuğrul, İ., & Karakaşoğlu, N. (2008). Comparison of fuzzy AHP and fuzzy TOPSIS methods for facility location selection. *International Journal of Advanced Manufacturing Technology*, *39*(7-8), 783–795. doi:10.1007/s00170-007-1249-8

Esmaelnezhad, D., Bahmani, J., Babgohari, A. Z., Taghizadeh-Yazdi, M., & Nazari-Shirkouhi, S. (2023). A fuzzy hybrid approach to analyse digital marketing strategies towards tourism industry. *International Journal of Tourism Policy*, *13*(5), 463–480. doi:10.1504/IJTP.2023.133201

Forde-Johnston, C., Butcher, D., & Aveyard, H. (2023). An integrative review exploring the impact of Electronic Health Records (EHR) on the quality of nurse–patient interactions and communication. *Journal of Advanced Nursing*, *79*(1), 48–67. doi:10.1111/jan.15484 PMID:36345050

Fornell, C., Morgeson, F. V. III, Hult, G. T. M., & VanAmburg, D. (2020). *The Reign of the Customer: Customer-Centric Approaches to Improving Satisfaction*. Springer Nature. doi:10.1007/978-3-030-13562-1

From, A. (n.d.). Humanoid Robots: A New Kind of Tool. Academic Press.

Gao, K., Liu, T., Yue, D., Simic, V., Rong, Y., & Garg, H. (2023). An Integrated Spherical Fuzzy Multi-criterion Group Decision-Making Approach and Its Application in Digital Marketing Technology Assessment. *International Journal of Computational Intelligence Systems*, *16*(1), 125. doi:10.1007/s44196-023-00298-3

Garbuio, M., & Lin, N. (2019). Artificial intelligence as a growth engine for health care startups: Emerging business models. *California Management Review*, *61*(2), 59–83. doi:10.1177/0008125618811931

Gerlich, M. (2023). The Power of Virtual Influencers: Impact on Consumer Behaviour and Attitudes in the Age of AI. *Administrative Sciences*, *13*(8), 178. doi:10.3390/admsci13080178

Ghahremani-Nahr, J., Najafi, S. E., & Nozari, H. (2022). A combined transportation model for the fruit and vegetable supply chain network. *Journal of Optimization in Industrial Engineering*, *15*(2), 131–145.

Ghahremani-Nahr, J., Nozari, H., Rahmaty, M., Zeraati Foukolaei, P., & Sherejsharifi, A. (2023). Development of a Novel Fuzzy Hierarchical Location-Routing Optimization Model Considering Reliability. *Logistics*, *7*(3), 64.

Gharaibeh, L., Eriksson, K. M., Lantz, B., Matarneh, S., & Elghaish, F. (2024). Toward digital construction supply chain-based Industry 4.0 solutions: Scientometric-thematic analysis. *Smart and Sustainable Built Environment*, *13*(1), 42–62. doi:10.1108/SASBE-12-2021-0224

Golovianko, M., Terziyan, V., Branytskyi, V., & Malyk, D. (2023). Industry 4.0 vs. Industry 5.0: Co-existence, Transition, or a Hybrid. *Procedia Computer Science*, *217*, 102–113. doi:10.1016/j.procs.2022.12.206

Greenspan, G. (2015). Multichain private blockchain-white paper. http://www. multichain. com/download/MultiChain-White-Paper. pdf

Groumpos, P. P. (2021). A critical historical and scientific overview of all industrial revolutions. *IFAC-PapersOnLine*, *54*(13), 464–471. doi:10.1016/j.ifacol.2021.10.492 PMID:38620687

Grubbs, F. E. (1969). Procedures for Detecting Outlying Observations in Samples. *Technometrics*, *11*(1), 21. doi:10.1080/00401706.1969.10490657

Haleem, A., Javaid, M., Qadri, M. A., Singh, R. P., & Suman, R. (2022). Artificial intelligence (AI) applications for marketing: A literature-based study. International Journal of Intelligent Networks.

Hammad, A. (2023). An improvement Of Blockchain and data mining in project Managemen. *International Journal of Computing and Digital Systems*, *14*(1), 1–xx.

Han, A., & Cai, Z. (2023, June). Design implications of generative AI systems for visual storytelling for young learners. In *Proceedings of the 22nd Annual ACM Interaction Design and Children Conference* (pp. 470-474). 10.1145/3585088.3593867

Han, H., & Trimi, S. (2018). A fuzzy TOPSIS method for performance evaluation of reverse logistics in social commerce platforms. *Expert Systems with Applications*, *103*, 133–145. doi:10.1016/j.eswa.2018.03.003

Hashemkhani Zolfani, S., Bazrafshan, R., Ecer, F., & Karamaşa, Ç. (2022). The suitability-feasibility-acceptability strategy integrated with Bayesian BWM-MARCOS methods to determine the optimal lithium battery plant located in South America. *Mathematics*, *10*(14), 2401. doi:10.3390/math10142401

Hazari, S., & Sethna, B. N. (2023). A Comparison of Lifestyle Marketing and Brand Influencer Advertising for Generation Z Instagram Users. *Journal of Promotion Management*, *29*(4), 491–534. doi:10.1080/10496491.2022.2163033

Hellani, H., Sliman, L., Samhat, A. E., & Exposito, E. (2021). On blockchain integration with supply chain: Overview on data transparency. *Logistics*, *5*(3), 46. doi:10.3390/logistics5030046

Herman, D., Googin, C., Liu, X., Sun, Y., Galda, A., Safro, I., ... Alexeev, Y. (2023). Quantum computing for finance. *Nature Reviews. Physics*, *5*(8), 450–465.

Hilal, W., Gadsden, S. A., & Yawney, J. (2022). Financial Fraud: A Review of Anomaly Detection Techniques and Recent Advances. *Expert Systems with Applications*, *193*, 193. doi:10.1016/j.eswa.2021.116429

Hongyan, J. (2024). Design and implementation of intelligent manufacturing system based on sensor networks and cloud computing technology. *Optical and Quantum Electronics*, *56*(3), 278. doi:10.1007/s11082-023-05923-1

Huang, L., Han, Y., Yuan, A., Xiao, T., Wang, L., Yu, Y., Zhang, X., Zhan, H., & Zhu, H. (2022). New business form of smart supply chain management based on "Internet of Things+Blockchain". *Mobile Information Systems*, *2022*, 2022. doi:10.1155/2022/1724029

Hura, A. (2022). Revealing consumer insights through visual analysis of social media images. *Journal of Digital & Social Media Marketing*, *10*(1), 69–75.

Hutson, J., & Cotroneo, P. (2023). Generative AI tools in art education: Exploring prompt engineering and iterative processes for enhanced creativity. Metaverse, 4(1).

Irani, H. R., & Nozari, H. (Eds.). (2024). *Smart and Sustainable Interactive Marketing*. IGI Global. doi:10.4018/979-8-3693-1339-8

Jaiganesh, S., Gunaseelan, K., & Ellappan, V. (2017, March). IOT agriculture to improve food and farming technology. In *2017 Conference on Emerging Devices and Smart Systems (ICEDSS)* (pp. 260-266). IEEE. 10.1109/ICEDSS.2017.8073690

Jaiwant, S. V. (2023). The Changing Role of Marketing: Industry 5.0-the Game Changer. In Transformation for Sustainable Business and Management Practices: Exploring the Spectrum of Industry 5.0 (pp. 187-202). Emerald Publishing Limited.

Jamil, F., Hang, L., Kim, K., & Kim, D. (2019). A novel medical blockchain model for drug supply chain integrity management in a smart hospital. *Electronics (Basel)*, 8(5), 505. doi:10.3390/electronics8050505

Jang, H., & Lee, J. (2017). An empirical study on modeling and prediction of bitcoin prices with bayesian neural networks based on blockchain information. *IEEE Access : Practical Innovations, Open Solutions*, 6, 5427–5437. doi:10.1109/ACCESS.2017.2779181

Jeyaraman, M., Nallakumarasamy, A., & Jeyaraman, N. (2022). Industry 5.0 in orthopaedics. *Indian Journal of Orthopaedics*, 56(10), 1694–1702. doi:10.1007/s43465-022-00712-6 PMID:36187596

Kannan, D., Khademolqorani, S., Janatyan, N., & Alavi, S. (2024). Smart waste management 4.0: The transition from a systematic review to an integrated framework. *Waste Management (New York, N.Y.)*, 174, 1–14. doi:10.1016/j.wasman.2023.08.041 PMID:37742441

Kartajaya, H., Kotler, P., & Hooi, D. H. (2019). Marketing 4.0: Moving from traditional to digital. World Scientific Book Chapters, 99-123.

Kazemi, A., Kazemi, Z., Heshmat, H., Nazarian-Jashnabadi, J., & Tomášková, H. (2024). Ranking factors affecting sustainable competitive advantage from the business intelligence perspective: Using content analysis and F-TOPSIS. *Journal of Soft Computing and Decision Analytics*, 2(1), 39–53. doi:10.31181/jscda21202430

Khan, I. S., Ahmad, M. O., & Majava, J. (2021). Industry 4.0 and sustainable development: A systematic mapping of triple bottom line, Circular Economy and Sustainable Business Models perspectives. *Journal of Cleaner Production*, 297, 126655. doi:10.1016/j.jclepro.2021.126655

Khatoon, N., Roy, S., & Narayan, R. Can ML Be Used in Cybersecurity? In Machine Learning in Healthcare and Security (pp. 174-183). CRC Press. doi:10.1201/9781003388845-15

Knezevic, D. (2018). Impact of blockchain technology platform in changing the financial sector and other industries. *Montenegrin Journal of Economics*, 14(1), 109–120. doi:10.14254/1800-5845/2018.14-1.8

Korucuk, S., Aytekin, A., Ecer, F., Karamaşa, Ç., & Zavadskas, E. K. (2022). Assessing green approaches and digital marketing strategies for twin transition via fermatean fuzzy SWARA-COPRAS. *Axioms*, 11(12), 709. doi:10.3390/axioms11120709

Koshariya, A. K., Kalaiyarasi, D., Jovith, A. A., Sivakami, T., Hasan, D. S., & Boopathi, S. (2023). Ai-enabled IoT and win-integrated smart agriculture system. In *Artificial Intelligence Tools and Technologies for Smart Farming and Agriculture Practices* (pp. 200–218). IGI Global. doi:10.4018/978-1-6684-8516-3.ch011

Kotler, P. (2007). *Marketing Management* (11th ed.). Pearson Education Asia LTD and Tsinghua University Press.

Kour, M., & Rani, K. (2023). Challenges and Opportunities to the Media and Entertainment Industry in Metaverse. Applications of Neuromarketing in the Metaverse, 88-102.

Kour, M. (2023), Blockchain Technology Changing Landscape of Banking Industry. *2nd International Conference on Applied Artificial Intelligence and Computing (ICAAIC)*, Salem, India, 2023, pp. 1212-1216, 10.1109/ICAAIC56838.2023.10140854

Kour, M., & Kaur, R. (2020). Impact of Social Media Marketing on Consumer Buying Behaviour: An Empirical Study. *International Journal of Advanced Science and Technology*, 29(11s), 975–984.

Kudeshia, C., & Mittal, A. (2015). The journey of Chumbak: From mail to mall – leveraging social media networks for on-going dialogue with customers. *Emerald Emerging Markets Case Studies*, 5(4), 1–20. doi:10.1108/EEMCS-09-2014-0209

Kudeshia, C., & Mittal, A. (2016). The effect of eWOM on brand attitude and purchase intention of consumers: A cross-sectional study on consumer electronics. *International Journal of Internet Marketing and Advertising*, 10(3), 131–151. doi:10.1504/IJIMA.2016.080162

Kumar, R., Kariminejad, A., Antonov, M., Goljandin, D., Klimczyk, P., & Hussainova, I. (2023). Progress in Sustainable Recycling and Circular Economy of Tungsten Carbide Hard Metal Scraps for Industry 5.0 and Onwards. *Sustainability (Basel)*, 15(16), 12249. doi:10.3390/su151612249

Lemon, K. N., & Verhoef, P. C. (2016). Understanding customer experience throughout the customer journey. *Journal of Marketing*, 80(6), 69–96. doi:10.1509/jm.15.0420

Leung, K. H., & Mo, D. Y. (2019, December). A fuzzy-AHP approach for strategic evaluation and selection of digital marketing tools. In 2019 IEEE international conference on industrial engineering and engineering management (IEEM) (pp. 1422-1426). IEEE. doi:10.1109/IEEM44572.2019.8978797

Li, X., & Ying, S. (2010). *Lib-SVMs Detection Model of Regulating-Profits Financial Statement Fraud Using Data of Chinese Listed Companies.* International Conference on E-Product E-Service and E-Entertainment, 4. 10.1109/ICEEE.2010.5660371

Li, X., & Hitt, L. M. (2018). How social media and big data analytics generate marketing insights. *Journal of Advertising Research*, 58(1), 81–85.

Lommeruda, K. E., & Sørgard, L. (2003). Entry in telecommunication: Customer loyalty, price-sensitive and access prices. *Information Economics and Policy*, 15(1), 55–72. doi:10.1016/S0167-6245(02)00086-0

Lou, C., & Yuan, S. (2019). Influencer marketing: How message value and credibility affect consumer trust of branded content on social media. *Journal of Interactive Advertising*, *19*(1), 58–73. doi:10.1080/15252019.2018.1533501

Low, S., Ullah, F., Shirowzhan, S., Sepasgozar, S. M., & Lin Lee, C. (2020). Smart digital marketing capabilities for sustainable property development: A case of Malaysia. *Sustainability (Basel)*, *12*(13), 5402. doi:10.3390/su12135402

Machkour, B., & Abriane, A. (2020). Industry 4.0 and its Implications for the Financial Sector. *Procedia Computer Science*, *177*, 496–502. doi:10.1016/j.procs.2020.10.068

Madushanki, A. R., Halgamuge, M. N., Wirasagoda, W. S., & Syed, A. (2019). Adoption of the Internet of Things (IoT) in agriculture and smart farming towards urban greening: A review. *International Journal of Advanced Computer Science and Applications*, *10*(4), 11–28. doi:10.14569/IJACSA.2019.0100402

Majeed, Y., Fu, L., & He, L. (2024). Artificial intelligence-of-things (AIoT) in precision agriculture. *Frontiers in Plant Science*, *15*, 1369791. doi:10.3389/fpls.2024.1369791 PMID:38344185

Makki, S. (2017). *Fraud Analysis Approaches in the Age of Big Data-A Review of State of the Art.* 2017 IEEE 2nd International Workshops on Foundations and Applications of Self* Systems, 17.

Malio, S. (2022). *Strengthening Humanitarian Disaster Response Value Chain Using Robotic Process Automation: a Case for World Food Programme* [Doctoral dissertation]. University of Nairobi.

Malthouse, E. C., & Hofacker, C. F. (2018). Looking back and looking forward on the twenty-fifth anniversary of "Integrated Marketing Communications: Putting it together and making it work". *Journal of Advertising*, *47*(1), 3–12.

Martin-Consuegra, D., Molina, A., & Esteban, A. (2007). An integrated model of price, satisfaction, and loyalty: An empirical analysis in the service sector. *Journal of Product and Brand Management*, *16*(7), 459–468.

McCartney, G., & McCartney, A. (2020). Rise of the machines: Towards a conceptual service-robot research framework for the hospitality and tourism industry. *International Journal of Contemporary Hospitality Management*, *32*(12), 3835–3851. doi:10.1108/IJCHM-05-2020-0450

McCulloch, W. S., & Pitts, W. (1943). A logical calculus of the ideas immanent in nervous activity. *The Bulletin of Mathematical Biophysics*, *5*(4), 19. doi:10.1007/BF02478259

Mehta, S. (2022). The Evolution of Marketing 1.0 to Marketing 5.0. *Issue 4 Int'l JL Mgmt. &. Human.*, *5*, 469.

Miao, F., & Holmes, W. (2021). International Forum on AI and the Futures of Education, developing competencies for the AI Era, 7-8 December 2020: synthesis report. Academic Press.

Mohammadi, M., & Rezaei, J. (2020). Bayesian best-worst method: A probabilistic group decision making model. *Omega*, *96*, 102075. doi:10.1016/j.omega.2019.06.001

Compilation of References

Monamo, Marivate, & Twala. (2016). *Unsupervised learning for robust Bitcoin fraud detection.* Information Security for South Africa (ISSA), 6.

Movahed, A. B., Aliahmadi, A., Parsanejad, M., & Nozari, H. (2023). A Systematic Review of Collaboration in Supply Chain 4.0 with Meta-Synthesis Method. Supply Chain Analytics, 100052.

Movahed, A. B., Movahed, A. B., & Nozari, H. (2024). Opportunities and Challenges of Smart Supply Chain in Industry 5.0. *Information Logistics for Organizational Empowerment and Effective Supply Chain Management*, 108-138.

Movahed, A. B., Movahed, A. B., & Nozari, H. (2024a). Opportunities and Challenges of Marketing 5.0. *Smart and Sustainable Interactive Marketing*, 1-21.

Movahed, A. B., Movahed, A. B., & Nozari, H. (2024a). Opportunities and Challenges of Smart Supply Chain in Industry 5.0. Information Logistics for Organizational Empowerment and Effective Supply Chain Management, 108-138.

Movahed, A. B., Movahed, A. B., & Nozari, H. (2024b). Opportunities and Challenges of Marketing 5.0. *Smart and Sustainable Interactive Marketing*, 1-21.

Movahed, A. B., Movahed, A. B., & Nozari, H. (2024b). Opportunities and Challenges of Smart Supply Chain in Industry 5.0. *Information Logistics for Organizational Empowerment and Effective Supply Chain Management*, 108-138.

Muhammad, T., & Munir, M. (2023). Network Automation. *European Journal of Technology*, 7(2), 23–42. doi:10.47672/ejt.1547

Mukul, E., Büyüközkan, G., & Güler, M. (2019, April). Evaluation of digital marketing technologies with MCDM methods. In *Proceedings of the 6th International Conference on New Ideas in Management Economics and Accounting,* France, Paris (pp. 19-21). 10.33422/6th.imea.2019.04.1070

Murugan, M., & Prabadevi, M. N. (2023). Impact of Industry 6.0 on MSME Entrepreneur's Performance and Entrepreneur's Emotional Intelligence in the Service Industry in India. *Revista de Gestão Social e Ambiental*, 17(4), e03340–e03340. doi:10.24857/rgsa.v17n4-007

Nair, N., Jayachandran, S., & Park, M. (2022). Digital customer engagement, customer satisfaction, and loyalty: Evidence from US retail industry. *Journal of Retailing and Consumer Services*, 66, 102895.

Najafi, Nozari, & Edalatpanah. (2022). Artificial Intelligence of Things (AIoT) and Industry 4.0–Based Supply Chain (FMCG Industry). *A Roadmap for Enabling Industry 4.0 by Artificial Intelligence*, 31-41.

Nakamoto. (2008). Bitcoin: A peer-to-peer electronic cash system. *Decentralized Business Review*, 21260.

Ngai, E., Hu, Y., Wong, Y. H., Chen, Y., & Sun, X. (2011a). The application of data mining techniques in financial fraud detection: A classification framework and an academic review of literature. *Decision Support Systems*, *50*(3), 10. doi:10.1016/j.dss.2010.08.006

Nielsen. (2023). State of the Media: The Social Media Report Q32023. Nielsen.

Nikkel, B. (2020). Fintech forensics: Criminal investigation and digital evidence in financial technologies. *Forensic Science International Digital Investigation*, *33*, 33. doi:10.1016/j.fsidi.2020.200908

Nissenbaum, H. (2020). Protecting privacy in an information age: The problem of privacy in public. In *The ethics of information technologies* (pp. 141–178). Routledge. doi:10.4324/9781003075011-12

Nozari, H. (2024). Supply Chain 6.0 and Moving Towards Hyper-Intelligent Processes. In Information Logistics for Organizational Empowerment and Effective Supply Chain Management (pp. 1-13). IGI Global.

Nozari, H., Ghahremani-Nahr, J., & Najafi, E. (2023). The Role of Internet of Things and Blockchain in the Development of Agile and Sustainable Supply Chains. In Digital Supply Chain, Disruptive Environments, and the Impact on Retailers (pp. 271-282). IGI Global. doi:10.4018/978-1-6684-7298-9.ch015

Nozari, H., Ghahremani-Nahr, J., & Szmelter-Jarosz, A. (2023). AI and machine learning for real-world problems. *Advances In Computers*, (online first).

Nozari, H., Szmelter-Jarosz, A., & Rahmaty, M. (2024). Smart Marketing Based on Artificial Intelligence of Things (AIoT) and Blockchain and Evaluating Critical Success Factors. In Smart and Sustainable Interactive Marketing (pp. 68-82). IGI Global.

Nozari, H., Tavakkoli-Moghaddam, R., Ghahremani-Nahr, J., & Najafi, E. (2023). A conceptual framework for Artificial Intelligence of Medical Things (AIoMT). In Computational Intelligence for Medical Internet of Things (MIoT) Applications (pp. 175-189). Academic Press.

Nozari, H., Tavakkoli-Moghaddam, R., Rohaninejad, M., & Hanzalek, Z. (2023, September). Artificial Intelligence of Things (AIoT) Strategies for a Smart Sustainable-Resilient Supply Chain. In *IFIP International Conference on Advances in Production Management Systems* (pp. 805-816). Cham: Springer Nature Switzerland. 10.1007/978-3-031-43670-3_56

Nozari, H. (Ed.). (2023). *Building Smart and Sustainable Businesses With Transformative Technologies*. IGI Global. doi:10.4018/979-8-3693-0210-1

Nozari, H., & Aliahmadi, A. (2023). Analysis of critical success factors in a food agile supply chain by a fuzzy hybrid decision-making method. [Formerly known as Iranian Journal of Management Studies]. *Interdisciplinary Journal of Management Studies*, *16*(4), 905–926.

Nozari, H., Fallah, M., Kazemipoor, H., & Najafi, S. E. (2021). Big data analysis of IoT-based supply chain management considering FMCG industries. *Бизнес-информатика*, *15*(1, 1 (eng)), 78–96. doi:10.17323/2587-814X.2021.1.78.96

Nozari, H., Ghahremani-Nahr, J., & Szmelter-Jarosz, A. (2023). A multi-stage stochastic inventory management model for transport companies including several different transport modes. *International Journal of Management Science and Engineering Management*, *18*(2), 134–144. doi:10.1080/17509653.2022.2042747

Nozari, H., Najafi, E., Fallah, M., & Hosseinzadeh Lotfi, F. (2019). Quantitative analysis of key performance indicators of green supply chain in FMCG industries using non-linear fuzzy method. *Mathematics*, *7*(11), 1020. doi:10.3390/math7111020

Nozari, H., & Rahmaty, M. (2023). Modeling the make-to-order problem considering the order queuing system under uncertainty. *International Journal of Industrial Engineering*, *34*(4), 1–20.

Nozari, H., Sadeghi, M. E., Eskandari, J., & Ghorbani, E. (2012). Using integrated fuzzy AHP and fuzzy TOPSIS methods to explore the impact of knowledge management tools in staff empowerment (Case study in knowledge-based companies located on science and technology parks in Iran). *International Journal of Information, Business and Management*, *4*(2), 75–92.

Nozari, H., & Szmelter-Jarosz, A. (2024). An Analytical Framework for Smart Supply Chains 5.0. In *Building Smart and Sustainable Businesses With Transformative Technologies* (pp. 1–15). IGI Global.

Nozari, H., Szmelter-Jarosz, A., & Ghahremani-Nahr, J. (2021). The Ideas of Sustainable and Green Marketing Based on the Internet of Everything—The Case of the Dairy Industry. *Future Internet*, *13*(10), 266. doi:10.3390/fi13100266

Nuseir, M. T., El Refae, G. A., Aljumah, A., Alshurideh, M., Urabi, S., & Kurdi, B. A. (2023). Digital Marketing Strategies and the Impact on Customer Experience: A Systematic Review. *The Effect of Information Technology on Business and Marketing Intelligence Systems*, 21-44.

Nwagor Offor. (n.d.). *Simulation of Oil Production with Simultaneous Inclusion of a Hydrocarbon Constituent Driven Random Environmental Perturbation Value of 0.08.*

O'Neill, J. (2011). *The growth map: Economic opportunity in the BRICs and beyond*. Penguin UK.

Oh, S., Park, M. J., Kim, T. Y., & Shin, J. (2023). Marketing strategies for fintech companies: Text data analysis of social media posts. *Management Decision*, *61*(1), 243–268. doi:10.1108/MD-09-2021-1183

Oliver, R. L. (1997). *Satisfaction: A Behavioral Perspective on the Consumer*. McGraw Hill.

Omanović-Mikličanin, E., & Maksimović, M. (2018). *Application of nanotechnology in agriculture and food production—Nanofood and nanoagriculture. IcETRAN. Palic*. Serbia.

Pansari, A., & Kumar, V. (2018). Customer engagement: The construct, antecedents, and consequences. *Journal of the Academy of Marketing Science*, *46*(2), 252–270.

Parasuraman, A., Zeithaml, V. A., & Berry, L. L. (2018). A conceptual model of service quality and its implications for future research. *Journal of Marketing*, *49*(4), 41–50. doi:10.1177/002224298504900403

Park, S. M., & Kim, Y. G. (2022). A metaverse: Taxonomy, components, applications, and open challenges. *IEEE Access : Practical Innovations, Open Solutions*, *10*, 4209–4251. doi:10.1109/ACCESS.2021.3140175

Pathak, S., Arora, K., & Quraishi, S. J. (2024). Strategic Challenges of Human Resources Management in the Industry 6.0. In Futuristic e-Governance Security With Deep Learning Applications (pp. 169-190). IGI Global.

Patterson, P. G., & Spreng, R. A. (1997). Modelling the relationship between perceived value, satisfaction, and repurchase intentions in a business-to-business, services context: An empirical examination. *International Journal of Service Industry Management*, *8*(5), 414–434. doi:10.1108/09564239710189835

Payne, A., Storbacka, K., & Frow, P. (2013). Managing the co-creation of value. *Journal of the Academy of Marketing Science*, *41*(2), 133–150.

Peltier, J. W., Dahl, A. J., & Schibrowsky, J. A. (2023). Artificial intelligence in interactive marketing: A conceptual framework and research agenda. *Journal of Research in Interactive Marketing*, (ahead-of-print).

Peng & You. (2016). *The Health Care Fraud Detection Using the Pharmacopoeia Spectrum Tree and Neural Network Analytic Contribution Hierarchy Process*. IEEE Trustcom/BigDataSE/ISPA, 6.

Peng, J. (2018). *Fraud Detection of Medical Insurance Employing Outlier Analysis*. IEEE 22nd International Conference on Computer Supported Cooperative Work in Design (CSCWD), 6. 10.1109/CSCWD.2018.8465273

Peres, Schreier, Schweidel, & Sorescu. (2022). Blockchain meets marketing: Opportunities, threats, and avenues for future research. Academic Press.

Peres, R. S., Jia, X., Lee, J., Sun, K., Colombo, A. W., & Barata, J. (2020). Industrial artificial intelligence in industry 4.0-systematic review, challenges and outlook. *IEEE Access : Practical Innovations, Open Solutions*, *8*, 220121–220139. doi:10.1109/ACCESS.2020.3042874

Perreault, J., McCarthy, E. J., Parkinsen, S., & Stewda, K. (2000). *Basic Marketing*. McGraw Hill.

Perry, A., Lawrence, V., & Henderson, C. (2020). Stigmatization of those with mental health conditions in the acute general hospital setting. A qualitative framework synthesis. *Social Science & Medicine*, *255*, 112974. doi:10.1016/j.socscimed.2020.112974 PMID:32388323

Petersen, J. A., Paulich, B. J., Khodakarami, F., Spyropoulou, S., & Kumar, V. (2022). Customer-based execution strategy in a global digital economy. *International Journal of Research in Marketing*, *39*(2), 566–582. doi:10.1016/j.ijresmar.2021.09.010

Peters, G. M., Peelen, R. V., Gilissen, V. J., Koning, M. V., van Harten, W. H., & Doggen, C. J. (2023). Detecting Patient Deterioration Early Using Continuous Heart rate and Respiratory rate Measurements in Hospitalized COVID-19 Patients. *Journal of Medical Systems*, *47*(1), 12. doi:10.1007/s10916-022-01898-w PMID:36692798

Pine, B. J., & Gilmore, J. H. (2013). *The experience economy: Work is theatre & every business a stage.* Harvard Business Press.

Poornachandrika, V., & Venkatasudhakar, M. (2020, September). Quality transformation to improve customer satisfaction: Using product, process, system, and behavior model. []. IOP Publishing.]. *IOP Conference Series. Materials Science and Engineering*, *923*(1), 012034. doi:10.1088/1757-899X/923/1/012034

Primasiwi, C., Irawan, M. I., & Ambarwati, R. (2021, May). Key Performance Indicators for Influencer Marketing on Instagram. In 2nd International Conference on Business and Management of Technology (iconbmt 2020) (pp. 154-163). Atlantis Press. Retrieved from https://www2.deloitte.com/content/dam/Deloitte/cn/Documents/about-deloitte/deloitte-cn-dtt-thriving-in-the-era-of-persuasive-ai-en-200819.pdf

Rahmaty, M., & Nozari, H. (2023). Optimization of the hierarchical supply chain in the pharmaceutical industry. *Edelweiss Applied Science and Technology*, *7*(2), 104–123. doi:10.55214/25768484.v7i2.376

Rai, A. K., & Srivastava, R. K. (2018). Role of social media engagement in creating brand experience and loyalty. Vision. *The Journal of Business Perspective*, *22*(3), 311–322.

Rajasekaran, A. S., Azees, M., & Al-Turjman, F. (2022). A comprehensive survey on blockchain technology. *Sustainable Energy Technologies and Assessments*, *52*, 102039. doi:10.1016/j.seta.2022.102039

Ranzani, O. T., Bastos, L. S., Gelli, J. G. M., Marchesi, J. F., Baião, F., Hamacher, S., & Bozza, F. A. (2021). Characterization of the first 250 000 hospital admissions for COVID-19 in Brazil: A retrospective analysis of nationwide data. *The Lancet. Respiratory Medicine*, *9*(4), 407–418. doi:10.1016/S2213-2600(20)30560-9 PMID:33460571

Ravisankar, P., Ravi, V., Raghava Rao, G., & Bose, I. (2011). Detection of financial statement fraud and feature selection using data mining techniques. *Decision Support Systems*, *50*(2), 491–500. doi:10.1016/j.dss.2010.11.006

RB. (2021). Credit card fraud detection using artificial neural network. *Global Transitions Proceedings*, *2*(1), 6.

Reichheld, F., Markey, R. G. J., & Hopton, C. (2000). The loyalty effect: The relationship between loyalty and profits. *European Business Journal*, *12*, 134–139.

Reinartz, W. J., & Ulaga, W. (2016). How to sell services more profitably. *Harvard Business Review*, *94*(3), 90–97. PMID:18543811

Reis, J. L., Peter, M. K., Cayolla, R., & Bogdanovic, Z. (2021). Marketing and smart technologies. *Proceedings of ICMarkTech, 1.*

Rezaei, J. (2015). Best-worst multi-criteria decision-making method. *Omega*, *53*, 49–57. doi:10.1016/j.omega.2014.11.009

Reznik, O. M., Hetmanets, O. P., Kovalchuk, A., Nastyuk, V., & Andriichenko, N. (2020). Financial security of the state. Academic Press.

Rizki, A. A., Surjandari, I., & Wayasti, R. A. (2017). Data mining application to detect financial fraud in Indonesia's public companies. *3rd International Conference on Science in Information Technology*, 5. 10.1109/ICSITech.2017.8257111

Roetzer, P., & Kaput, M. (2022). *Marketing Artificial Intelligence: AI, Marketing, and the Future of Business*. BenBella Books.

Ronaghi, M. H. (2021). A blockchain maturity model in agricultural supply chain. *Information Processing in Agriculture*, *8*(3), 398–408. doi:10.1016/j.inpa.2020.10.004

Roy, R., & George, K. T. (2017). Detecting insurance claims fraud using machine learning techniques. *International Conference on Circuit, Power and Computing Technologies*, 6. 10.1109/ICCPCT.2017.8074258

Saaty, T. L. (1980). *The analytical hierarchy process, planning, priority. Resource allocation*. RWS publications.

Sadeghi, M. E., Nozari, H., Dezfoli, H. K., & Khajezadeh, M. (2021). Ranking of different of investment risk in high-tech projects using TOPSIS method in fuzzy environment based on linguistic variables. *arXiv preprint arXiv:2111.14665*.

Sampson, J. R. (1976). Adaptation in natural and artificial systems (John H. Holland). Society for Industrial and Applied Mathematics.

Sarker, I. H. (2021). Data science and analytics: An overview from data-driven smart computing, decision-making and applications perspective. *SN Computer Science*, *2*(5), 377. doi:10.1007/s42979-021-00765-8 PMID:34278328

Sartoretti, T., Wildberger, J. E., Flohr, T., & Alkadhi, H. (2023). Photon-counting detector CT: Early clinical experience review. *The British Journal of Radiology*, *95*, 20220544. doi:10.1259/bjr.20220544 PMID:36744809

Schnatz, J., Guerrero-Ruiz, A., & Sachin, K. (2022). *Aligning development co-operation to the SDGs in lower middle-income countries: A case study of Bangladesh (No. 105)*. OECD Publishing.

Schwartz, D., Youngs, N., & Britto, A. (2014). The ripple protocol consensus algorithm. *Ripple Labs Inc White Paper*, *5*(8), 151.

Sedlmeir, J., Lautenschlager, J., Fridgen, G., & Urbach, N. (2022). The transparency challenge of blockchain in organizations. *Electronic Markets*, *32*(3), 1–16. doi:10.1007/s12525-022-00536-0 PMID:35602109

Sereshti, N., Adulyasak, Y., & Jans, R. (2024). Managing flexibility in stochastic multi-level lot-sizing problems with service level constraints. *Omega*, *122*, 102957. doi:10.1016/j.omega.2023.102957

Seyed-Hosseini, S. M., Safaei, N., & Asgharpour, M. J. (2006). Reprioritization of failures in a system failure mode and effects analysis by decision making trial and evaluation laboratory technique. *Reliability Engineering & System Safety*, *91*(8), 872–881. doi:10.1016/j.ress.2005.09.005

Sharma, J., & Tripathy, B. B. (2023). An integrated QFD and fuzzy TOPSIS approach for supplier evaluation and selection. *The TQM Journal*, *35*(8), 2387–2412. doi:10.1108/TQM-09-2022-0295

Sheth, J. N., Mittal, B., & Newman, B. I. (1999). *Customer Behaviour: Consumer Behaviour and Beyond*. Dryden.

Sheth, J. N., & Sisodia, R. S. (2018). The future of marketing is human. *Journal of Business Research*, *86*, 374–376.

Shuyi, J., Mamun, A. A., & Naznen, F. (2024). Social media marketing activities on brand equity and purchase intention among Chinese smartphone consumers during COVID-19. *Journal of Science and Technology Policy Management*, *15*(2), 331–352. doi:10.1108/JSTPM-02-2022-0038

Silva, A. R., Almeida-Xavier, S., Lopes, M., Soares-Fernandes, J. P., Sousa, F., & Varanda, S. (2023). Is there a time window for an MRI in Wernicke encephalopathy—A decade of experience from a tertiary hospital? *Neurological Sciences*, *44*(2), 703–708. doi:10.1007/s10072-022-06477-y PMID:36335281

Singh, R., Tyagi, A. K., & Arumugam, S. K. (2024). Imagining the Sustainable Future With Industry 6.0: A Smarter Pathway for Modern Society and Manufacturing Industries. In Machine Learning Algorithms Using Scikit and TensorFlow Environments (pp. 318-331). IGI Global.

Singha, S., Arha, H., & Kar, A. K. (2023). Healthcare analytics: A techno-functional perspective. *Technological Forecasting and Social Change*, *197*, 122908. doi:10.1016/j.techfore.2023.122908

Singh, R., Tyagi, A. K., & Arumugam, S. K. (2024). Imagining the sustainable future with Industry 6.0: A smarter pathway for modern society and manufacturing industries. In *Machine Learning Algorithms Using Scikit and TensorFlow Environments* (pp. 318–331). IGI Global.

Singleton, T. W. (2006). *Fraud auditing and forensic accounting*. John Wiley & Sons.

Sookkaew, J., & Saephoo, P. (2021). "Digital influencer": Development and coexistence with digital social groups. *International Journal of Advanced Computer Science and Applications*, *12*(12). Advance online publication. doi:10.14569/IJACSA.2021.0121243

Statista. (2023a). https://www.statista.com/statistics/1365145/artificial-intelligence-market-size/

Statista. (2023b). https://www.statista.com/statistics/1293758/ai-marketing-revenue-worldwide/#:~:text=In%202021%2C%20the%20market%20for,than%20107.5%20billion%20by%202028

Sun, C. C. (2010). A performance evaluation model by integrating fuzzy AHP and fuzzy TOPSIS methods. *Expert Systems with Applications*, *37*(12), 7745–7754. doi:10.1016/j.eswa.2010.04.066

Sutaguna, I. N. T., Achmad, G. N., Risdwiyanto, A., & Yusuf, M. (2023). Marketing strategy for increasing sales of cooking oil shoes in Barokah trading business. *International Journal of Economics and Management Research*, 2(1), 132–152. doi:10.55606/ijemr.v2i1.73

Szetela, Mentel, & Stanis-Law. (2016). Dependency analysis between bitcoin and selected global currencies. *Dynamic Econometric Models*, 16, 133–144.

Tariq, S., & Syed, J. (2018). Impact of customer-centric marketing on customer loyalty: Moderating role of customer involvement. *Journal of Marketing and Consumer Research*, 46, 10–18.

Tezel, A., Febrero, P., Papadonikolaki, E., & Yitmen, I. (2021). Insights into blockchain implementation in construction: Models for supply chain management. *Journal of Management Engineering*, 37(4), 04021038. doi:10.1061/(ASCE)ME.1943-5479.0000939

Thomas, M. R., & Shivani, M. P. (2020). Customer profiling of alpha: The next generation marketing. *Ushus Journal of Business Management*, 19(1), 75–86.

Tran, H. A. M., Ngo, H. Q. T., Nguyen, T. P., & Nguyen, H. (2018, November). Design of green agriculture system using the Internet of things and image processing techniques. In *2018 4th International Conference on Green Technology and Sustainable Development (GTSD)* (pp. 28-32). IEEE. 10.1109/GTSD.2018.8595663

Tretina, K. (2023). Top 10 Cryptocurrencies In India. https://www.forbes.com/advisor/in/investing/cryptocurrency/top-10-cryptocurrencies/

Treviño, L. K., Den Nieuwenboer, N. A., & Kish-Gephart, J. J. (2014). (Un)ethical behavior in organizations. *Annual Review of Psychology*, 65(1), 635–660. doi:10.1146/annurev-psych-113011-143745 PMID:23834354

Trung, N. Q., & Thanh, N. V. (2022). Evaluation of digital marketing technologies with fuzzy linguistic MCDM methods. *Axioms*, 11(5), 230. doi:10.3390/axioms11050230

Tuş, A., Öztaş, G. Z., Öztaş, T., Özçil, A., & Aytaç Adalı, E. (2023). *An alternative approach for calculating Turkey's digital transformation index: Bayesian BWM*. Pamukkale University Journal of Engineering Sciences-Pamukkale Universitesi Muhendislik Bilimleri Dergisi.

Tyagi, A. K., Mishra, A. K., Vedavathi, N., Kakulapati, V., & Sajidha, S. A. (2024). Futuristic technologies for smart manufacturing: Research statement and vision for the future. *Automated Secure Computing for Next-Generation Systems*, 415-441.

Uddin, M. H., Ali, M. H., & Hassan, M. K. (2020). Cybersecurity hazards and financial system vulnerability: A synthesis of the literature. *Risk Management*, 22(4), 239–309. doi:10.1057/s41283-020-00063-2

Underwood, S. (2016). Blockchain beyond bitcoin. *Communications of the ACM*, 59(11), 15–17. doi:10.1145/2994581

van Agtmael, A. (2007). Industrial Revolution 2.0. *Foreign Policy*, 158, 40.

Verhoef, P. C., Broekhuizen, T., Bart, Y., Bhattacharya, A., Dong, J. Q., Fabian, N., & Haenlein, M. (2021). Digital transformation: A multidisciplinary reflection and research agenda. *Journal of Business Research*, *122*, 889–901. doi:10.1016/j.jbusres.2019.09.022

Vrontis, D., Christofi, M., Pereira, V., Tarba, S., Makrides, A., & Trichina, E. (2022). Artificial intelligence, robotics, advanced technologies and human resource management: A systematic review. *International Journal of Human Resource Management*, *33*(6), 1237–1266. doi:10.1080/09585192.2020.1871398

Wang, S., Zhang, J., Wang, P., Law, J., Calinescu, R., & Mihaylova, L. (2024). A deep learning-enhanced Digital Twin framework for improving safety and reliability in human–robot collaborative manufacturing. *Robotics and Computer-integrated Manufacturing*, *85*, 102608. doi:10.1016/j.rcim.2023.102608

Wang, Z., Li, M., Lu, J., & Cheng, X. (2022). Business Innovation based on artificial intelligence and Blockchain technology. *Information Processing & Management*, *59*(1), 102759. doi:10.1016/j.ipm.2021.102759

Wang, Z., Zheng, Z., Jiang, W., & Tang, S. (2021). Blockchain-enabled data sharing in supply chains: Model, operationalization, and tutorial. *Production and Operations Management*, *30*(7), 1965–1985. doi:10.1111/poms.13356

Wan, J., & Xia, H. (2023, March). How Advanced Practice Nurses Can Be Better Managed in Hospitals: A Multi-Case Study. *Health Care*, *11*(6), 780. PMID:36981438

Wells, J. T. (2014). *Principles of fraud examination*. John Wiley & Sons.

Westberg, J., & Jason, H. (2004). *Fostering Learning in Small Groups: A Practical Guide*. Springer Publishing Company.

West, J., & Bhattacharya, M. (2016). Intelligent financial fraud detection: A comprehensive review. *Computers & Security*, *57*, 47–66. doi:10.1016/j.cose.2015.09.005

Wu, L., Dodoo, N. A., Wen, T. J., & Ke, L. (2022). Understanding Twitter conversations about artificial intelligence in advertising based on natural language processing. *International Journal of Advertising*, *41*(4), 685–702. doi:10.1080/02650487.2021.1920218

Xia, L., Li, K., Wang, J., Xia, Y., & Qin, J. (2023). Carbon emission reduction and precision marketing decisions of a platform supply chain. *International Journal of Production Economics*, 109104.

Xia, L., Monroe, K., & Cox, J. (2004). The price is unfair! A conceptual framework of price fairness perceptions. *Journal of Marketing*, *68*(4), 1–15. doi:10.1509/jmkg.68.4.1.42733

Xu, B., Luo, C., & Xie, S. (2022). *Research and Design of "AI+ Agriculture" Disease Detection System Based on Deep Learning. In 3D Imaging—Multidimensional Signal Processing and Deep Learning: Multidimensional Signals, Images, Video Processing and Applications* (Vol. 2). Springer Nature Singapore.

Xu, W., & Liu, Y. (2012). *An optimized SVM model for detection of fraudulent online credit card transactions.* In *2012 International Conference on Management of e-Commerce and e-Government.* IEEE. 10.1109/ICMeCG.2012.39

Xu, Z., & Kuang, D. (2023, July). Evaluation of Economic Development Data Management System Based on Particle Swarm Optimization Algorithm. In *2023 International Conference on Data Science and Network Security (ICDSNS)* (pp. 1-5). IEEE. 10.1109/ICDSNS58469.2023.10245900

Yadav, R., Arora, S., & Dhull, S. (2022). A path way to Industrial Revolution 6.0. *Int. J. Mech. Eng, 7*, 1452–1459.

Yadav, S. P., Agrawal, K. K., Bhati, B. S., Al-Turjman, F., & Mostarda, L. (2022). Blockchain-based cryptocurrency regulation: An overview. *Computational Economics, 59*(4), 1659–1675. doi:10.1007/s10614-020-10050-0

Yang, F., Qi, W., & Han, J. (2023). Research on the mechanism of promoting coordinated development of ecological well-being in rural counties through industrial transformation. *PLoS One, 18*(9), e0291232. doi:10.1371/journal.pone.0291232 PMID:37682965

Yang, K. C., Varol, O., Davis, C. A., Ferrara, E., Flammini, A., & Menczer, F. (2019). Arming the public with artificial intelligence to counter social bots. *Human Behavior and Emerging Technologies, 1*(1), 48–61. doi:10.1002/hbe2.115

Yuan, J. (2023). Application of micro film advertising communication under new media form. *The Frontiers of Society, Science and Technology, 5*(15).

Yue, D. (2009). *Logistic Regression for Detecting Fraudulent Financial Statement of Listed Companies in China. International Conference on Artificial Intelligence and Computational Intelligence,* 5.

Zadeh, L. A. (1965). Fuzzy sets. *Information and Control, 8*(3), 338–353. doi:10.1016/S0019-9958(65)90241-X

Zeadally, S., & Bello, O. (2021). Harnessing the power of Internet of Things-based connectivity to improve healthcare. *Internet of Things : Engineering Cyber Physical Human Systems, 14*, 100074. doi:10.1016/j.iot.2019.100074

Zhang, A. X., Muller, M., & Wang, D. (2020). How do data science workers collaborate? roles, workflows, and tools. Proceedings of the ACM on Human-Computer Interaction, 4, 1-23. 10.1145/3392826

Zheng, Z., Xie, S., Dai, H., Chen, X., & Wang, H. (2017). *An overview of blockchain technology: Architecture, consensus, and future trends. In 2017 IEEE international congress on big data (BigData congress).* IEEE.

Zheng, Z., Xie, S., Dai, H.-N., Chen, X., & Wang, H. (2018). Blockchain challenges and opportunities: A survey. *International Journal of Web and Grid Services, 14*(4), 352–375. doi:10.1504/IJWGS.2018.095647

Related References

To continue our tradition of advancing information science and technology research, we have compiled a list of recommended IGI Global readings. These references will provide additional information and guidance to further enrich your knowledge and assist you with your own research and future publications.

Abdul Razak, R., & Mansor, N. A. (2021). Instagram Influencers in Social Media-Induced Tourism: Rethinking Tourist Trust Towards Tourism Destination. In M. Dinis, L. Bonixe, S. Lamy, & Z. Breda (Eds.), *Impact of New Media in Tourism* (pp. 135-144). IGI Global. https://doi.org/10.4018/978-1-7998-7095-1.ch009

Abir, T., & Khan, M. Y. (2022). Importance of ICT Advancement and Culture of Adaptation in the Tourism and Hospitality Industry for Developing Countries. In C. Ramos, S. Quinteiro, & A. Gonçalves (Eds.), *ICT as Innovator Between Tourism and Culture* (pp. 30–41). IGI Global. https://doi.org/10.4018/978-1-7998-8165-0.ch003

Abir, T., & Khan, M. Y. (2022). Importance of ICT Advancement and Culture of Adaptation in the Tourism and Hospitality Industry for Developing Countries. In C. Ramos, S. Quinteiro, & A. Gonçalves (Eds.), *ICT as Innovator Between Tourism and Culture* (pp. 30–41). IGI Global. https://doi.org/10.4018/978-1-7998-8165-0.ch003

Abtahi, M. S., Behboudi, L., & Hasanabad, H. M. (2017). Factors Affecting Internet Advertising Adoption in Ad Agencies. *International Journal of Innovation in the Digital Economy*, 8(4), 18–29. doi:10.4018/IJIDE.2017100102

Afenyo-Agbe, E., & Mensah, I. (2022). Principles, Benefits, and Barriers to Community-Based Tourism: Implications for Management. In I. Mensah & E. Afenyo-Agbe (Eds.), *Prospects and Challenges of Community-Based Tourism and Changing Demographics* (pp. 1–29). IGI Global. doi:10.4018/978-1-7998-7335-8.ch001

Agbo, V. M. (2022). Distributive Justice Issues in Community-Based Tourism. In I. Mensah & E. Afenyo-Agbe (Eds.), *Prospects and Challenges of Community-Based Tourism and Changing Demographics* (pp. 107–129). IGI Global. https://doi.org/10.4018/978-1-7998-7335-8.ch005

Agrawal, S. (2017). The Impact of Emerging Technologies and Social Media on Different Business(es): Marketing and Management. In O. Rishi & A. Sharma (Eds.), *Maximizing Business Performance and Efficiency Through Intelligent Systems* (pp. 37–49). Hershey, PA: IGI Global. doi:10.4018/978-1-5225-2234-8.ch002

Ahmad, A., & Johari, S. (2022). Georgetown as a Gastronomy Tourism Destination: Visitor Awareness Towards Revisit Intention of Nasi Kandar Restaurant. In M. Valeri (Ed.), *New Governance and Management in Touristic Destinations* (pp. 71–83). IGI Global. https://doi.org/10.4018/978-1-6684-3889-3.ch005

Alkhatib, G., & Bayouq, S. T. (2021). A TAM-Based Model of Technological Factors Affecting Use of E-Tourism. *International Journal of Tourism and Hospitality Management in the Digital Age*, 5(2), 50–67. https://doi.org/10.4018/IJTHMDA.20210701.oa1

Altinay Ozdemir, M. (2021). Virtual Reality (VR) and Augmented Reality (AR) Technologies for Accessibility and Marketing in the Tourism Industry. In C. Eusébio, L. Teixeira, & M. Carneiro (Eds.), *ICT Tools and Applications for Accessible Tourism* (pp. 277-301). IGI Global. https://doi.org/10.4018/978-1-7998-6428-8.ch013

Anantharaman, R. N., Rajeswari, K. S., Angusamy, A., & Kuppusamy, J. (2017). Role of Self-Efficacy and Collective Efficacy as Moderators of Occupational Stress Among Software Development Professionals. *International Journal of Human Capital and Information Technology Professionals*, 8(2), 45–58. doi:10.4018/IJHCITP.2017040103

Aninze, F., El-Gohary, H., & Hussain, J. (2018). The Role of Microfinance to Empower Women: The Case of Developing Countries. *International Journal of Customer Relationship Marketing and Management*, 9(1), 54–78. doi:10.4018/IJCRMM.2018010104

Antosova, G., Sabogal-Salamanca, M., & Krizova, E. (2021). Human Capital in Tourism: A Practical Model of Endogenous and Exogenous Territorial Tourism Planning in Bahía Solano, Colombia. In V. Costa, A. Moura, & M. Mira (Eds.), *Handbook of Research on Human Capital and People Management in the Tourism Industry* (pp. 282–302). IGI Global. https://doi.org/10.4018/978-1-7998-4318-4.ch014

Related References

Arsenijević, O. M., Orčić, D., & Kastratović, E. (2017). Development of an Optimization Tool for Intangibles in SMEs: A Case Study from Serbia with a Pilot Research in the Prestige by Milka Company. In M. Vemić (Ed.), *Optimal Management Strategies in Small and Medium Enterprises* (pp. 320–347). Hershey, PA: IGI Global. doi:10.4018/978-1-5225-1949-2.ch015

Aryanto, V. D., Wismantoro, Y., & Widyatmoko, K. (2018). Implementing Eco-Innovation by Utilizing the Internet to Enhance Firm's Marketing Performance: Study of Green Batik Small and Medium Enterprises in Indonesia. *International Journal of E-Business Research*, *14*(1), 21–36. doi:10.4018/IJEBR.2018010102

Asero, V., & Billi, S. (2022). New Perspective of Networking in the DMO Model. In M. Valeri (Ed.), *New Governance and Management in Touristic Destinations* (pp. 105–118). IGI Global. https://doi.org/10.4018/978-1-6684-3889-3.ch007

Atiku, S. O., & Fields, Z. (2017). Multicultural Orientations for 21st Century Global Leadership. In N. Baporikar (Ed.), *Management Education for Global Leadership* (pp. 28–51). Hershey, PA: IGI Global. doi:10.4018/978-1-5225-1013-0.ch002

Atiku, S. O., & Fields, Z. (2018). Organisational Learning Dimensions and Talent Retention Strategies for the Service Industries. In N. Baporikar (Ed.), *Global Practices in Knowledge Management for Societal and Organizational Development* (pp. 358–381). Hershey, PA: IGI Global. doi:10.4018/978-1-5225-3009-1.ch017

Atsa'am, D. D., & Kuset Bodur, E. (2021). Pattern Mining on How Organizational Tenure Affects the Psychological Capital of Employees Within the Hospitality and Tourism Industry: Linking Employees' Organizational Tenure With PsyCap. *International Journal of Tourism and Hospitality Management in the Digital Age*, *5*(2), 17–28. https://doi.org/10.4018/IJTHMDA.2021070102

Ávila, L., & Teixeira, L. (2018). The Main Concepts Behind the Dematerialization of Business Processes. In M. Khosrow-Pour, D.B.A. (Ed.), Encyclopedia of Information Science and Technology, Fourth Edition (pp. 888-898). Hershey, PA: IGI Global. https://doi.org/ doi:10.4018/978-1-5225-2255-3.ch076

Ayorekire, J., Mugizi, F., Obua, J., & Ampaire, G. (2022). Community-Based Tourism and Local People's Perceptions Towards Conservation: The Case of Queen Elizabeth Conservation Area, Uganda. In I. Mensah & E. Afenyo-Agbe (Eds.), *Prospects and Challenges of Community-Based Tourism and Changing Demographics* (pp. 56–82). IGI Global. https://doi.org/10.4018/978-1-7998-7335-8.ch003

Baleiro, R. (2022). Tourist Literature and the Architecture of Travel in Olga Tokarczuk and Patti Smith. In R. Baleiro & R. Pereira (Eds.), *Global Perspectives on Literary Tourism and Film-Induced Tourism* (pp. 202-216). IGI Global. https://doi.org/10.4018/978-1-7998-8262-6.ch011

Barat, S. (2021). Looking at the Future of Medical Tourism in Asia. *International Journal of Tourism and Hospitality Management in the Digital Age, 5*(1), 19–33. https://doi.org/10.4018/IJTHMDA.2021010102

Barbosa, C. A., Magalhães, M., & Nunes, M. R. (2021). Travel Instagramability: A Way of Choosing a Destination? In M. Dinis, L. Bonixe, S. Lamy, & Z. Breda (Eds.), *Impact of New Media in Tourism* (pp. 173-190). IGI Global. https://doi.org/10.4018/978-1-7998-7095-1.ch011

Bari, M. W., & Khan, Q. (2021). Pakistan as a Destination of Religious Tourism. In E. Alaverdov & M. Bari (Eds.), *Global Development of Religious Tourism* (pp. 1-10). IGI Global. https://doi.org/10.4018/978-1-7998-5792-1.ch001

Bartens, Y., Chunpir, H. I., Schulte, F., & Voß, S. (2017). Business/IT Alignment in Two-Sided Markets: A COBIT 5 Analysis for Media Streaming Business Models. In S. De Haes & W. Van Grembergen (Eds.), *Strategic IT Governance and Alignment in Business Settings* (pp. 82–111). Hershey, PA: IGI Global. doi:10.4018/978-1-5225-0861-8.ch004

Bashayreh, A. M. (2018). Organizational Culture and Organizational Performance. In W. Lee & F. Sabetzadeh (Eds.), *Contemporary Knowledge and Systems Science* (pp. 50–69). Hershey, PA: IGI Global. doi:10.4018/978-1-5225-5655-8.ch003

Bechthold, L., Lude, M., & Prügl, R. (2021). Crisis Favors the Prepared Firm: How Organizational Ambidexterity Relates to Perceptions of Organizational Resilience. In A. Zehrer, G. Glowka, K. Schwaiger, & V. Ranacher-Lackner (Eds.), *Resiliency Models and Addressing Future Risks for Family Firms in the Tourism Industry* (pp. 178–205). IGI Global. https://doi.org/10.4018/978-1-7998-7352-5.ch008

Bedford, D. A. (2018). Sustainable Knowledge Management Strategies: Aligning Business Capabilities and Knowledge Management Goals. In N. Baporikar (Ed.), *Global Practices in Knowledge Management for Societal and Organizational Development* (pp. 46–73). Hershey, PA: IGI Global. doi:10.4018/978-1-5225-3009-1.ch003

Bekjanov, D., & Matyusupov, B. (2021). Influence of Innovative Processes in the Competitiveness of Tourist Destination. In J. Soares (Ed.), *Innovation and Entrepreneurial Opportunities in Community Tourism* (pp. 243–263). IGI Global. https://doi.org/10.4018/978-1-7998-4855-4.ch014

Related References

Bharwani, S., & Musunuri, D. (2018). Reflection as a Process From Theory to Practice. In M. Khosrow-Pour, D.B.A. (Ed.), Encyclopedia of Information Science and Technology, Fourth Edition (pp. 1529-1539). Hershey, PA: IGI Global. doi:10.4018/978-1-5225-2255-3.ch132

Bhatt, G. D., Wang, Z., & Rodger, J. A. (2017). Information Systems Capabilities and Their Effects on Competitive Advantages: A Study of Chinese Companies. *Information Resources Management Journal*, *30*(3), 41–57. doi:10.4018/IRMJ.2017070103

Bhushan, M., & Yadav, A. (2017). Concept of Cloud Computing in ESB. In R. Bhadoria, N. Chaudhari, G. Tomar, & S. Singh (Eds.), *Exploring Enterprise Service Bus in the Service-Oriented Architecture Paradigm* (pp. 116–127). Hershey, PA: IGI Global. doi:10.4018/978-1-5225-2157-0.ch008

Bhushan, S. (2017). System Dynamics Base-Model of Humanitarian Supply Chain (HSCM) in Disaster Prone Eco-Communities of India: A Discussion on Simulation and Scenario Results. *International Journal of System Dynamics Applications*, *6*(3), 20–37. doi:10.4018/IJSDA.2017070102

Binder, D., & Miller, J. W. (2021). A Generations' Perspective on Employer Branding in Tourism. In V. Costa, A. Moura, & M. Mira (Eds.), *Handbook of Research on Human Capital and People Management in the Tourism Industry* (pp. 152–174). IGI Global. https://doi.org/10.4018/978-1-7998-4318-4.ch008

Birch Freeman, A. A., Mensah, I., & Antwi, K. B. (2022). Smiling vs. Frowning Faces: Community Participation for Sustainable Tourism in Ghanaian Communities. In I. Mensah & E. Afenyo-Agbe (Eds.), *Prospects and Challenges of Community-Based Tourism and Changing Demographics* (pp. 83–106). IGI Global. https://doi.org/10.4018/978-1-7998-7335-8.ch004

Biswas, A., & De, A. K. (2017). On Development of a Fuzzy Stochastic Programming Model with Its Application to Business Management. In S. Trivedi, S. Dey, A. Kumar, & T. Panda (Eds.), *Handbook of Research on Advanced Data Mining Techniques and Applications for Business Intelligence* (pp. 353–378). Hershey, PA: IGI Global. doi:10.4018/978-1-5225-2031-3.ch021

Boragnio, A., & Faracce Macia, C. (2021). "Taking Care of Yourself at Home": Use of E-Commerce About Food and Care During the COVID-19 Pandemic in the City of Buenos Aires. In M. Korstanje (Ed.), *Socio-Economic Effects and Recovery Efforts for the Rental Industry: Post-COVID-19 Strategies* (pp. 45–71). IGI Global. https://doi.org/10.4018/978-1-7998-7287-0.ch003

Borges, V. D. (2021). Happiness: The Basis for Public Policy in Tourism. In A. Perinotto, V. Mayer, & J. Soares (Eds.), *Rebuilding and Restructuring the Tourism Industry: Infusion of Happiness and Quality of Life* (pp. 1–25). IGI Global. https://doi.org/10.4018/978-1-7998-7239-9.ch001

Bücker, J., & Ernste, K. (2018). Use of Brand Heroes in Strategic Reputation Management: The Case of Bacardi, Adidas, and Daimler. In A. Erdemir (Ed.), *Reputation Management Techniques in Public Relations* (pp. 126–150). Hershey, PA: IGI Global. doi:10.4018/978-1-5225-3619-2.ch007

Buluk Eşitti, B. (2021). COVID-19 and Alternative Tourism: New Destinations and New Tourism Products. In M. Demir, A. Dalgıç, & F. Ergen (Eds.), *Handbook of Research on the Impacts and Implications of COVID-19 on the Tourism Industry* (pp. 786–805). IGI Global. https://doi.org/10.4018/978-1-7998-8231-2.ch038

Bureš, V. (2018). Industry 4.0 From the Systems Engineering Perspective: Alternative Holistic Framework Development. In R. Brunet-Thornton & F. Martinez (Eds.), *Analyzing the Impacts of Industry 4.0 in Modern Business Environments* (pp. 199–223). Hershey, PA: IGI Global. doi:10.4018/978-1-5225-3468-6.ch011

Buzady, Z. (2017). Resolving the Magic Cube of Effective Case Teaching: Benchmarking Case Teaching Practices in Emerging Markets – Insights from the Central European University Business School, Hungary. In D. Latusek (Ed.), *Case Studies as a Teaching Tool in Management Education* (pp. 79–103). Hershey, PA: IGI Global. doi:10.4018/978-1-5225-0770-3.ch005

Camillo, A. (2021). *Legal Matters, Risk Management, and Risk Prevention: From Forming a Business to Legal Representation*. IGI Global. doi:10.4018/978-1-7998-4342-9.ch004

Căpusneanu, S., & Topor, D. I. (2018). Business Ethics and Cost Management in SMEs: Theories of Business Ethics and Cost Management Ethos. In I. Oncioiu (Ed.), *Ethics and Decision-Making for Sustainable Business Practices* (pp. 109–127). Hershey, PA: IGI Global. doi:10.4018/978-1-5225-3773-1.ch007

Chan, R. L., Mo, P. L., & Moon, K. K. (2018). Strategic and Tactical Measures in Managing Enterprise Risks: A Study of the Textile and Apparel Industry. In K. Strang, M. Korstanje, & N. Vajjhala (Eds.), *Research, Practices, and Innovations in Global Risk and Contingency Management* (pp. 1–19). Hershey, PA: IGI Global. doi:10.4018/978-1-5225-4754-9.ch001

Charlier, S. D., Burke-Smalley, L. A., & Fisher, S. L. (2018). Undergraduate Programs in the U.S: A Contextual and Content-Based Analysis. In J. Mendy (Ed.), *Teaching Human Resources and Organizational Behavior at the College Level* (pp. 26–57). Hershey, PA: IGI Global. doi:10.4018/978-1-5225-2820-3.ch002

Chumillas, J., Güell, M., & Quer, P. (2022). The Use of ICT in Tourist and Educational Literary Routes: The Role of the Guide. In C. Ramos, S. Quinteiro, & A. Gonçalves (Eds.), *ICT as Innovator Between Tourism and Culture* (pp. 15–29). IGI Global. https://doi.org/10.4018/978-1-7998-8165-0.ch002

Dahlberg, T., Kivijärvi, H., & Saarinen, T. (2017). IT Investment Consistency and Other Factors Influencing the Success of IT Performance. In S. De Haes & W. Van Grembergen (Eds.), *Strategic IT Governance and Alignment in Business Settings* (pp. 176–208). Hershey, PA: IGI Global. doi:10.4018/978-1-5225-0861-8.ch007

Damnjanović, A. M. (2017). Knowledge Management Optimization through IT and E-Business Utilization: A Qualitative Study on Serbian SMEs. In M. Vemić (Ed.), *Optimal Management Strategies in Small and Medium Enterprises* (pp. 249–267). Hershey, PA: IGI Global. doi:10.4018/978-1-5225-1949-2.ch012

Daneshpour, H. (2017). Integrating Sustainable Development into Project Portfolio Management through Application of Open Innovation. In M. Vemić (Ed.), *Optimal Management Strategies in Small and Medium Enterprises* (pp. 370–387). Hershey, PA: IGI Global. doi:10.4018/978-1-5225-1949-2.ch017

Daniel, A. D., & Reis de Castro, V. (2018). Entrepreneurship Education: How to Measure the Impact on Nascent Entrepreneurs. In A. Carrizo Moreira, J. Guilherme Leitão Dantas, & F. Manuel Valente (Eds.), *Nascent Entrepreneurship and Successful New Venture Creation* (pp. 85–110). Hershey, PA: IGI Global. doi:10.4018/978-1-5225-2936-1.ch004

David, R., Swami, B. N., & Tangirala, S. (2018). Ethics Impact on Knowledge Management in Organizational Development: A Case Study. In N. Baporikar (Ed.), *Global Practices in Knowledge Management for Societal and Organizational Development* (pp. 19–45). Hershey, PA: IGI Global. doi:10.4018/978-1-5225-3009-1.ch002

De Uña-Álvarez, E., & Villarino-Pérez, M. (2022). Fostering Ecocultural Resources, Identity, and Tourism in Inland Territories (Galicia, NW Spain). In G. Fernandes (Ed.), *Challenges and New Opportunities for Tourism in Inland Territories: Ecocultural Resources and Sustainable Initiatives* (pp. 1-16). IGI Global. https://doi.org/10.4018/978-1-7998-7339-6.ch001

Delias, P., & Lakiotaki, K. (2018). Discovering Process Horizontal Boundaries to Facilitate Process Comprehension. *International Journal of Operations Research and Information Systems*, *9*(2), 1–31. doi:10.4018/IJORIS.2018040101

Denholm, J., & Lee-Davies, L. (2018). Success Factors for Games in Business and Project Management. In *Enhancing Education and Training Initiatives Through Serious Games* (pp. 34–68). Hershey, PA: IGI Global. doi:10.4018/978-1-5225-3689-5.ch002

Deshpande, M. (2017). Best Practices in Management Institutions for Global Leadership: Policy Aspects. In N. Baporikar (Ed.), *Management Education for Global Leadership* (pp. 1–27). Hershey, PA: IGI Global. doi:10.4018/978-1-5225-1013-0.ch001

Deshpande, M. (2018). Policy Perspectives for SMEs Knowledge Management. In N. Baporikar (Ed.), *Knowledge Integration Strategies for Entrepreneurship and Sustainability* (pp. 23–46). Hershey, PA: IGI Global. doi:10.4018/978-1-5225-5115-7.ch002

Dezdar, S. (2017). ERP Implementation Projects in Asian Countries: A Comparative Study on Iran and China. *International Journal of Information Technology Project Management*, *8*(3), 52–68. doi:10.4018/IJITPM.2017070104

Domingos, D., Respício, A., & Martinho, R. (2017). Reliability of IoT-Aware BPMN Healthcare Processes. In C. Reis & M. Maximiano (Eds.), *Internet of Things and Advanced Application in Healthcare* (pp. 214–248). Hershey, PA: IGI Global. doi:10.4018/978-1-5225-1820-4.ch008

Dosumu, O., Hussain, J., & El-Gohary, H. (2017). An Exploratory Study of the Impact of Government Policies on the Development of Small and Medium Enterprises in Developing Countries: The Case of Nigeria. *International Journal of Customer Relationship Marketing and Management*, *8*(4), 51–62. doi:10.4018/IJCRMM.2017100104

Durst, S., Bruns, G., & Edvardsson, I. R. (2017). Retaining Knowledge in Smaller Building and Construction Firms. *International Journal of Knowledge and Systems Science*, *8*(3), 1–12. doi:10.4018/IJKSS.2017070101

Edvardsson, I. R., & Durst, S. (2017). Outsourcing, Knowledge, and Learning: A Critical Review. *International Journal of Knowledge-Based Organizations*, *7*(2), 13–26. doi:10.4018/IJKBO.2017040102

Related References

Edwards, J. S. (2018). Integrating Knowledge Management and Business Processes. In M. Khosrow-Pour, D.B.A. (Ed.), Encyclopedia of Information Science and Technology, Fourth Edition (pp. 5046-5055). Hershey, PA: IGI Global. doi:10.4018/978-1-5225-2255-3.ch437

Eichelberger, S., & Peters, M. (2021). Family Firm Management in Turbulent Times: Opportunities for Responsible Tourism. In A. Zehrer, G. Glowka, K. Schwaiger, & V. Ranacher-Lackner (Eds.), *Resiliency Models and Addressing Future Risks for Family Firms in the Tourism Industry* (pp. 103–124). IGI Global. https://doi.org/10.4018/978-1-7998-7352-5.ch005

Eide, D., Hjalager, A., & Hansen, M. (2022). Innovative Certifications in Adventure Tourism: Attributes and Diffusion. In R. Augusto Costa, F. Brandão, Z. Breda, & C. Costa (Eds.), *Planning and Managing the Experience Economy in Tourism* (pp. 161-175). IGI Global. https://doi.org/10.4018/978-1-7998-8775-1.ch009

Ejiogu, A. O. (2018). Economics of Farm Management. In *Agricultural Finance and Opportunities for Investment and Expansion* (pp. 56–72). Hershey, PA: IGI Global. doi:10.4018/978-1-5225-3059-6.ch003

Ekanem, I., & Abiade, G. E. (2018). Factors Influencing the Use of E-Commerce by Small Enterprises in Nigeria. *International Journal of ICT Research in Africa and the Middle East*, 7(1), 37–53. doi:10.4018/IJICTRAME.2018010103

Ekanem, I., & Alrossais, L. A. (2017). Succession Challenges Facing Family Businesses in Saudi Arabia. In P. Zgheib (Ed.), *Entrepreneurship and Business Innovation in the Middle East* (pp. 122–146). Hershey, PA: IGI Global. doi:10.4018/978-1-5225-2066-5.ch007

El Faquih, L., & Fredj, M. (2017). Ontology-Based Framework for Quality in Configurable Process Models. *Journal of Electronic Commerce in Organizations*, 15(2), 48–60. doi:10.4018/JECO.2017040104

Faisal, M. N., & Talib, F. (2017). Building Ambidextrous Supply Chains in SMEs: How to Tackle the Barriers? *International Journal of Information Systems and Supply Chain Management*, 10(4), 80–100. doi:10.4018/IJISSCM.2017100105

Fernandes, T. M., Gomes, J., & Romão, M. (2017). Investments in E-Government: A Benefit Management Case Study. *International Journal of Electronic Government Research*, 13(3), 1–17. doi:10.4018/IJEGR.2017070101

Figueira, L. M., Honrado, G. R., & Dionísio, M. S. (2021). Human Capital Management in the Tourism Industry in Portugal. In V. Costa, A. Moura, & M. Mira (Eds.), *Handbook of Research on Human Capital and People Management in the Tourism Industry* (pp. 1–19). IGI Global. doi:10.4018/978-1-7998-4318-4.ch001

Gao, S. S., Oreal, S., & Zhang, J. (2018). Contemporary Financial Risk Management Perceptions and Practices of Small-Sized Chinese Businesses. In I. Management Association (Ed.), Global Business Expansion: Concepts, Methodologies, Tools, and Applications (pp. 917-931). Hershey, PA: IGI Global. doi:10.4018/978-1-5225-5481-3.ch041

Garg, R., & Berning, S. C. (2017). Indigenous Chinese Management Philosophies: Key Concepts and Relevance for Modern Chinese Firms. In B. Christiansen & G. Koc (Eds.), *Transcontinental Strategies for Industrial Development and Economic Growth* (pp. 43–57). Hershey, PA: IGI Global. doi:10.4018/978-1-5225-2160-0.ch003

Gencer, Y. G. (2017). Supply Chain Management in Retailing Business. In U. Akkucuk (Ed.), *Ethics and Sustainability in Global Supply Chain Management* (pp. 197–210). Hershey, PA: IGI Global. doi:10.4018/978-1-5225-2036-8.ch011

Gera, R., Arora, S., & Malik, S. (2021). Emotional Labor in the Tourism Industry: Strategies, Antecedents, and Outcomes. In V. Costa, A. Moura, & M. Mira (Eds.), *Handbook of Research on Human Capital and People Management in the Tourism Industry* (pp. 73–91). IGI Global. https://doi.org/10.4018/978-1-7998-4318-4.ch004

Giacosa, E. (2018). The Increasing of the Regional Development Thanks to the Luxury Business Innovation. In L. Carvalho (Ed.), *Handbook of Research on Entrepreneurial Ecosystems and Social Dynamics in a Globalized World* (pp. 260–273). Hershey, PA: IGI Global. doi:10.4018/978-1-5225-3525-6.ch011

Glowka, G., Tusch, M., & Zehrer, A. (2021). The Risk Perception of Family Business Owner-Manager in the Tourism Industry: A Qualitative Comparison of the Intra-Firm Senior and Junior Generation. In A. Zehrer, G. Glowka, K. Schwaiger, & V. Ranacher-Lackner (Eds.), *Resiliency Models and Addressing Future Risks for Family Firms in the Tourism Industry* (pp. 126–153). IGI Global. https://doi.org/10.4018/978-1-7998-7352-5.ch006

Glykas, M., & George, J. (2017). Quality and Process Management Systems in the UAE Maritime Industry. *International Journal of Productivity Management and Assessment Technologies*, 5(1), 20–39. doi:10.4018/IJPMAT.2017010102

Glykas, M., Valiris, G., Kokkinaki, A., & Koutsoukou, Z. (2018). Banking Business Process Management Implementation. *International Journal of Productivity Management and Assessment Technologies, 6*(1), 50–69. doi:10.4018/IJPMAT.2018010104

Gomes, J., & Romão, M. (2017). The Balanced Scorecard: Keeping Updated and Aligned with Today's Business Trends. *International Journal of Productivity Management and Assessment Technologies, 5*(2), 1–15. doi:10.4018/IJPMAT.2017070101

Gomes, J., & Romão, M. (2017). Aligning Information Systems and Technology with Benefit Management and Balanced Scorecard. In S. De Haes & W. Van Grembergen (Eds.), *Strategic IT Governance and Alignment in Business Settings* (pp. 112–131). Hershey, PA: IGI Global. doi:10.4018/978-1-5225-0861-8.ch005

Goyal, A. (2021). Communicating and Building Destination Brands With New Media. In M. Dinis, L. Bonixe, S. Lamy, & Z. Breda (Eds.), *Impact of New Media in Tourism* (pp. 1-20). IGI Global. https://doi.org/10.4018/978-1-7998-7095-1.ch001

Grefen, P., & Turetken, O. (2017). Advanced Business Process Management in Networked E-Business Scenarios. *International Journal of E-Business Research, 13*(4), 70–104. doi:10.4018/IJEBR.2017100105

Guasca, M., Van Broeck, A. M., & Vanneste, D. (2021). Tourism and the Social Reintegration of Colombian Ex-Combatants. In J. da Silva, Z. Breda, & F. Carbone (Eds.), *Role and Impact of Tourism in Peacebuilding and Conflict Transformation* (pp. 66-86). IGI Global. https://doi.org/10.4018/978-1-7998-5053-3.ch005

Haider, A., & Saetang, S. (2017). Strategic IT Alignment in Service Sector. In S. Rozenes & Y. Cohen (Eds.), *Handbook of Research on Strategic Alliances and Value Co-Creation in the Service Industry* (pp. 231–258). Hershey, PA: IGI Global. doi:10.4018/978-1-5225-2084-9.ch012

Hajilari, A. B., Ghadaksaz, M., & Fasghandis, G. S. (2017). Assessing Organizational Readiness for Implementing ERP System Using Fuzzy Expert System Approach. *International Journal of Enterprise Information Systems, 13*(1), 67–85. doi:10.4018/IJEIS.2017010105

Haldorai, A., Ramu, A., & Murugan, S. (2018). Social Aware Cognitive Radio Networks: Effectiveness of Social Networks as a Strategic Tool for Organizational Business Management. In H. Bansal, G. Shrivastava, G. Nguyen, & L. Stanciu (Eds.), *Social Network Analytics for Contemporary Business Organizations* (pp. 188–202). Hershey, PA: IGI Global. doi:10.4018/978-1-5225-5097-6.ch010

Hall, O. P. Jr. (2017). Social Media Driven Management Education. *International Journal of Knowledge-Based Organizations*, *7*(2), 43–59. doi:10.4018/IJKBO.2017040104

Hanifah, H., Halim, H. A., Ahmad, N. H., & Vafaei-Zadeh, A. (2017). Innovation Culture as a Mediator Between Specific Human Capital and Innovation Performance Among Bumiputera SMEs in Malaysia. In N. Ahmad, T. Ramayah, H. Halim, & S. Rahman (Eds.), *Handbook of Research on Small and Medium Enterprises in Developing Countries* (pp. 261–279). Hershey, PA: IGI Global. doi:10.4018/978-1-5225-2165-5.ch012

Hartlieb, S., & Silvius, G. (2017). Handling Uncertainty in Project Management and Business Development: Similarities and Differences. In Y. Raydugin (Ed.), *Handbook of Research on Leveraging Risk and Uncertainties for Effective Project Management* (pp. 337–362). Hershey, PA: IGI Global. doi:10.4018/978-1-5225-1790-0.ch016

Hass, K. B. (2017). Living on the Edge: Managing Project Complexity. In Y. Raydugin (Ed.), *Handbook of Research on Leveraging Risk and Uncertainties for Effective Project Management* (pp. 177–201). Hershey, PA: IGI Global. doi:10.4018/978-1-5225-1790-0.ch009

Hawking, P., & Carmine Sellitto, C. (2017). Developing an Effective Strategy for Organizational Business Intelligence. In M. Tavana (Ed.), *Enterprise Information Systems and the Digitalization of Business Functions* (pp. 222–237). Hershey, PA: IGI Global. doi:10.4018/978-1-5225-2382-6.ch010

Hawking, P., & Sellitto, C. (2017). A Fast-Moving Consumer Goods Company and Business Intelligence Strategy Development. *International Journal of Enterprise Information Systems*, *13*(2), 22–33. doi:10.4018/IJEIS.2017040102

Hawking, P., & Sellitto, C. (2017). Business Intelligence Strategy: Two Case Studies. *International Journal of Business Intelligence Research*, *8*(2), 17–30. doi:10.4018/IJBIR.2017070102

Hee, W. J., Jalleh, G., Lai, H., & Lin, C. (2017). E-Commerce and IT Projects: Evaluation and Management Issues in Australian and Taiwanese Hospitals. *International Journal of Public Health Management and Ethics*, *2*(1), 69–90. doi:10.4018/IJPHME.2017010104

Hernandez, A. A. (2018). Exploring the Factors to Green IT Adoption of SMEs in the Philippines. *Journal of Cases on Information Technology*, *20*(2), 49–66. doi:10.4018/JCIT.2018040104

Hollman, A., Bickford, S., & Hollman, T. (2017). Cyber InSecurity: A Post-Mortem Attempt to Assess Cyber Problems from IT and Business Management Perspectives. *Journal of Cases on Information Technology, 19*(3), 42–70. doi:10.4018/JCIT.2017070104

Ibrahim, F., & Zainin, N. M. (2021). Exploring the Technological Impacts: The Case of Museums in Brunei Darussalam. *International Journal of Tourism and Hospitality Management in the Digital Age, 5*(1), 1–18. https://doi.org/10.4018/IJTHMDA.2021010101

Igbinakhase, I. (2017). Responsible and Sustainable Management Practices in Developing and Developed Business Environments. In Z. Fields (Ed.), *Collective Creativity for Responsible and Sustainable Business Practice* (pp. 180–207). Hershey, PA: IGI Global. doi:10.4018/978-1-5225-1823-5.ch010

Iwata, J. J., & Hoskins, R. G. (2017). Managing Indigenous Knowledge in Tanzania: A Business Perspective. In P. Jain & N. Mnjama (Eds.), *Managing Knowledge Resources and Records in Modern Organizations* (pp. 198–214). Hershey, PA: IGI Global. doi:10.4018/978-1-5225-1965-2.ch012

Jain, P. (2017). Ethical and Legal Issues in Knowledge Management Life-Cycle in Business. In P. Jain & N. Mnjama (Eds.), *Managing Knowledge Resources and Records in Modern Organizations* (pp. 82–101). Hershey, PA: IGI Global. doi:10.4018/978-1-5225-1965-2.ch006

James, S., & Hauli, E. (2017). Holistic Management Education at Tanzanian Rural Development Planning Institute. In N. Baporikar (Ed.), *Management Education for Global Leadership* (pp. 112–136). Hershey, PA: IGI Global. doi:10.4018/978-1-5225-1013-0.ch006

Janošková, M., Csikósová, A., & Čulková, K. (2018). Measurement of Company Performance as Part of Its Strategic Management. In R. Leon (Ed.), *Managerial Strategies for Business Sustainability During Turbulent Times* (pp. 309–335). Hershey, PA: IGI Global. doi:10.4018/978-1-5225-2716-9.ch017

Jean-Vasile, A., & Alecu, A. (2017). Theoretical and Practical Approaches in Understanding the Influences of Cost-Productivity-Profit Trinomial in Contemporary Enterprises. In A. Jean Vasile & D. Nicolò (Eds.), *Sustainable Entrepreneurship and Investments in the Green Economy* (pp. 28–62). Hershey, PA: IGI Global. doi:10.4018/978-1-5225-2075-7.ch002

Joia, L. A., & Correia, J. C. (2018). CIO Competencies From the IT Professional Perspective: Insights From Brazil. *Journal of Global Information Management, 26*(2), 74–103. doi:10.4018/JGIM.2018040104

Juma, A., & Mzera, N. (2017). Knowledge Management and Records Management and Competitive Advantage in Business. In P. Jain & N. Mnjama (Eds.), *Managing Knowledge Resources and Records in Modern Organizations* (pp. 15–28). Hershey, PA: IGI Global. doi:10.4018/978-1-5225-1965-2.ch002

K., I., & A, V. (2018). Monitoring and Auditing in the Cloud. In K. Munir (Ed.), *Cloud Computing Technologies for Green Enterprises* (pp. 318-350). Hershey, PA: IGI Global. https://doi.org/ doi:10.4018/978-1-5225-3038-1.ch013

Kabra, G., Ghosh, V., & Ramesh, A. (2018). Enterprise Integrated Business Process Management and Business Intelligence Framework for Business Process Sustainability. In A. Paul, D. Bhattacharyya, & S. Anand (Eds.), *Green Initiatives for Business Sustainability and Value Creation* (pp. 228–238). Hershey, PA: IGI Global. doi:10.4018/978-1-5225-2662-9.ch010

Kaoud, M. (2017). Investigation of Customer Knowledge Management: A Case Study Research. *International Journal of Service Science, Management, Engineering, and Technology*, 8(2), 12–22. doi:10.4018/IJSSMET.2017040102

Katuu, S. (2018). A Comparative Assessment of Enterprise Content Management Maturity Models. In N. Gwangwava & M. Mutingi (Eds.), *E-Manufacturing and E-Service Strategies in Contemporary Organizations* (pp. 93–118). Hershey, PA: IGI Global. doi:10.4018/978-1-5225-3628-4.ch005

Khan, M. Y., & Abir, T. (2022). The Role of Social Media Marketing in the Tourism and Hospitality Industry: A Conceptual Study on Bangladesh. In C. Ramos, S. Quinteiro, & A. Gonçalves (Eds.), *ICT as Innovator Between Tourism and Culture* (pp. 213–229). IGI Global. https://doi.org/10.4018/978-1-7998-8165-0.ch013

Kinnunen, S., Ylä-Kujala, A., Marttonen-Arola, S., Kärri, T., & Baglee, D. (2018). Internet of Things in Asset Management: Insights from Industrial Professionals and Academia. *International Journal of Service Science, Management, Engineering, and Technology*, 9(2), 104–119. doi:10.4018/IJSSMET.2018040105

Klein, A. Z., Sabino de Freitas, A., Machado, L., Freitas, J. C. Jr, Graziola, P. G. Jr, & Schlemmer, E. (2017). Virtual Worlds Applications for Management Education. In L. Tomei (Ed.), *Exploring the New Era of Technology-Infused Education* (pp. 279–299). Hershey, PA: IGI Global. doi:10.4018/978-1-5225-1709-2.ch017

Kővári, E., Saleh, M., & Steinbachné Hajmásy, G. (2022). The Impact of Corporate Digital Responsibility (CDR) on Internal Stakeholders' Satisfaction in Hungarian Upscale Hotels. In M. Valeri (Ed.), *New Governance and Management in Touristic Destinations* (pp. 35–51). IGI Global. https://doi.org/10.4018/978-1-6684-3889-3.ch003

Kożuch, B., & Jabłoński, A. (2017). Adopting the Concept of Business Models in Public Management. In M. Lewandowski & B. Kożuch (Eds.), *Public Sector Entrepreneurship and the Integration of Innovative Business Models* (pp. 10–46). Hershey, PA: IGI Global. doi:10.4018/978-1-5225-2215-7.ch002

Kumar, J., Adhikary, A., & Jha, A. (2017). Small Active Investors' Perceptions and Preferences Towards Tax Saving Mutual Fund Schemes in Eastern India: An Empirical Note. *International Journal of Asian Business and Information Management*, 8(2), 35–45. doi:10.4018/IJABIM.2017040103

Latusi, S., & Fissore, M. (2021). Pilgrimage Routes to Happiness: Comparing the Camino de Santiago and Via Francigena. In A. Perinotto, V. Mayer, & J. Soares (Eds.), *Rebuilding and Restructuring the Tourism Industry: Infusion of Happiness and Quality of Life* (pp. 157–182). IGI Global. https://doi.org/10.4018/978-1-7998-7239-9.ch008

Lavassani, K. M., & Movahedi, B. (2017). Applications Driven Information Systems: Beyond Networks toward Business Ecosystems. *International Journal of Innovation in the Digital Economy*, 8(1), 61–75. doi:10.4018/IJIDE.2017010104

Lazzareschi, V. H., & Brito, M. S. (2017). Strategic Information Management: Proposal of Business Project Model. In G. Jamil, A. Soares, & C. Pessoa (Eds.), *Handbook of Research on Information Management for Effective Logistics and Supply Chains* (pp. 59–88). Hershey, PA: IGI Global. doi:10.4018/978-1-5225-0973-8.ch004

Lechuga Sancho, M. P., & Martín Navarro, A. (2022). Evolution of the Literature on Social Responsibility in the Tourism Sector: A Systematic Literature Review. In G. Fernandes (Ed.), *Challenges and New Opportunities for Tourism in Inland Territories: Ecocultural Resources and Sustainable Initiatives* (pp. 169–186). IGI Global. https://doi.org/10.4018/978-1-7998-7339-6.ch010

Lederer, M., Kurz, M., & Lazarov, P. (2017). Usage and Suitability of Methods for Strategic Business Process Initiatives: A Multi Case Study Research. *International Journal of Productivity Management and Assessment Technologies*, 5(1), 40–51. doi:10.4018/IJPMAT.2017010103

Lee, I. (2017). A Social Enterprise Business Model and a Case Study of Pacific Community Ventures (PCV). In V. Potocan, M. Ünğan, & Z. Nedelko (Eds.), *Handbook of Research on Managerial Solutions in Non-Profit Organizations* (pp. 182–204). Hershey, PA: IGI Global. doi:10.4018/978-1-5225-0731-4.ch009

Leon, L. A., Seal, K. C., Przasnyski, Z. H., & Wiedenman, I. (2017). Skills and Competencies Required for Jobs in Business Analytics: A Content Analysis of Job Advertisements Using Text Mining. *International Journal of Business Intelligence Research*, 8(1), 1–25. doi:10.4018/IJBIR.2017010101

Levy, C. L., & Elias, N. I. (2017). SOHO Users' Perceptions of Reliability and Continuity of Cloud-Based Services. In M. Moore (Ed.), *Cybersecurity Breaches and Issues Surrounding Online Threat Protection* (pp. 248–287). Hershey, PA: IGI Global. doi:10.4018/978-1-5225-1941-6.ch011

Levy, M. (2018). Change Management Serving Knowledge Management and Organizational Development: Reflections and Review. In N. Baporikar (Ed.), *Global Practices in Knowledge Management for Societal and Organizational Development* (pp. 256–270). Hershey, PA: IGI Global. doi:10.4018/978-1-5225-3009-1.ch012

Lewandowski, M. (2017). Public Organizations and Business Model Innovation: The Role of Public Service Design. In M. Lewandowski & B. Kożuch (Eds.), *Public Sector Entrepreneurship and the Integration of Innovative Business Models* (pp. 47–72). Hershey, PA: IGI Global. doi:10.4018/978-1-5225-2215-7.ch003

Lhannaoui, H., Kabbaj, M. I., & Bakkoury, Z. (2017). A Survey of Risk-Aware Business Process Modelling. *International Journal of Risk and Contingency Management*, 6(3), 14–26. doi:10.4018/IJRCM.2017070102

Li, J., Sun, W., Jiang, W., Yang, H., & Zhang, L. (2017). How the Nature of Exogenous Shocks and Crises Impact Company Performance?: The Effects of Industry Characteristics. *International Journal of Risk and Contingency Management*, 6(4), 40–55. doi:10.4018/IJRCM.2017100103

Lopez-Fernandez, M., Perez-Perez, M., Serrano-Bedia, A., & Cobo-Gonzalez, A. (2021). Small and Medium Tourism Enterprise Survival in Times of Crisis: "El Capricho de Gaudí. In D. Toubes & N. Araújo-Vila (Eds.), *Risk, Crisis, and Disaster Management in Small and Medium-Sized Tourism Enterprises* (pp. 103–129). IGI Global. doi:10.4018/978-1-7998-6996-2.ch005

Mahajan, A., Maidullah, S., & Hossain, M. R. (2022). Experience Toward Smart Tour Guide Apps in Travelling: An Analysis of Users' Reviews on Audio Odigos and Trip My Way. In R. Augusto Costa, F. Brandão, Z. Breda, & C. Costa (Eds.), *Planning and Managing the Experience Economy in Tourism* (pp. 255-273). IGI Global. https://doi.org/10.4018/978-1-7998-8775-1.ch014

Malega, P. (2017). Small and Medium Enterprises in the Slovak Republic: Status and Competitiveness of SMEs in the Global Markets and Possibilities of Optimization. In M. Vemić (Ed.), *Optimal Management Strategies in Small and Medium Enterprises* (pp. 102–124). Hershey, PA: IGI Global. doi:10.4018/978-1-5225-1949-2.ch006

Malewska, K. M. (2017). Intuition in Decision-Making on the Example of a Non-Profit Organization. In V. Potocan, M. Üngan, & Z. Nedelko (Eds.), *Handbook of Research on Managerial Solutions in Non-Profit Organizations* (pp. 378–399). Hershey, PA: IGI Global. doi:10.4018/978-1-5225-0731-4.ch018

Maroofi, F. (2017). Entrepreneurial Orientation and Organizational Learning Ability Analysis for Innovation and Firm Performance. In N. Baporikar (Ed.), *Innovation and Shifting Perspectives in Management Education* (pp. 144–165). Hershey, PA: IGI Global. doi:10.4018/978-1-5225-1019-2.ch007

Marques, M., Moleiro, D., Brito, T. M., & Marques, T. (2021). Customer Relationship Management as an Important Relationship Marketing Tool: The Case of the Hospitality Industry in Estoril Coast. In M. Dinis, L. Bonixe, S. Lamy, & Z. Breda (Eds.), Impact of New Media in Tourism (pp. 39-56). IGI Global. https://doi.org/doi:10.4018/978-1-7998-7095-1.ch003

Martins, P. V., & Zacarias, M. (2017). A Web-based Tool for Business Process Improvement. *International Journal of Web Portals*, 9(2), 68–84. doi:10.4018/IJWP.2017070104

Matthies, B., & Coners, A. (2017). Exploring the Conceptual Nature of e-Business Projects. *Journal of Electronic Commerce in Organizations*, 15(3), 33–63. doi:10.4018/JECO.2017070103

Mayer, V. F., Fraga, C. C., & Silva, L. C. (2021). Contributions of Neurosciences to Studies of Well-Being in Tourism. In A. Perinotto, V. Mayer, & J. Soares (Eds.), *Rebuilding and Restructuring the Tourism Industry: Infusion of Happiness and Quality of Life* (pp. 108–128). IGI Global. https://doi.org/10.4018/978-1-7998-7239-9.ch006

McKee, J. (2018). Architecture as a Tool to Solve Business Planning Problems. In M. Khosrow-Pour, D.B.A. (Ed.), Encyclopedia of Information Science and Technology, Fourth Edition (pp. 573-586). Hershey, PA: IGI Global. doi:10.4018/978-1-5225-2255-3.ch050

McMurray, A. J., Cross, J., & Caponecchia, C. (2018). The Risk Management Profession in Australia: Business Continuity Plan Practices. In N. Bajgoric (Ed.), *Always-On Enterprise Information Systems for Modern Organizations* (pp. 112–129). Hershey, PA: IGI Global. doi:10.4018/978-1-5225-3704-5.ch006

Meddah, I. H., & Belkadi, K. (2018). Mining Patterns Using Business Process Management. In R. Hamou (Ed.), *Handbook of Research on Biomimicry in Information Retrieval and Knowledge Management* (pp. 78–89). Hershey, PA: IGI Global. doi:10.4018/978-1-5225-3004-6.ch005

Melian, A. G., & Camprubí, R. (2021). The Accessibility of Museum Websites: The Case of Barcelona. In C. Eusébio, L. Teixeira, & M. Carneiro (Eds.), *ICT Tools and Applications for Accessible Tourism* (pp. 234–255). IGI Global. https://doi.org/10.4018/978-1-7998-6428-8.ch011

Mendes, L. (2017). TQM and Knowledge Management: An Integrated Approach Towards Tacit Knowledge Management. In D. Jaziri-Bouagina & G. Jamil (Eds.), *Handbook of Research on Tacit Knowledge Management for Organizational Success* (pp. 236–263). Hershey, PA: IGI Global. doi:10.4018/978-1-5225-2394-9.ch009

Menezes, V. D., & Cavagnaro, E. (2021). Communicating Sustainable Initiatives in the Hotel Industry: The Case of the Hotel Jakarta Amsterdam. In F. Brandão, Z. Breda, R. Costa, & C. Costa (Eds.), *Handbook of Research on the Role of Tourism in Achieving Sustainable Development Goals* (pp. 224-234). IGI Global. https://doi.org/10.4018/978-1-7998-5691-7.ch013

Menezes, V. D., & Cavagnaro, E. (2021). Communicating Sustainable Initiatives in the Hotel Industry: The Case of the Hotel Jakarta Amsterdam. In F. Brandão, Z. Breda, R. Costa, & C. Costa (Eds.), *Handbook of Research on the Role of Tourism in Achieving Sustainable Development Goals* (pp. 224-234). IGI Global. https://doi.org/10.4018/978-1-7998-5691-7.ch013

Mitas, O., Bastiaansen, M., & Boode, W. (2022). If You're Happy, I'm Happy: Emotion Contagion at a Tourist Information Center. In R. Augusto Costa, F. Brandão, Z. Breda, & C. Costa (Eds.), *Planning and Managing the Experience Economy in Tourism* (pp. 122-140). IGI Global. https://doi.org/10.4018/978-1-7998-8775-1.ch007

Mnjama, N. M. (2017). Preservation of Recorded Information in Public and Private Sector Organizations. In P. Jain & N. Mnjama (Eds.), *Managing Knowledge Resources and Records in Modern Organizations* (pp. 149–167). Hershey, PA: IGI Global. doi:10.4018/978-1-5225-1965-2.ch009

Mokoqama, M., & Fields, Z. (2017). Principles of Responsible Management Education (PRME): Call for Responsible Management Education. In Z. Fields (Ed.), *Collective Creativity for Responsible and Sustainable Business Practice* (pp. 229–241). Hershey, PA: IGI Global. doi:10.4018/978-1-5225-1823-5.ch012

Monteiro, A., Lopes, S., & Carbone, F. (2021). Academic Mobility: Bridging Tourism and Peace Education. In J. da Silva, Z. Breda, & F. Carbone (Eds.), *Role and Impact of Tourism in Peacebuilding and Conflict Transformation* (pp. 275-301). IGI Global. https://doi.org/10.4018/978-1-7998-5053-3.ch016

Muniapan, B. (2017). Philosophy and Management: The Relevance of Vedanta in Management. In P. Ordóñez de Pablos (Ed.), *Managerial Strategies and Solutions for Business Success in Asia* (pp. 124–139). Hershey, PA: IGI Global. doi:10.4018/978-1-5225-1886-0.ch007

Murad, S. E., & Dowaji, S. (2017). Using Value-Based Approach for Managing Cloud-Based Services. In A. Turuk, B. Sahoo, & S. Addya (Eds.), *Resource Management and Efficiency in Cloud Computing Environments* (pp. 33–60). Hershey, PA: IGI Global. doi:10.4018/978-1-5225-1721-4.ch002

Mutahar, A. M., Daud, N. M., Thurasamy, R., Isaac, O., & Abdulsalam, R. (2018). The Mediating of Perceived Usefulness and Perceived Ease of Use: The Case of Mobile Banking in Yemen. *International Journal of Technology Diffusion*, *9*(2), 21–40. doi:10.4018/IJTD.2018040102

Naidoo, V. (2017). E-Learning and Management Education at African Universities. In N. Baporikar (Ed.), *Management Education for Global Leadership* (pp. 181–201). Hershey, PA: IGI Global. doi:10.4018/978-1-5225-1013-0.ch009

Naidoo, V., & Igbinakhase, I. (2018). Opportunities and Challenges of Knowledge Retention in SMEs. In N. Baporikar (Ed.), *Knowledge Integration Strategies for Entrepreneurship and Sustainability* (pp. 70–94). Hershey, PA: IGI Global. doi:10.4018/978-1-5225-5115-7.ch004

Naumov, N., & Costandachi, G. (2021). Creativity and Entrepreneurship: Gastronomic Tourism in Mexico. In J. Soares (Ed.), *Innovation and Entrepreneurial Opportunities in Community Tourism* (pp. 90–108). IGI Global. https://doi.org/10.4018/978-1-7998-4855-4.ch006

Nayak, S., & Prabhu, N. (2017). Paradigm Shift in Management Education: Need for a Cross Functional Perspective. In N. Baporikar (Ed.), *Management Education for Global Leadership* (pp. 241–255). Hershey, PA: IGI Global. doi:10.4018/978-1-5225-1013-0.ch012

Nedelko, Z., & Potocan, V. (2017). Management Solutions in Non-Profit Organizations: Case of Slovenia. In V. Potocan, M. Üngan, & Z. Nedelko (Eds.), *Handbook of Research on Managerial Solutions in Non-Profit Organizations* (pp. 1–22). Hershey, PA: IGI Global. doi:10.4018/978-1-5225-0731-4.ch001

Nedelko, Z., & Potocan, V. (2017). Priority of Management Tools Utilization among Managers: International Comparison. In V. Wang (Ed.), *Encyclopedia of Strategic Leadership and Management* (pp. 1083–1094). Hershey, PA: IGI Global. doi:10.4018/978-1-5225-1049-9.ch075

Nedelko, Z., Raudeliūnienė, J., & Črešnar, R. (2018). Knowledge Dynamics in Supply Chain Management. In N. Baporikar (Ed.), *Knowledge Integration Strategies for Entrepreneurship and Sustainability* (pp. 150–166). Hershey, PA: IGI Global. doi:10.4018/978-1-5225-5115-7.ch008

Nguyen, H. T., & Hipsher, S. A. (2018). Innovation and Creativity Used by Private Sector Firms in a Resources-Constrained Environment. In S. Hipsher (Ed.), *Examining the Private Sector's Role in Wealth Creation and Poverty Reduction* (pp. 219–238). Hershey, PA: IGI Global. doi:10.4018/978-1-5225-3117-3.ch010

Obicci, P. A. (2017). Risk Sharing in a Partnership. In *Risk Management Strategies in Public-Private Partnerships* (pp. 115–152). Hershey, PA: IGI Global. doi:10.4018/978-1-5225-2503-5.ch004

Obidallah, W. J., & Raahemi, B. (2017). Managing Changes in Service Oriented Virtual Organizations: A Structural and Procedural Framework to Facilitate the Process of Change. *Journal of Electronic Commerce in Organizations, 15*(1), 59–83. doi:10.4018/JECO.2017010104

Ojo, O. (2017). Impact of Innovation on the Entrepreneurial Success in Selected Business Enterprises in South-West Nigeria. *International Journal of Innovation in the Digital Economy, 8*(2), 29–38. doi:10.4018/IJIDE.2017040103

Okdinawati, L., Simatupang, T. M., & Sunitiyoso, Y. (2017). Multi-Agent Reinforcement Learning for Value Co-Creation of Collaborative Transportation Management (CTM). *International Journal of Information Systems and Supply Chain Management, 10*(3), 84–95. doi:10.4018/IJISSCM.2017070105

Olivera, V. A., & Carrillo, I. M. (2021). Organizational Culture: A Key Element for the Development of Mexican Micro and Small Tourist Companies. In J. Soares (Ed.), *Innovation and Entrepreneurial Opportunities in Community Tourism* (pp. 227–242). IGI Global. doi:10.4018/978-1-7998-4855-4.ch013

Ossorio, M. (2022). Corporate Museum Experiences in Enogastronomic Tourism. In R. Augusto Costa, F. Brandão, Z. Breda, & C. Costa (Eds.), Planning and Managing the Experience Economy in Tourism (pp. 107-121). IGI Global. https://doi.org/doi:10.4018/978-1-7998-8775-1.ch006

Ossorio, M. (2022). Enogastronomic Tourism in Times of Pandemic. In G. Fernandes (Ed.), *Challenges and New Opportunities for Tourism in Inland Territories: Ecocultural Resources and Sustainable Initiatives* (pp. 241–255). IGI Global. https://doi.org/10.4018/978-1-7998-7339-6.ch014

Özekici, Y. K. (2022). ICT as an Acculturative Agent and Its Role in the Tourism Context: Introduction, Acculturation Theory, Progress of the Acculturation Theory in Extant Literature. In C. Ramos, S. Quinteiro, & A. Gonçalves (Eds.), *ICT as Innovator Between Tourism and Culture* (pp. 42–66). IGI Global. https://doi.org/10.4018/978-1-7998-8165-0.ch004

Pal, K. (2018). Building High Quality Big Data-Based Applications in Supply Chains. In A. Kumar & S. Saurav (Eds.), *Supply Chain Management Strategies and Risk Assessment in Retail Environments* (pp. 1–24). Hershey, PA: IGI Global. doi:10.4018/978-1-5225-3056-5.ch001

Palos-Sanchez, P. R., & Correia, M. B. (2018). Perspectives of the Adoption of Cloud Computing in the Tourism Sector. In J. Rodrigues, C. Ramos, P. Cardoso, & C. Henriques (Eds.), *Handbook of Research on Technological Developments for Cultural Heritage and eTourism Applications* (pp. 377–400). Hershey, PA: IGI Global. doi:10.4018/978-1-5225-2927-9.ch018

Papadopoulou, G. (2021). Promoting Gender Equality and Women Empowerment in the Tourism Sector. In F. Brandão, Z. Breda, R. Costa, & C. Costa (Eds.), Handbook of Research on the Role of Tourism in Achieving Sustainable Development Goals (pp. 152-174). IGI Global. https://doi.org/ doi:10.4018/978-1-7998-5691-7.ch009

Papp-Váry, Á. F., & Tóth, T. Z. (2022). Analysis of Budapest as a Film Tourism Destination. In R. Baleiro & R. Pereira (Eds.), *Global Perspectives on Literary Tourism and Film-Induced Tourism* (pp. 257-279). IGI Global. https://doi.org/10.4018/978-1-7998-8262-6.ch014

Patiño, B. E. (2017). New Generation Management by Convergence and Individual Identity: A Systemic and Human-Oriented Approach. In N. Baporikar (Ed.), *Innovation and Shifting Perspectives in Management Education* (pp. 119–143). Hershey, PA: IGI Global. doi:10.4018/978-1-5225-1019-2.ch006

Patro, C. S. (2021). Digital Tourism: Influence of E-Marketing Technology. In M. Dinis, L. Bonixe, S. Lamy, & Z. Breda (Eds.), *Impact of New Media in Tourism* (pp. 234-254). IGI Global. https://doi.org/10.4018/978-1-7998-7095-1.ch014

Pawliczek, A., & Rössler, M. (2017). Knowledge of Management Tools and Systems in SMEs: Knowledge Transfer in Management. In A. Bencsik (Ed.), *Knowledge Management Initiatives and Strategies in Small and Medium Enterprises* (pp. 180–203). Hershey, PA: IGI Global. doi:10.4018/978-1-5225-1642-2.ch009

Pejic-Bach, M., Omazic, M. A., Aleksic, A., & Zoroja, J. (2018). Knowledge-Based Decision Making: A Multi-Case Analysis. In R. Leon (Ed.), *Managerial Strategies for Business Sustainability During Turbulent Times* (pp. 160–184). Hershey, PA: IGI Global. doi:10.4018/978-1-5225-2716-9.ch009

Perano, M., Hysa, X., & Calabrese, M. (2018). Strategic Planning, Cultural Context, and Business Continuity Management: Business Cases in the City of Shkoder. In A. Presenza & L. Sheehan (Eds.), *Geopolitics and Strategic Management in the Global Economy* (pp. 57–77). Hershey, PA: IGI Global. doi:10.4018/978-1-5225-2673-5.ch004

Pereira, R., Mira da Silva, M., & Lapão, L. V. (2017). IT Governance Maturity Patterns in Portuguese Healthcare. In S. De Haes & W. Van Grembergen (Eds.), *Strategic IT Governance and Alignment in Business Settings* (pp. 24–52). Hershey, PA: IGI Global. doi:10.4018/978-1-5225-0861-8.ch002

Pérez-Uribe, R. I., Torres, D. A., Jurado, S. P., & Prada, D. M. (2018). Cloud Tools for the Development of Project Management in SMEs. In R. Perez-Uribe, C. Salcedo-Perez, & D. Ocampo-Guzman (Eds.), *Handbook of Research on Intrapreneurship and Organizational Sustainability in SMEs* (pp. 95–120). Hershey, PA: IGI Global. doi:10.4018/978-1-5225-3543-0.ch005

Petrisor, I., & Cozmiuc, D. (2017). Global Supply Chain Management Organization at Siemens in the Advent of Industry 4.0. In L. Saglietto & C. Cezanne (Eds.), *Global Intermediation and Logistics Service Providers* (pp. 123–142). Hershey, PA: IGI Global. doi:10.4018/978-1-5225-2133-4.ch007

Pierce, J. M., Velliaris, D. M., & Edwards, J. (2017). A Living Case Study: A Journey Not a Destination. In N. Silton (Ed.), *Exploring the Benefits of Creativity in Education, Media, and the Arts* (pp. 158–178). Hershey, PA: IGI Global. doi:10.4018/978-1-5225-0504-4.ch008

Pipia, S., & Pipia, S. (2021). Challenges of Religious Tourism in the Conflict Region: An Example of Jerusalem. In E. Alaverdov & M. Bari (Eds.), *Global Development of Religious Tourism* (pp. 135-148). IGI Global. https://doi.org/10.4018/978-1-7998-5792-1.ch009

Poulaki, P., Kritikos, A., Vasilakis, N., & Valeri, M. (2022). The Contribution of Female Creativity to the Development of Gastronomic Tourism in Greece: The Case of the Island of Naxos in the South Aegean Region. In M. Valeri (Ed.), *New Governance and Management in Touristic Destinations* (pp. 246–258). IGI Global. https://doi.org/10.4018/978-1-6684-3889-3.ch015

Radosavljevic, M., & Andjelkovic, A. (2017). Multi-Criteria Decision Making Approach for Choosing Business Process for the Improvement: Upgrading of the Six Sigma Methodology. In J. Stanković, P. Delias, S. Marinković, & S. Rochhia (Eds.), *Tools and Techniques for Economic Decision Analysis* (pp. 225–247). Hershey, PA: IGI Global. doi:10.4018/978-1-5225-0959-2.ch011

Radovic, V. M. (2017). Corporate Sustainability and Responsibility and Disaster Risk Reduction: A Serbian Overview. In M. Camilleri (Ed.), *CSR 2.0 and the New Era of Corporate Citizenship* (pp. 147–164). Hershey, PA: IGI Global. doi:10.4018/978-1-5225-1842-6.ch008

Raghunath, K. M., Devi, S. L., & Patro, C. S. (2018). Impact of Risk Assessment Models on Risk Factors: A Holistic Outlook. In K. Strang, M. Korstanje, & N. Vajjhala (Eds.), *Research, Practices, and Innovations in Global Risk and Contingency Management* (pp. 134–153). Hershey, PA: IGI Global. doi:10.4018/978-1-5225-4754-9.ch008

Raman, A., & Goyal, D. P. (2017). Extending IMPLEMENT Framework for Enterprise Information Systems Implementation to Information System Innovation. In M. Tavana (Ed.), *Enterprise Information Systems and the Digitalization of Business Functions* (pp. 137–177). Hershey, PA: IGI Global. doi:10.4018/978-1-5225-2382-6.ch007

Rao, Y., & Zhang, Y. (2017). The Construction and Development of Academic Library Digital Special Subject Databases. In L. Ruan, Q. Zhu, & Y. Ye (Eds.), *Academic Library Development and Administration in China* (pp. 163–183). Hershey, PA: IGI Global. doi:10.4018/978-1-5225-0550-1.ch010

Ravasan, A. Z., Mohammadi, M. M., & Hamidi, H. (2018). An Investigation Into the Critical Success Factors of Implementing Information Technology Service Management Frameworks. In K. Jakobs (Ed.), *Corporate and Global Standardization Initiatives in Contemporary Society* (pp. 200–218). Hershey, PA: IGI Global. doi:10.4018/978-1-5225-5320-5.ch009

Rezaie, S., Mirabedini, S. J., & Abtahi, A. (2018). Designing a Model for Implementation of Business Intelligence in the Banking Industry. *International Journal of Enterprise Information Systems*, *14*(1), 77–103. doi:10.4018/IJEIS.2018010105

Richards, V., Matthews, N., Williams, O. J., & Khan, Z. (2021). The Challenges of Accessible Tourism Information Systems for Tourists With Vision Impairment: Sensory Communications Beyond the Screen. In C. Eusébio, L. Teixeira, & M. Carneiro (Eds.), *ICT Tools and Applications for Accessible Tourism* (pp. 26–54). IGI Global. https://doi.org/10.4018/978-1-7998-6428-8.ch002

Rodrigues de Souza Neto, V., & Marques, O. (2021). Rural Tourism Fostering Welfare Through Sustainable Development: A Conceptual Approach. In A. Perinotto, V. Mayer, & J. Soares (Eds.), *Rebuilding and Restructuring the Tourism Industry: Infusion of Happiness and Quality of Life* (pp. 38–57). IGI Global. https://doi.org/10.4018/978-1-7998-7239-9.ch003

Romano, L., Grimaldi, R., & Colasuonno, F. S. (2017). Demand Management as a Success Factor in Project Portfolio Management. In L. Romano (Ed.), *Project Portfolio Management Strategies for Effective Organizational Operations* (pp. 202–219). Hershey, PA: IGI Global. doi:10.4018/978-1-5225-2151-8.ch008

Rubio-Escuderos, L., & García-Andreu, H. (2021). Competitiveness Factors of Accessible Tourism E-Travel Agencies. In C. Eusébio, L. Teixeira, & M. Carneiro (Eds.), *ICT Tools and Applications for Accessible Tourism* (pp. 196–217). IGI Global. https://doi.org/10.4018/978-1-7998-6428-8.ch009

Rucci, A. C., Porto, N., Darcy, S., & Becka, L. (2021). Smart and Accessible Cities?: Not Always – The Case for Accessible Tourism Initiatives in Buenos Aries and Sydney. In C. Eusébio, L. Teixeira, & M. Carneiro (Eds.), *ICT Tools and Applications for Accessible Tourism* (pp. 115–145). IGI Global. https://doi.org/10.4018/978-1-7998-6428-8.ch006

Ruhi, U. (2018). Towards an Interdisciplinary Socio-Technical Definition of Virtual Communities. In M. Khosrow-Pour, D.B.A. (Ed.), Encyclopedia of Information Science and Technology, Fourth Edition (pp. 4278-4295). Hershey, PA: IGI Global. doi:10.4018/978-1-5225-2255-3.ch371

Ryan, L., Catena, M., Ros, P., & Stephens, S. (2021). Designing Entrepreneurial Ecosystems to Support Resource Management in the Tourism Industry. In V. Costa, A. Moura, & M. Mira (Eds.), *Handbook of Research on Human Capital and People Management in the Tourism Industry* (pp. 265–281). IGI Global. https://doi.org/10.4018/978-1-7998-4318-4.ch013

Sabuncu, I. (2021). Understanding Tourist Perceptions and Expectations During Pandemic Through Social Media Big Data. In M. Demir, A. Dalgıç, & F. Ergen (Eds.), *Handbook of Research on the Impacts and Implications of COVID-19 on the Tourism Industry* (pp. 330–350). IGI Global. https://doi.org/10.4018/978-1-7998-8231-2.ch016

Safari, M. R., & Jiang, Q. (2018). The Theory and Practice of IT Governance Maturity and Strategies Alignment: Evidence From Banking Industry. *Journal of Global Information Management*, 26(2), 127–146. doi:10.4018/JGIM.2018040106

Sahoo, J., Pati, B., & Mohanty, B. (2017). Knowledge Management as an Academic Discipline: An Assessment. In B. Gunjal (Ed.), *Managing Knowledge and Scholarly Assets in Academic Libraries* (pp. 99–126). Hershey, PA: IGI Global. doi:10.4018/978-1-5225-1741-2.ch005

Saini, D. (2017). Relevance of Teaching Values and Ethics in Management Education. In N. Baporikar (Ed.), *Management Education for Global Leadership* (pp. 90–111). Hershey, PA: IGI Global. doi:10.4018/978-1-5225-1013-0.ch005

Sambhanthan, A. (2017). Assessing and Benchmarking Sustainability in Organisations: An Integrated Conceptual Model. *International Journal of Systems and Service-Oriented Engineering*, 7(4), 22–43. doi:10.4018/IJSSOE.2017100102

Sambhanthan, A., & Potdar, V. (2017). A Study of the Parameters Impacting Sustainability in Information Technology Organizations. *International Journal of Knowledge-Based Organizations*, 7(3), 27–39. doi:10.4018/IJKBO.2017070103

Sánchez-Fernández, M. D., & Manríquez, M. R. (2018). The Entrepreneurial Spirit Based on Social Values: The Digital Generation. In P. Isaias & L. Carvalho (Eds.), *User Innovation and the Entrepreneurship Phenomenon in the Digital Economy* (pp. 173–193). Hershey, PA: IGI Global. doi:10.4018/978-1-5225-2826-5.ch009

Sanchez-Ruiz, L., & Blanco, B. (2017). Process Management for SMEs: Barriers, Enablers, and Benefits. In M. Vemić (Ed.), *Optimal Management Strategies in Small and Medium Enterprises* (pp. 293–319). Hershey, PA: IGI Global. doi:10.4018/978-1-5225-1949-2.ch014

Sanz, L. F., Gómez-Pérez, J., & Castillo-Martinez, A. (2018). Analysis of the European ICT Competence Frameworks. In V. Ahuja & S. Rathore (Eds.), *Multidisciplinary Perspectives on Human Capital and Information Technology Professionals* (pp. 225–245). Hershey, PA: IGI Global. doi:10.4018/978-1-5225-5297-0.ch012

Sarvepalli, A., & Godin, J. (2017). Business Process Management in the Classroom. *Journal of Cases on Information Technology*, *19*(2), 17–28. doi:10.4018/JCIT.2017040102

Saxena, G. G., & Saxena, A. (2021). Host Community Role in Medical Tourism Development. In M. Singh & S. Kumaran (Eds.), *Growth of the Medical Tourism Industry and Its Impact on Society: Emerging Research and Opportunities* (pp. 105–127). IGI Global. https://doi.org/10.4018/978-1-7998-3427-4.ch006

Saygili, E. E., Ozturkoglu, Y., & Kocakulah, M. C. (2017). End Users' Perceptions of Critical Success Factors in ERP Applications. *International Journal of Enterprise Information Systems*, *13*(4), 58–75. doi:10.4018/IJEIS.2017100104

Saygili, E. E., & Saygili, A. T. (2017). Contemporary Issues in Enterprise Information Systems: A Critical Review of CSFs in ERP Implementations. In M. Tavana (Ed.), *Enterprise Information Systems and the Digitalization of Business Functions* (pp. 120–136). Hershey, PA: IGI Global. doi:10.4018/978-1-5225-2382-6.ch006

Schwaiger, K. M., & Zehrer, A. (2021). The COVID-19 Pandemic and Organizational Resilience in Hospitality Family Firms: A Qualitative Approach. In A. Zehrer, G. Glowka, K. Schwaiger, & V. Ranacher-Lackner (Eds.), *Resiliency Models and Addressing Future Risks for Family Firms in the Tourism Industry* (pp. 32–49). IGI Global. https://doi.org/10.4018/978-1-7998-7352-5.ch002

Scott, N., & Campos, A. C. (2022). Cognitive Science of Tourism Experiences. In R. Augusto Costa, F. Brandão, Z. Breda, & C. Costa (Eds.), Planning and Managing the Experience Economy in Tourism (pp. 1-21). IGI Global. https://doi.org/ doi:10.4018/978-1-7998-8775-1.ch001

Seidenstricker, S., & Antonino, A. (2018). Business Model Innovation-Oriented Technology Management for Emergent Technologies. In M. Khosrow-Pour, D.B.A. (Ed.), Encyclopedia of Information Science and Technology, Fourth Edition (pp. 4560-4569). Hershey, PA: IGI Global. doi:10.4018/978-1-5225-2255-3.ch396

Selvi, M. S. (2021). Changes in Tourism Sales and Marketing Post COVID-19. In M. Demir, A. Dalgıç, & F. Ergen (Eds.), *Handbook of Research on the Impacts and Implications of COVID-19 on the Tourism Industry* (pp. 437–460). IGI Global. doi:10.4018/978-1-7998-8231-2.ch021

Senaratne, S., & Gunarathne, A. D. (2017). Excellence Perspective for Management Education from a Global Accountants' Hub in Asia. In N. Baporikar (Ed.), *Management Education for Global Leadership* (pp. 158–180). Hershey, PA: IGI Global. doi:10.4018/978-1-5225-1013-0.ch008

Sensuse, D. I., & Cahyaningsih, E. (2018). Knowledge Management Models: A Summative Review. *International Journal of Information Systems in the Service Sector*, *10*(1), 71–100. doi:10.4018/IJISSS.2018010105

Seth, M., Goyal, D., & Kiran, R. (2017). Diminution of Impediments in Implementation of Supply Chain Management Information System for Enhancing its Effectiveness in Indian Automobile Industry. *Journal of Global Information Management*, *25*(3), 1–20. doi:10.4018/JGIM.2017070101

Seyal, A. H., & Rahman, M. N. (2017). Investigating Impact of Inter-Organizational Factors in Measuring ERP Systems Success: Bruneian Perspectives. In M. Tavana (Ed.), *Enterprise Information Systems and the Digitalization of Business Functions* (pp. 178–204). Hershey, PA: IGI Global. doi:10.4018/978-1-5225-2382-6.ch008

Shaqrah, A. A. (2018). Analyzing Business Intelligence Systems Based on 7s Model of McKinsey. *International Journal of Business Intelligence Research*, *9*(1), 53–63. doi:10.4018/IJBIR.2018010104

Sharma, A. J. (2017). Enhancing Sustainability through Experiential Learning in Management Education. In N. Baporikar (Ed.), *Management Education for Global Leadership* (pp. 256–274). Hershey, PA: IGI Global. doi:10.4018/978-1-5225-1013-0.ch013

Shetty, K. P. (2017). Responsible Global Leadership: Ethical Challenges in Management Education. In N. Baporikar (Ed.), *Innovation and Shifting Perspectives in Management Education* (pp. 194–223). Hershey, PA: IGI Global. doi:10.4018/978-1-5225-1019-2.ch009

Sinthupundaja, J., & Kohda, Y. (2017). Effects of Corporate Social Responsibility and Creating Shared Value on Sustainability. *International Journal of Sustainable Entrepreneurship and Corporate Social Responsibility*, *2*(1), 27–38. doi:10.4018/IJSECSR.2017010103

Škarica, I., & Hrgović, A. V. (2018). Implementation of Total Quality Management Principles in Public Health Institutes in the Republic of Croatia. *International Journal of Productivity Management and Assessment Technologies*, *6*(1), 1–16. doi:10.4018/IJPMAT.2018010101

Skokic, V. (2021). How Small Hotel Owners Practice Resilience: Longitudinal Study Among Small Family Hotels in Croatia. In A. Zehrer, G. Glowka, K. Schwaiger, & V. Ranacher-Lackner (Eds.), *Resiliency Models and Addressing Future Risks for Family Firms in the Tourism Industry* (pp. 50–73). IGI Global. doi:10.4018/978-1-7998-7352-5.ch003

Smuts, H., Kotzé, P., Van der Merwe, A., & Loock, M. (2017). Framework for Managing Shared Knowledge in an Information Systems Outsourcing Context. *International Journal of Knowledge Management, 13*(4), 1–30. doi:10.4018/IJKM.2017100101

Sousa, M. J., Cruz, R., Dias, I., & Caracol, C. (2017). Information Management Systems in the Supply Chain. In G. Jamil, A. Soares, & C. Pessoa (Eds.), *Handbook of Research on Information Management for Effective Logistics and Supply Chains* (pp. 469–485). Hershey, PA: IGI Global. doi:10.4018/978-1-5225-0973-8.ch025

Spremic, M., Turulja, L., & Bajgoric, N. (2018). Two Approaches in Assessing Business Continuity Management Attitudes in the Organizational Context. In N. Bajgoric (Ed.), *Always-On Enterprise Information Systems for Modern Organizations* (pp. 159–183). Hershey, PA: IGI Global. doi:10.4018/978-1-5225-3704-5.ch008

Steenkamp, A. L. (2018). Some Insights in Computer Science and Information Technology. In *Examining the Changing Role of Supervision in Doctoral Research Projects: Emerging Research and Opportunities* (pp. 113–133). Hershey, PA: IGI Global. doi:10.4018/978-1-5225-2610-0.ch005

Stipanović, C., Rudan, E., & Zubović, V. (2022). Reaching the New Tourist Through Creativity: Sustainable Development Challenges in Croatian Coastal Towns. In M. Valeri (Ed.), *New Governance and Management in Touristic Destinations* (pp. 231–245). IGI Global. https://doi.org/10.4018/978-1-6684-3889-3.ch014

Tabach, A., & Croteau, A. (2017). Configurations of Information Technology Governance Practices and Business Unit Performance. *International Journal of IT/Business Alignment and Governance, 8*(2), 1–27. doi:10.4018/IJITBAG.2017070101

Talaue, G. M., & Iqbal, T. (2017). Assessment of e-Business Mode of Selected Private Universities in the Philippines and Pakistan. *International Journal of Online Marketing, 7*(4), 63–77. doi:10.4018/IJOM.2017100105

Tam, G. C. (2017). Project Manager Sustainability Competence. In *Managerial Strategies and Green Solutions for Project Sustainability* (pp. 178–207). Hershey, PA: IGI Global. doi:10.4018/978-1-5225-2371-0.ch008

Tambo, T. (2018). Fashion Retail Innovation: About Context, Antecedents, and Outcome in Technological Change Projects. In I. Management Association (Ed.), Fashion and Textiles: Breakthroughs in Research and Practice (pp. 233-260). Hershey, PA: IGI Global. https://doi.org/ doi:10.4018/978-1-5225-3432-7.ch010

Tantau, A. D., & Frăţilă, L. C. (2018). Information and Management System for Renewable Energy Business. In *Entrepreneurship and Business Development in the Renewable Energy Sector* (pp. 200–244). Hershey, PA: IGI Global. doi:10.4018/978-1-5225-3625-3.ch006

Teixeira, N., Pardal, P. N., & Rafael, B. G. (2018). Internationalization, Financial Performance, and Organizational Challenges: A Success Case in Portugal. In L. Carvalho (Ed.), *Handbook of Research on Entrepreneurial Ecosystems and Social Dynamics in a Globalized World* (pp. 379–423). Hershey, PA: IGI Global. doi:10.4018/978-1-5225-3525-6.ch017

Teixeira, P., Teixeira, L., Eusébio, C., Silva, S., & Teixeira, A. (2021). The Impact of ICTs on Accessible Tourism: Evidence Based on a Systematic Literature Review. In C. Eusébio, L. Teixeira, & M. Carneiro (Eds.), *ICT Tools and Applications for Accessible Tourism* (pp. 1–25). IGI Global. doi:10.4018/978-1-7998-6428-8.ch001

Trad, A., & Kalpić, D. (2018). The Business Transformation Framework, Agile Project and Change Management. In M. Khosrow-Pour, D.B.A. (Ed.), Encyclopedia of Information Science and Technology, Fourth Edition (pp. 620-635). Hershey, PA: IGI Global. https://doi.org/ doi:10.4018/978-1-5225-2255-3.ch054

Trad, A., & Kalpić, D. (2018). The Business Transformation and Enterprise Architecture Framework: The Financial Engineering E-Risk Management and E-Law Integration. In B. Sergi, F. Fidanoski, M. Ziolo, & V. Naumovski (Eds.), *Regaining Global Stability After the Financial Crisis* (pp. 46–65). Hershey, PA: IGI Global. doi:10.4018/978-1-5225-4026-7.ch003

Trengereid, V. (2022). Conditions of Network Engagement: The Quest for a Common Good. In R. Augusto Costa, F. Brandão, Z. Breda, & C. Costa (Eds.), *Planning and Managing the Experience Economy in Tourism* (pp. 69-84). IGI Global. https://doi.org/10.4018/978-1-7998-8775-1.ch004

Turulja, L., & Bajgoric, N. (2018). Business Continuity and Information Systems: A Systematic Literature Review. In N. Bajgoric (Ed.), *Always-On Enterprise Information Systems for Modern Organizations* (pp. 60–87). Hershey, PA: IGI Global. doi:10.4018/978-1-5225-3704-5.ch004

Vargas-Hernández, J. G. (2017). Professional Integrity in Business Management Education. In N. Baporikar (Ed.), *Management Education for Global Leadership* (pp. 70–89). Hershey, PA: IGI Global. doi:10.4018/978-1-5225-1013-0.ch004

Varnacı Uzun, F. (2021). The Destination Preferences of Foreign Tourists During the COVID-19 Pandemic and Attitudes Towards: Marmaris, Turkey. In M. Demir, A. Dalgıç, & F. Ergen (Eds.), *Handbook of Research on the Impacts and Implications of COVID-19 on the Tourism Industry* (pp. 285–306). IGI Global. https://doi.org/10.4018/978-1-7998-8231-2.ch014

Vasista, T. G., & AlAbdullatif, A. M. (2017). Role of Electronic Customer Relationship Management in Demand Chain Management: A Predictive Analytic Approach. *International Journal of Information Systems and Supply Chain Management*, *10*(1), 53–67. doi:10.4018/IJISSCM.2017010104

Vieru, D., & Bourdeau, S. (2017). Survival in the Digital Era: A Digital Competence-Based Multi-Case Study in the Canadian SME Clothing Industry. *International Journal of Social and Organizational Dynamics in IT*, *6*(1), 17–34. doi:10.4018/IJSODIT.2017010102

Vijayan, G., & Kamarulzaman, N. H. (2017). An Introduction to Sustainable Supply Chain Management and Business Implications. In M. Khan, M. Hussain, & M. Ajmal (Eds.), *Green Supply Chain Management for Sustainable Business Practice* (pp. 27–50). Hershey, PA: IGI Global. doi:10.4018/978-1-5225-0635-5.ch002

Vlachvei, A., & Notta, O. (2017). Firm Competitiveness: Theories, Evidence, and Measurement. In A. Vlachvei, O. Notta, K. Karantininis, & N. Tsounis (Eds.), *Factors Affecting Firm Competitiveness and Performance in the Modern Business World* (pp. 1–42). Hershey, PA: IGI Global. doi:10.4018/978-1-5225-0843-4.ch001

Wang, C., Schofield, M., Li, X., & Ou, X. (2017). Do Chinese Students in Public and Private Higher Education Institutes Perform at Different Level in One of the Leadership Skills: Critical Thinking?: An Exploratory Comparison. In V. Wang (Ed.), *Encyclopedia of Strategic Leadership and Management* (pp. 160–181). Hershey, PA: IGI Global. doi:10.4018/978-1-5225-1049-9.ch013

Wang, J. (2017). Multi-Agent based Production Management Decision System Modelling for the Textile Enterprise. *Journal of Global Information Management*, *25*(4), 1–15. doi:10.4018/JGIM.2017100101

Wiedemann, A., & Gewald, H. (2017). Examining Cross-Domain Alignment: The Correlation of Business Strategy, IT Management, and IT Business Value. *International Journal of IT/Business Alignment and Governance*, *8*(1), 17–31. doi:10.4018/IJITBAG.2017010102

Wolf, R., & Thiel, M. (2018). Advancing Global Business Ethics in China: Reducing Poverty Through Human and Social Welfare. In S. Hipsher (Ed.), *Examining the Private Sector's Role in Wealth Creation and Poverty Reduction* (pp. 67–84). Hershey, PA: IGI Global. doi:10.4018/978-1-5225-3117-3.ch004

Yablonsky, S. (2018). Innovation Platforms: Data and Analytics Platforms. In *Multi-Sided Platforms (MSPs) and Sharing Strategies in the Digital Economy: Emerging Research and Opportunities* (pp. 72–95). Hershey, PA: IGI Global. doi:10.4018/978-1-5225-5457-8.ch003

Yaşar, B. (2021). The Impact of COVID-19 on Volatility of Tourism Stocks: Evidence From BIST Tourism Index. In M. Demir, A. Dalgıç, & F. Ergen (Eds.), *Handbook of Research on the Impacts and Implications of COVID-19 on the Tourism Industry* (pp. 23–44). IGI Global. https://doi.org/10.4018/978-1-7998-8231-2.ch002

Yusoff, A., Ahmad, N. H., & Halim, H. A. (2017). Agropreneurship among Gen Y in Malaysia: The Role of Academic Institutions. In N. Ahmad, T. Ramayah, H. Halim, & S. Rahman (Eds.), *Handbook of Research on Small and Medium Enterprises in Developing Countries* (pp. 23–47). Hershey, PA: IGI Global. doi:10.4018/978-1-5225-2165-5.ch002

Zacher, D., & Pechlaner, H. (2021). Resilience as an Opportunity Approach: Challenges and Perspectives for Private Sector Participation on a Community Level. In A. Zehrer, G. Glowka, K. Schwaiger, & V. Ranacher-Lackner (Eds.), *Resiliency Models and Addressing Future Risks for Family Firms in the Tourism Industry* (pp. 75–102). IGI Global. https://doi.org/10.4018/978-1-7998-7352-5.ch004

Zanin, F., Comuzzi, E., & Costantini, A. (2018). The Effect of Business Strategy and Stock Market Listing on the Use of Risk Assessment Tools. In *Management Control Systems in Complex Settings: Emerging Research and Opportunities* (pp. 145–168). Hershey, PA: IGI Global. doi:10.4018/978-1-5225-3987-2.ch007

Zgheib, P. W. (2017). Corporate Innovation and Intrapreneurship in the Middle East. In P. Zgheib (Ed.), *Entrepreneurship and Business Innovation in the Middle East* (pp. 37–56). Hershey, PA: IGI Global. doi:10.4018/978-1-5225-2066-5.ch003

About the Contributors

Hamed Nozari is an assistant professor in Industrial engineering at the Azad University of the Emirates branch. He holds a Ph.D. in Industrial Engineering with a focus on Production Management and Planning and PostDoc in Industrial Engineering from the Iran University of Science and Technology. He has taught various courses in the field of Industrial Engineering and has published many books and papers as well. Now he is a researcher in the field of digital developments and smart systems and optimization.

* * *

Renuka Devi D. is Assistant Professor, in the Department of Computer Science, Stella Maris College, Chennai, India. Having 14+ years of rich teaching experience, Ph.D in University of Madras. Her Research interests include Data mining, Machine Learning, Big Data and Artificial Intelligence. She has published a book "Research Practitioner's Handbook on Big Data Analytics" Apple Academic Press, CRC Press, USA, book chapter and 20+ research articles (National and International), including IEEE, Springer, Scopus, and Web of Science. She has published patents. She has also presented papers at International conferences and received the best paper award and she is also presented with Best Researcher award. She has been a reviewer in international peer reviewed Scopus and SCI indexed journals. She has been invited for talks in conferences and workshops. Her commitment to innovation is evident through patents, including Innovation patent for Un Nanban, an AI-based interactive web and voice application, and a Design patent for a "Smart Walking Stick" for visually impaired individuals in 2023. Represented India as a panelist in the "Global Perspectives on Artificial Intelligence in Higher Education - A virtual roundtable on AI" in 2023 organised by Alamo Colleges District, San Antonio, USA.

Sowmiya K. C., an accomplished Ph.D. scholar at Sri Vasavi College in Erode, emerges as a dynamic and vibrant researcher with a rich educational background. Having laid the foundation with a B.Ed. degree and furthered her academic pursuits with post-graduation at PSGR Krishnammal College for Women, she has adeptly positioned herself at the forefront of scholarly exploration. Her commitment to advancing knowledge is exemplified through her proactive involvement in two conferences in 2023, where she not only showcased her research prowess but also actively engaged with peers and experts, fostering meaningful discussions. Notably, the recognition garnered from presenting her research findings at these conferences has resulted in the acceptance of her journal article for publication later this year. This noteworthy achievement not only underscores Sowmiya's dedication to the academic realm but also highlights her impactful contributions to the scholarly discourse. As a Ph.D. scholar, she stands as a vibrant and influential contributor to the ever-evolving landscape of research and academic exploration, leaving an indelible mark on her field.

Manjit Kour is a dedicated and experienced Academician with zeal for research and providing quality education. Currently she is working as Professor at University Business School at Chandigarh University. She has 18 years of experience in the education sector. Her research interests revolve around fintech, sustainable finance, and social marketing, where she has contributed significantly.

Rajinder Kour is working as Professor at University School of Business, Chandigarh University. She is a PhD in finance and has about two decades of experience in academia. Her areas of research include fintech, business ethics, sustainability and online marketing. Her research papers are published in reputed journals (Scopus indexed, ABDC listed and UGC care). She is on editorial board of many reputed journals as well.

Aditya Kumar is a Ph.D. scholar at the Central University of South Bihar, pursuing research in the field of computer science and engineering. He holds a Master of Technology (M.Tech.) degree in Computer Science and Engineering, which he completed in 2021. Aditya's research interests primarily revolve around feature set partitioning methods in machine learning. Along with achieving major accolades like the Junior Research Fellowship (JRF), UGC-NET, and GATE credentials, he made a substantial academic contribution.

Swetha Margaret T. A. is an accomplished professional with a diverse background in academia, research, and industry, specializing in Cyber and Network Security, Cloud Computing, Computer Networks, IoT, IIoT, Big Data, and Artificial Intelligence. With 12 years of experience, she currently serves as an Assistant Professor in the Department of Computer Science at Stella Maris College, bringing seven years of dedicated teaching expertise. Dr. Margaret holds a Ph.D., earned during her three-year tenure as a full-time Doctoral Research Scholar at Quaid E Millath College, Chennai. Prior to her academic pursuits, she gained valuable industry experience with IBM and Citrix, focusing on IBM mainframe back-end support, task management, and load creation. Her commitment to professional development is evident through various international certifications, including those from IBM, Big Data University, and Udemy, covering Cloud Computing, Data Science Methodology, and more. As the Chief Information Security Officer (CISO) at Stella Maris College since 2023, she has demonstrated leadership in securing information assets. Dr. Margaret's research contributions extend to over 20 publications in international journals, including Scopus, IEEE, and Springer. Her expertise has been recognized through accolades such as the "Best Researcher Award" from D K International Research Foundation and the 'Young Faculty in Science' Award during the Contemporary Academic Meet-CAM by Venus International Foundation, both in 2018-2019. Her commitment to innovation is evident through patents, including Innovation patent for "Un Nanban," an AI-based interactive web and voice application, and a Design patent for a "Smart Walking Stick" for visually impaired individuals in 2023. Represented India as a panelist in the "Global Perspectives on Artificial Intelligence in Higher Education - A virtual roundtable on AI" in 2023 organised by Alamo Colleges District, San Antonio, USA.

Vetrivel S. C. is a faculty member in the Department of Management Studies, Kongu Engineering College (Autonomous), Perundurai, Erode Dt. Having experience in Industry 20 years and Teaching 16 years. Awarded with Doctoral Degree in Management Sciences in Anna University, Chennai. He has o rganized various workshops and Faculty Development Programmes. He is actively involved in research and consultancy works. He acted as a resource person to FDPs & MDPs to various industries like, SPB ltd, Tamilnadu Police, DIET, Rotary school and many. His areas of interest include Entrepreneurship, Business Law, Marketing and Case writing. Articles published more than 100 International and National Journals. Presented papers in more than 30 National and International conferences including IIM Bangalore, IIM Kozhikode, IIM Kashipur and IIM Indore. He was a Chief Co-ordinator of Entrepreneurship and Management Development Centre (EMDC) of Kongu Engineering College, he was instrumental in organizing various Awareness Camps, FDP, and TEDPs to aspiring entrepreneurs which was funded by NSTEDB – DST/GoI.

Gomathi T. served in various reputed institutions. Currently employed as an Assistant Professor (Department In charge) at Gnanamani College of Technology, Namakkal. His area of specialization are Human Resource and Finance Management. She has 13 years of Teaching experience. A soft skill trainer. She has published papers in International and national Journals and participated in more than 20 national and international conferences, Seminars, FDPs, Workshops. She served as a question paper setter in various autonomous colleges. She has also delivered various guest talks and soft skill training in various schools and colleges.

Reza Tavakkoli-Moghaddam is a Professor of Industrial Engineering at the College of Engineering, University of Tehran, Iran. He obtained his Ph.D., M.Sc. and B.Sc. degrees in Industrial Engineering from Swinburne University of Technology in Melbourne (1998), University of Melbourne in Melbourne (1994), and Iran University of Science and Technology in Tehran (1989), respectively. He serves as the Editor-in-Chief of "Advances in Industrial Engineering" journal published by the University of Tehran and the Editorial Board member of nine reputable academic journals. He is the recipient of the 2009 and 2011 Distinguished Researcher Awards and the 2010 and 2014 Distinguished Applied Research Awards at University of Tehran, Iran. He has been selected as the National Iranian Distinguished Researcher in 2008 and 2010 by the MSRT (Ministry of Science, Research, and Technology) in Iran. He has obtained the outstanding rank as the top 1% scientist and researcher in the world elite group since 2014. Also, he received the Order of Academic Palms Award as a distinguished educator and scholar for the insignia of Chevalier dans l'Ordre des Palmes Academiques by the Ministry of National Education of France in 2019. He has published 5 books, 39 book chapters, and more than 1000 journal and conference papers.

Sabareeshwari V. currently serves as Assistant Professor in Department of Soil Science, Amrita School of Agricultural Sciences, Coimbatore. Having more than 5 years of research experience and more than 2 years of teaching experience. She got 7 awards in the field of agriculture. Her field of expertise are soil genesis, soil pedological studies as well as soil fertility mapping using advanced software like Arc GIS. She had published 22 research papers and more than 10 book chapters and books in high- impact reputed journals. She has actively participated and presented her papers in more than 20 conferences and seminars. She not only restrict her contribution only in the academic and research part, she had extension experience at farm level (lab to land) with varied crop research.

Jainath Yadav is an accomplished Associate Professor who joined the Central University of South Bihar in 2013. He holds an M. Tech and a Ph.D. degree from the prestigious Indian Institute of Technology Kharagpur. With a strong academic background, Jainath Yadav's journey has been marked by excellence. He not only secured notable achievements such as Junior Research Fellowship (JRF), UGC-NET, and GATE qualifications but also contributed significantly to academia. Throughout his academic career, Jainath Yadav has demonstrated his dedication to both learning and research. He received teach- ing assistantship from 2009 to 2011 and research assistantship from June 2011 to March 2013 at IIT Kharagpur, gaining valuable experience in teaching and research methodologies. As an Associate Professor, he continues to inspire and guide students in their academic pursuits. Jainath Yadav's impact on the research community is evident through his numerous research papers published in renowned journals including IEEE Transactions on Audio Speech and Language Processing, IEEE Signal Processing Letters, and Speech Communication. His work has been recognized on the international stage through presentations at esteemed international conferences.

Index

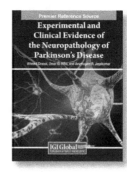
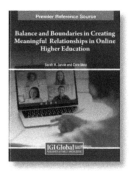

www.igi-global.com

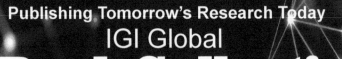